D1161656

# MAN'S ESTATE

*Adventures in Economic Discovery*

*Books by Alfred M. Bingham*

MAN'S ESTATE: *Adventures in Economic Discovery*
INSURGENT AMERICA: *The Revolt of the Middle-Classes*

# MAN'S ESTATE

## *Adventures in Economic Discovery*

ALFRED M. BINGHAM

*New York* · W · W · NORTON & COMPANY · INC ·

70 Fifth Avenue, New York, N. Y.

*First Edition*

MANUFACTURED IN THE UNITED STATES
BY QUINN & BODEN COMPANY, INC., RAHWAY, N. J.

To S. K. B.

# CONTENTS

## *PART I. MOSTLY AUTOBIOGRAPHICAL*



## *PART II. A SELECTION OF RELEVANT FACTS*



## *PART III. THROUGH MARXISM DARKLY*

## *PART IV. A THEORY TO EXPLAIN THE FACTS*



## *PART V. EXPERIMENT IN POLITICAL ECONOMY*

# *PART I*

# MOSTLY AUTOBIOGRAPHICAL

# Chapter One

## BY WAY OF FOREWORD, PREFACE AND INTRODUCTION

THE relation between an author and his reader should be one of mutual confidence. The author is claiming a good many hours of the reader's attention. Why he feels justified in asking so much should be made perfectly clear. He ought not to retire into an oracular anonymity merely because he is using the written rather than the spoken word.

In the usual serious treatise the author speaks candidly as a human being only in the Preface. He speaks in the first person singular, he identifies himself by date and place, he mentions the friends who helped him, he explains how he happened to write the book and what it is about. And then, just as you begin to feel you rather like him, he disappears, and Chapter One appears in his place, all dressed up in judicial robe and false whiskers. The human touch is lost. But something even more important may be lost: by putting on the semblance of infallible logic the author may be deceiving both the reader and himself. Especially will this be the case when he is dealing with a subject in which his own personality is deeply involved, like morals, or politics, or the social order. Syllogisms will appear to march to categorical conclusions, when the author is in fact merely airing his personal prejudices.

As the author of this book, I am going to try to avoid that pitfall. There is no special Preface to these pages. I shall attempt to keep the frankness and directness, that usually are confined to a Preface, throughout the book, though often, no doubt, I shall fail; the date and place I shall write at the end, when I have finished.

It is a book with a big subject: no less than the state of the present-day world. Because I believe the principal causes of the world's present distress are economic, it is a book on economics.* Yet it is more than that. You will find a certain amount of history, philosophy and sociology in it, because it is a book about human beings and their limitations and their possibilities. You will find a certain amount of autobiography in it, too, for the same reason.

You and I, and about two billion others like us, are on a planet whirling through space. The terrestrial existence of each one of us is only a flash of cosmic time, but we are quite concerned with it nevertheless. Like all other forms of life we need air, water and food, and, unlike even the higher animals, we have come to need clothing and shelter and a growing number of other amenities. The vast majority of us—probably four-fifths of the two billion—are living at the edge of starvation and desperate exposure to the weather. Though it is beginning to appear that our mastery of the natural environment can now provide for all our material needs, our mastery over ourselves and over our social environment is not yet sufficiently developed, and even the most essential goods are still generally scarce. Economics—to venture a preliminary definition—has to do with the production and rationing of scarce goods.

Want, however, is not the only trouble that afflicts our human race. Every one of us has an indeterminate sentence of death hanging over him. Accident, disease and old age are our common lot. Famines and plagues capable of wiping out millions are ready to leap out of nowhere, when certain of our social arrangements—sanitation or transportation, for instance—break down. Worse still, the most basic arrangements of all, the ways we have organized ourselves, seem to be breaking down. Alarming symptoms are appearing in the institutional devices by which the work of the world is done. Even in a rich country like America babies go without enough milk. The political institutions, by which these two billion people manage to keep some sort of order among themselves and not step on each other's toes, are working so badly that we have started killing each other in sizable batches in various parts of the globe, and wholesale killing seems likely to begin any minute. Even this is not the worst. A billion people less on the

* Some of the political and social aspects of the same problems were dealt with three years ago in my previous book, *Insurgent America*.

earth would leave more room for the remainder; but in this indiscriminate killing process we may destroy the knowledge that has enabled us to get thus far from the jungle stage. Scientists and libraries and laboratories are no more immune to bombs than babies and bathrooms.

I don't know how you feel about bombs, but I am afraid of them. Not that I have ever been bombed; but there are so many bombs already dropping on the earth's surface that I don't feel permanently out of range. Some people who have been within range seem to feel chiefly anger at the aviator dropping the bombs, or at the people who gave him his orders; and their prompt reaction is to want to drop bombs on the other people. Yet the humiliating peace of Munich was due not a little to the fact that so many people today think almost anything is better than being bombed.

If it is true that one of the primary reasons for the breakdown of our national and international arrangements is economic, then it is highly important that we examine the economic problem in as objective and scientific a spirit as possible before it is too late. It will be too late so far as you and I are concerned when either of us is killed, and so far as the world is concerned when the possibility of scientific inquiry has been killed by the destruction of libraries, laboratories and objectivity.

A scientific or objective attitude in this field is, however, peculiarly difficult. An investigator in any of the natural sciences—a chemist, for instance—is careful not to get himself into any experiment, not merely for fear of being burned or of losing a finger, but because if his finger, or a piece of his prejudices about what ought to happen, gets into the test-tube the whole experiment is ruined. But in this research I am conducting, I *am* part of the experiment. I am one of the people temporarily living on this chaotic planet, trying to make sure that I don't die prematurely of hunger, cold or violence. My own prejudices are part of the mixture in the test-tube, and there is no use pretending they are not.

Is it possible, then, to apply the scientific method to our social problems? Is it possible to be objective toward an enemy bombing plane? or toward hunger? or toward a strike? or toward such abstract concepts as "capitalism" or "socialism"?

A partial answer to those questions I discovered just as I was beginning work on this book. I read Thurman Arnold's *Folklore of Capitalism* and Stuart Chase's *Tyranny of Words*.* They pointed out that much of our thinking is done with emotional symbols and "verbal monsters." There can be no scientific approach to the social problems of which we are so much an active part without what Chase called the "semantic discipline." We must honestly try to discover where the words we use derived their meaning in our own experiences. How otherwise can we achieve any understanding of our problems?

It is possible, of course, to solve problems without understanding them. We get lost in the woods and somehow find our way out without making a chart. Most of man's progress has been of that kind. At most he has had myths and magic to guide him, and sometimes his magic has been so ill adapted to his survival that he has perished. Our chance for survival ought to be better because we have learned to substitute science for magic. Unfortunately, however, the most important areas of human thought and action today—economics and politics—are virtually untouched by the scientific method, though cloistered scholars have long made the attempt.

In this book on economics I am making an attempt myself. Why I think I have a better chance at understanding than some of those cloistered scholars is not important: most of us have enough vanity and curiosity to want to work out answers for ourselves, if we get the opportunity. In any case we have far more data for any scholar to work over today than ever before, especially with the communist and fascist countries as proving grounds; and if in addition we have a growing awareness of the nature of the words we use as tools, better results should now be possible. Certainly it should be possible to improve on such an analysis as Marx made in the middle of the nineteenth century, yet many intelligent and well-intentioned people today think he said the last word in this field. Perhaps it is only now becoming possible to apply the scientific method here.

Perhaps it is becoming possible just in time, though it may be already too late to save our generation from frightful disaster. As

* Except for occasional references to important books in the text, most of the source material on which I have based the present volume is collected in the Bibliographical Notes in the final pages.

regards our general human arrangements today—our social institutions, our civilization, our political and economic organizations—a policy of blundering along from mistake to mistake with only myth and magic to guide us may have catastrophic results. If we can apply the scientific method in time, our chance of survival—whether as individuals, or as nations, or as a civilization—is greatly increased.

What is the scientific method? I have been asking myself that, and have been tempted to look up or work out a definition. But, following Thurman Arnold, I am going to be wary of definitions. Science is a "verbal monster" too. We tend to conjure up an image of an intent young man in a hospital orderly's coat peering through a microscope, and declaring that such and such a cough-drop is a "scientific" remedy. I will only make a few brief assertions about what I mean by the scientific method, and leave the rest to your imagination.

The word "method" suggests results: A good method "gets results." "Science" is another word for knowledge. The scientific method suggests a way of securing and using knowledge, in order to achieve certain objectives.

The engineers who built the Golden Gate Bridge had to stick rigorously to the scientific method. No myths or magic for them. They first gathered an array of facts. Some of these facts, about the tensile strength of steel, for instance, they could find in books. Others, about the nature of the terrain, they had to go out and discover. They had certain tools for getting the facts, surveying instruments and geologic boring instruments. They had certain other tools and certain materials for building the bridge, concrete and concrete mixers, wire, and devices to weave the wire into cables. They had to allow for the human factor, and string a safety net to catch men when they stumbled. Fortunately the human factor was one of the simplest elements in this complex engineering feat.

I am here suggesting plans for a bridge, too, a bridge from our present chaotic world, threatened by war, revolution, famine, and increasingly destructive habits of violence, to a reasonably well-ordered world. Unfortunately the human factor is almost everything in this problem. The terrain consists of human institutions, badly muddled ones on this side, workable ones over there. The getting of facts is not a matter of precision instruments but depends on human observations of human beings. Unlike the engineer of the Golden Gate Bridge, who could work on his blueprints without ever even getting his feet wet in San Francisco Bay, I am in this up to my neck. All my facts, like anyone else's, are selected from the great mass of facts according to my own human interests and limitations. The kind of bridge, and even my conception of what kind of world the bridge is to lead to, are determined by my own biased view of things.

To be scientific, then, in the treatment of such complex human problems as those of economics and politics requires a stricter honesty than in any other field. How can I evaluate my findings unless I know what my biases are? More important, how can you, unless you do? Our measuring instruments and our tools are mostly words. How can we get anywhere unless we are on the watch for "verbal monsters"? We cannot avoid them, for every word has something of the monster lurking in it, but we can at least not let the monster get the better of us.

Being human, we are fallible. There is no use pretending to infallibility. At the same time, we must seek to be as rigorously honest in our thinking as if we were infallible. It is in the interest of that kind of honesty—since I am in the test-tube—that the first part of this economic study is largely autobiography. It leads up to a definition of the economic problem in terms of my own mental search. At the end of this first part, I state the conclusion of my thinking as an hypothesis to be proved.

I am then in a position to select from the present-day world—Soviet socialism, fascism, dictatorship and democracy—those facts which seem to me relevant to the problem as I have defined it. They are presented in Part II, not without suggestive interpretation in the light of the hypothesis. Then, in Part III, it seemed to me necessary to test the Marxist economic theories, with their immense prestige, as an alternative explanation of the contemporary scene. Part IV is largely devoted to a synthesis of modern economic theory, as it bears on the basic issue and helps explain the facts. With a tentative Q.E.D. now tagged to my hypothesis, I go on in Part V to apply what theoretical conclusions I have reached to the practical problems of social and economic policy in America today.

# *Chapter Two*

## ABOUT MYSELF AND MY WORLD

THE world in which I grew up was an "economy of abundance." I cannot remember ever doing without anything I wanted because it cost more than my family was able to spend. Inherited wealth was the foundation of the spacious home in which I spent my childhood, and I early came to believe that having to "work for a living" was a comparatively rare misfortune in an otherwise ample and affluent world. Not that I didn't occasionally hear the phrase "we can't afford it," but this was always in reference to some remote and fantastic luxury like a steam yacht, which meant nothing to me.

I have few memories that go back farther than the time we moved into a big yellow-stuccoed red-tiled house on Prospect Hill in New Haven. A favorite story my brothers and I used to like to tell callers, though our parents mildly protested, was that some strangers once came and sat on the front porch thinking the house a hotel. We were a big family, and we filled the house pretty completely. There were sun-porches and sun-terraces, the sun flooded in the big windows in the nurseries and in the living-room—which was mostly a nursery, too. We were on the outskirts of the town, with woods and meadows to the north of us, and every summer the three months' vacation which my father as professor was usually able to share with us schoolboys, was spent in the smiling countryside of an old family estate fifty miles to the east.

Even with these ample and healthful surroundings we had our share of illness. Out of seven children not more than two would have lived to grow up if we had been born a hundred years earlier, without benefit of modern medical science. The little family graveyard in the country, dotted with the graves of great-great-aunts and uncles who had died in infancy, testified that even the gentry had never before been as protected as we. We survived, and grew to sound six-foot proportions, with sound hearts and sound lungs and sound muscles.

Most children, knowing no other environment but their own, can conceive no better till their critical faculties develop. In our case there was more than the usual reason for believing we were born into a perfect world, where no change was either desirable or possible.

Not that this meant happiness. I was annoyed when as a child sentimental grown-ups patted me on the head and said: "How wonderful to be a child. You'll never be so happy again." I still doubt whether childhood is a happy time. There are too many restraints and compulsions and inevitable disciplines. Freedom is a remote rainbow end. For a while I thought I would reach that goal when I was eleven. But eleven came and went, and I put it always a little farther ahead.

Freedom is a prerogative of the mature person whose environment permits it; and even then he must have learned that it has meaning only within disciplines. On the other hand happiness remains, in my opinion, largely an illusion, a permanent state of pleasurable enjoyment which is never attained in the perfection sought, and in so far as it is attained it has as much and as little significance for the "good life" as mere physical well-being.

Perhaps it was the pink socks and the candy rabbit that turned my mind at an early age from the pursuit of mere happiness. I took the candy rabbit because it was the biggest piece on the plate of candy offered me by my elderly Aunt Susan; for this I was roundly scolded as a greedy person without manners, and my newly roused conscience was confirmed in its sense of guilt when I found the rabbit of coarse texture and sickish flavor. The pink socks were perennial. We ran barefoot in the country in summers, but when we went to a party my mother, who always had wanted a daughter, could not resist putting us in pink socks, even after we looked rather gawky in them. I had it drilled into me that some things were right and proper though we didn't like them, and that my self-consciousness at being made to appear unconventional was something to be ashamed of. The result was that I developed a passion for freedom rather than for happiness. I had everything money could buy, but I was not my own master. Growing up, for me, has been a satisfying process of substituting my own disciplines for those imposed externally.

Yet, in spite of limitations, my childhood was almost Utopian. It was lived in an environment of sunshine and green fields, of nurtured health, of space to run in and grow in. Inseparable from these basic requirements of good food, shelter and fresh air, there was in our case an atmosphere of affection, and an earnest inculcation of moral and aesthetic standards. If there were imperfections in this ideal childhood environment I was not aware of them till much later.

My conception of an ideal social order is therefore derived, to no small extent, from this background. Since I have become convinced that the resources of this planet are sufficient to permit every growing child to have the advantages I had, I cannot be content merely to assure them to my own children. Even from the point of view of taste, the candy rabbit was disappointing.

### *First Lessons in Economics*

I was aware from an early age, of course, that there was poverty and misfortune in the world. A home as delicately keyed to finer sensibilities as mine was, no matter how much its refinement was colored by snobbery—and ours was shamefully snobbish—could not but make a child sensitive to others' pain. One of my most horrible recollections is of helping to kill three weaklings in a litter of Airedale puppies by awkwardly trying to break their backs.

Misfortune was exceptional, I believed. My nurse once pointed out a blind man to me as an object of pity specially arranged for by God so that we more fortunate ones would not be too proud in our blessings. That didn't quite satisfy me, but there was no other explanation available, and it was a convenient explanation of poverty as well as pain. At the age of eight I was taken with some other little boys from the select day school which my brothers and I attended, to distribute some Thanksgiving baskets in a tenement. The horror of poverty is still a vivid tangible blast of fetid air leaping out at me as we stood on a dark landing that smelled of urine. I got home as soon as I could, and tried not to think of the children I had been unable to count in that steaming flat.

My curiosity was not such that I wondered why this tenement life existed only a mile from Prospect Hill. But its smells remained in my nostrils, and I feared what I was only vaguely conscious of below the sunlit hilltop where we lived.

Fortunately there were barriers to keep the two worlds separate. Across the street from our house was a very large vacant lot, extending a quarter of a mile from the hill-crest down to the valley, where factory workers' dwellings clustered at the end of the carline. The lot was being held for some buyer who would build a mansion like those alongside, even more spacious than ours. In winter it was a favorite slope for coasting. Occasionally so many children from the factory district would come there to slide that the snow would be packed down to ice, and a smooth board or a dishpan would serve as a sled for the poorest. On such occasions my brothers and I, who had been taught not to associate with "muckers," would look on from a distance, a little disquieted by this noisy invasion of Prospect Hill. Later a wealthy old lady, related to us, built a big house on it, put a high wire fence all along the lower boundaries to keep out the "muckers," and installed an Italian caretaker, whose children knew their place, to see that the grounds were not invaded. We were permitted to coast there alone, in lordly style. If occasionally a couple of kids from the lower neighborhood, seeing us on the slide, climbed over to join us, we told them it was "private property"; they would look on us with new respect, as from some higher world, and wistfully turn away.

There must have been an unacknowledged germ of shame in my heart on such occasions, for as I look back now I loathe the very sound of the words "private property."

My school life, passed at private day schools, private boarding schools, and later at Yale, did little to alter the perspective of the world I had acquired at home. I never came in contact with the grimy world below my social class. In so far as I was aware of other social levels it was of those a little higher than mine, those to which Park Avenue and Southampton were as natural as my

Prospect Hill, rather than of those below me. Poverty, like death, was something well-bred people did not talk about.

I was only twelve years old when we went into the last war. I felt a good deal of pride, and much less alarm than I should have felt, when my father joined the Air Service (at forty-two!) and went to France. But I remember being much troubled by the inconsistencies between some of the new words and attitudes I was expected to learn and those I had been taught earlier. My father wrote a farewell letter to his sons, telling them always to hate the Germans. But I had been brought up in a definitely "Christian" home, and the belief that one should love one's enemies had, with some difficulty, been expounded to me. I had been taught the Ten Commandments, including "Thou shalt not kill," and now my father was going over to France to help kill Germans.

At twelve one has begun to reason for oneself, and obvious inconsistencies bother one more than a few years later, when the habit of rationalization and the separation of ideas in water-tight compartments have been developed. I was troubled by the way war news and war pictures came through. Allied attacks were "heroic"; German attacks "vicious." Allied resistance was a courageous defense of homes, wives and children; German resistance was that of cornered rats. I vividly remember a picture of British soldiers "mopping up" an enemy dug-out, by throwing hand-grenades down the entrance, while the Germans cowered in terror at being blown to pieces: I made myself believe this was "heroic" and "magnificent" and a "great victory," because the caption said so, but I found it difficult to be really enthusiastic.

At the same time I had mental difficulties with some other adult conceptions not immediately connected with fighting. I could not understand Liberty Bonds and War Savings Stamps, which I was encouraged to buy. Of course the country needed money to fight the war, though why it had to pay for what seemed to be its own anyway was difficult to understand. Wasn't the whole country fighting this war? But I was glad to do "my bit" and have some handsome engraved paper as a token of my patriotism; I was stumped, however, at the notion of being paid back in some mythical year in an infinite future, 1935, or something like that. How would the country be able to pay me back? Out of taxes, I was told; everybody would be paid back out of taxes. But who would pay the taxes? Why, everybody pays taxes, of course. Then we'll all be paying the money to ourselves? I couldn't understand it. The country was getting into debt to itself. It was a terrific "burden," this national debt, but it was one of the sacrifices made necessary by war, and some day we'd tax ourselves to pay the money back to ourselves.

The sneaking suspicion I had at that time, that there was something wrong about grown-ups' ways of thinking about the war and how it was paid for, stayed with me. I would hardly have admitted it to myself, as I went through my many years' schooling in conventionality. But when, at the age of twenty-five, I came up against radical criticism of capitalism, childhood doubts were revived, and made me receptive. Certainly there was nothing in my schooling to foster my doubts.

Yet my schooling was good in its way. The main emphasis, as at home, was on the humanities, literature, conventional history, Latin and modern languages. These studies sharpen one's critical and aesthetic susceptibilities, and while carefully skirting any embarrassing contact with the real world, they develop a humane sympathetic attitude toward one's fellow-man, which can be reconciled in later life with the cruelties and crudities of competitive capitalism only by the most rigorous maintenance of mental barriers between the "business" and domestic parts of one's mind.

A secondary emphasis of this education, no less valuable in its way, was on science. In the last generation schools have insisted on laboratory work in elementary courses in science, and the scientific method has involved a constant checking back and forth between what the books said and what could be observed. Within the careful limits of the laboratory experiments, in chemistry, physics and biology, there were no taboos or "verbal monsters" permitted. In drawing the dissected earthworm one faithfully included and properly labeled its anus along with its other visible parts, with perhaps a slight thrill that here at least one was in contact with the real world!

Economics was different. I only took one college course in economics, and there was no laboratory work. One could dwell in pure theory, rendered more or less visual through scrawled diagrams on a blackboard. No connection between economics and the real world was indicated. New Haven, where I had come back to college, was a manufacturing town, a railroad center, a favorite resort of sweatshops, only seventy-five miles from the nerve center of American finance. But the heads of the Economics Department lived on Prospect Hill, and I learned no more of the reasons for wealth and poverty than if I had still been living there. Yale's Gothic cloisters in the booming twenties were not likely to make one question the eternal verities of the economic and social order.

I had a guilty conscience, nevertheless. I was blood and bones of New England Puritan stock, with innumerable Congregational ministers in my ancestry, and something of grim old Calvin, by way of that expert in hell, Jonathan Edwards, must have come down to me in direct line. A slightly different steer somewhere in my past and I might have contented myself with organized charity, or even "social work"; in that case I could have conscientiously squared the parable of the talents with the admonition to the "rich young ruler"; I would have carefully conserved my investments, and at the same time given to good works as insurance against that alarming needle's eye.

Some practical economics, as distinguished from the theory taught in "Econ. 10," had been drilled into me from an early age by my father. Brought up himself in far-away Hawaii, by a missionary father, whose America was that of the 1850's, my father had in extraordinarily pure form the Calvinist economics that furnished such an impenetrable armor to nineteenth-century capitalism. Wealth is a reward for good works, as he taught us children by paying five cents for every excellent school report card. In business, competitive shrewdness is the criterion of success, as he believed it important to teach us by holding a monthly auction of knick-knacks and odds and ends—advertising calendars, duplicates of books in his library, old jack-knives and pencils. We little boys would bid avidly against each other, one cent at a time, being soundly laughed at if we bid up something to a price more than we could pay or more than it was worth. We were early taught to put money "to work" in the savings bank, quite unable to understand how pennies and dimes and dollar bills could do physical labor, but being duly awed when we were taken down to the marble-pillared temple and introduced to the banker, a much more mysterious and powerful person even than any minister we knew.

Perhaps you will think that, having everything money would buy, I could not know the value of money. But my father had had to save his pennies as a boy, and he was determined that we should have a proper respect for them, too. Pocket money was doled out in infinitesimal proportions. We were encouraged to do odd jobs like mowing the lawn around our country place, for which we would be paid ten cents an hour. It was then a thrilling experience to go to the village store and buy candy. Large candy sticks, striped like a barber pole, were a penny apiece. In my early thinking on economics the unit standard of value was the satisfaction to be derived from buying and eating one penny stick of candy, and larger sums of money were mentally transposed into terms of this unit. I was never permitted to buy so many that I learned anything about the law of diminishing utility or about marginal utility.

At the age of about fifteen, I was put on an allowance of two thousand dollars a year, out of which I was to pay all expenses, school tuition, clothing, and incidentals, leaving only vacation expenses to be borne at home. The allowance was half in cash and half derived from investments—diversification in sound common stocks was the only rule, but in practice I didn't make any changes from the excellent portfolio of securities turned over to me. Before my annual check could be deposited at the beginning of a new year I had to show a balanced account book for the previous year—which usually meant a couple of sweating days out of the Christmas vacation—and a balanced budget for the coming year. I was solemnly warned: "Neither a borrower nor a lender be."

I always tried to live up to these precepts, and accepted the economic system they vaguely indicated. Every Christmas I was asked what my stocks were worth, and I learned to look them up the day before in the financial columns of the newspaper. But my conscience still troubled me. I did not feel affluent with my two thousand dollars a year, even with all the vacation perquisites thrown in. I did not know that this income was larger than eighty per cent of the *families* lived on in America, let alone individuals. But I could not be entirely blind to the fact that most people were poorer than I, and I had heard vaguely of some idealist who had gone to live in the slums to see "how the other half lived."

After graduation from college, still innocent about most of the ways of the world, I decided to take the three-year course in the Law School, but, unwilling to spend more vacations in play or trips to European museums, I determined to devote the next three summers to seeing for myself "how the other half lived."

### *I Go Exploring*

The first summer, that of 1927, I worked two months as a farm hand. My first job, secured through an employment agency in Springfield, Massachusetts, lasted only a few days. The farmer made it clear that I wasn't worth what he was paying me: he said he didn't mind my inexperience but that I showed no ability to learn. I left, wondering what a Phi Beta Kappa key really signified. I got another job by answering a want ad, and my pride was so low that I was willing to work for a shamefully low wage, a dollar a day—with board and lodging.

I learned little except that the other farm hands who came and went were unenthusiastic about getting in someone else's hay, and that everyone in the little Massachusetts neighborhood was impatient to have Sacco and Vanzetti die. The old farmer, who did more work than any of his hands, was particularly bitter against the delays of the law: "Arnachists," as he called them, "ought to be shot at sunrise." But I acquired some idea of the amount of backbreaking work that is involved in producing food for city populations, and how much of the backbreaking work can be saved by such machines as trucks, power hay-forks, automatic hay-loaders, and an overhead trolley to carry manure out of the cow barn.

In the summer of 1928 I used a little "pull" to get work in a brass mill in Waterbury. The first job was in the rivet shop, on a night shift—thirteen hours, five nights a week—a nightmare of feeding rivets into a shaping machine, deafening clamor, the nauseous smell of hot oil, piecework speed, and a hideous endless monotony. I watched the clock hands crawl around the dial. Talk was impossible in the din, and the workers were far apart. I decided then and there that unskilled factory labor made a horrible travesty of human life. Of course anyone can get used to it. But only by a kind of encysting process: all mental activity must withdraw into a tiny inner shell, and the more it can simulate death the better the adjustment. I survived in that shrunken inner world by a conscious and elaborate organization of day-dreams.

Transferred to another department, as an inspector of the product of a number of machines operated mostly by women, I found myself far enough up the hill of purgatory to get a considerable perspective. I developed a new appreciation of the marvelous and intricate ingenuity of the machine, and at the same time of the relative cheapness of human labor. Many small processing operations on light brass products—electric light sockets, vanity cases, automobile hub caps—were being performed in this shop. The principal operation was feeding the machines. In some cases this was performed by hand, in others again by automatic mechanisms. The automatic feeders seemed to break down frequently enough so that the cost of using them was very close to feeding by hand, and many of the girls would be working alongside of machines which were performing the same operation. A slight increase in efficiency and added investment—or perhaps a slight rise in wages—would have made it economical to dispense with at least half the workers in that shop.

I was filled with a vague disquiet. This balancing of costs, this failure to utilize the automatic process to the full, so the girls could get out into the summer greenery, the urge to see them free—free from this prison-like confinement—over against the realization that freedom meant unemployment and empty pocketbooks, all puzzled me. The hideousness of Waterbury spread out for several miles in every direction. But I knew that out beyond was a vacation land, where my friends were playing, breathing the deep fragrance of newly mown golf courses in the sun. I saw the automatic machine as a bringer of freedom—and fear.

In my smug Republicanism I found comfort in the fact that the plant maintained a trade school open to any bright young worker, and that it would even send a particularly promising youngster to engineering school. It was undoubtedly possible for the ambitious and able to rise in the world. But somehow that did not quite make up for the fact that the elderly woman who was stamping "Made in U.S.A." on brass thimbles down in the corner had been working there for thirty-seven years, and that she was humbly grateful to the company for giving her an annual week's vacation with pay ever since her twenty-fifth year.

The next summer, the last of the glorious 1920's, I left New England and wandered westward. I had a week of selling magazine subscriptions from door to door in Pittsburgh, and then, after a long jump, another week in Oklahoma City. I learned that salesmanship is a more horrible killer of humanity than factory labor. The smart young white-collar men who sold sixteen-dollar club subscriptions in working-class homes made good money if they sold three or four a day, but they sold whatever souls they had at the same time. I could see not the slightest connection between the possible value of the product sold and the making of a sale. The sale depended entirely on the extent to which the salesman could lie, bluff, wheedle and cajole the badgered housewife into signing her name—there was little chance of a sale if the man of the house were at home. Every house was already littered with tawdry magazines which were admittedly not read. I was congratulated by the "crew manager" when I made a sale my first day—to a wan little woman who had sprained her back a week before and was unable to get out of an armchair even to change her baby's diapers, much less put up any effective "sales resistance."

Every house interior in Oklahoma City was exactly like every house interior in Pittsburgh, a cheap imitation of the furnishings depicted in the garish advertisements in the magazines I was selling. I was looking for what was left of the Frontier and I had to escape. I bought a battered little Chevrolet—not out of my earnings—and followed the wheat harvest north. I was a plutocrat, of course, compared to the thousands of harvest hands who hitchhiked or rode the rails. With constantly changing companions I followed rumors of ripe harvests and many jobs, up through Oklahoma, Kansas, Nebraska. Every little grain center we came to was packed with gaunt sunburned men on the same quest, getting one, two, three days of work a month. The combine had conquered the grain belt, and the men it had displaced were tramping the roads in forlorn thousands. I got two or three jobs of a couple of days each, and was appalled at the bleakness and ugliness of these dung-encrusted farm homes, the "backbone of America." In one house, on marginal land, at the end of the Bad Lands, where the wheat seemed too scrawny to harvest, the farmer and his wife hated each other with a murderous hate, and the "great open spaces" outside seemed to squeeze in the tiny world of their discontent. I did not know then that depression had hit agriculture in 1920, and that this failing struggle with failing land was already almost a decade old.

I fled once more, into my own familiar world, visiting some friends at Swan Lake in the Montana Rockies. I drove up in my now tottering Chevrolet, with my clothes still grimy from the harvest fields, and I had a sense of relief at being back among my own kind when the maid who answered the bell referred me to the "service entrance." Swan Lake is a summer refuge of the lords of Anaconda Copper, who, though I did not know it then, virtually own the state of Montana. Their daughters, with whom I went riding, wore immaculate riding habits tailored in Fifth Avenue shops. I could not help liking their company, but I felt uneasy at their contrast to the gaunt men who sat silent and dusty on the curbstones of the little wheat towns a few hundred miles away. And I had no further illusions about the Frontier.

## *A World in Transition*

I had one more year in the Law School. In November there was a stock-market crash, which I read about indifferently. My own discontent with the laws of personal and real property was getting unbearable. My fellow-students were focused on the big Wall Street firms, where the most lucrative business was in reorganizing copper companies and farm implement manufacturing corporations and brass factories. But they never expected to handle copper or farm machinery or brass, only Class A and Class B stock and junior debentures and waivers and estoppels and equities. Unemployment was a word more and more in use. But I had difficulty linking its abstractness to the girls I had known making brass gadgets, or the tramping harvest hands.

I was still far from questioning the economic system around me. It rested on eternal verities, though I knew there was always room for improvement and reform. I had a dim Utopian yearning to see the rank wilderness I had glimpsed in my summer wanderings reclaimed to the same carefully tended trimness and beauty and comfort of the garden world in which I had been brought up. But I was still too much concerned with straightening out inner personal problems to bother overmuch with social problems.

The prospect of settling into law practice immediately on taking the bar examinations was one I could not face. Again I took flight, this time with a generous letter of credit in my pocket. In some mysterious fashion I could not understand, this piece of paper would enable me to draw money in Allahabad or Singapore, Tokyo or Constantinople, and live in the style to which I was accustomed, while I explored the great world in a larger circle. I still felt as ignorant of the real world as when I lived on Prospect Hill.

For a year I went toward the rising sun, by way of Europe to the Near East, India and on to the Far East, and then for another year westward, first across the length of the Soviet Union and finally, after zigzagging around Europe, back home.

From the moment I first left America I found myself in an atmosphere tense with change. The whole political structure of the post-war era was tottering and shifting, as the economic foundations under it gave way little by little. The people I talked with, the strangely detached, international-minded, traveling population—it was not in tourist season—spoke in familiar terms of catastrophes impending. I was lugging a heavy suitcase of books, picked out, not by my father, but by a mildly liberal economics professor. I read anthropology, the history of morals, a Fabian Socialist book or two, a volume of American muck-raking. My preconceptions slowly began to disintegrate as I pursued my journey.

I had been brought up on Kipling. The special mission of the Anglo-Saxon race in bringing enlightenment to the world—the "white man's burden"—was something to be taken for granted. But as I traveled out by way of Egypt and the Arab Near East to India I became aware of the seamy side of imperialism. I saw picture-book Englishmen—beautiful, charming, arrogant—living in "oriental luxury," where the per capita income for all of India was five cents a day. As an American without undue race prejudice I made friends easily with Hindus who were never considered anything but menials by their British rulers and exploiters. I talked to Gandhi and Jawaharlal Nehru, and realized that ideas on politics, economics and social relationships—drawn not only from the cultural past of India but from modern Russia and the Western socialist movement—were leading toward conclusions "not dreamt of in my philosophy."

A vague sense of a whole world in convulsions began to grip me. India was obviously headed for independence, whether rightly or wrongly, peacefully or violently; and then what would happen to the British Empire and the tight little world of Anglo-Saxon snobbery in which I had been brought up?

I went on to China. The revolt against foreign imperialism was at its height. I had the chilling experience of being spat at as I drove through the noisome slums of Shanghai. I visited the vast tomb of Sun Yat-sen, symbol of the new China, in Nanking, and read the principles he enunciated for the coming era—almost socialist in their emphasis on the role of government in the building up of a China for the Chinese. I could understand why the European and American business men feared the rising Chinese nationalism, which was obviously destined some day to sweep them, and their "concessions," and "international settlements," and "open door" for profits, into limbo. As I dined luxuriously in an air-conditioned dining-room at the top of one of Shanghai's skyscraper hotels I was vaguely disquieted at the thought that the ideals driving China were not the ideals of American democracy (which somehow had produced American skyscrapers), but of something newer and more radical. Yet when I interviewed Chiang Kai-shek—former ally of Communists, now fighting them, later once again to become their ally—I felt in his piercingly direct black eyes some kind of spiritual force against which Western domination of China could not long contend.

I went north. I found the Forbidden City of Peiping and the cherry blossoms of Japan stale postcard stuff in comparison to the great drama of clashing world interests that was then coming to a head in Manchuria—imperialism, nationalism, the Western world versus the Eastern, American technology taken up and as it seemed improved by the Japanese, to begin some great venture about which nothing could yet be guessed except that it would follow no pattern yet known to history.

By the time I tremulously stacked my possessions on a "hard car" bench on the Trans-Siberian express in Manchouli, the ideas in which I had been brought up, my conceptions of the world and its economic and social order, were riddled through and through. Soviet Russia put a new strain on them, and they crumbled completely.

I entered the Soviet Union with only the knowledge of the average conservative outsider. I feared I was coming to the center of the disintegrating forces that were wrecking civilization. Even if the Russians were still human and friendly—I had half-expected to be spotted as a capitalist, taken out at some Siberian way station and shot—nevertheless the whole Bolshevik way of thinking was in too many respects the precise opposite of all I had been taught to believe, for me to take to it except as a frightened patient takes to some drastic medicine. The workers in factories, the "toilers" of every kind, were exalted; cultured refinement, in which I had been brought up, was held in contempt. Moreover, I was aware from the first of the contradictions and inconsistencies of this new world of universal brotherhood. I saw terror in the faces of some who looked over their shoulder before they talked to me. I sensed tragedy in pitifully ragged and uprooted peasant travelers. I saw furtive beggars, who had no bread-cards, devouring crusts which the more fortunate could spare. As a "hard class" traveler I resented the well-groomed officials who traveled in the luxury of "soft."

But I began learning a new economics. It was concerned with production rather than finance, with making goods rather than with making money.

The tractor was then the symbol of the machine world this country was building. Tractors and combines were being built, not to sell haphazardly to farmers who would then have no use for hired hands, but to enable more food to be grown with less human labor. I was taken into factories, where the sight of hundreds of grimy humans tending countless implacable roaring machines filled me with the old horror of my Waterbury experience; but at least there was meaning and purpose here that lent hope: the more machines, the more products, the higher the standard of living, the more leisure. There was some sense to this. It was inconceivable that automatic machinery would be idle until everybody had enough; it was inconceivable that it would be a curse instead of a blessing.

There were banks, but they were not marble-pillared temples. I saw all sorts of bookkeeping entries being made while I waited endlessly for travelers' checks to be cashed. But the whole bookkeeping mechanism of the country was explained in comparatively simple and obvious terms in the propaganda I read. There were confusing hangovers: a theoretical gold standard, government bond issues, and others. But it was not hard to understand that the monetary system was thought of as wholly subordinate to the production schedule of the Five Year Plan.

As for the consumer and his standard of living, obviously something was wrong. I was told how so much production was going into building factories and making machines and developing resources—which would later make possible much more ample consumption—that the present consumer goods were few. The shelves in the shops were mostly bare; it was clear that consumers had more than enough tokens in their pockets—money, food cards, identification cards entitling workers to factory meals or special allotments of shoes and other goods—to absorb all the goods produced as soon as they were made available. But goods were woefully short.

Thrift was laughed at. After all, was not the government practicing thrift to the extent of diverting half the country's productive energies into capital construction? A girl teased me for my "bourgeois" habits when she caught me ordering the less expensive items on the hotel menu, while I had a pocketbook full of rubles. What is money for, if not to spend?

This was the third and biggest year of the first Five Year Plan. Everywhere on billboards, on street corners, in newspapers, were the latest figures on the production schedules. The economic system came into diagrammatic relief. It was easy to understand. There were vast resources in the land, and vast numbers of hands to work these resources—and to make machines to work these resources—in order to produce and distribute goods.

Meanwhile I read, as an echo from some strange mythical world I had left, of the pound going "off" gold, and of the panic in the money markets of Europe. And the only American news that reached me was of lengthening breadlines in the shadow of bursting warehouses, of "hunger marches" while wheat was burned, of idle men and idle machines and idle resources.

This Russian economy was devastatingly logical. I did not know how to refute it. Life was brutal and crude, to be sure, and the lack of skilled administrators, which a year later brought parts of the Five Year Plan near to collapse, was apparent enough. But permeating the whole was an appealing ideal—plenty for all—and a stark common sense in the business of going out to secure it, in sharp contrast to the oblique mythology of the economics I had learned at home.

I spent three months wandering over the Soviet Union—Siberia, Turkestan, the Caucasus, Moscow, Leningrad, Kiev, Odessa. I spoke enough Russian to make my way alone, and for a while I had a job in Moscow teaching English, to give me the feeling that in a small way I was part of the picture. The warm kindly humanity of the Russian people, whether or not due to their economic system, had certainly not been destroyed by it, and the eager confidence of the young people won me to tolerance as nothing else could have done. I left in a state of complete moral and intellectual indigestion.

That winter I spent in Italy. If communism was to be studied seriously as an alternative to the ways I had been taught, then fascism was to be studied equally seriously. I was without prejudices or preconceptions by this time, desperately searching, knowing only that the greatest sin was a closed mind.

Mussolini's Italy struck me at every point with its parallels to Russia, except that at every point it was on a lower level. There was the same fanatical enthusiasm of the young people, but not quite so fanatical. There was the same emphasis on collective action as a national group, but without the clear-cut simplicity of direct socialist planning. There was the same arrogant ignorant superiority to the "capitalist" world outside, though the differences from capitalism were often not apparent on the surface. There was a little building construction going on, but not on anything like the Russian scale; and I was not taken to see new factories. The atmosphere was not quite so tense, either with terror or exuberance.

One strange fact struck me as soon as I left Russia; it amazed me when I landed in Constantinople from Odessa, and it stayed with me when I got to Italy. It was the display of foodstuffs and other wares in innumerable shops. My first impression was one of returning to lands of milk and honey. But ragged poverty and pinched faces were everywhere for the looking. Apparently Italy had been unable to solve that basic problem: her people couldn't consume what she could produce, because they couldn't buy it. There was no integration between productive capacity and purchasing power. I vaguely sensed that this was crucial.

I went on to Social Democratic Germany, where the only choice for people rendered desperate by depression seemed to be between the Communists and the Nazis. I spent a few months in England, where at least I hoped to find a safe and familiar stability. Could England, with its centuries-long traditions which were also my traditions, conceivably have a revolution?

One of the political leaders I sought out was a member of the House of Lords. I was ushered down the cathedral-like corridors of the Houses of Parliament by impressive flunkies, and shown into a great Gothic room that might have been a bishop's study. A grave and elegant gentleman received me, every inch a Lord. Here, I felt, was the British Empire itself, in all its dignity. What if the Lord was a member of the Labour party? England could absorb anything, even the Labour party, and turn it into a pillar of strength. But when I asked the Lord his views on England, on Europe, on the state of the world generally, I was appalled. Nothing but revolution could sweep away the decadent institutions that were impeding progress. Never mind the cost. It was better to have a thorough house-cleaning and start again.

If such ideas could be quietly intoned in the chambers of a peer there was no longer any use my trying to pretend the old world was not vanishing. Everything in my past had conspired to make me a conservative. Yet now I had to adjust myself to radical change as a fact.

Of course I had always known that history must mean change. But apparently in certain periods the pace is speeded, the stresses and strains of growth and decay become intolerable, events move suddenly and swiftly. I knew now that I was living in such a period. It was even conceivable that civilization would be unable to make the adjustments necessary to survival. I already sensed everywhere the consciousness of impending doom which was to grow in the following years.

I found at the end of my world tour, almost to my horror, that I was arguing the inevitability of revolution with everyone I met.

## *Myself in Transition*

In one sense, to be sure, I was prepared to be a rebel against the *status quo* for some time before the crucial shift in my thinking. The grim realities of American life as I had, if only superficially, discovered them in the summers between studying law, had struck me most of all for their ugliness. The contrast between the industrial wastelands and the sunny green pastures where I had been brought up was too vivid. I resented the ethical contrast between the standards of generosity and affection and mutual consideration of my own home and the injustices and brutalities of the commercial system. Yet my revolt was more aesthetic than ethical. The disorder and planless anarchy of the workaday world horrified me; the sordidness of poverty filled me with disgust rather than pity. So there was something in me that welcomed, almost from the first, the idea of an orderly planned economy.

Yet to accept a really radical concept of change warred with my natural conservatism; even more it warred with my idealized craving for freedom. How could I fit my individuality into the stern requirements of communism? Fascism had no appeal. It seemed a poor substitute for communism and offered no more scope for the precious values of individualism and individual freedom. I finally concluded that there was little chance for the individual in the world as I had seen it, and that there might be vastly greater chances in the new world I saw ahead.

By the time I left Europe to come home, I was converted: The capitalist system was passing and must be replaced by a socialist system. Since Russia seemed to be having immense successes in solving the basic economic problem—its industrial production doubled in four years while the rest of the world was slumping to desperate depths—I was ready to call myself a communist. Since Marx was the father of Russian communism, I was ready to be a Marxist. Since the dictatorship of the proletariat was the slogan under which the political changes had been carried out, I was even ready to admit that this might be the only way, though, with my background, this required a greater religious consecration than the rest.

Yet, having thrown off one ready-made mythology with infinite pain, I was skeptical from the first about the new mythology that was offered instead. I got back to New York expecting to see signs everywhere of the uprising of the American working class, as I had read about it in Russia. But New York looked much the same. I couldn't see the uprising. I wandered in Union Square and bought the revolutionary Marxist publications for sale around the edges, but the knot of jobless men clustered near a soap-box orator looked forlorn and hardly sufficient to terrorize the "bourgeoisie." I went in the subway to Coney Island on a Sunday afternoon, and "the revolution" seemed as remote as did Moscow.

From the little I had been able to observe of the real America in my summer vacation explorations, I found it difficult to believe that "Tovarich," or its American equivalent "Comrade," would ever be the common mode of address. I could not imagine American schools propounding "dialectical materialism," though I knew we had plenty of nonsense of our own. I could not visualize the America of Jefferson's Declaration of Independence, of Andrew Jackson's frontier boots, of Lincoln's log-cabin-to-White-House tradition, becoming a Soviet America.

So I put this all aside for the time being, and set out on what seemed an immediate and obvious task, helping other Americans to think at least as far as I had thought.

How far was that? I knew that the arrangements by which we worked and produced and distributed goods in this country—I called them the capitalist system—did not work well, and that new arrangements had to be devised. For eight months after I got back from my world tour, through March, 1933, it looked as though they soon would break down completely.

I was aware that there were immense possibilities for the creation of wealth in this country, unused resources, unused labor power, unused machines, and on the basis of what Russia had already done, it seemed reasonable to assume that with some common sense in our economic arrangements we could produce plenty for everybody and abolish poverty. I had seen enough of poverty in my travels in this country so that the idea of abolishing it filled me with enthusiasm. I knew enough about the amenities and potentialities of life if it were lived in a well-tended garden, with freedom, and the opportunity to create, to make me want to shout from the housetops that such a life could be made available for everybody.

Moreover, poverty by that year 1932 was on every street corner. And I became aware of the permanent casualties of the "American system," tottering old bums, empty hulks of men who had had no solid food inside them for longer than I liked to think—though somehow they could usually find how to get a drink. When one of them would ask me for a nickel for a cup of coffee, it made me feel utterly futile. For they were past helping. I had a sense of emptiness in my own stomach when I saw those hollow phantoms. I compared the gray stubble in their sunken cheeks with the full smoothness of my Wall Street friends, and the hideous ramshackleness of not only the Bowery but most of New York, with the velvety finish of the comfortable homes I had an intimate knowledge of, and I had a craving to see these hulks washed and shaved and tailored and comfortably ensconced in an armchair by a club window drinking highballs in gentlemanly fashion. I had a craving to take a huge sponge and wipe all these ugly tenements off the face of Manhattan and begin again, with some fantastic sunny "city of the future" for a plan.

I had no doubt that the problem was basically economic. I had no inclination to preach at these old bums, as I had once done at a "mission" when I was in college.

So, with a like-minded colleague, I launched a magazine. We felt we were following in the footsteps of Thomas Paine, whose pamphlet, *Common Sense*, had done much to bring another great crisis to a head; so we took that name. Our message was direct if oversimplified. The economic system was breaking down, with consequent poverty and misery "in the midst of plenty." The alternative was "production for use." It seemed obvious to us that the Marxist parties, socialist and communist, were too deeply involved in European dogmas to meet a response in America. We looked to the more spontaneous native revolts—Populist, Progressive, Farmer-Labor—as indications of the kind of movement that might succeed. And we called for a reassertion of the "ideals of 1776" as the logical slogans under which the American people might be aroused to action.

At the same time I welcomed the opportunity to speak from every platform that invited me. If I were asked embarrassing questions about objectives and methods, there were always easy answers ready. But they were only tentative ones, and many of them were sheer bluff.

I suspected that I was only at the beginning of my problem, rather than at the end. Innumerable questions were rising in my own mind which I could not answer.

The only people I found who had answers to every question were the Marxists. They often gave different answers, and they fought bitterly among themselves. But they had an overwhelmingly voluminous literature, from Marx down to contemporary thinkers; more than any of the non-Marxist groups they appreciated the profundity and complexity of the change from one kind of economic system to another. What they seemed to lack was freshness of perception. They considered all problems in terms of mid-nineteenth-century concepts, and even their language had a slight savor of antiquity. Their answers did not satisfy me.

The next half-dozen years have been so swift and full as to leave rationalization and understanding always panting in the rear. The New Deal came in six months after we started *Common Sense*. It seemed to fit none of the categories in which radicals, including myself, were thinking. Was it socialism or capitalism? Even today the debate rages. At the same time as the New Deal, Hitler appeared on the front of the world stage. Was Nazism socialism or capitalism? Americans pretty generally agreed that they did not like the Nazis, but with equal unanimity they did not understand them. Meanwhile more and more was being written and thought about the Soviet Union, and with the recognition of its government by Roosevelt an era of almost wistful admiration set in among American liberals; yet even in the case of communist Russia the old categories of thought did not seem to fit. Business men went to see for themselves and came back saying Stalin's system was not socialism or communism, but a form of state capitalism. The Trotskyites, at the other extreme, were becoming more and more vocal in their insistence that "the revolution" had been "betrayed."

Two conclusions began to emerge in my own thinking. One was not given clear expression till, as I mentioned in the introductory chapter, "semantics" burst on my consciousness. It was that the words we were using were inadequate and dangerous tools. The "revolution," the "working class," "socialism," "communism," "fascism," "capitalism," "liberalism," the "profit system," "production for use"—all these were abstractions being used variously and incongruously. As Stuart Chase said, following Korzybski and Bridgman, what we needed was more "operational" thinking, more testing of our concepts in the real world, to find what they referred to—their "referents."

The second conclusion was that, while we were in a period of historical transition from one system of economic practices to another, no one had clearly defined the beginning and the end. What were the essential features of the system we were leaving behind? And what were the essential features of the new system toward which we were tending? Transition, yes; but transition *from* what, *to* what? Until they knew the answers to that, how could intelligent men decide on *methods* of transition?

Before I went any farther it was necessary to determine just what this slippery word "capitalism" referred to. I never became enough a rebel to want to sweep away the whole past, just for the sake of starting again. The more gradual the transition, I was sure, the better, on all scores. What were the minimum changes that were necessary? I had to go backward, into my own past and into the historical past, back before the Great War, or at least before the Great Depression, to find what specific "referents" made up this abstract term "capitalism." Then only could I begin to define my problem.

# Chapter Three

## WHAT IS CAPITALISM?

IN 1914 I was nine years old. Few of my useful memories go back to the mythical pre-war world. My nursery view of it was a part of my nursery view of home and family. Though I might not always like its constraints, it was perfection. My parents and the rules they made were unalterable and infallible. The world had reached the final stage of progress. Once there had been ogres, cannibals, wars, pestilences, hunger and greed and cruelty and oppression. But these things, except in a few out-of-the-way corners not yet reached by the American and British flags, had been cleared up. The world was now as clean and bright and sunny as our nursery.

My knowledge of that well-ordered world which was shattered by the war is thus only a memory of an atmosphere impregnated with smug assumptions.

The earlier voices of protest and revolt had been almost stilled. In my especially sheltered world I had never even heard of them. The Utopians and Christian Socialists, Owen, William Morris, Charles Kingsley, whose revolt against the ugliness and iniquity of mid-nineteenth-century industrialism had given the first idealistic drive to the British Labour party, and their late American counterpart, Edward Bellamy, had been forgotten in the glittering promise of the twentieth century. I read Kingsley's *Water Babies:* its chimney-sweep victim of child labor was only a lay figure in an ancient fairy tale. I read Dickens, and the grim horror of England's factory slums frightened me, but this was long ago, before humanitarianism had triumphantly legislated poverty out of sight.

As for Karl Marx and Marxian socialism, which had flared briefly in the more backward countries of Central and Eastern Europe, not even their echo had reached my world. They had given way to social legislation and an increasingly respectable trade unionism in Europe. Though, without my being aware of it, there was a buoyant and growing socialist movement in every advanced country, including America, in those pre-war years, it carried no menace of Marxian revolution.

One of the basic assumptions of the pre-war world, which still has its many stubborn adherents today, is that capitalism was the final achievement of a long struggle for liberty. The history books I read did not even say this, so basic was the assumption. In fact I never heard the word capitalism.

### *Two Simple Answers*

The trouble with history is that it is always told with ulterior ends in view. We justify our biases by citing our own interpretation of events. It has taken me some time to realize that of two completely opposing views of the origins of laissez faire capitalism each may contain parts of the truth. On the one hand is the view that capitalism grew out of the triumph over despotism. On the other is the Marxist view that capitalism is merely a new form of exploitation of one class by another.

Adherents of the Marxist view are inclined to be cynical of the older view, as a mere rationalization of ugly facts. Yet it was none the less true that capitalism came to full flower as a result of the liberating and enlightening tendencies brought on by the Renaissance and Reformation. Two paramount ideas came to affect men's minds powerfully in the seventeenth and eighteenth centuries: we may call them science and humanism. Science meant a new and more efficient method of thinking, and brought on the great technological achievements of the Industrial Revolution—the age of the machine. Humanism meant a belief in the value of the individual human personality, carrying as a corollary the belief in self-discipline—"freedom"—as opposed to an externally imposed discipline, and hence democracy, as a technique of group organization.

Simultaneous with this development—I think it fruitless to

argue whether it was cause or effect—came certain economic practices, which were ultimately given philosophic content as laissez faire: let the individual alone to seek his personal economic welfare free of governmental restraints, and the social welfare will follow naturally. The principle did indeed seem to produce remarkable results in terms of economic progress and the production of wealth. An "economic system" of amazing efficiency spread over the world.

The French Revolution and the whole transition from feudalism to capitalism is baffling and confusing because, while men like Voltaire were revolting against stupidity and superstition and autocracy, other men were reaping an economic reward through the establishment of "free enterprise," which meant a new form of exploitation. For understanding the latter development, the Marxist view is essential.

Down through history there have been a number of forms of exploitation by which the many were kept in subjection by the few. The three classical divisions have been slavery, serfdom, and the wage system. In all of them there has been some chance of recruiting up from the bottom, to strengthen the rulers' line. In all of them the great mass produced enough wealth above their own subsistence to enable the privileged few to live without themselves producing wealth. Parasitism and extravagance were not their only features, however. In every system the rulers performed the indispensable function of organizing and administering the group, without which it could not have survived as a group and most of its individuals would have perished. When the rulers failed to perform this function new individuals rose to take their places as rulers, and occasionally a deep social change occurred, as in the shift from slavery to feudalism, sufficient to change the nature of the class division.

The emergence of modern industry from the Middle Ages accompanied the growth of science and democracy. Ambitious business men, merchants, traders, manufacturers, gradually won scope to carry on their business enterprises without arbitrary interference. In France the monarchy was violently overthrown, and business men became assured of control under the Directorate and all future governments. In England there was some violent struggle in the seventeenth century, but for the most part the old land-holding nobility who controlled the King merged insensibly with the rising business magnates. In other countries business won only tentative concessions. But in every case it is important to note that the national state never relinquished its authority; it merely fell under the control of varying interests.

For his concept of the class state Marx must be given fullest credit. Other students of politics had idealized the State as some kind of divine and ultimate Reality. Marx showed how the political struggles, such as those of the period of the French Revolution, were struggles of classes representing conflicting economic interests, for control of the governmental machinery. Unfortunately he vastly oversimplified this class struggle; he believed that there must always be only two basic classes at odds, until finally one class, the proletariat, would abolish all class distinctions.

It is essential, then, to realize that laissez faire capitalism, while apparently thrusting government into a backstage, passive role, represented to an equal degree the coming to governmental power of a new class. It is true, however, that as compared to the previous ruling class, they wished to minimize direct governmental intervention in economic processes.

The outward picture, on which the laissez faire economists fastened, was that of the entrepreneur or free enterpriser. The driving incentive to production and efficiency was the margin of profit the enterpriser could derive from selling the product his workers turned out for more than it cost him. His enterprise was free, in the sense that no one gave him any orders. The workers were free in the sense that they could enter or leave his employment at will, unlike slaves or serfs.

The discrepancy between the theoretical freedom of the workers and the conditions under which they actually lived, particularly in the early nineteenth century in England (but capable of duplication any time anywhere, from the cotton mills of Shanghai to those of our southern mill towns), has always lent plenty of support to the Marxists' argument that this was a new system of slavery, not one of freedom. Actually, I think it fairer to say it was both.*

* If we wanted to take a long view we might say that the need for new disciplines and new administrative techniques had raced ahead of the possibilities of developing the self-disciplines which spell freedom. Self-discipline—

What I am concerned with here, however, is to emphasize how unreal, from the beginning, was the laissez faire ideal of complete freedom of individual enterprise, entirely unrestrained by government interference. First of all, there were intrinsic limitations in the concept, because of the fact that capitalism arrived on the scene as the expression of a new ruling class, exercising political as well as economic dominance. And, secondly, as it grew mightily in the nineteenth century, it evolved in ways which removed it farther and farther from the laissez faire ideal.

### *The State and the Corporation*

That first limitation may be stated thus: laissez faire, instead of being an absence of governmental policy, was itself a policy, and a policy of new and increasingly powerful political organizations, the national states.

The national states first claimed sovereign and absolute powers when the kings, supported by the rising business men of the towns, sought to eliminate the hampering restrictions of feudalism, with its conflicting allegiances to church and noble. The governments of those national states have claimed sovereign and absolute powers ever since, which necessarily has meant that they have always had the authority to interfere with or control economic activity at any stage. Yet that first alliance, between king and business man, symbolized a continuing division of function and interest between government and business. Perhaps less than any other ruling class, the business class has left the actual functions of government to underlings.

Thus, in spite of the fact that the state had sovereign powers, several factors contributed to the concept of a government with limited powers. The new democratic spirit of the Enlightenment, which furnished the rationale for the capitalist rise to dominance, also meant that final power resided in the people, not in a monarch or a ruling class. At the same time the business class put "checks and balances" on arbitrary power, to make sure that its

democracy—under the circumstances of the new machine age required a comparatively adult and intelligent personality. We are only now beginning to see how better and freer techniques can be worked out. The necessary development of personality is still far off.

underlings should never set themselves up once again as arbitrary monarchs.

The curious conflict of interest that resulted here—a conflict which upsets both the laissez faire assumptions and the Marxist assumptions—can be exemplified in a talk I once had with an old-fashioned political boss. This was at the time I was still a student in law school, before the Great Depression brought the old system down in ruins. I was interested in entering Republican politics in Connecticut, and I called on J. Henry Roraback, unquestioned boss of the party. He was also president of the Connecticut Light & Power Company. The electric utilities were dominating many state governments for favorable franchises and privileges, but only in Connecticut, so far as I know, was the leading utility magnate and the leading political figure the same person. Though no express dishonesty was ever charged against Roraback (after all, there was no occasion for him to offer bribes to himself) there was plenty of protest from liberals against this tie-up or virtual merger between business and government. Yet in my conversation with Roraback he rose wrathfully to denounce the tendencies in Washington toward government interference with private enterprise, particularly, of course, as regards the utilities.

Roraback was a sort of hangover from the nineteenth century. Business had its puppets in Washington and the state capitals, when it did not act for itself. Its railroads and banks and oil companies and utility corporations were dependent upon if not created by the government, so it made certain that the government was its own. Yet all the time it was afraid that its own government would use the sovereign power against it, instead of on its behalf.

The Connecticut Light & Power Company went back even farther than the nineteenth century for its first ancestor. For the corporation as the creation of the sovereign political power is over three centuries old.

The East India Company was a group of merchants given a monopoly franchise by Queen Elizabeth to carry on trade with India. It was delegated all kinds of powers, so that when it set up trading posts in India it established virtually its own governments, able to raise armies and carry on wars, issue money, dispense justice. It proceeded to undertake the greatest feat of robbery in history. Unlike any other "government," its sole purpose was loot. It had not even the traditions of *noblesse oblige*, which the robber barons of Europe early developed. Later, after the cruder forms of rapine had been exhausted, its functions were taken back by the government that had granted them, and India was more subtly exploited by an administrative machine that had some standards of governmental responsibility.

When I went to India in 1931 I found from my first day that the British rulers were split into two sections. I had met some army officers on the steamer and was invited by them to the Yacht Club overlooking Bombay harbor. Here the elite of officialdom, civil and military, foregathered for a highball in the dusk. Never has there been a ruling group so physically perfect, so courteously arrogant, as the soldiers and civil servants of British India. Not a brown native skin was to be seen, except for the servants; neither was there to be seen any person "in trade." The traders had originally been given supreme power; and gradually the officials who had come out in their interest, for more orderly exploitation, had encroached on that power, till the traders found themselves completely outside the sixty-two orders of precedence that govern British social functions in India.*

The East India Company was a joint-stock company. The modern corporation is its descendant. A corporation is given a charter by a sovereign state, and granted certain powers therein. The power to grant charters to corporations is one of the remaining attributes of sovereignty left in the various "states" of the United States.

It is well to look for a moment at this curious creature, the corporation. It is a method of group organization for group activity in the economic field, whose powers come from and are enforced by the more inclusive national group working through a government. It is an artificial legal creation. Its activities have no more to do with "free enterprise" than, let us say, the post office: the only difference is that the persons in administrative authority (able to fix prices or wages, for instance) derive their authority according to different procedures. In each case there is a compli-

* Was this perhaps a portent? Will the English aristocracy of Eton and Harrow who survived the transition from feudalism to capitalism, again come out on top, after a transition known as Tory socialism? See below, page 217.

cated functional group with certain powers not inconsistent with the functioning of the whole national group.

The management of the United States Steel Corporation, for instance, has at various times had the power of government: it could build and govern towns, or wipe them out, it could raise a private army of armed "deputies," it could control its own subservient courts of justice, it could create millions of dollars of purchasing power by using its credit with bankers, and it could give orders to a hundred thousand people. Some of these powers were inherent in its charter, some of them were derived from the fact that the government was its own government, some from the mere climate of opinion and social habits in which it operated. It was able to carry on its vast undertakings, not in some "natural" environment of "liberty," but in a complex network of laws, whose final authority was governmental. The flow of materials, from iron ore to finished steel rails, was governed, not alone by the skill and brawn of its many workers, nor alone by the managerial and organizing techniques of those who gave the orders, but equally by numerous pieces of paper, currency, checks, bills, notes, acceptances, commercial paper, whose efficacy was maintained by constituted legal authorities. Let a worker take home with him some of the tools with which he works, even so much as a screw driver, and the whole machinery of The Law, by which the national group is held together and ruled, will be set in motion to say that the tool is not his. United States Steel is not "free enterprise" operating in accordance with "natural" economic principles, but group action in one of its highest forms, and close to the national state itself.

"Free enterprise" has never been other than on sufferance of the national state, and in so far as it is corporate enterprise it is wholly an artificial creation which would collapse if the state collapsed and whose prerogatives depend on its own influence over the machinery of the state.

It is often pointed out that even when exercising mere "police powers" and maintaining "law and order" the state is actually providing the sanction for all economic activity.

For long the whole bent of our courts and executive authorities was toward the protection of the business man's artificially defined "rights." The slogans might be private property, and noninterference with private enterprise, but actually the whole state machinery stood behind the false front of the business man's independence, in a way sufficient to justify the Marxian argument that the state was only the "executive committee of the ruling class."

The classic instance of the ever-present latent interference of state power on behalf of the business man is the strike. Today, with American business men complaining that the Labor Relations Act has put all the state power behind the worker, the case is no longer obvious. But for generations the strike was an occasion when the state's machinery came out into the open, whether through policemen or courts or troops, and the pretense that economic activity was carried on independently of political activity was dropped.

Actually the degree of governmental intervention is much greater than might appear from mere consideration of pickets being carted off in police wagons. The sit-down strike in General Motors in 1937 indicated how the whole fabric of governmental rules was woven into an economic situation.

My conservative friends would always have a rush of emotion when they denounced the fact that the strikers were permitted to "trespass on private property."

"Whose private property?" I might ask.

"The property of General Motors, of course," would be the answer.

"That's the name of a corporation. What people own the property?"

"The stockholders, I suppose."

Assume that my conservative friend is one of the two hundred and fifty thousand stockholders of General Motors.

"You are one of the owners, whose property is being violated, then?" I might ask. "Have you been prevented from going into your plants?"

"No, but the management is kept out. It's outrageous."

"Why has the management any more right on the property than the strikers? Aren't they all alike paid employees of the company?"

"The management has the authority to run the plants. They can hire and fire the workers. Actually the strikers aren't workers any more, and they don't have any right to stay in the plants."

"Who says they haven't any right? And how does the management get its authority to say they aren't workers?"

"It's the law. Didn't a judge just tell them to get out?"

Actually the management gets its authority through various procedures of stockholders' and directors' meetings, procedures defined in its charter of incorporation, which in turn conforms to the highly intricate corporation laws under which it was set up. The corporation is legalistically and practically the creature of the state. Only in so far as the state decrees and acts, through its government, are the complex relations of stockholders, management and workers maintained.

The common law rules perpetuated in the courts, and the legislation amplifying these rules, which legislatures pass and executives apply and courts enforce, these provide the network of property rights and personal relations in which "private" business operates. Without them the corporation would be impossible. If they ceased to operate the corporation would become nothing but some files of waste paper.

In Delaware and New Jersey business interests have influenced legislatures to pass especially favorable enabling laws. The state has spoken in clear terms. It has taken decisive action in sponsoring the creation of business entities, which would have been impossible in a world of pure laissez faire.*

It is not only corporate business that exists by virtue of state action. Every individual enterpriser carries on his business in an all-pervasive atmosphere of enabling laws, laid down and enforced by governmental sanction, though usually arising originally from

* A long tradition in the Supreme Court declares that corporations are "persons," though a distinction is made from "natural" persons. Legal fictions cannot change nature, fortunately. As "persons," corporations are held to be protected by the Bill of Rights. They have never insisted on their right to bear arms, and they have never been threatened with "jeopardy of life or limb," for they have neither legs nor arms. But they have property, and this must not be taken "without due process." Justice Hugo L. Black, within a few months of his appointment, shocked "all right-thinking men" by stating in a dissent that corporations should not be considered "persons." This is symptomatic of the breaking-down of much of the old folklore about corporations. Also symptomatic is a growing demand that government once more reassert its prerogatives over corporations, and in particular that all corporations engaged in interstate commerce be federally incorporated or licensed, and thus subjected to more integrated control.

mere habitual conventions. The property laws, the laws of contract, the various types of credit and commercial paper, never existed in a state of nature; they arose out of commercial practice under governmental protection and sanction; and it is the sovereign collectivity, the national state and its lesser subdivisions, which give them continuing validity.

This then is an intrinsic limitation on the laissez faire idea. Out of its historic origins "private enterprise" has always been subject to the sovereign national state, and its most highly developed form, the corporation, is the very creature of the state.

### *What Is Private and What Is Public?*

Certain evolutionary changes have come about in the course of the last hundred and fifty years which have prevented the conservative's concept of individual or private enterprise from ever approaching reality, even if its origins had not tied it to the state. The corporation itself became a form of private collectivism, having little if any resemblance to individual enterprise. In addition, the government, even in the heyday of capitalist glory, was "encroaching" steadily on "free enterprise." The words private and public were losing their meaning not only in the case of "public" utilities and "private" corporations but all through the economic system.

The first time I ever went to Philadelphia alone I wasted several nickels and badly frayed my temper before I discovered that there were two sets of telephone booths in the railroad station, the Keystone and the Bell. What idiocy, I thought. How can the people of Philadelphia keep from going mad with two competing telephone companies? There was a frightening sense of the imminence of anarchy, in this challenge to the otherwise well-ordered world of the American Telephone and Telegraph Company's monopoly.

I was given some shares of American Tel. & Tel. as part of my economic education, and I used to be mystified and a little flattered by the annual reports which always spoke of the company as "your company." Of course, I knew it wasn't mine. All I had was a piece of paper called "stock," and the name and address on this paper was the same as that on the envelope that brought the annual reports and "dividend checks." I could trace the "$45.00" that appeared on my dividend check into my checking account, and could do the simple addition and subtraction—though with a good deal of sweating—that made my book jibe with the bank statement after I had paid my school tuition and Christmas expenses. If I had known enough I could have traced my name on my stock certificate and on the check and on the envelope back to a stencil in some vast filing room in a New York office. That was the extent to which it was "my company": a stencil filed somewhere with my name on it, and some figures that appeared periodically in certain bookkeeping transactions.

Later I learned that the American Telephone and Telegraph Company is the largest "private" corporation in the world, and that its income and employees rival the income and population of whole nations. Its cables under the streets, its poles along the highways, its rights of way, its working conditions, its bookkeeping methods, have long been subject to various governmental rules and regulations, and its rates and business practices generally are becoming more and more subject to the Federal Communications Commission. But these are mostly only checks and balances. As a vast, efficient, going concern the telephone company runs itself; it has administrative autonomy. It is free to exact an income from high rates, sufficient to distribute largess to hundreds of thousands of beneficiaries like myself. Mr. Gifford and his friends, who happen to head the company, are interested in maintaining their power to distribute this largess partly because they can distribute so much of it to themselves. But at the same time they are reported to be public-spirited and honest men who like to see telephone service constantly improved.

When I have used telephones in foreign countries, where they are run by the government along with the post offices, I have found their service exasperatingly bad in comparison. I have been told many times that this proves the superior efficiency of "private ownership" over socialism. But can either the word "private" or the word "ownership" be properly applied to the American Tel. & Tel.? Is this not rather a form of "collectivism" with a high degree of administrative autonomy?

Other kinds of group action are presented to me as alternatives every day when I leave my office to go out to lunch. A block and a half in one direction is a co-operative cafeteria, and half a block in another is one of Stewart's cafeterias. Being lazy I generally choose the latter, as between the two. The food and the service and the prices are about the same. Both are parts of chains of cafeterias throughout the city. Both are efficiently managed and run, though the executives of Stewart's probably get higher salaries. Profits from operating Stewart's go to a number of people called "stockholders," profits from the co-operative go to a number of people called "members," and the bookkeeping methods are not quite the same; the chief difference between the two is that the owners ("members") of the co-op eat there frequently, and the owners ("stockholders") of Stewart's probably never do. Moreover, the members of the co-op became members chiefly because they are informed people who are well aware of the fact that economic activity dependent on the urge for profits is giving way to economic activity directly motivated by consumer needs, and they feel they are helping along a "cause." (I have not become a member, because I calculated that it would take me eight years to recover my membership investment from patronage dividends on my irregular purchases, and I have other "causes" to help.)

The kinds of group economic activity no longer to be described as individual enterprise are by this time legion. Co-operatives motivated by idealism or the desire of consumers to get good quality at a cheap price, chain stores looking for profit from volume of business, corporations under all sorts of governmental regulations, and corporations comparatively free from governmental regulation, businesses trying to take advantage of a monopoly of some profitable field, labor unions trying to take advantage of a monopoly of some line of work, banks operating under complex rules by which the government tries to bring their functions into some sort of predictable order—these are all institutions for organizing human activities in groups. As the machine has tied individuals into larger and ever more complex groups the tendency has been steadily toward community activity on a wider and wider scale, a constant growth of nation-wide organizations, a constant tendency for the more responsible forms of governmental and public organization to supersede "private" organizations.

The country estate where I used to spend the summers as a boy was in Salem in eastern Connecticut, and when I became twenty-one I was made a voter in the township where my great-great-great-grandfather had once been a leading citizen. I attended town meetings whenever I could. Being a very small town of not more than two hundred voters, of whom seldom more than half attended the semi-annual town meetings, it provided a microscopic demonstration of democratic government. A perennial topic for consideration was roads. The primitive dirt roads were maintained by the town, and the selectmen would be hauled on the carpet if they had been too inefficient in filling the mudholes with gravel, or had shown favoritism in repairing a stretch by the house of the Republican chairman, or had given too many jobs to their sons-in-law. A number of years before, a section of road had been macadamized at a cost that could be met only by borrowing from a bank in New London, and for years the burden of this debt was a damper on any enthusiasm for further paving by the town. Fortunately the main highway through the town had been paved with concrete by the state, with federal aid; it was a main artery, between Hartford and New London, and the federal government had a special interest, so it was said, because New London was of military importance, having a submarine base and serving the coast defenses of Long Island Sound. Crossing this highway was another state road, recently paved. If you went down this road a few miles toward Lyme you passed a little white house, right at the edge of the paving, which had once maintained a toll gate—a reminder that until comparatively recently highways were built and maintained by "private enterprise" for "private profit."

My father used to make speeches at that time for what he called "the little red schoolhouse." It was the symbol for the "self-reliance" of the small town, which ought not to accept domination by state or federal educational authorities in his opinion, even if it was bribed by offer of a big modernized central schoolhouse in place of the half-dozen little shacks scattered over the township. When it came to roads I could see the problem a little more clearly: on the one hand centralized governmental action was very much more effective; the straight concrete trunk-line highway was in every way superior to the other roads—thanks to federal aid in the financing and construction—while the town's own roads were execrable, and the mysteries of the banking process kept them from improvement. On the other hand there was no doubt that the wranglings in the town meetings gave far more people the fun and the responsibilities and the sense of free participation in running their own affairs than would have been possible if all the roads had been "federal aid" roads. But I wondered if the citizens who lived beyond the mudholes on the backroads, and the children who said their lessons to a low salaried teacher in a one-room schoolhouse, were not paying too high a price for "self-reliance."

Schooling had once been a private profit enterprise like toll roads. The providing of educational "service" and the providing of highways and the providing of telephones can all be considered economic activities which have gone through various phases, private operation, corporate operation, local government operation, state and federal government operation, with all sorts of cross currents, and interdependences and variations. There has been a steady tendency for the economic unit to get larger and more inclusive, and for it to come more and more directly under governmental rather than "private" control. For the most part this results in increases in efficiency. The only possible loss worth considering seems to lie in depriving individuals of an active participation in running these activities themselves; but even in the case of those which first went into public hands, schools and roads, this active participation is still very large.

It should be noted that "ownership" is of little consequence in any of these examples. Under the common law the Salem farmers through whose land these roads ran might "own" to the center of the highway; but let them try to assert their "ownership" on a summer Sunday when the traffic to the shore is heavy. Who "owns" the Salem schoolhouses? The teacher is boss in school hours, but each child has a right to a desk; the selectmen have to keep the buildings in repair; the state and federal governments may have more or less influence on what is taught and how. A lawyer could tell you in whose name the title stood, but would that be of any special significance? The question of ownership is indeed increasingly irrelevant.

But there is another way in which the concept of private enterprise is breaking down. The basic assumption and excuse for private enterprise is that it operates in a competitive market. I have mentioned how the corporation has from its birth been more or less a monopoly, granted franchises by the sovereign state. The story of the corporation's long struggle to eliminate the competitive market has been often told.

The corporation has not been alone in this. Labor, the farmer, and the consumer have likewise sought in various ways to avoid the brutal costs of the competitive market, through group organization of various kinds. Where the business man has eliminated his competitors, by absorption and amalgamation, by holding companies and trusts, by inside manipulation and open trade associations, the working man has sought a union with his fellows to prevent them from underbidding his wages. Both capital and labor instinctively and naturally seek a monopoly of the market, so that they can determine the price of their product, whether goods or labor, free from the limitations of the open market. The business man always had the edge, and his multifarious techniques for establishing monopolistic prices were always a step ahead of any governmental attempt to check him.

The farmer and the consumer have been even less successful than the worker. The advantages of large-scale mechanized farming could not outweigh the disadvantages of slave or wage labor, in comparison to the farmer's own individual sun-up-to-sun-down self-exploitation. So there was nothing in the agricultural field to compare with the giant corporations and trusts of industry. But the farmer has occasionally found a way to beat the market for his products through marketing co-operatives. In the United States he has also been markedly successful in bringing his collective strength to bear to influence legislation.

The benefits which co-operation in selling their products brought the farmers led naturally to their co-operation in buying. The consumers' co-operative had a large growth in Europe among city workers, beginning with the Rochdale weavers almost a century ago, but its chief impetus in this country came from the farmers. The purpose of a co-operative is to beat the market by replacing the individual buyer, helpless to bring down prices and to determine quality, with a collective buyer. The co-operator may insist that he is not beating the market, but restoring it, by pitting the organized consumer against the organized producer. But when, as in Sweden, the co-ops break a monopoly in electric light bulbs by setting up their own plant there is no return to free price competition; something new, production-for-the-consumer, appears, and is glorified as the goal of the co-operative movement.

Regardless of how far the co-operative movement can go in completely transforming the system, clearly it is another instance of the decay of "private enterprise" operating through a free market. Workers and farmers have organized for collective bargaining, both as buyers and sellers, and so replaced the individual as the economic unit. In so doing they have merely sought to imitate, afar off, what the business man was doing.

The mechanisms that tended toward private collectivism in business and finance were first clearly analyzed and their automatic nature emphasized by Marx. The various types of Big Business and monopoly have been explored and analyzed many times since his day, and there is no need to go into them here (though I shall later discuss the changes in economic theory that are just now coming to a head because of monopoly prices). The two chief impulsions to private collectivism pointed out by Marx are, first, technological: the advantages of large-scale production enable the big business to squeeze out the smaller; and second, monetary: capital accumulations tend to snowball up, thanks to the fact that the larger the amount of productive wealth owned, the less the proportion the owner himself consumes.

### *Collectivism Under Capitalism*

The simple world of economic concepts in which I was brought up, where private enterprise pursues its private profit in its own way in a competitive market, turns out then to have been so far from the truth as to be almost imaginary. And in spite of the preachers of laissez faire it was not "let alone" by the government. Even in the pre-war world there were at least four types of "interference," taxation,. regulation, direct government operation, money and banking controls.

The power to tax is in effect made use of for all sorts of other purposes than securing revenue. The obvious instance of government interference with business in such a way as directly to flout laissez faire, yet entirely at the instance of business men themselves, is the tax on imports, the protective tariff. Progressive income and inheritance taxes, which impose a disproportionate burden on the wealthy, provide a political weapon for achieving a social end, the redistribution of wealth. This interference with "natural economic law" was denounced as the entering wedge of communism when first proposed.

Governmental regulation, the second type of "interference," has steadily encroached. As a heritage of the pre-capitalist era the government had the power to regulate any business, as to virtually any matter, price, standards, conditions of work. Under the influence of the laissez faire doctrine regulation was restricted to a very few fields, such as common carriers (stage-coaches, canals, railroads), and other businesses that were considered so essential that they were called public or "quasi-public." In the latter part of the nineteenth century all sorts of "public utilities" and "businesses affected with a public interest" began to be recognized once more as subject to regulation. We shall see in a moment where the compulsions came from that demanded these interferences with private business. Here it need only be noted that the continuing concept of "police power" or "public interest" was a fatal breach in the dam that separated business and government, and it has been widening steadily till governmental regulation has come to be a rushing flood.

After all, every business, no matter how small, affects the public to some extent. A little sweatshop in a small town can tend to undermine the living standards of workers in a whole industry. The Jersey City tailor whose conviction under the NRA for pressing a suit for twenty-five cents instead of thirty-five was used to arouse public opinion against the Act, was affecting the whole cleaning and pressing business in his small way. When the Supreme Court ruled on the Wagner Labor Relations Act, declaring that labor conditions in a local factory affect all interstate commerce, and thus can be regulated under the Constitution, little remained of the old fiction that a man's business is his private affair, to be carried on in his own way, without governmental intervention. No European country had carried this fiction so far; consequently America's new regulatory social regulation for the most part merely followed precedents laid down decades earlier in Europe.

Direct government operation of enterprises has always been an accepted procedure, though it has expanded and grown with increasing rapidity of late years. Even in the days when American law seemed to forbid most government *regulation* of business, it was never claimed that government could not *carry on* business. Our government postal system started with Benjamin Franklin and the founding of the Republic, though when the parcel post was proposed a generation ago, as a natural extension, the private express companies discovered once again the menace of "socialism."

A government business can drive a private business out of the field if it chooses, just as in the case of the taxing power it was long ago emphasized that "the power to tax is the power to destroy." Publicly owned power plants can be used either as "yardsticks" to keep down rates, or as means of driving the private utilities out of business.*

Public ownership is not necessarily the distinguishing feature of government operation of a business. Ownership, as we have seen, may be relatively unimportant. One does not think of the ownership of a post office as of any significance. A post office building may be leased from a private owner. A public highway may be legally owned by the farmer across whose land it runs. In the case of the United States Shipping Board, the government built and owned a fleet of merchant vessels, but they were leased to and operated by private firms. The various New York subway lines are all operated alike, with a uniform five-cent fare, and all have been built with government sanction, though by private contractors: actual management and operation have in different circumstances been by private companies, by receivers in bankruptcy appointed by courts, and by the city directly; in either case the question of private and public operation is no more important than the question of public or private ownership, for government regulation of every important detail is complete, the business being of vital public concern.

Government enterprise falls into two major classes, that in which the service or product is furnished free and that in which there is a charge. In the former there is complete production for use, limited only by the general resources of the governmental authority.

* In the case of the TVA the government has not yet made up its mind which it wants to do.

Financially it may be reimbursed out of taxation or special assessments, out of borrowing or the creation of government credit, or by printing paper money. Most government enterprise is of this first kind: schools, fire and police protection, national defense, navigation aids in rivers and harbors, highways, most bridges, parks, playgrounds, water for certain purposes, sewage disposal, and so on through a constantly expanding list. Most of these goods and services have in other times and places been left to be provided by private enterprise.

Government enterprise supplying goods or services for a price includes the post office, and a growing number of local utilities and public services, including transportation, light and power, water. In some cases these public businesses are operated like private businesses, competing in the market, seeking to show a profit margin between prices and costs, adjusting their prices to supply and demand; but more often the social purpose to be served is considered more important, and prices are fixed more or less arbitrarily, deficits being made up out of the public funds where they arise. Thus the post office, responding to the demands of publishers, and in accordance with a theory that it is good public policy to encourage a wide dissemination of printed periodicals, carries newspapers and magazines at a price far below cost, even when those periodicals carry vitriolic denunciations of "government in business."

The fourth type of governmental interference mentioned is that of monetary and banking controls, operating for the most part in a shadow-land, where private and public ownership, private and public management, supervisory and regulatory devices are bewilderingly mixed. The average layman is baffled by the nature of National Banks, the Federal Reserve System, rediscount rates, gold sterilization, paper money, gold clause bonds, token coins, and all the rest of our ill-assorted family of monetary institutions. They are a natural but fantastically jumbled evolutionary product of a long history during which a dimly felt public interest, expressing itself often through people's champions like Jackson and Bryan, battled with private profit interests, which claimed that banking was a purely private business. The end of the battle and the solution of our monetary difficulties are not yet in sight. The implications of monetary policy will be considered later in this book. But it may be observed that there is a large field here for the interference of government with business, a field which has been steadily growing until there is widespread acceptance of the idea that the monetary and banking system should become wholly a public service, and should be used to give direction to all other economic processes.

Here, again, note that the question of ownership is irrelevant. The banking system is not affected by the question who owns the marble palaces known as banks: the postal savings system has no banking buildings at all, but operates through the post offices, which may or may not be situated on public property. The ownership of the Federal Reserve System is a meaningless concept: what is important is how the members of its board of governors are appointed and what functions they perform. The coins in your pocket may seem to be yours, but they are stamped with a United States eagle, marked "In God We Trust," and if you deface or imitate them you are liable to get into trouble. Your paper money may say that you are entitled to five dollars on demand, but hand in your bill and ask for five dollars and you will merely get another bill marked the same way. Who owns the gold buried at Fort Knox? Ask the official in charge and see if he knows. Banking and money are largely bookkeeping phenomena, backed up occasionally by a ceremonial handling of gold bars. The important question is merely who lays down the rules by which the bookkeeping is carried on. If it is a private banker, deciding whether or not to issue a loan to a business man, the determining factor is his expectation of profit; a public agency can issue credit in direct relation to some concept of public policy, to stimulate low-cost housing, for instance.

### *Why Does the Government Encroach?*

In every field governmental agencies are pushing out farther and farther over areas formerly left to private enterprise. What is the reason for this constant encroachment of public enterprise?

Private business men are naturally inclined to view it with alarm, and to consider that there are insidious forces at work. Under the New Deal, the fact that the President was professedly more interested in catering to the needs of the "forgotten man" than to the special interests of the wealthy, seemed to lend color to the theory that he was intent on becoming a dictator. The memory of business men is short, or they would recall that in the days of Hoover, when the Cabinet was packed with Wall Street lawyers and millionaires, complaints were continuous against "government by commission," the "new despotism," and spreading administrative powers.

Time after time the cry of "socialism" and "communism" has been raised when the government went into new fields, public schools, parcel post, postal savings banks. Today, since Soviet Russia and the fascist powers have made the government dominant over economic activities, the words Moscow, Nazism and fascism have been added to the vocabulary of alarm, and people as far apart as Union Square and Wall Street hint darkly of Revolution.

Yet the process as it goes on today is not greatly different in kind from the process as it went on in pre-war days. Then as now the expansion of public enterprise was in response to specific practical demands. Ambition for personal dictatorship played little or no part. "Subversive" movements and propaganda, whether inspired by socialist doctrines or not, were clearly impotent. The demands came partly from such a widespread consumer need that it can hardly be specified, as in the case of highway expansion in general, and partly from special interest groups, such as a group of farmers on a back road insisting the town fill in the mudholes.

Group pressure is usually more effective than the general consumer interest, as is obvious from the protective tariffs. Any one import duty was likely to increase the cost of the product to the whole country, and might benefit only one manufacturer or small group of manufacturers. But the victimized public was unaware and voiceless, and the manufacturer got his way, unless there was another special interest group opposed.

The lobby is an old institution. Sometimes it worked from a distance, "building fires" under Congressmen in their home districts, sometimes it went to Washington or a state legislature and by entertaining lavishly or wheedling or threatening sought to secure some governmental action.

During the early days of the capitalist system, in the eighteenth and early nineteenth centuries, the dominant lobby was of business men who wanted favors and freedom from earlier restrictions. But with the increasing complexity of economic processes, and the increasing vocality of workers' and farmers' groups, the pressure on government for ever more positive action grew. (The climax was reached in March, 1933, when every section of the population clamored in unison for "Action!" though with little coherent idea of what action was needed.)

The three major lobbies in Washington in all the pre-war period were, in this order, business, the farmers and labor. Today the order may be the same, but the difference in their relative strength is almost gone, and occasionally the voice of labor may be the dominant one. The fact that business always had the inside track was due to several obvious facts. It had money, for carfare, and entertainment and staffs, to say nothing of financing political campaigns. It had social position, and even machine politicians respect and envy the social graces. To a very considerable extent, in most countries, in most of the states of the Union, over a long period of time, governments were in effect the creatures of the business class. There was enough of this to justify Marx and his followers in the generalizations about class rule. The generalizations were made absolute and thus were not true, for in fact the other groups exercised continuous influence and occasionally controlled local or state governments. The New Deal probably represents a definite change, with the business influence frequently in the minority.

The early trade unions were the first to bring pressure for a free public school system. The farmers' Grange was responsible for railroad legislation. The Populists of the eighties and nineties, drawing their strength from workers, farmers, and all the poorer elements, pressed for income taxes, regulation of trusts, and a wide extension of public enterprises: most of their demands were enacted into law by Republican and Democratic politicians trying to win votes.

The business interest itself consisted of a great many often conflicting elements. Regulation of railroad rates was imposed not only because of the demands of farmers but also because it was to the interest of the shippers of industrial products generally to have standard freight rates. The express companies' lobby was powerless to prevent the setting up of the parcel post system demanded by the mail order houses. The consumer interest is often represented by a powerful capitalist group: thus poor fishermen and holiday yachtsmen may make use of the buoys and charts of our waterways maintained free by the government, but it was the wealthy shipowners who from the beginning insisted that this service be furnished.

These isolated instances indicate the chief reason why the government has gone into business. For the most part it has been because of business pressure. But all the multifarious pressures that are brought to bear in all sorts of ways on governmental institutions have played their part.

Nevertheless there are two special incentives to governmental encroachment which spring from government itself. They may be considered under the headings of war and bureaucracy. They have become dominant incentives today, though they have been operative for a long time.

The development of modern methods of waging war has been in the direction of a more and more inclusive and integrated national enterprise. The market place and the battlefield have always been at odds. With the modern concept of the nation at war the old economics based on the market place has been retreating in utter rout. This phenomenon is considered in other parts of this book. Here we are concentrating on the world before 1914. Even then in many countries the collective organization of the war-making power was encroaching on the capitalist economy, and the armies and navies were themselves organized on completely totalitarian collectivist lines. The decision between war and peace was still left in political hands, subject to all sorts of lobbying pressures, and it was financial and commercial rivalries that led to the armed tension which finally produced war in 1914. But, once at war, military considerations tended to outweigh profit considerations, and it is not to be supposed that the American railroads asked to be taken over by Mr. McAdoo just because they were assured a continuance of their profits.

Bureaucracy is an even more subtle impulse. It involves a consistent pressure to extend governmental activities.

A special commission is set up to study a problem with the assumption that when its job is done it will disband. But a whole staff begins to function as an entity, all the way from the executive chief to the lowliest stenographer. Job stakes are set up, loyalties develop, habit patterns are formed, an institution has been born. It develops a will to live, like any other organism. At the conclusion of its formal work it discovers that there is a continuing task to be performed, and it becomes a permanent government bureau.

A government job usually has certain features of security and permanence, particularly as Civil Service laws are enacted. Mr. Smith, who has a government job, is approached by Mr. Jones, his nephew, or an old friend. Mr. Smith finds he needs another assistant. The next Appropriation Bill provides a place for Mr. Jones.

Some people enjoy power, as a gratification to their ego. This may be true of the janitor of the Podunk post office as well as of a successful aspirant to the Presidency. While it is true that most people are lazy, ambition often gets the better of their laziness, and they look for new fields to conquer. Workers in the government service have an interest in seeing the field of their operations enlarged.

All of these things are true of private business, and the bureaucratic tendencies are as visible there as anywhere. But hard times, with deficits and bankruptcy, mean recurrent retrenchment and business casualties in the field of private enterprise, while government is subject to no such check: it never knows permanent bankruptcy, and hard times may see it grow even more rapidly than good times.

I am not here concerned with whether bureaucracy is a menace or not. And I am not now considering it in relation to the problem of administrative efficiency. My only purpose here is to mention it as one of the incentives to the extension of governmental activity. In succeeding chapters which analyze the communist and fascist states it will be noted that the office-holding bureaucracy becomes the dominant economic interest. With 40 per cent or 50 per cent of the national income going through government hands in the fascist states, and with the beneficiaries of these funds all close to the inner machinery of the governmental structure, those outside capitalist interests that may still have an interest in the laissez faire market mechanism are feeble voices in comparison. It would seem as if the bureaucratic drive itself had reached a point where it was beyond further check, and would stop only when it had embraced all economic activities and there were no more worlds to conquer. How it can be squared with individual freedom is a part of our basic problem.

The nineteenth century, and the twentieth up to 1914, witnessed a great expansion of our wealth-producing machinery, mostly at the initiative of individuals trying to get rich. In the early period they sought freedom from governmental interference, because the interferences inherited from the Middle Ages and from the mercantilist period hampered their pursuit of wealth. But the national state, also inherited from the Middle Ages, never resigned or disappeared. It always maintained its absolute sovereignty. It maintained an atmosphere of law and order, common law property rights, and enabling legislation, under which individual business men could organize hundreds and even thousands of people into complex collective enterprises.

As these enterprises grew in size and complexity individual freedom of action was more and more subordinated to collective disciplines. Moreover, the interference of government was more and more sought, by business men themselves as well as by all sorts of other interested groups, both selfish and humanitarian. Governmental interference took myriad forms, but there was a steady substitution of "public" enterprise in place of "private" enterprise.

The pre-war era, then, contained a complex jumble of capitalism, liberalism, nationalism, socialism, private and public collectivism.

Clearly the "capitalist system" was not a simple concept. If it was true, as the conservatives said, that the closer the approach to laissez faire the greater the liberty, then liberty had been increasingly imperiled for some time. And what was the enemy that imperiled it?—public ownership? bureaucracy? Did "socialism" necessarily mean dictatorship? Or, on the other hand, was "capitalism" an enemy of freedom? Or, putting both questions at once, what must be done to bring about an efficient economic system capable of producing abundance, and at the same time conserve past freedoms and enlarge them?

The issue was beginning to take shape. But it was not yet strictly defined. Apparently I was still having "word trouble."

# Chapter Four

## DEFINING THE PROBLEM

AMONG the words which spread an inky cloud over our present confusion is the word "liberalism." Herbert Hoover and Earl Browder both appeal to it. For a while I was inclined to scorn it, and call myself a "radical." But it will not down. And I have come to feel that the basic problem before us is, to no small degree, tied up with our understanding of that word. It is a word that has been identified with what is best in the older era. If the new era is to conserve the best of the old it too must be "liberal."

Liberalism, it seems to me, can be analyzed into four components, corresponding to four tendencies of nineteenth-century political thought: laissez faire liberalism, international liberalism, humanitarian liberalism and socialist liberalism.

Laissez faire liberalism was the oldest and most correct use of the term. The revolt of "free enterprise" against feudal and mercantilist restrictions was rationalized in a logical theory by the economists and philosophers of the early nineteenth century. The Liberal party in England was the champion of the business man. The United States Supreme Court became on this side of the Atlantic the final oracle of the doctrine that the government must leave business alone.

The governmental ideal of democracy and the social ideal of individual liberty were tied in closely, partly by accident, partly by design, with the theory that the welfare of all is best promoted by leaving free enterprise to pursue its own untrammeled way, with government merely in the combined role of umpire and policeman. This concept of liberalism reached its fullest flower in America, for free land to the West perpetuated the possibility of every man an enterpriser, government could approach zero, and the anarchistic goal of social harmony without government could seem attainable.

Karl Marx was the first to show that free competition would inevitably tend to grow into its opposite, monopoly. But the older liberalism would not accept the inevitable. In Europe special fields were marked off for monopoly; salvation was sought in state ownership or state regulated cartels in those fields, and the theory was considered valid elsewhere. In America liberalism sought to ban monopoly, through anti-trust laws. To this day every American political party does homage in its pronouncements to the old liberal idea that the protection of competition from monopolistic practices is the way to prosperity and freedom.

International liberalism was a natural and logical extension of the idea of laissez faire, but it suffered from a much more acute inner contradiction, the dispute between protection and free trade. This was partly a dispute between the academic mind, which sought consistency in the extension of the free market to all the world, and the practical man of affairs, who found protective tariffs long established in such a way that the whole price and business structure would be imperiled by their removal. But this division of opinion was long true only in America, not in England, whose commercial empire grew to greatness with free trade. The dispute was in reality much more a dispute between different interests of varying strength and coherence. In America the interests on the side of free trade were, first, as we saw, the great unvocal and unenlightened consuming public, which paid higher prices for all protected goods without realizing it, and, second, the importers and, to a lesser extent, the exporters, whose dollar interest (and whose voice in Washington therefore) was small compared to that of the great manufacturers who fattened on the protected domestic market. In England the manufacturers saw their goods flowing out over all the world's trade channels, and they were glad to see raw materials flow back without barriers to pay for their exports. England was the world's banker before the war, and her prestige gave the free trade doctrine the upper hand in economic theory.

Even today, with American protection as effective as it ever was, and with England long forced to abandon free trade, the ideas of international liberalism retain their appeal. Diplomats and professors alike still dream of a world of peace and plenty without trade barriers, where there are no quotas and restrictions, where commodities and gold flow in an automatic adjustment of prices between supply and demand. Most of those professors and diplomats, after all, were brought up in the pre-war world when the laissez faire ideal on an international scale seemed to be on the verge of fulfillment.

There was another strong tendency, humanitarianism, in the pre-war liberalism. The eighteenth-century age of Enlightenment, out of which capitalism grew, gave dignity to the individual personality, condemned oppression and exploitation, stimulated the traits of sympathy and compassion. The philosophers and economists who developed the theories of laissez faire were eminently humane men. They could not carry their hands-off policy to the extent of condoning the horrors of the early factory conditions depicted by Marx. Logical consistency was saved by the concept of "abuses." The war between reformers and vested interests began early. The reformers saw the stunted children, and the maimed laborers, and the women driven into wage slavery and prostitution, as "abuses" to be remedied by governmental action; the vested interests stood pat on the original logic of laissez faire doctrine.

Liberals, as the advance guard of progress, who first had fought against all governmental interference, now came to demand more and more governmental interference. The confusion was augmented in England by the fact that it was usually Tory governments which put through factory acts, minimum wage laws, eight-hour days, child labor legislation, for the more feudal tradition of the Tories was also more easily paternalistic. In America the demand for reforms came from farm organizations and labor unions, and it was intimately bound up with Populism and cheap money panaceas; but the old parties stole the reform thunder when they had to. The liberal came to be thought of by politicians as a sentimentalist and a soft-hearted crank, whose nuisance value could not be permanently ignored. This humanitarian liberalism, moreover, being constantly aroused by injustices and "abuses," made itself unpopular by its insistent finger-pointing, viewing with alarm, and cantankerous muck-raking. Such journals as *The Nation* and *The New Republic* bear much of the glory and much of the odium that still surround the word "liberal" in the public mind.

The humanitarian liberal who sought to mitigate abuses by governmental action found himself, much as he might dislike it, on the way to a complete contradiction of the original laissez faire doctrines. Perhaps this is the reason for his proverbial unhappiness. He was always divided against himself. He believed passionately in capitalism, which was to him almost a synonym for freedom; yet he found himself pushed over into the socialist camp. If it was the function of government directly to promote the welfare of all the people, what was to be the safeguard of the precious individual rights so hardly won a century earlier? Over in the conservative camp, reactionaries could honestly pose as the only true liberals, protecting individual freedom from the encroachment of despotism. The Supreme Court of the United States was inclined (until 1937) to view every social reform as a violation of the Bill of Rights. It echoed the conservatives' alarm at the advance of "socialism," and many a liberal felt it necessary to choose between "socialism" and "freedom." For intellectuals it was a painful choice: Walter Lippmann's life has been spent in agonized indecision between the two lines of logic. The pre-war American socialist movement, having managed to slough off its intellectuals, throve for a while, blithely ignoring the inconsistencies of socialist liberalism: it combined Populism, anti-monopoly laissez faire and free trade doctrines with a belief in the reform of all abuses by governmental action. To a real Marxian Socialist like De Leon the movement was hopelessly naïve. When, after 1917, it beheld the realities of revolutionary expropriation and the dictatorship of the proletariat in Russia, it was horrified. It never recovered its élan.

The forces we loosely call liberal or progressive today still suffer from the confusions and contradictions that had not yet come to a head in the golden age before the Great War. The historical development of the term liberalism can be traced by anyone so inclined. But the basic social and economic problem confronting the advanced thinker, the problem of devising free institutions that will be both efficient and democratic, that will serve both our individual and our social welfare, is still unsolved; and where, under the compulsion of actual conditions, practical adjustments are made, they face a terrific handicap of apparent contradictions. The fact is that the historic origins of liberalism have perpetuated a completely false and illogical notion, that there is necessarily an opposition between individualism and group action. This notion of a basic conflict runs through all thought today, on both left and right.

Yet, as a few isolated voices are beginning to insist, the basic conflict does not exist. Of course there is an opposition of interest between rulers and ruled, between exploiters and exploited, between bureaucrats and individualists, between dictatorship and democracy. *But there is no real conflict between individualism and group action.*

All around us we see individuals living their lives in groups, finding expression in group activity. We all accept the fact that the Robinson Crusoe, the hermit, who is isolated from group contacts, is only half a human being. We know that in the responsibilities and disciplines and co-operative activities of the family, the church, the school, the club, there is a growth of the individual personality rather than a restriction.

The dilemma between individual freedom and social controls, which has been the plague of progressive social thinking, is a false dilemma. The issue is not between individual freedom and collective dictatorship, as a Walter Lippmann would attempt to draw it. The collective controls are inevitable and desirable. The only question is how they come about and in what form. In short, are the new group institutions being brought about and operated democratically or dictatorially?

### *The Fighting Ism Words*

One of the real problems raised by conservatives, and recognized by radicals as well, is that of bureaucracy. It is, as I pointed out in the last chapter, one of the incentives to governmental action. The essence of the problem is to discover institutional devices which will not strangle the individual. But the word bureaucracy is an excellent instance of how our mental concepts may inhibit real thought.

The word brings to my mind an image of a bureau with many

drawers and musty cubby-holes. If I were asked to define it I should probably do so in terms of red tape (another visual image) and hordes of lazy people watching the clock. It is like all the other words ending in -cracy or -ism: democracy, liberalism, capitalism, autocracy, despotism, fascism, socialism, communism. Not that these words have no proper meaning or use. Their proper use is as abbreviations, shorthand descriptions of complex interrelated facts. The trouble with them is that our minds are seldom disciplined enough to keep all the background material in our mental vision when we use them. We think in concrete terms, often derived from cartoons—visual images stamped out in black and white.

There is magic in these words too. I remember the sense of vague mystery surrounding the word "ism" all by itself, when I first ran into it. It is the essence of all essences, the abstraction of abstractions, something deep and dark, no doubt awfully fundamental. Yet in our thought processes it is almost a zoological term. Stuart Chase pictured in his *Tyranny of Words* that queer menagerie where the ism words gambol and roar. Just as some people have more fondness for animals than others, some, because of race or upbringing or mere personal peculiarity, find greater satisfaction in isms. By and large I think Americans take their isms less seriously than Europeans. They play with them in their leisure hours, but seldom die for them.

When I came back to America from my travels I was saturated with European ism words. Most of all I was convinced, as I have said, that the change through which the world was passing was a change from one ism to another, from "capitalism" to "socialism." I sought out all the people and movements in America who were on the side of progress, on the side of "socialism." Among others I talked to a political leader of the typically American stamp, a pragmatic progressive. I was baffled to find my isms meant nothing to him. "Capitalism" and "socialism"? He waved them aside. I thought he was merely a straddler, refusing to take sides on the vital issue of the hour. I have since come to realize that these words really did mean nothing to him. The abstract words with which he would play before an American political audience—"American People," "vested interests," "Wall Street," "monopoly," and the like—were of a lesser order of abstraction than the ism words of Europe.

Do the words "capitalism" and "socialism" then mean nothing? We might pick out certain features of what we call capitalism, and say that they are crucial and that when they dominate we have a "capitalist system"; and we might take certain features of socialism, and say that when they dominate we have a "socialist system." But the previous chapter has indicated that my first inquiry did not prove very profitable. For what were the crucial features?

An average man's definition of capitalism might be in terms of "free enterprise," competition without governmental interference. But even a cursory glance into the history of capitalism, particularly in the nineteenth century, indicated that this laissez faire conception never existed in anything like a pure form. With the growth of big business, particularly, "freedom" of enterprise had come to be more and more artificial a conception: are the workers free? is the management free? are the stockholders free? Each has certain "freedoms," and somewhere you are likely to come on the boss; but even he is a prisoner of his business. Moreover, individual competition drops farther and farther into the background, while governmental interferences come more and more to the fore.

Capitalism is thought of as a system of private ownership and the profit motive. All these words turn out on analysis to be slippery monsters. The modern corporation especially is in no proper sense private. Ownership is so often separated from control, and is such a multiple personality of crisscrossing interests and claims, that it no longer has any exact relevance.

I can recall my childish curiosity in 1918 when all railroad tickets began to carry the signature "Wm. G. McAdoo, Director General of Railroads" or some such title. The new standards of discipline and order required by the war had compelled the government to "take over" the railroads. Yet the same people "owned" the railroads: or at least "owned" the pieces of paper which the courts recognized as constituting legal "ownership." The same people managed them, though there were undoubtedly more gatherings about mahogany desks, to eliminate wasteful competition between different lines. The same people operated them, though possibly on somewhat altered schedules: when next I took a trip I saw the same little stationmaster with the trim beard, with whom my father had always passed the time of day in the station, and though I didn't know the locomotive engineer, up on his dignified height in the engine cab, I could not see that he looked any different.

Suppose the government were to establish public ownership of the railroads tomorrow, according to one of the several bills recently presented in Congress. There might be a few changes in schedules and rates, a few soft jobs might be eliminated, and a few new soft jobs created, the "owners" would be given slightly different pieces of paper in exchange for their former certificates. But in the "real world" the difference would be scarcely observable. Go to Canada and travel west: on the Canadian Pacific Route you are being transported by "private enterprise," on the Canadian National by "public enterprise," but you would not know which was which without being told.*

The words private and public simply do not carry meanings of any scientific precision in the case of corporations. They are of purely legalistic (which generally means imaginary) significance. What, for instance, is a "public utility"?

I have sometimes been startled in crossing the Jersey meadows between New York and Newark by the great looming electric signs displaying the words "PUBLIC SERVICE." The powerful electric power company that uses this name has often been the object of attacks by liberals and reformers, who claim that it corrupts the whole state government, to say nothing of local governments, in order to multiply its exorbitant profits. I have no doubt that it is politically pernicious. But suppose that instead of government being controlled by it, it were controlled by the government, and, so as not to complicate the argument, suppose that the latter is good government, genuinely interested in "public service." What will happen in the real world? The service is good now, for those who can pay for it, and there is no reason to expect any marked

* The Canadian National happens to be a "burden on the taxpayers": it is saddled with a large debt left over from the days of "private" operation, and its traffic is not heavy enough to pay the interest without governmental subsidy. The alternative to the taking over of the line originally was to "tax" the consumer with heavier rates, which the government did not want to permit for political reasons; so the tax was levied on the general public instead.

improvement: the same engineers, electricians, line-men, bill-collectors and the like would probably be on the same jobs. Rates would be probably somewhat lower, so that a few housewives would be able to use electric washing machines who cannot afford to now. But most of the Jersey housewives would still have to wash laboriously by hand even though the wires were never carrying as much current as they could.

The difference between public and private enterprise does not seem on close inspection to be very useful. What about profit? Is not capitalism basically a "profit system"?

But profit is likewise a slippery word. The individual worker who works for a wage or a salary and is stimulated by the hope of a raise, may be thought of as acting under the profit motive; but this will apply alike to the day laborer and the general manager, to the shopkeeper and the "captain of industry," whether they are working for themselves, for a "private corporation," or for the government. Profit is also used as a bookkeeping term, the difference between cost and selling price, for instance: but a municipal electric light plant may show this kind of profit, and so may a co-operative. Is it a matter of "private" profit then? But the profit of a big corporation may accrue to hundreds of thousands of stockholders, bank depositors or insurance policy holders.

I do not mean to claim that these criteria of capitalism may not be important. What I am arguing is that they are anything but crisp and clear. They are of little value in determining the essential differences between "capitalism" and "socialism." *

I have found that the only general agreement among conservatives and radicals alike is that the terms "capitalism" and "socialism" are used as fighting words. The conservatives insist that "capitalism" means freedom and democracy, and that "socialism" is slavery. The radicals consider "capitalism" a system of oppression and exploitation, where the rich and powerful ride on the backs of the toiling masses, while "socialism" means economic democ-

* A later chapter will describe to what extent the Soviet Union retains profit, both as an incentive and as a bookkeeping device to keep privately run but publicly owned enterprises up to schedule. Towards the end of the book I shall have to analyze "profit" from a somewhat more technical point of view. See page 326.

racy and freedom.* All alike move in a dream-world of abstractions, seeing only what will fit their scheme of things.

If "capitalism" is a difficult word to handle, how much worse is "capital"! What is "capital"?—a dollar in the savings bank, a threshing machine, a share of A. T. & T., the Ford plant, a locomotive, a factory, an apartment house, a post office?

A skillful little propaganda leaflet issued by a Big Business advertising firm recently defined "capital," in terms of its root word, "cattle," as the source of wealth. You can kill and eat your cow, but you will then get no more milk and no more calves. In a modern world capital is machinery. But machinery cannot be eaten. Capital then is conceived of as a saving of wealth which might otherwise be consumed, in order to have more wealth produced in future. Or more accurately, capital consists of tools and raw materials, the result of labor which might have been expended merely for immediate consumption, but which through foresight and self-restraint was put into more far-reaching benefits. Out of these simple concepts it is argued that capitalism is merely a system which stores and uses capital. People who think along this line are likely then to conceive of socialism as a system which, by dividing all wealth equally, dissipates accumulated capital, and thus tends to return to primitivism. When it is observed that the Soviet Union puts half its energy into capital goods construction, while the workers remain poor in consumer goods, these people say that Russia has abandoned socialism and is building "state capitalism" in place of "free" or "private capitalism."

Another variant of this approach is to think of capital as accumulated money, which is used to accumulate still more money. This, crudely put, is Marx's conception. It is also likely to be that of those who deal in money as a business, bankers, brokers, speculators, investors. If you enjoy an income from investments you think of the money value of your securities as your "capital," and

* When the radicals look at the Soviet Union they have two alternatives: one is to deny that there is anything "socialist" about it, since it has so little democracy. This is virtually Norman Thomas's position. The other alternative is to insist, through ignoring or interpreting facts, that what appears as a bloody dictatorship is in reality a free democracy. In between others use words like state capitalism and state socialism, further evidence of the vagueness of "capitalism" and "socialism."

"capitalism" as a system where this kind of capital is widespread. The means of production—factories, tools, power plants—are created out of money savings properly invested. According to this theory, if nobody saves money there will be no capital goods accumulated, no factories built, and the system will run down. An elderly gentleman of my acquaintance who had spent most of his life in Wall Street, long felt that the Russian Communists were merely living on the accumulated savings of previous capitalists; when they built a new factory it was with some of this confiscated money; and when they had run through all these savings they would be bankrupt and finished. It is only fair to say that as Russia has become the first industrial nation of Europe he has partially changed his mind. But he, too, feels that Russia has abandoned socialism for state capitalism.

It should be clear from all these horrible examples of the attempt to fit complex facts into verbal strait-jackets, that capitalism is not a sharply marked concept. We can define it in almost any way we choose. Consequently it is folly to think of the transition from capitalism to a new economic system in terms of an apocalyptic day, the day of "the revolution," when, all of a sudden, one system supersedes another.*

That a transition has been going forward I am not denying. That there are certain crucial elements in it is one of my major assumptions. This book is in a sense a record of my search to find what those elements are. In a long and difficult journey, I found little guidance from previous travelers. Much of the difficulty arose from the fact that I started out with all the old verbal baggage. Having finally reached the point where I could treat the ism words with proper disrespect—as well as these other concepts of "property," "profit," "capital," and "freedom of enterprise"—I was ready to attempt an appraisal of the economic problem in terms of the real world.

* This concept is most common among the non-Marxist radicals like the Technocrats. The Marxists distinguish between the political change—the revolutionary shift of power from the capitalist class to the working class—which they believe must be sudden, and the economic change, which may be gradual. But it is not easy to separate the two; and because Marxists have not thought how the transition is to be accomplished, their view of "the revolution" is often quite naïve. See below, pages 93-97, 282-288.

*Economics in the Real World*

If I draw a check for ten dollars, payable to "cash," and sign my name at the bottom, I have performed an operation that is of almost no significance in the real world of matter and energy—it takes only a minute of my time, a scrap of paper (any paper will do if I write in the name of my bank) and a drop of ink. So far as my material wants are concerned, I cannot use this marked-up piece of paper as food or as clothing. About the only useful thing that might be done with it would be to transfer a light from a fire to a pipe, in which case the ink would make it less rather than more effective. I would be none the poorer if I used my piece of paper in this way.

But some remarkable events may occur in my mind and the minds of other people because of the arrangement of symbols on the paper. For the moment no one else knows I have written the check. The significance of the check is wholly in my own mind. If I have a bank account and a balance against which the check is drawn I know that my piece of paper is now as good as money. I can buy groceries with it. I can give it to a friend of mine from whom I borrowed ten dollars, and he can buy groceries with it, though he will be asked to sign his name on the back. I have these same feelings even if I am mistaken about having a balance in the bank. Perhaps I have overdrawn my account. Perhaps I am a little mad and I never had a bank account. Still my own mental concept of what this check means remains the same.

Suppose I take the check out and try to buy groceries with it at the A. & P. Another mind comes into play. The clerk will take it if he knows me, and believes I have a balance in the bank. Whether he trusts me or not is a matter of his private judgment, his mental processes on the basis of his past experience with me, and with other customers like me. In other words, whether this check performs a function of money or not depends on purely psychological factors, what is going on in somebody's head. But whether I eat or not depends on whether I get my groceries in the physical world.

Economics is constantly dealing with two worlds. We may call them the real world and the mental world, though of course the mental world is part of the real world. Economic activities involve the production and distribution and consumption of goods and services in the real world, and certain mental processes that accompany and affect the physical processes.

In a sense the goods and services exist both in the real world and in our minds. The difference between a "cultured" pearl and a "real" pearl is almost entirely in our minds, yet in each case the pearl is in the real world. Certain services, like the services of a psychiatrist, are almost wholly mental. But, in general, goods and services come from the physical environment, are produced by physical labor, and cater to our physical wants. On the other hand the money end of economics is almost entirely in the mental world. There was a time when real cattle in the real world constituted money, and later gold and silver, which were weighed out in any transaction. When the metal was stamped or coined the mental element became stronger, and the effectiveness of money depended on people's confidence (a mental attitude) in its being what it purported to be. With the coming of bank notes and government notes redeemable in gold the physical world drew farther into the background. Today in this country most transactions are by check. Only in international transactions is there even any convertibility to gold. The paper and ink constituting the checks in the real world are of negligible importance. Money has become a mental attitude. Any scrap of paper may pass as money if the persons concerned consider it money. A seller will part with his goods in return for a check if he *thinks* he can buy goods in his turn. In fact, with the extension of credit (*credo*, I believe; *credit*, he believes), checks are often used only to settle balances at the end of the month, or longer periods, and money has been pushed even farther into the mental world: it becomes merely figures in various account books.

If, instead of writing my check with a figure 1 followed by a zero, I were to write 1 with six zeros, neither I nor my grocer would take it very seriously, though the Treasurer of the United States might do the same any day of the week. But suppose there were twelve zeroes, or as many as the piece of paper would hold, it would become meaningless for the Treasurer of the United States as well. Even at the height of the German inflation it was easy for any child to write enough zeroes after a number to make it meaningless as a measure of money. The numbers we write in our account books then ought to bear some relation to the real world. But they need not be limited by the real world in the way the older money was: today it is easy to create money with the turn of a printing press or the flick of a fountain pen; a weight of gold bullion on the other hand could be hammered very thin to cover a church dome but could not be increased by one gram.

In the real world there are very concrete and definite limitations on economic processes. The limitations in the mental world are of quite a different sort. The breeding of chickens is limited by their feeding and environment as well as their natural biological constitution. The counting of chickens before they hatch is a different matter.

For our present purposes we may state the real limits of economic processes as two: the capacity to consume and the capacity to produce. The capacity to consume in the real world is not, as the Brookings Institution has measured it, a matter of money income, but of physical limitations. As regards food for a small boy it may be defined as so many pancakes, or so much soda pop. As regards clothes it might be measured as four suits a year. More might be bought and used occasionally and hung in the closet where the moths would get at them, but this would be waste, not consumption. It is not difficult to measure capacity to consume. One study found that it would be virtually impossible for a family to consume much more than $3,000 worth of standard goods in a year.*

The capacity to produce is likewise subject to measurement. The Ford plant has a capacity to turn out so many cars a day. The automobile industry as a whole can turn out a certain larger number. It is necessary to check back to the sources of raw materials and the various processing operations (like the rubber supply and tire factories) to determine whether or not that capacity of the automobile industry can be maintained all year round. But it is

* This figure covers food, clothing, shelter, furniture, and other personal requirements of the mass production type; families with higher incomes spend them on hand-made goods, domestic servants, and other scarce luxuries, in regard to which demand is virtually infinite. For further data on this survey, and on the relation of services to a standard of living, see below, page 319 and note.

possible to go even farther and determine the capacity of the whole industrial plant of the United States, with the "bottle necks" of raw materials or processing or transportation all taken into consideration. A study was once made of our productive capacity, and it was found that in 1929 we could have produced 135 billion dollars' worth of goods and services (arbitrarily measured in 1929 prices), with many of our plants even then not operated at their maximum capacity.*

Now, if our standard of living were determined solely by these two limiting factors in the real world, capacity to consume and capacity to produce, it is clear that it would be much higher than it is. Unfortunately all sorts of mental factors enter into the economic mechanism, of which money is only one of the most obvious. All our social arrangements affect the production and distribution of goods. Inefficiency in management and administration is the most legitimate. In certain industries, such as our telephone system, capacity as measured by cables and connections may be vastly affected by efficiency in management and administration, though the human factor is being eliminated more and more by automatic equipment. Fads and consumer trends created by advertising have a vast effect. A social system so disorganized as to lead to a general strike may cut down production almost to zero. A money system dependent on the vagaries of "confidence" and "panic" may likewise bring operations in the real world almost to a stop.

With this crude analysis of the limiting factors of economics it should be easier to answer our first and major question: What are the fundamental economic elements in this period of change? *From* what sort of prevailing economic practices *to* what sort of new economic practices are we changing?

### *Transition from What to What?*

The most compact statement I could find at this stage of my inquiry, to describe what has been happening, was to say that there has been a trend from *production for the market* to *production for use.*

* See page 318 below, for a fuller discussion of productive capacity.

Both of those phrases need a good deal of analyzing and defining. Even the words "for" and "the" raise questions. Later, as will appear in the course of this book, I found that the problem is much more subtle than even these terms would indicate. But they are helpful nonetheless. Let me apply them to some of the examples I have cited from the "real" world.

When roads were built "for the market" toll gates were put up to bar those who could not pay the toll. The "market" for roads was small, the tolls collected amounted to limited sums, and the roads were execrable. The growing American community felt it was worth while for public authorities to build roads out of tax money or borrowings, for public "use." The labor and materials (mostly gravel and cement) available to build roads in the real world are ample, but our road building is still hampered by events in the mental world ("Where is the money coming from?"). On the whole these financial considerations have carried less and less weight, for "state aid" and "federal aid" have made them more remote from local communities. Thus road building is largely "for use." Estimates of the need of those who drive, whether in passenger cars or trucks, increasingly determine how and when and where roads are built. Mountains are slashed to meet consumer specifications.

Once all schools were private ventures; they were supported by tuition fees or charity. Only those children got a schooling who could pay the tuition or who the givers of the charity felt were worthy of it. While it may be stretching a point to use the term "market" to apply to parochial and charitable schools, the term is apt in the case of the ordinary private schools dependent on tuition fees. Production in this case is not of goods but of a service, the professional service performed by a teacher, education: the product is a more or less educated person. Only a limited number of parents, with ample bank accounts, can afford the product of a girls' finishing school or a boys' country day school. But the "little red schoolhouse" has gone on a different principle. Money is no bar. The teaching is free. The school system is organized to meet a generally felt need. Schools appear in every town and city budget, along with fire and police protection, sewage and sanitation, parks, varied public services, usually the provision of water, sometimes the provision of electricity. Where no special payment or fee is required, as in the case of fire protection (an alarm system, a staff of firemen, equipment in the shape of fire engines and hose, accessible fire hydrants), there is production for use in purest form, though it was not so long ago that private fire-fighting companies would bargain with a householder (in "the market") while his house was burning. Where payment is required (as for electricity produced in a municipally owned plant) the motive is indeed to produce for use, but the economic effect is so little different that it may still be considered production for the market.

"For" use or "for" the market is then not merely a question of intent. Most private schools are run by altruistic individuals primarily concerned with filling an obvious need for better education. Publicly owned power plants are built to give more people more electric power. But the functions they perform within the economic system are limited by the amount they can sell on "the market." We might arbitrarily say that one-quarter of each is "production for use" and three-quarters "production for the market." If a municipal plant has the capacity to produce more power and does not produce it because certain would-be consumers cannot pay for it, to that extent surely it is not producing "for use." In fact it is engaging in a practice that is becoming increasingly better known as "nonproduction."

When we went to war in 1917 it became a matter of life and death to produce guns and ammunition and uniforms and army food rations, and it was equally important that these goods when produced should be shipped by train and boat to Europe as rapidly as possible. To increase efficiency the American government set up a War Industries Board to plan production, and it took over the railroads and went into the shipping business. (Transportation, of course, is a part of the productive process.) None of this was free, however. All those munitions and uniforms and foodstuffs had to be paid for, mostly by the government, occasionally by the individual consumers. Where did the money come from?

Some of it was borrowed from savings, some was raised by taxation. But a large part was "new" money, created by the government and the banks for the purpose. There are many names for this, which we shall ultimately have to analyze—"deficit financing," "credit inflation," "putting the burden on posterity," "economic insanity," and things even worse. But what I am interested in showing here is that there may be production of wealth when there is no "market" for that wealth, the money with which to buy it being created as production goes on—and that this is just as much "production for use" when the consumer has to pay for it (like an army officer buying his uniform) as when the consumer uses it free (like the same officer firing a sixteen-inch battery made in a government owned arsenal).*

Observe that production for use is a method of getting things done in the real world, and that its effectiveness has nothing to do with whether the ends sought may be good or bad.

It should be possible now to suggest some of the implications of this economic method, in contrast to the old method of production for the market.

Under production for use the only limits are the physical limits already mentioned: the capacity to consume and the capacity to produce. Under production for the market all sorts of mental limits are imposed by the mental world.†

Production for use is production controlled by a more or less governing plan. Production for the market is production according to a hundred thousand guesses by a hundred thousand business men—how much can they sell?—and hence necessarily unplanned. There is a certain rough common sense in the minds of business men, which keeps some sort of order and prevents complete unpredictability: we shall analyze the "law" of supply and demand in a later section. Economists who want to defend the *status quo* will argue that if left to themselves the business men and the "laws" of economics will result in economic "planning" in every way better, because more automatic, than the planning of a governmental agency. But in the real world production for the market gives us millions of jobless men and underfed children, and lack

* Don't be bothered by the fact that the "wealth" produced may be for destruction: an officer's uniform, a sixteen-inch battery, are wealth which is produced for consumption, just as truly as a hunter's togs and his shotgun.

† It is only necessary to cite the slump that began in August, 1937, caused by a failure of "confidence": by "fear" that the budget would not be balanced (or that it had been balanced), by an appearance of "overproduction" (not in relation to real physical need, but in relation to what people might be expected to buy), by a fear of "inflation" or a fear of "deflation," or of the effects of certain taxes—by millions of people reacting unpredictably to a changing business situation.

of integrated planning leaves production far short of productive capacity and consumptive capacity.

Since production for use can be planned, with regard only for those real limits, it can provide an economy of abundance, if the limit of productive capacity permits it—specifically if the man-power and the natural resources are available up to the limits of consumption. The capacity to consume so far as food is concerned ought to be measured by health standards, as to what constitutes the best diet known. If the capacity to produce is limited, say, by inadequate soil and a poor climate, so that it cannot provide everybody with this optimum diet, then an economy of abundance, "plenty for all," is an empty dream. But if the capacity to produce food, and all other staple articles of an ample standard of living, is at or above the capacity to consume, then an economy of abundance is possible.

Why cannot production for the market achieve such abundance? That is not as easy a question to answer as I first thought. Here I will merely venture this generalization: When production is for the market the amount produced is determined by innumerable factors in the mental world. Business men produce what they think they can sell, and they can sell only what customers can buy, and the amount of money the customers can spend, once more, is determined haphazardly by a million unpredictables, including such abstractions as what a group of bankers may think the rediscount rate should be. Why these unpredictables once resulted in a fairly efficient system and why they no longer do is our most difficult problem. But there can be no doubt of the facts: production for the market now falls chronically short of capacity production.

### *Freedom as End and as Means*

With this tentative statement of the economic problem, let me look back to see how far I have come on my inquiry. What is the nature of this hectic period of change? Its origins are familiar and obvious, though it is well to remind ourselves of them if we are to keep up our courage.

Origins cannot legitimately be isolated in a world of intricate interrelationships and multiple causation, but they can be roughly emphasized. The beginnings of the scientific method, with Galileo, Copernicus, and Newton, coincided with a release of the Western mind from the rigid absolutisms of the Middle Ages. These developments were followed on the one hand by the application of science in technology, bringing on the Industrial Revolution and the modern machine, and on the other by the Great Enlightenment, with the ideals of individual freedom and political democracy which found expression in the eighteenth century.

For about a hundred and fifty years—a short period, be it noted, in human history—man has been struggling to assimilate these two ideas, science and democracy. They have meant power and the widespread opportunity to take advantage of that power. They have meant a long series of revolutionary upheavals, as old institutions—economic, political, religious, social—have had to give place to new.

The difficulty of adjusting to the new factors is exemplified by the naïve faith prevailing during most of the period, that popular education would insure a successful adjustment. When everybody had at least a grammar school education democracy would work. Later the goal was set at a high school education, and some even went so far as to call for a universal college education. But the new literacy seemed quite incompetent, even to choose presidents or representatives, much less decide complex policies like a protective tariff, or anti-monopoly legislation; and the greater literacy the people had the more susceptible they were to fraud, whether of advertising or propaganda.

Now the naïve faith is shattered, and there are those who preach the virtues of illiteracy, relying instead on racial or tribal instincts. But the failure is not of education. Rather is it the failure to develop adequate social arrangements, workable institutions, administrative techniques, that would enable us to take full advantage both of our new-found control over our environment and of our new-found freedom.

What the end product of this particular readjustment may be it is not possible to predict but only to guess and hope. In a sense there is no "end" product, for we are merely at one stage in an endless process of changing social life. But we may think of the immediate end as the provision of the basic goods in abundance to all, as water comes out of a tap in abundance. With poverty abolished, riches will cease to have much if any significance. With the wide margins for error and experimentation that become possible under conditions of plenty the widest conceivable range for expression of individual choice, or idiosyncrasy, or even idle whim, becomes possible.

If this trend is indeed a natural result of the unleashed forces of science and democracy then it is probably not only an inevitable trend, but an irreversible one: there is no use either bemoaning it or trying to go back to the good old days.

At the same time it is not a trend that can safely be left to work itself out. The dangers of a failure to understand and control it are too obvious to need much emphasis. Having mastered our natural environment—shut out the weather, spanned space, harnessed energy—our survival now depends on mastering our social environment. The real alternatives are between an orderly transition to a better ordered social environment, and a transition so chaotic that it comes to rely on bayonets and concentration camps. The latter alternative may destroy both the science and the democracy that inspired the transition, and thus halt further progress.

The chance of its being a free, humane, democratic, intelligent and orderly process depends on our discovering the rules (laws, hypotheses, theories) that govern it. This simply means the further use of the scientific method.

Yet the scientific method cannot define the end. In the last analysis that depends on personal "value judgments." At bottom there are biases which are not reasoned. They are intuitive, emotional, perhaps "spiritual." My thinking is necessarily conditioned by what I *want*. And what I want is conditioned by my past.

I know something of what used to be called the "good life," for I have had the opportunity to live it virtually dumped in my lap. I know that health and happiness and creative living depend in no small degree on the level of material well-being which economic arrangements might make possible for each of us: ample food, clothing and shelter, with all the amenities of modern living. I believe that every one of these can and should be available to all.

Yet in my own life these material things have been so much a matter of course that they have seemed to be of only elementary and preliminary importance. I want to use the machine to the limit, to flood the world with goods; but I want to be able to forget both the machine and the goods, as I forget the telephone system or the water supply system or the sewage system. Yet if I were a machinist, I would want to have a share in the controls of the machine. If there is to be economic planning, let every human being have a share in it, let no one be a mere pawn in the hands of planners.

The "end" so far as I am concerned can only be described in terms of the much overworked words, freedom and democracy. I have hated to be told what to do and what not to do; yet disciplines are essential. Creative work is the highest prerogative of man. The only opportunity most people now have for it is in what they call "leisure." Freedom means the opportunity to find creative work, in which the essential disciplines can be self-imposed. The whole problem of the relation of freedom to economic collectivism can be summed up in some such way as this: *Since, in this complex and crowded world, work is of necessity mostly collective, everyone must have a share in the controls over that work, and the fullest opportunity for individualism apart from it.*

Yet even this statement of the problem is not quite adequate, for in setting a goal it seems to separate means and ends too sharply. Even if we agreed that the transition was from A to B, and we were able to determine just what we meant by A and what we meant by B, so that B became a concrete goal and a definite end to be achieved, then it might be assumed that what happened between A and B was unimportant so long as B was achieved. In other words, the only concern was to find means and methods that worked in bringing result B.

The Moscow trials, beginning in 1936 and continuing through 1938, aroused in many of us the disquieting realization that twenty years after "the revolution" a reign of terror might still be necessary. Apparently you could not overlook means. Apparently means and ends merge so imperceptibly that it is impossible to keep them sharply distinct. Perhaps after all it is not a question of a transition from a definite system A to a definite system B, but a question of a continuous process of historical evolution, in which A and B are merely shorthand ways of describing prevailing characteristics at different periods, which yet interpenetrate throughout.

When, a few years ago, I first became aware of the changes that were being made and that had to be made in our social folkways, I was inclined to scoff at the conservative argument that capitalism is a system of "free enterprise," and therefore essential to the continuance of freedom. Who were the conservatives to argue that socialism would destroy freedom, when the capitalist system they upheld left freedom illusory for all but a few?

The basic problem, as I first saw it, was the hastening of the transition from capitalism to socialism. No need to worry unduly about freedom, for that was impossible under capitalism, and would follow naturally from the achievement of socialism. I was even willing to accept the possible necessity of an interim dictatorship.

But if means and ends are so closely interrelated that they merge constantly one into the other, liberty cannot be so cavalierly treated. The problem is not how to achieve a democratic socialist society as an end product. Nor is it merely how to achieve a transition to such a society by democratic means. The problem is one much more familiar to Americans with their conviction of the possibility of progress: how to facilitate an evolutionary process which involves the gradual attainment of *more* liberty and *more* abundance for all people.

This book is the record of my own pursuit of understanding in the field of economic change. My education in this field began with my two years of travel abroad. In the eight years since I started that voyage of discovery I have been gathering facts and making tentative hypotheses to explain the facts. And all the time I have been looking for results—not merely in terms of a satisfying and complete theory, but in terms of a theory that would facilitate more intelligent action. Yet no education in this field of swift change can ever be finished.

From now on this book will be less directly autobiographical. It is necessary for my purposes to marshal the facts that I think most relevant—about Soviet socialism, about fascism, about all the experiments in social and economic control launched in other countries, under the spur of war preparation or democratic demand or merely the instinct for survival. It is necessary for my purposes to examine the Marxist interpretation of world change, because, as I have said, it is the most impressive in its claim to completeness and authoritativeness. It is necessary to dig into the theories of the more orthodox economists. And finally, if I am to do the job I have set myself, I must inquire what are the practical possibilities for effective and intelligent action in the American political scene.

I have come to a point where I can make a tentative statement of the conclusion to which this book is directed. To state a conclusion as an hypothesis to be proved is, I take it, in the accepted scientific manner.

The argument of this book is that the difference between capitalism and socialism is in so many respects verbal and unreal, that the transition through which we are now passing may be of a far less drastic character than commonly supposed. The capitalist economy of the nineteenth century was far more collectivist than any of its present defenders appreciate. The controlled economy—call it collectivism or socialism—into which we are emerging in the twentieth century, is one in which there is and will continue to be far more capitalism than any of the radicals appreciate.

I have become convinced that the type of "free enterprise" which laissez faire economists assumed to prevail under capitalism will only become possible in a controlled or planned economy—paradoxical as that may sound. To present the issue as one between private enterprise and public enterprise, or between private ownership and public ownership, or between the profit motive and the service motive, as I was at first inclined to do, now seems to me meaningless and irrelevant, if not false.

The controls necessary to make the economic system function to produce abundance and freedom will emerge in this book from a study of collectivism in practice all over the world, and from a theoretical analysis of the economic problem itself. As a necessary first step, I have wanted to get rid of some of the confusion that surrounds our concepts.

So long as we think in terms of such hard and distinct yet incredibly vague words as capitalism and socialism, free enterprise and planned economy, the transition through which we are passing by evolutionary necessity will arouse a maximum of hatred and fear and painful conflict. If I am right in my hypothesis—that a few "reforms" of the existing system will facilitate a process already far advanced; that the difficulties of this dangerous period are features of a social readjustment which, while profound in its effect, is institutionally a comparatively minor one; that when we achieve an efficient economic system it will look so familiar that we shall continue to call it capitalism, though it will be in every essential respect a socialist system—if this hypothesis is correct, then, by the very fact that the old labels cease to be fighting slogans, perhaps the conflicts will be minimized. The wars and revolutions and ideological crusades may be largely due to a misunderstanding of the process itself, battles over words and dogmas in spite of widespread agreement on what is to be done.

As for me, I have determined to be an optimist. This period of danger and difficulty represents a stage in modern man's efforts to adapt his social habits to the power brought by science and the machine, and to an ideal of individual freedom that is still new. It is a dangerous time. Any of us may be blown to bits by a bomb before we are a year older; and our civilization itself may be set back for centuries by a disastrous series of wars. Even humane and intelligent men, aware of the constructive forces at work in the world, are so wrought up over what seem to them destructive symptoms as to feel that war is the only way out. This to me is what is most profoundly disquieting. If civilization does "collapse" it may be as much because of lack of tolerance and perspective on the part of "men of good will" as because of the blind forces they are fighting. For behind our unrest, behind communism and behind fascism, even behind the menace of war, there are forces of great promise.

The liberation of the human spirit—that vague process of growing up which we symbolize under such words as freedom of thought and democracy and science—has not been arrested. But it is demanding new disciplines, individual and social. If we do not all rush out to mutual slaughter, time will help us work them out.

# *PART II*

# A SELECTION OF RELEVANT FACTS

# Chapter Five

## FROM OCTOBER TO FIVE YEAR PLANS

WHEN I was in Leningrad I was taken by my Intourist guide to the Smolny Institute, that vast palace seminary for princesses, duchesses and other gentle female snobs, which suddenly became the focal point of revolution. It was late on a fall day, after museum visiting hours, and the incalculably long corridors were dark and empty. I was shown a little well-like room with an iron cot, on which Lenin snatched a few hours of feverish sleep during the October days of 1917, when men lived too fast to have time either for eating or sleeping. My guide got the key to the classic-columned hall where the Congress of Soviets had met in continuous session fourteen years before. He could find no light near the door so he groped up to the rostrum and switched on the light at the reading desk. Immediately a gigantic shadow leaped from him up to the rear wall of the dim auditorium. It might have been the shadow of the maker of the revolution himself, as he appeared before the tense multitude on the evening after the Winter Palace two miles away had fallen and the Kerensky government had disappeared, and declared: "We shall now proceed to construct the socialist order."

A few months before, Lenin had considered the fact that he might soon have to undertake the "reorganization of the capitalist system into a socialist one"; yet he had been forced to admit: "I do not know of any socialist who has dealt with these problems." Now here they were, he and the Bolsheviks; by a swift and decisive coup they had seized power over the largest compact national area in the world, intent on transforming its every way of living, yet without any plan of procedure. John Reed, in his magnificent account of the *Ten Days That Shook the World,* describes the comrade who had been appointed Commissar of Finance in the new regime because he had "once been clerk in a French bank"; he was sitting in a corner, "anxiously figuring on a dirty envelope, and biting his pencil"; while the new Commissar of Commerce humorously admitted that he knew "nothing whatever of business."

This was the beginning of the first and still the only conscious attempt to fashion a socialist economy. I am inclined to believe there will never again be a similar experiment because there will never be another "socialist revolution." In this case it was possible to carry through "the" revolution because of a combination of extraordinary circumstances: disintegration of a corrupt regime under the strain of a great war, absence of any effective democratic institutions, and the existence of a trained and disciplined revolutionary group, uniquely led and utterly ruthless in their seizure and maintenance of power because of an utter conviction of the righteousness of their cause. But even if there is never again to be a similar situation, the experience of the Soviet Union in the last twenty-odd years is of paramount importance to all those who believe a planned collectivist economy is the pattern of the future.

The Bolsheviks started in almost complete ignorance of the economic problems they had to face. Their minds were cluttered up with Marxist notions that constantly led to false steps whenever an attempt was made to apply them. They were guilty of virtually every mistake they could have made. Their mistakes were horribly costly, resulting in millions of unnecessary deaths and untold suffering: if the dictatorship had been any less brutal than it was it could never have survived these errors, and if the country had been any farther developed from a primitive agricultural base than it was no regime could have kept order in the chaos that would have ensued. Yet the mistakes are as instructive as the successes.

In the twenty-one years since the October Revolution there has been a vast amount of argument and discussion in the outside world about the failures and successes of the Soviet "experiment." But they have been almost wholly in political terms. And a great part of the discussion, particularly as between the various Marxist groups, has been over abstractions—like the "dictatorship of the proletariat"—whose referents were mostly emotional states in the sectarian mind.

It is perhaps not entirely surprising that there has been little analysis of Soviet progress in strictly economic terms. For the Marxists have always been taught to believe that any analysis of the workings of socialism (even apparently when it was contemporary!) was "Utopian." Capitalist economists have been biased, and have either disregarded the Soviet Union or pointed to its failures as horrible examples.

When, in the course of my own inquiry, I sought to understand exactly what constituted the difference between "production for use" and "production for the market," I found only two or three books in all the wealth of available material that were helpful in interpreting Soviet economics. My own brief visits to the Soviet Union had merely given me an oversimplified version of the Soviet planned economy: a blueprint was drafted for a five-year period, then the people did as the central planners directed. But apparently there had been several shifts of ground; there was no doubt that there had been frightful failures as well as magnificent successes; and the outward results still seemed to me doubtful.

When I went back to Soviet economic history in search of economic principles I found there was much to be learned which had been almost entirely neglected, alike by partisans and enemies of the regime.

## *How Not to Do It*

Soviet history is easily divisible into three parts, the period of "War Communism" from the Revolution to 1921, the period of the "New Economic Policy" or "NEP" from 1921 to 1928, and the period of the Five Year Plans from 1928 to the present. During the first period the economic mechanism ran down till it almost stopped, during the second it was revived by a judicious return to laissez faire, and only in the last did the "constitution of a socialist order" begin in earnest. To be sure, these periods merged into each other, and so did both the destructive and constructive elements in each of them; but the division is near enough the truth to be helpful.

When I went to Russia my head was full of tales of destruction.

The outside "bourgeois" world got its most vivid impression of the Russian Revolution from those who fled famine, terror and economic collapse in the first period, and that impression has remained. The idea some of my conservative friends still have, that the Bolsheviks have been living off the accumulated wealth of past generations of Russians, was true enough when it first became current.

For a few months after the Revolution the old order still had momentum. People went about their jobs as a matter of habit. Lenin wisely tried to hold back the enthusiasm of the workers, who knew only that, in Marxian lingo, the "expropriators" were to be "expropriated." In the beginning only the Imperial State Bank was taken over, and the attempt was made to check any wholesale socialization of business and industrial enterprises. The pace quickened nonetheless. The whole credit structure—the innumerable pieces of paper that are inscribed with promises to pay—collapsed almost at once as the private banks disappeared. The syndicalist tradition, that the workers take over the factories, was given added impetus in the excitement of the Revolution: there was no stopping the process by which the workers drove out their employers. With business management gone and credit gone the factories slowed to a stop.

A year or two later the factory workers in Italy followed suit; their "occupation of the factories" was one of the stimulants of fascism. In both cases stocks of raw materials shortly ran out and could not be replaced, and the finished products tended to pile up without any mechanism to move them on toward consumers; there was no money coming in for wages or for the purchase of additional raw materials.

It was believed that money would soon disappear—Marx was vague on this point as on every point connected with the building of socialism—so the People's Bank merely printed rubles for day-to-day governmental purposes, without regard to consequences. State and municipal services were free, and it was apparently thought that the communist goal, "from each according to his ability, to each according to his needs," could be quickly realized.

Lenin rightly emphasized that "socialism is the keeping of accounts," but he thought it a comparatively simple matter, which any worker with a knowledge of arithmetic would easily master.

By 1920 it was apparent that industries merely under the control of the workers would not run themselves; the disciplines required by war and dictatorship were again imposed in the factories, particularly in the munitions plants, and centralized control took the place of the decentralized syndicalist operation. But the tools for intelligent planning were lacking. A decree "abolished" banking, and set up the "Central Budget and Accounting Administration" in place of the People's Bank, but this was only a change of label: the new institution did little but keep the printing presses running. Another decree, inspired by Marx's labor theory of value, declared that all values were to be measured in terms of labor; this was ignored at the time, but the notion was to plague Soviet economists for many years yet.

Meanwhile economic processes stagnated more and more. With shortages of everything the only recourse was the recourse of shipwrecked mariners or of an army beleaguered far from its sources of supply: the rationing of goods in meager doles. A great migration occurred from the cities back to the villages, where at least people were close to the one essential source of supply. Leningrad and Moscow were empty shells. But even in the case of basic foodstuffs the incentive to production had been lacking. At the end of 1921 a frightful famine took place, and the already weakened population died like flies.

At the low point in this first period industrial production fell to 13 per cent of the pre-war level. Railway traffic fell to 12 per cent; only a few locomotives were still functioning, the rest rusting in idle repair shops. Consumption of bread in the towns, which was always the staple food, was at 50 per cent. Never has a great country slipped so rapidly back towards savagery. In some of the villages there were stories of cannibalism.

The orthodox Communist explains the failure of War Communism as due merely to war conditions. It is true that intervention and civil war, on top of the disastrous years of the Great War, and finally complicated by the war with Poland, ravaged the country and left it prostrate. Yet if there had been an understanding of the nature of socialism in the beginning the disruption need not have been so catastrophic. The fiasco of War Communism was the fiasco of socialist economic thinkers, who, following Marx, considered it "Utopian" to plan for the transition to socialism, and never "dealt with these problems." The heritage of that first period of degradation and suffering, and "the Terror" that was added to it as the only means of retaining any semblance of order, is still a blight on the Soviet Union.

The New Economic Policy or NEP was admittedly a temporary "step backward" toward "capitalism," to permit recovery of lost ground. Ownership of the basic means of production was not returned to private hands nor was private banking permitted. But private trade and business-for-profit were encouraged. Most important of all, the peasants were induced to produce food for the cities once again, by the re-establishment of commodity markets and a money economy. Prices were once more left to the play of supply and demand. A vast growth of speculation followed, especially as the ruble was not stabilized till 1924 (at 50 billion to 1); but speculation at least meant that the life-blood of economic activity was pumping through the country's veins.

Walter Duranty gives a striking picture of Moscow at the end of the original period, a crumbling, ragged city, which had not even kept up such essential services as streets and drainage and electricity, and where a dwindling population lived from hand to mouth: a few more years of drawing on past accumulations without replacement and the city would have been like an H. G. Wells ruin, inhabited only by a few cave men. Then Duranty describes the startling transformation that occurred on the introduction of the New Economic Policy. In a capitalist system economic wheels are kept turning by the market, where goods are traded under the spur of monetary profit. The Bolsheviks had destroyed the market and put nothing in its place: gradually the wheels had stopped turning and money had become more and more worthless paper. The NEP restored the market. Trade was once more permitted. The wheels began to turn. Money began to flow. Even its depreciation was now an incentive to keep it moving. Gambling flourished like a weed after a drought. The Moscow authorities put the heaviest of punitive taxation on the gambling dens, yet still they throve. And out of the taxes on gambling, says Duranty, the city at last was able to get the resources to repair the streets and the municipal services. A dead economy began to revive, thanks in part to a restoration of some of the worst features of capitalism. The dead economy was a "socialist" one, and the NEP represented a return to "capitalism."

For a while the retreat threatened to become a rout. The dogmatism of the earlier period so far relaxed that Boris Brutzkus, a Leningrad University economist, was permitted to publish an attack on the economics of socialism which is still one of the most penetrating in the field, and was even given a responsible post in the regional agricultural planning bureau, though he was exiled shortly thereafter. Many of the former business men who were left were called back, and the socialized industries were instructed to operate along capitalist lines.

The Bolshevik leaders, however, never seem to have had any doubts that it was more than a temporary stratagem. The "bosses" might be called back in the guise of "experts" or "specialists," but their tenure was precarious and their status dubious. They were watched by the triple hawk-eyes of the Communist party cells, the secret police, and the trade union representatives. And the "Nepmen" proper, the petty traders and business men whose initiative and greed made the NEP recovery possible, were a tolerated but despised class.

When I went to Russia in 1931 the NEP was still recent history. The older people looked back to it as a brief and partial but nonetheless blessed return to the good old days. The younger people, who by that time had had fourteen years of drilling in the ideals of the Revolution, betrayed a noble scorn for the profit motive and for money-making. To this attitude I readily responded, having come from an aristocracy where these "bourgeois" traits were held in equal contempt, however useful they might be to make my capitalist system (or the Russian NEP) function. Occasionally I lunched in a restaurant where a furtive Nepman lingered on, or had my hair cut by an independent barber who complained of being taxed out of existence. And on one occasion I talked to an "expert" manager of a plant who might have been a pre-war business executive, and felt his irritation at the bumptious, red-haired youth sitting beside him, "representing the workers, and with equal authority."

No, the NEP had been only a deceptive Indian summer for the old free market. And behind the scenes the Bolsheviks were taking to heart the lessons of War Communism.

### *Learning How to Plan*

The idea of planning had survived the fiasco of "natural socialism." The Gosplan or State Planning Commission had been set up under the Council of Labor and Defense as early as 1921. Plans for electrification were pushed at Lenin's insistence, and the capacity of Soviet power plants increased 50 per cent during the NEP.

With the stabilization of the ruble in 1924, planning on an extensive scale for the first time became possible: after all, it is not possible to make an integrated plan without a reasonably stable unit of measure. An over all economic plan for the national economy was adopted for the year 1925-26, and for each year thereafter. But these plans were tentative and experimental. Even with a fairly stable ruble, prices were so variable under private trade that there seemed no way of predicting where and how goods would flow. In particular, there seemed no way of counting on adequate supplies of grain for export, to buy the machinery needed to rehabilitate home industries: foreign trade was still a socialized monopoly, but between the independence of the peasants and the unpredictables of the open market, these early plans broke down.

The idea of the first Five Year Plan began to take shape in 1926. If prices were not to be permitted to fluctuate on the open market then it was felt that private trading must give way to planned distribution as well as planned production. The Plan became more and more elaborate. It began to take on a fourfold aspect. The first was the construction of new plants, already begun in the field of electric power. Second was the production of raw materials, especially oil and coal, iron and steel, without which there could be no industrial expansion, but which demanded in turn that the building of new plants must be concentrated in this field—steel mills, oil wells, mines and smelters—rather than in the consumer goods field. Third was the production and distribution of consumer goods. And last were the monetary aspects of the Plan.

Apparently during the formulation of the first Five Year Plan there was a good deal of caution in high places. The disasters of War Communism were still fresh. The experiments in doing without money had resulted in a return to orthodoxy in financial matters. A whole series of new banks had been founded in 1922, and interest up to 8 and 10 per cent was paid on deposits to encourage the accumulation of monetary capital. The currency had been given a gold base when it was stabilized, though notes were not redeemable in gold and the gold had no significance for the internal economy, other than its psychological effect on those who had charge of the printing presses.

Capitalist banking practices flourished under the NEP, with the banks discounting the commercial paper brought to them by the private and socialized businesses. This type of free commercial credit continued well into the Five Year Plan. But commercial banking and investment banking were separated in 1927. The Gosbank or State Bank concentrated all short-term or commercial credit in its hands, and for a while it had sufficient cash deposits to take care of the demand. The other banks, founded to promote investment in industry (the "Prombank"), electrification, and public works, came to rely on grants from the Treasury as the chief source of funds.

With all of this conventional monetary and banking framework around them, the framers of the Five Year Plan conceived of its monetary aspects in fairly conventional terms. A "market equilibrium" was to be sought between the goods produced and the amount of money in circulation, with prices gently falling. Under expanded production, and with costs lowered because of increased mechanization, businesses would make handsome profits, and new construction would be financed by way of investment of these profits as well as out of Treasury funds raised by taxation and loans.

It has been said by such an otherwise hostile critic as Brutzkus, that the Five Year Plan as it finally evolved after two years of work was the "result of the collaboration of the best Russian minds." One of the chief planners, Strumilin, had moved far enough from Marxist orthodoxy, according to Brutzkus, to "discover" the theory of "marginal utility."

To begin with, the planners had a country rich in resources—no one knew how rich till the geologists, explorers and prospectors began to come back from their expeditions. They had a fair number of large and centralized industries and a good railway network (though in ghastly disrepair) built with foreign capital in the days of the Czar. They had an enormous population. And they had a dictatorship, one of the most effective ever seen because fired by an infectious zeal.

To "build socialism in one country" and "outstrip the capitalist countries" they must not merely put labor to work on resources but they must seek to increase their productive capacity. This meant a special emphasis on machines, since in this modern era it is machines which make abundance possible. Machines became a fetish: the flower plot in the center of Theatre Square in Moscow was laid out in the design of a tractor when I was there. But machines are made of steel, and steel is made from iron and coal. Machines need power, and power comes from falling water and from burning fuel. Czarist Russia imported its machines but Soviet Russia aimed to build its own. Czarist Russia had opened coal and iron mines and oil wells, but these were inadequate for a great expansion program, and they were operated by primitive hand methods, which would never do when every worker's labor must be made to count: Soviet Russia must not only open new mines and wells and factories but must increase the productivity of every worker. Productivity, however, is not merely a matter of new machines but of new skill, and new technical schools would have to be provided.

Here were half a dozen herculean tasks to be done at once. And on top of them all the Five Year Plan aimed to increase the production of consumer goods so that the standard of living could rise and be the reward of the great effort. But to raise the standard of living in just one item, say the production of cotton shirts, is an infinitely complex and roundabout process. With inadequate understanding of the magnitude of the task, but a willingness to make mistakes, a readiness to be ruthless, and a vast enthusiasm, the Plan got under way.

My first visit to the Soviet Union was in its third year. I found myself at once confronted with the hardships and the courage of the Soviet leaders. Coming across Siberia my first stop was at Novosibirsk. Seeking someone who could speak a language I knew, I went sightseeing under the amateur guidance of a young newspaperwoman who spoke French. She took me out to the site of a new factory for manufacturing mining machinery. It was out on the cold rainy prairie, and little was visible but vast muddy excavations where struggled hundreds of ragged men and straining horses. My girl companion was insufficiently clad and she shivered as she told me what it was all about. I felt as ignorant as a man from Mars.

An almost incandescent heat began to light her as she warmed to her subject—the new world she was helping to build. Here will be the schools, and here the workers' homes, and there the largest machine shop of its kind in the world. She and these fellow-workers are poor. They need clothes (as I can easily see). Cotton, and machines to weave the cotton, are necessary. That means steel, and coal, the two basic raw materials of a standard of living. The Kuznetsk coal fields nearby are newly discovered. Novosibirsk will be a center for a great mining region. This factory will help speed the production of coal. Meanwhile cotton is being grown, a thousand miles to the south, in Turkestan. To take advantage of the warm cotton-growing soil to the full, it should not be used to grow wheat. Wheat will grow here, in the Siberian prairie. Therefore we must build a railroad, from here to there, to carry our wheat to feed the cotton growers of Turkestan, and bring back cotton to clothe us. Railroads, too, need steel and coal.

The whole scheme fitted together like a picture puzzle. I was able to handle many of the pieces and put them together myself. I traveled down over the new "Turk-Sib" railroad and in warm Tashkent saw a vast factory going up to build cultivators and other implements for the cotton fields, not accidentally but according to plan. I began to study the figures of the Five Year Plan by which these factories and railroads and fields were plotted against each other. Increase the wheat acreage here, the cotton acreage there; open up a coal mine here, increase productivity per worker so much with the latest mechanical devices used in America, build a plant here, more there, a railroad to link these efforts.

I never even thought of asking, "Where's the money coming from?" It seemed clear enough that the money question was merely the bookkeeping end of an engineering problem. They had the coal and the soil and the hands. Why worry about how little black marks were made on pieces of paper?

The Soviet planners were not worrying over those little black marks any more than I. In a sense they were right. Yet the most intelligent economists, who were thrust aside after drafting the original plans, knew that there must be a close correspondence between the "real world" and the "mental world," and that the Financial Plan might be as important as the Production Plan. A new series of colossal blunders was piling up, ready to bring disaster the year after my first visit. The only way the Plan could be carried through without collapse was by reviving the terror and the dictatorship in full force, once more under the excuse of imminent war.

Nonetheless, the first Five Year Plan marked the beginning of the building of a planned socialist economy. There was no further turning back. Historians a hundred years from now will be inclined to overlook the victims—suffering is an old story—and view this period as one of the most truly heroic in all history. The Soviet planners were carried away by the very magnitude of their own conception. Under the spell of their blueprints they visualized a country leaping ahead at one stroke from a backward agricultural economy with a low standard of living, to an advanced industrial economy with a high standard of living. Their accomplishment fell far short of their expectations, their statistics failed the test of practical application, they made major miscalculations, yet they succeeded in doubling their industrial production by the end of the first Five Year Plan, and quadrupling it by the end of the second. No other country at any other time had ever done anything like that.

The quantitative achievement, particularly in the building of new plants, has been often described. But the reasons for both failure and success are only just beginning to be studied by the objective historian. Four principal errors made at the beginning of the first Five Year Plan are beginning to become apparent.

### *Failures*

First of all, the planners failed to work out a mechanism to assure an adequate supply of foodstuffs and other agricultural products from individualistic peasants, whose economic perspective was confined to a village market. When the NEP markets were abolished the Bolsheviks knew no other way than compulsion to get the peasants to produce food for the industrial population.

The crude method they developed was collective farms and compulsory grain deliveries. The peasants countered by planting only enough for their own use, and by eating up half their livestock, virtually their only capital. The Bolsheviks' answer to this was to unleash a new reign of terror, directed ostensibly at "kulaks" or rich peasants, and to let the people starve wherever the crops were short. The whole country was demoralized by the famine conditions which began in 1931, reached a peak in 1932 and continued even into 1933. At the end of the first Five Year Plan there were half as many horses, cattle and hogs as at the beginning, and only one-third as many sheep and goats; production of grain was 10 per cent less than before the war and 5 per cent less than at the beginning of the Plan, and consumption of meat and fats had fallen to one-half and of milk to two-thirds of what it had been at the beginning of the Plan. The price of these mistakes of the first Five Year Plan had still not been paid by the end of the second, for herds take time to build up.

Secondly, the planners miscalculated the ability of unskilled workers to use machines, and to learn new industrial techniques, and they underestimated the problem of achieving efficient management. Costly new machines bought abroad were promptly spoiled by Soviet workers. All the work took longer than planned, and required more workers. The cost of the vast production and construction programs was essentially a labor cost, since the state owned all the plants and bought raw materials and semi-finished goods from itself, but the labor cost was constantly far in excess of estimates. Shock-brigades and later Stakhanovites were called into action to make up for lagging productivity by speed-ups, but the artificially induced enthusiasm of a few could not make up for the inefficiency of the many. Quality of product was constantly sacrificed to achieve quantity quotas. The result of all these miscalculations was that many new plants were not yet finished at the end of the Plan, production was lagging behind schedule in many fields, and the monetary aspects of the Plan had been thrown completely out of joint.

Thirdly, the roundabout nature of production had been underestimated. The means of production—raw materials, fuels, existing capital plant—had to be used to produce more "means of production," which in turn were used to produce more "means of production," which again were used to produce more "means of production." Inevitably the production of consumer goods was slighted. In an effort to meet this difficulty, which loomed up in the first year of the Plan, the schedules for capital goods expansion were revised upward—in place of a threefold expansion of pig iron production a fivefold increase was now put down in the Plan—but to no avail: actually production was not quite doubled by the last year of the Plan.

More important for our purposes were the monetary errors. The original Plan had been sound enough, in its monetary aspects, thanks to the conservatism of many of its economic experts. They apparently realized that if a billion rubles were being paid out in wages in the construction of new plants, and another billion to workers manufacturing consumer goods in existing plants (and if under the labor theory of value the consumer goods were valued at a billion rubles), no consumer goods would be available in the stores to match the first billion paid out to the workers building the new plants. They planned, as noted above, to restore a balance by taxes, loans and profits.

But the Plan was no sooner under way than the enthusiasts, who had always clung to the notion that money was an unnecessary evil in a socialist economy, threw caution to the winds. Because of lagging efficiency industrial operations everywhere required more labor than estimated, and the increased payrolls were met by means of direct currency inflation. "Private" commercial credit was wisely abandoned in 1930—that is, different enterprises ceased to extend credit for supplies to each other, and the granting of short-term credit was concentrated in the Gosbank, which at least could keep track of it; but for the first two years the ease of creating credit by merely writing it in a book was deceptive. The managers of enterprises paid little attention to costs, they hired extra workers, they let stocks accumulate till they spoiled before they could be sold; they had little incentive to efficiency, since the Gosbank could always pay their bills; and behind the Gosbank were the printing presses.

Meanwhile the expected profits did not materialize, because costs rose so much faster than prices. And the taxes and loans were quite inadequate. The new investment required more and more inflation. The turnover tax, which was a sales tax levied on wholesale prices and hence easiest to impose and collect, went up to 50 and even 80 per cent on some articles. Workers were forced time after time to give up a month's pay in the guise of a loan. In spite of everything far more money kept coming to the shops than there were goods to buy.*

I saw queues in front of empty shops all over Russia. These were not necessarily a sign of mere temporary shortages due to lags in production schedules, as I was glibly told and as glibly believed, but of continuing shortages: shortages of goods in relation to the money seeking to buy at the given prices. They were the surest sign of currency inflation. The Soviet leaders were slow in taking proper measures. They went back to rationing the meager supply in various complicated ways, at the prices they considered correct, and allocating a part of the products to "open" stores where prices soared to a point of balance between supply and demand. This practice of having more than one price for each article according to whether it was bought in a "closed" (which usually meant rationed) store or an "open" one, greatly complicated all bookkeeping and accounting. Its only conceivable advantage was that

* Between 1928 and 1932, the years of the first Five Year Plan, currency in circulation increased from 2 billion rubles to 8. At the same time the figures for retail trade turnover indicate a rise only from 15.2 billion to 40.4. No figures on general price levels were published after 1930, and obviously with shifting and variable prices they would have been difficult to determine. One competent investigator estimated that average prices were five times as high in 1935 as in 1929. Since the currency in circulation rose little more between 1932 and 1935 (it was only 9.3 billion in 1935), it is probable that prices were near the maximum in 1932, at the end of the first Five Year Plan. Suppose we assume, however, that prices were only four times as high in 1932 as in 1928, then the threefold rise of retail trade turnover would still indicate a considerable drop in consumption.

The additional flow of money that is represented by the difference in a fourfold currency inflation over against a threefold increase in retail turnover, is partly explainable by the increase in taxes, loans and savings, all virtually compulsory, which in 1932 totaled 5.7 billion rubles out of a total payroll of 32.7. There was still extra money in people's pockets, however. Some of this was spent on railroad travel, expenditures on which increased six times in this period; the labor turnover implied in this great migration was one of the special headaches of the planners. But part of the inflation was probably counterbalanced by a drop in velocity: if you couldn't spend your money today you left it in your pockets till tomorrow.

it made possible special privileges for special workers, as political or economic incentives.

Inflation, to be sure, had no direct effect on production, since production was pushed to capacity in the first place and paid for afterward. But indirectly it must have had a serious effect, since the difficulty of planning in all its monetary aspects was increased: both for the Gosplan experts and for each individual enterpriser it was a constant handicap to try to keep up with the Plan while prices gyrated.

There have been other excuses given for the difficulties of the first Five Year Plan. The capitalist depression did make the question of paying for the planned imports of machinery with exports of raw materials a serious one, but this difficulty was exaggerated to justify hardship. Actually tonnage of grain exported in the first three years of the Plan never reached 8 per cent of the total production, which under other circumstances would not have greatly affected consumption. Then the railroads proved inadequate to the burden imposed on them, creating an unforeseen difficulty. And in addition, as has been often emphasized, the growing danger of war required a growing emphasis on armaments. But the invasion of Manchuria did not begin till 1931 and Hitler did not come to power till 1933, so that the war scare in the first Five Year Plan was also chiefly an excuse for failures arising from other causes. In so far as war preparations did have an effect it was in further speeding up the heavy and extractive industries at the expense of the consumer goods industries.

The difficulties that piled up in 1931 and 1932 were further complicated by the rash decision to complete the Plan at the end of the latter year, which was only four and a quarter years since its inception in October, 1928. It was apparently hoped that by sheer will power and artificially induced enthusiasm the Plan could be carried through in that last year. But too much damage had been done by previous mistakes. The pace continued to slow down, and even though an additional year was permitted to go by (to finish plants that had been started and to consolidate gains) before the second Five Year Plan was announced, even by the end of 1933 the original goals in many fields were not yet achieved.*

* For a statistical summary of the successes and failures of Soviet planning, see table at end of this chapter, pages 114 and 115.

### *Successes*

By the time the second Five Year Plan was announced at the end of 1933 (it was considered to have begun at the beginning of that year) most of the mistakes of the first Plan were well on the way to rectification. Progress during the next three years was at an astounding rate. Tonnage of freight carried by the railroads is one of the best single indices of economic activity. In 1928 it was 156,000,000 tons, and in 1933 it was 268,000,000, an increase of 112,000,000. By 1936 it had leaped to 484,000,000, a further increase of 216,000,000.* The increase for those three years of the second Five Year Plan was twice as great as the increase of the preceding five years. Production of iron, steel, coal, and other basic industrial products, except oil, was leaping ahead, and some of the consumer goods industries began to move.

Let us look at the way the particular errors mentioned above were ironed out.

In agriculture, the collectivization program so recklessly undertaken at the beginning of the first Plan was carried through, though at a slower pace, during the remainder of the first and the whole of the second, until today at least 93 per cent of the peasants and 99 per cent of the sown area are collectivized. But the emphasis shifted after the first costly mistakes. The giant state farms run with wage labor like factories turned out to be uneconomic and were not pushed after 1931. The more complete type of collective, where all the land, equipment and livestock were owned in common, gave way to a form more nearly approaching that of a producers' co-operative. The Russian peasant today is permitted to own his own house and garden and a certain amount of livestock. And each collective farm is in effect a private enterprise, owned by the peasants as if they were stockholders; they seek to divide as large a profit as possible among themselves.

More important still was the relaxation of compulsion in grain collections, and the re-establishment of market conditions, both for the sale of produce and the purchase of consumer goods. A

* These figures are for tonnage "despatched." "Ton-kilometers" carried increased at about the same rate, but the figures, while more significant, happen to be less complete.

certain compulsory quota has been retained at an arbitrary low price, which covers the requirements of the army and other direct state functions; but most agricultural produce is bought by the state trading organizations, apparently with a fair amount of bargaining over price, and peasant markets in the cities for individual consumers have been increasingly permitted.

It is not strictly true that agriculture has been socialized. The farms are owned by the farmers themselves, though in co-operative groups; the profit motive has been increasingly relied on; and the distribution of the product has been more and more on what approaches an open market. Back of this increase in economic freedom has been no relaxation of political controls, rather an increase in their efficiency. The machine-tractor stations were started in 1930 as centers for both economic and political education and control; the collective farms have been made increasingly dependent on them, until in 1935, 72 per cent of the sown area of the collective farms was served from these four thousand centers.

As for the second difficulty listed above as arising from rapid technological advance, that of training and organizing skilled workers and technicians, and estimating and accounting for costs of production, by the time the second Five Year Plan got under way this problem was pretty well mastered. The most important step was the concentrating of responsibility in the manager of the individual enterprise, with complete discipline over his workers. Trade unions became the instruments of scientific management, the kind of "company union" which every personnel manager in American industry dreams of. Piece wages and extreme wage differentials (some Soviet earnings are said to be eighty times those of the lowest paid) were increasingly resorted to, as monetary incentives to more efficient work. Emphasis was put more and more on the earning of a book profit, as the only check on efficiency. A part of any profit earned went to the expansion of the enterprise, and to the improvement of the social amenities of the workers (workers' clubs, crêches, restaurants, etc.), as well as a small fraction to the management in the shape of a bonus, thus providing additional incentives. In all these features we see increasing resemblances to capitalist procedures.

In regard to the third problem, the development of adequate

means of production as a foundation for roundabout industrial development, there was no tendency to minimize its importance in the drafting of the second Five Year Plan. Even though for purposes of propaganda it was announced that the emphasis in the second Plan would be shifted from capital goods to consumer goods, actually the second Plan proposed an even more rapid building of new plants and expansion of the basic industries like coal and iron. Under the first Plan the production of coal and iron had doubled; under the second it doubled again, which meant a fourfold increase altogether. At the same time there was more and more emphasis on machinery. The planners paid little enough attention to machinery to produce finished consumers' goods: they concentrated on machinery that would increase the production of machinery which in turn would increase the production of more machinery. Between 1928 and 1936 they stepped up the production of machinery eleven times. Electric motors, Diesel engines, metal-cutting machine tools, mining machinery, railroad equipment, all these and hundreds of special technological devices were turned out in a steady stream in the second Five Year Plan, to lay a firm foundation for a modern industrial civilization. The consumer goods industries began to get attention (3,600 looms were built in 1935 as compared to 300 in 1932), so that by the end of the second Plan the standard of living was at last definitely showing signs of rising.*

* The failure of the standard of living to rise—in fact the best evidence seems to show that it fell—during the first two Five Year Plans, in contrast to the extraordinary rise in industrial production, presents something of a paradox. Several partial explanations may be given. First, the consumption of food fell. Collectivization and mechanization involved a social upheaval which tended to reduce production at first rather than increase it; livestock is not yet back to what it was, hence meat and milk products have lagged; grain production has remained fairly stationary, yield falling as sown area increased. On the other hand, canned goods show a tenfold increase, which boosts the industrial index but may have a negligible effect on total food consumption. Recently there has been a considerable rise in beet sugar production.

Second, consumption of clothing declined. The increase in cotton grown domestically merely balanced the drop in imports, hence cotton textiles have no more than kept up with the growth in population, and are said to have declined in quality; woolen goods have of course not been able to surmount the shortage of sheep; the increase in manufactured shoes has apparently not

As for the fourth problem mentioned, it took the Soviet planners six years to correct the monetary mistakes they made in two years of the first Plan. In 1931 they began to insist on a rigid accounting from the managers of plants, and the State Bank began to keep a constant watchful check on every disbursement, to see that it conformed to the Plan or was otherwise vitally necessary. The uncontrolled credit expansion was halted, and with it the currency stabilized, by the end of 1932. But the awkward two-price system remained for several years. In one set of stores goods continued to be "correctly" valued at the labor cost of production, in another prices soared to absorb the surplus money resulting from inflation. A rational pricing system was only achieved by degrees during 1935 and 1936, when the "closed stores" were gradually abolished, and single prices were set at five or ten times the 1928 level.* This involved new difficulties, for certain low-paid workers, who had previously depended on the artificially low

yet been able to compensate for the liquidation of hand-made footware of better quality, and of course leather is scarce.

Housing, the third major item in a standard of living, has notoriously fallen behind the demand caused by the great influx into the cities.

On the other hand, in the last few years the production of luxuries—silk goods, cosmetics, cameras, bicycles, sporting goods—has increased considerably, but these are still within the reach of only a few. L. E. Hubbard, whose books on the Soviet economy are more informative than any other writer's, considers that the standard of living of the higher income groups has risen and that of the majority of workers and peasants has fallen. But he does not take into account the enormous increase in social and cultural facilities of the last ten years, schools, clubs, holiday trips, and the like, which would partially counterbalance the drop in the essential goods.

In looking at the future, there are two possibilities. One, which I am inclined to favor, is that, having mastered the techniques of planning, built their basic industrial plant, and gone "over the hump" with the basic agricultural raw materials under the new social dispensation, the standard of living can be expected to rise consistently from now on, at an increasingly rapid rate. The other is the more pessimistic one, that having still failed to master the techniques of planning (which of these two assumptions is correct will be further analyzed in the next chapter), a terrific amount of human labor will continue to be wasted in piling up an industrial plant which merely feeds on itself, and thus the production of consumer goods will continue where it is.

* Bread was the first article derationed, in January, 1935. Meat and other foodstuffs followed in October of that year, and manufactured articles in January, 1936.

prices of rationed goods, then had to be given wage rises, and inventory values had to be marked up, both of which involved further adjustment and further inflation.

But it appears that within the last two or three years most of the planners' monetary troubles came to an end. The Financial Plan is now the reflection of the Production Plan, and permits a really effective control by the banking system. At the same time better pricing procedures have been developed; and the flow of money into investment, production, distribution, and through the central government's "budgets," has come under adequate control.

The end result, as I have sought to measure it recently, with the completion of the second Five Year Plan, has indeed been an extraordinary achievement. While the rest of the world has been floundering in depression and the social ills that accompany depression, production in the Soviet Union has been leaping ahead.

The League of Nations publishes comparable statistics supplied it by various countries, and its key figure is the index of industrial production, for which it takes 1929 as 100. This was the first full year of the first Five Year Plan, and it was the last year of the old capitalist prosperity. By 1932, the end of the first Plan, the Soviet index was at 183.4 (it had been 79.5 in 1928 when the Plan was launched); the indices for other countries in 1932 were: United States 53.8, Germany 53.3, France 68.8, England 83.5. By 1937 the Soviet Union had pushed industrial production to 424. The average for 1937 in the other important countries was: United States 92.2, Germany 117.2, France 82.8, England 124.0. In other words, while the rest of the world virtually stood still between 1929 and 1937, the Soviet Union more than quadrupled its industrial production.

While index numbers are never wholly reliable, actual physical quantities reported bear out that estimate. Between 1928 and 1937 the Soviet Union increased railroad freight tonnage 3½ times, production of electricity 7 times, coal 3½ times, pig iron 4 times, cement 3 times, and machines 11 times. In the consumer goods industries, cotton textile production increased less than 20 per cent, but production of leather shoes multiplied 6 times; soap production had apparently about doubled and paper tripled.

The following table summarizes the Soviet achievement.

## Statistics of Soviet Production Under the Five Year Plans

| | 1913 | 1928 | 1932 Plan | 1932 Actual | 1937 Plan | 1937 Actual | 1942 Plan |
|---|---|---|---|---|---|---|---|
| *Industrial Production* | | | | | | | |
| Index (1929 = 100)[a] | | 79.5 | | 183.4 | | 424.0 | |
| Value (billion rubles)[b] | | 18.3 | 43.2 | 43.3 | 92.7 | 95.5 | 180.0 |
| *Heavy Industry* | | | | | | | |
| Coal (million tons) | 29.1 | 35.5 | 75.0 | 64.7 | 152.5 | 122.6 | 230.0 |
| Oil (million tons) | 9.2 | 11.7 | 21.7 | 22.3 | 46.8 | 27.8 | 54.0 |
| Pig iron (million tons) | 4.2 | 3.3 | 10.0 | 6.2 | 16.0 | 14.5 | 22.0 |
| Cement (million tons) | 1.5 | 1.9 | 6.8 | 3.5 | 7.4[c] | 5.8 | |
| Autos and trucks (thousands) | | .7 | | 23.9 | 220.0[c] | 163.3 | 400.0 |
| Tractors (thousands) | | 1.3 | | 50.6 | | 115.6[d] | |
| Machine and metal working industry (billion rubles)[b] | 1.1 | 2.2 | | 9.4 | 30.3[c] | 24.7[d] | |
| Electric power (billion kwh.) | 1.9 | 5.0 | 22.0 | 13.5 | 38.0 | 35.7 | 75.0 |
| *Consumer Goods Industry* | | | | | | | |
| Cotton textiles (billion meters) | | 2.8 | 3.6 | 2.7 | 5.1 | 3.2 | |
| Woolen textiles (million meters) | | 99.0 | 270.0 | 93.3 | 226.0 | 100.3 | |
| Shoes (million pairs, manufactured, leather) | 8.3 | 29.6 | 80.0 | 84.7 | 180.0 | 183.0 | |
| Soap (household, thousand tons) | 95.0 | 183.6 | | 261.0 | 1000.0 | | |
| Paper (thousand tons) | 197.0 | 284.5 | | 478.5 | 955.0[c] | 763.0[d] | |
| Bicycles (thousands) | | 10.8 | | 128.4 | 900.0[c] | 268.0[d] | |
| Cameras (thousands) | | | | 29.6 | | 557.0[d] | |
| Books (millions) | 113.4 | 266.7 | | 518.3 | | | |
| *Agriculture and Foodstuffs* | | | | | | | |
| Grain (million tons) | 80.1 | 73.3 | 106.0 | 69.9 | 110.0 | 83.0[d] | |
| Cotton (million centners) | | 8.2 | | 12.7 | | 22.0[d] | |

| | | | | | | | |
|---|---|---|---|---|---|---|---|
| Livestock:[e] Horses (millions) | 35.8 | 34.6 | | 19.6 | | 16.6[d] | |
| Cattle (millions) | 60.6 | 67.1 | | 40.7 | | 56.5[d] | |
| Hogs (millions) | 20.9 | 20.4 | | 11.6 | | 30.4[d] | |
| Sheep and goats (millions) | 121.2 | 147.0 | | 52.1 | | 73.3[d] | |
| Fishery products (million centners) | | 9.5[f] | | 13.3 | | | |
| Meat and fats (billion rubles)[b] | | 2.4[f] | | 1.2 | | 1.4[d] | |
| Milk (billion rubles)[b] | | 2.1[f] | | 1.4 | | | |
| Sugar (granulated, million centners) | 9.9 | | | 8.2 | 25.0 | 24.0 | |
| Canned goods (million cans) | | 130.0 | | 900.0 | 1400.0 | 800.0 | |
| *Railroad Freight* (million tons despatched) | 132.0 | 156.0 | | 268.0 | 475.0 | 517.0 | |
| (million ton-kilometers carried) | | 113.0[f] | | 169.0 | | | |
| *National Income*[g] | | | | | | | |
| Total (billion rubles)[b] | 21.0 | 25.0 | | 45.5 | 100.0 | 95.7 | |
| Retail trade turnover (billion rubles)[g] | | 15.2 | | 40.4 | 122.0 | 125.0 | |
| Average annual wage (rubles)[g] | 300 | 730 | | 1427 | | 2776[d] | |
| Retail price level (1928 = 100)[g] | 30 | 100 | | 400 | | 500 | |
| Notes in circulation (billion rubles)[h] | | 2.0 | 3.2 | 8.0 | | 10.8[d] | |
| Social and cultural budget (billion rubles)[g] | | 1.4[i] | | 4.4 | | 30.8 | 53.0 |
| Total state budget (billion rubles)[g] | | 6.7[i] | | 30.3 | | 104.1 | |

[a] League of Nations, *Monthly Bulletin of Statistics.* For other sources see Bibliographical Notes at end of volume.

[b] These figures are given in terms of a statistical ruble of constant purchasing power (1926-27 prices); since no price levels are published there is no assurance that these figures are at all reliable.

[c] Production plan adopted at beginning of 1937, second Five Year Plan figures as adopted in 1933 being unavailable.

[d] 1936 figures.

[e] Livestock figures represent total number as of July 1st in each year; first column figures are for 1916 instead of 1913; second column figures are 1929 instead of 1928.

[f] 1929 figures.

[g] Estimates of the national income and the standard of living are highly unreliable. The total is given in 1926-27 rubles (see [b] above), but all other figures are in current rubles. The 1913 wage and the retail price level represent guesses from L. E. Hubbard, *Soviet Money and Finance* (1936) and *Soviet Trade and Distribution* (1938).

[h] Current rubles, end of year.

[i] 1928-1929 fiscal year.

# *Chapter Six*

## SAVING AND SPENDING UNDER STALIN

NOTHING better indicates how Soviet economic practices have been ignored by the outside world and attention concentrated on political factors than the descriptions most commonly given of the planning process. The political aspects of the planning mechanism have been described over and over again, while until recently there was virtually no knowledge of the financial procedures.

Thus every student knows that a Five Year Plan and its component yearly plans start at the top with a request for information from the Planning Commission. The information is gathered at the bottom: each worker and each workshop is induced to estimate how much can be produced in the ensuing year. Where new plants and new machinery are about to be put into operation the estimates are engineering estimates, but everywhere else estimates are based on past operation. Each plant and each industry (organized with varying degrees of complexity into national, regional and local Trusts, Combines and Central Administrations) sends its estimate for a new program of production back to the Planning Commission. The Planning Commission then fits the different estimates together, incorporates the amount of new construction it believes possible, adapts the whole plan to the political objectives set by the Communist leaders (war preparations, social services, more consumer goods, etc.), and then sends it back down the ladder. It is subject to revision and amendment at any point, even the individual quota for the individual work bench. Then it once more goes back up to the top, to be whipped into shape in the light of the suggested revisions, and is adopted. The whole process may take eight or ten months.

On the other hand the Financial Plan, which mirrors the Production Plan, has been little publicized. It answers the question, "Who's going to pay for it?" Yet, unlike the dominating importance given this question in capitalist countries, the financial problem is never a primary concern. Though the Soviet economists were wrong when they thought for a while they could get along without a Financial Plan, or at least without adhering to it, they were right in considering it secondary. Financial considerations should have no limiting effect on a Production Plan. The only limit is properly the capacity to produce, in the "real world" of human and natural resources. Thus the Production Plan or "material" plan is expressed in tons of coal, yards of cloth, units of machinery. The Financial Plan, expressed in rubles, does not control the other; it facilitates or hinders its execution.

### *The Role of the Ruble*

The Financial Plan is in three parts, providing for long-term credit, short-term credit and cash.

The long-term credit or investment capital has, since the first year or so, been largely in the form of a direct grant from the Treasury, not requiring repayment. These figures appear in the government's budget. An additional amount of funds for the construction of new plants and the expansion of old plants is derived from earnings, such as are set aside for amortization and depreciation. The whole question of financing investment will require more extended treatment later.

The second part is concerned with short-term credit, or, as it is usually known in a capitalist country, commercial credit. The long-term investment goes into a plant and is not repayable any more than stock in a capitalist corporation is repayable, but the short-term credit is to tide enterprises over the time between production and sale of the product; hence it can and must be repaid. In the case of agriculture, for instance, the farmer harvests all his crop in a comparatively short period of time, but it is consumed throughout the year. He is paid out of credit when he sells his crop. The Grain Trust sells it to the Food Trust, and so on down the line till an ultimate consumer buys bread, when the last debt can be repaid. Even in an industry without such seasonal variation there is a period, beginning with the purchase of raw materials, through the processes of production and distribution, to the ultimate sale; and if the bookkeeping or monetary aspect of the economic system is to mirror the physical aspect, there must be a creation of credit to cover this intervening period, and the Plan must provide for this short-term credit.

But all this credit, both long-term and short-term, ultimately ends up as currency in a worker's or farmer's pay envelope: hence the "cash plan." If the worker is a construction worker building a new textile mill, the paper rubles he gets as wages started in the books as long-term credit for capital construction. If he is a worker in a textile mill producing cloth, his wages may have been advanced out of short-term credit which will be repaid when the cloth is sold. For ordinary operations the textile mill is supposed to have a balance in the form of "working capital" or "turnover capital" to provide its minimum demands for wages and materials till its goods are sold; but everything it needs above that minimum is a short-term credit advance from the bank. All of this must be considered in the cash plan as well as the credit plan.

It should by now be apparent how important the banking system is in Soviet planning. It is up to the banks to see that the Financial Plan in its three parts, long-term investment, short-term credit, and cash, is carried out. Since the chaos of the first years the Soviet authorities have learned the technique of "ruble control" through the banks. If the manager of a plant is not keeping up with the Plan it shows up at once in the bank's books. At the same time the cash aspects of the Plan, which were so badly bungled in the first few years as to result in a fivefold inflation of the currency, have now apparently been mastered. The Soviet monetary authorities should now be able to maintain a steady proportion between the flow of purchasing power in cash and the appearance of goods and services for sale. So long as purchasing power and goods continue to rise at an equal rate there will be no further inflation.

This of course assumes that prices have been properly fixed, and that the general price level is kept steady. Sound pricing policies are only slowly being learned by a process of trial and error.

Beginning in 1935 the Soviet planners "accepted market prices as the natural price level." They abandoned the idea of a "correct" price in terms of the Marxian labor concept of value, which had had such disastrous consequences, and could be made to work only by having two sets of stores. For each article a price was now determined on somewhere between the two old prices. Then by trial and error it was adjusted until demand (the money offered in the stores by consumers who wanted these goods) just equaled supply (that is, just cleared the shelves). Errors would show up either in queues, where the demand was greater than the supply, or in unsold goods. The first prices chosen under the new pricing system turned out to be too high. Presumably the goods were not cleared off the shelves. Foreign visitors who previously had been unfavorably impressed by queues were now favorably impressed because there appeared to be so much for sale in the shops. But one mistake was as bad as the other. The Soviet pricing authorities quite properly reduced prices.

The balance between purchasing power, goods, and prices, which is possible under the Soviet system, is in sharp contrast to the prevailing practice in the capitalist system, where production is geared not to productive capacity and needs, but to whatever purchasing power happens to be—and purchasing power is an accidental unplanned quantity dependent on an intricate combination of unpredictable events. To be sure, Soviet practice has not been up to its possibilities, due no doubt to a failure fully to understand what was required; but at least the Soviet planners erred on the other side. There was never a shortage of purchasing power; instead there has been more money than goods during most of the Five Year Plans. The inflation during the first Five Year Plan never imposed a direct restriction on production, as deflation is capable of doing. And in the last few years the total flow of purchasing power seems to have been fairly well adjusted to balance the total flow of goods produced.

This, then, seems to be one of the criteria of "production for use," as against "production for the market" or "capitalism": that money as purchasing power shall not limit production, but shall be merely an efficient instrument for facilitating distribution.

It may be felt that the Soviet Union is hardly a good exponent of the principle of "production for use," since there has been famine and universal shortage of most consumer goods. But the Soviet Union, through the sovereign power of the state as represented by Stalin, has determined what use is to be first sought. It has determined to produce factories and raw materials and armaments rather than consumer goods. In either case production is planned "for use," to meet the needs determined on, and the amount of money that happens to be in purchasers' pockets has no effect on the Plan.

But if production is "for use" why is "profit" retained? Conservatives who don't like to admit the achievements of "socialism" insist that the Soviet Union has gone back to production for profit, because of the wide differences in wages, which lavishly reward the most useful workers, and because of the emphasis on requiring managers of enterprises to show a book profit. Yet here again the monetary aspect appears as an instrument rather than a directive. The profit motive operates as an incentive, to induce managers and workers to do a job as efficiently as possible. Book profit operates also as a test, within the mechanism of accounting, to determine whether a plant as a whole is economic. Thus, if a mistake in planning is made, and coal is being mined in a field where the seams are too thin to justify operation, the excess labor costs per ton will show up on the books as a deficit or absence of profit, and the mistake will be corrected. But this is very different from production *for* profit. Production is planned in advance, without regard to profitability. Then the profit motive is brought into play *afterward*, as a spur to efficiency and as a check on inefficiency.

Under the capitalist system not only are businesses operated in order to earn a profit, and closed down when they cannot earn a profit, but new enterprises are undertaken only when they are expected to be profitable—except, of course, in the case of public enterprises like schools and highways. In the Soviet Union all investment tends to be determined by the same kind of criteria as our public investment. In so far as profitability is taken into account—and I shall suggest in a moment that it should play an increasing part—it is once again as a test rather than a decisive control.

The Russian ruble is, in all respects, the humblest and most obedient currency in the world today.

### *Saving and Investment*

The tyranny of the dollar and the other capitalist currencies is nowhere more evident than in their effect on investment. The very terms "saving" and "investment" are so overlaid with monetary connotations that it is hard for us to get at the reality underneath. The Soviet planners have had a great advantage. In this field their scorn of monetary considerations was their strength.

In looking forward to a moneyless "communism" they were looking back as well to a theoretical type of primitive "communism" also lacking money. There was something starkly primitive, yet very sensible, about the way they set about building up their capital equipment.

The Stone Age savage who took a day off from chasing rabbits, and went hungry while he chipped a flint to a sharp edge and constructed a weapon with which he could kill a wild goat, would not have understood the distinction between saving and investing. Yet he was abstaining from current consumption even at the cost of some physical discomfort, in order to acquire capital with which to increase the effectiveness of his future labor.

Another savage, with a little more foresight and will power, might have saved some of his food for a day or two, so that on the day he made his ax he still could eat. But on the other hand, he might have saved some of his food anyway—for a rainy day when the hunting was not so good. He might then be able to distinguish between saving and investing: the food he saved was not invested until he consumed it while making an ax, that is, in new capital construction. But while he had the surplus food he would feel rich, and he might equally well consider his hoard was an "investment"—his "capital"—to permit him to take his ease on another day; he, too, would do better to avoid the slippery words altogether.

Let us look at the primitive communist tribe. If its members needed more stone axes they could store up food, and then spend a month on fashioning weapons. But they would be much more likely to develop a division of labor: a number of men would become specialized as ax-makers, while the rest would secure more food in their daily hunting than they needed for themselves and would turn the surplus over to the ax-makers. If we define axes as capital, and the process by which capital is secured as "saving and investing," then there is a constant process of "saving and investing" going on in that tribe, but it would be hard to say just what was "saved" and what was "invested."

In a modern industrial society, where division of labor is carried to extraordinary lengths, it is even more difficult to say exactly what work and what goods correspond to saving and investing. Some workers are building factories and making machines, others are digging raw materials and fuels out of the ground, others are working on a single process in a long chain of processes between raw materials and the final sale of goods to consumers, others are growing food for themselves and all the rest.

It is only when you look at the money end of a capitalist system that saving and investing seem to take on clear meanings. You can either spend your money for your own consumption, or you can save it. If you save it, you can either put it aside and hoard it, say in a strong-box, or invest it—in which case, according to the older economists, you spend it on capital goods. But the newer economists aren't so sure about any of these things.

It is no wonder that the terms saving and investing are difficult to apply to the Soviet Union, where money has been reduced to its proper subservient role. It is no wonder that there has been a vast amount of discussion as to whether the Soviet system is socialism or capitalism. It uses capital, obviously, hence some foolish people say it is "state capitalism." Again, opponents of socialism have argued in the past that because there would be no wealthy persons to save their money, there could be no expansion of capital goods through investment. Yet under the Soviet system, capital equipment has been expanded with unique rapidity, and this is taken for further evidence that it is "state capitalism." Obviously there has been more saving and investing in the Soviet Union than in any other country. Yet how is it to be measured?

Soviet production statistics are divided between "means of production" and consumer goods, and attention is called to a rise in the percentage of "means of production" from 43 per cent of all industrial production in 1928 to 59 per cent in 1935: but this is no adequate measure, for much of these "means of production" ended up not as capital equipment but as consumer goods. Coal mining, for instance, is listed in Soviet figures as "production of means of production," yet when it is burned in a cook stove it is being used directly for consumption purposes. Even steel, which is everywhere considered a "capital goods industry," goes into razor blades as well as railroad rails.

Yet if the answer is sought in monetary figures, new difficulties arise. Figures for capital investment are necessarily given in ruble values of the respective year, since they come out of the budget; but the only figures for the national income are in terms of a stable price level—the price level of the year 1926-27. In 1929, when the inflation had not yet made comparison of the two figures impossible, the national income was given as 28.9 billion rubles and capital investment as 5.9 billion or a little over 20 per cent. It is probable that as the Five Year Plans proceeded the rate of capital investment approached 30 per cent of the national income.*

It was this capital investment that tourists were shown in the Soviet Union, chiefly new factories, mines, power plants and machines. The machines were perhaps the most important, for factories, mines and power plants are merely places where machines are put to work. In the early years of the first Five Year Plan most of the machines were imported. But the Soviet planners were determined to be independent of imports in this most essential of all fields, and they spurred the machine-building industry. By 1935 it was by far the most important of Soviet industries: including agricultural machines, automobiles and railroad equipment, it amounted to one-quarter of all industrial production.

Now, while certain Soviet workers were turning out tractors and freight cars, boilers and electric generators, and machine tools of various kinds, other workers were turning out a meager supply of foodstuffs, clothing and other essential consumer goods to enable both themselves and the other group of workers to live. Looking at the Soviet economy as a whole during the first two Five Year Plans we may say that it was taking about 30 per cent of its workers away from work that would have increased the amount of goods available for consumption at that time, and putting them into work that would increase the production of goods for con-

* The Webbs suggest it may have reached 40 per cent.

sumption at some future time. The savage who made a flint ax increased his productivity. The Soviet Union in making machines has increased the productivity of each of its workers enormously, by well over 100 per cent in the last ten years. With modern machinery the "savings and investment" process can result in extraordinarily rapid progress.

The startling result of pyramiding savings can be illustrated in some such way as this: Imagine a colony of people whose total production of goods and services is $100,000 a year. Their income is likewise $100,000 a year. They use primitive hand methods and few tools. Suppose they decide to increase their production and therefore their income by introducing modern machine methods. To buy the machines abroad they pull in their belts and save $30,000 the first year; they spend only 70 per cent of their effort and $70,000 of their income on consumer goods. The next year they are able to produce, say, $10,000 worth of additional goods, thanks to the new machines. But they keep down their consumption to $70,000, so they have $40,000 to invest in more machinery that year. Each year, if they keep consumption down to the original level, they can save more. Suppose after ten years they had stepped up their productivity to four times what it was, or to $400,000, which is quite possible on our assumptions: if they still kept their belts buckled in tight and consumed no more than $70,000, they could save $330,000, or eleven times as much as they saved the first year!

These figures are not as far-fetched as they sound. The Soviet Union increased industrial production four times in two Five Year Plans, partly by doubling their productivity, partly by doubling their labor force, through drafting women and peasants into industry. Their production of machinery, as we have seen, increased eleven times. However, they permitted some increase in consumer goods production, and the wastage and inefficiency in the use of machinery kept the rate of "saving" from increasing with equal rapidity; yet the amount of capital construction in the last year of the second Five Year Plan was about three times what it was when the first Five Year Plan started.

There seems no reason why the Soviet Union cannot continue to go ahead at a constantly accelerating rate. The more capital equipment it has, the more rapidly it can add to its capital equipment. The more machines it has, the more rapidly it can construct new machines. Progress is cumulative, like compound interest. In the first Five Year Plan industrial output was doubled; in the second it was doubled again, making a fourfold increase all told. Why should it not double again in the third, and perhaps again in the fourth? The Soviet planners aimed at rapidly surpassing the industrial development of the capitalist countries. Their speed was not quite as great as they hoped, but it seems likely that they will surpass even the United States, if the trends of the last ten years hold, much sooner than any of their critics thought conceivable. And the day is probably soon coming when they will choose to enjoy their wealth instead of saving it. An "American standard of living" is not at all a remote possibility in the Soviet Union.*

There are several important things to be noted about this rapid progress. For one thing, the tightening of belts was done by the Soviet dictators rather than by the people themselves: the saving was compulsory, not voluntary. Presumably, therefore, it could have been accomplished in like fashion by any absolute dictatorship, whether it called itself "Socialist" or "Communist" or what not. If the Soviet Union had been as truly a slave state as its most violent critics claimed, it could have forced the same proportion of workers to produce capital goods, and therefore have made equally rapid progress.† At the same time it follows as another aspect of the same situation that if the Soviet Union had not been a dictatorship it could not have gone ahead as rapidly, for a people with democratic rights would never have chosen such heroic abstinence.

There is another limiting observation to be made. The Soviet Union was industrially backward, and was able to take advantage

* Since this chapter was written the first reports of the third Five Year Plan have appeared. Like the second Plan it was announced a year late. The Plan calls for an industrial output in 1942 88 per cent above 1937, which comes pretty close to another five-year doubling of output.

† However, a pure slave state would not have had the advantage of the enthusiasm which the Soviet Union aroused through political propaganda, "socialist competition" between factories, the setting up of new production records to be attained in the Plan figures, as well as "shock-brigades" and Stakhanovism. Yet much doubt has been thrown on the efficacy of these stimulants.

of what the more advanced countries had developed in the way of machines. If it had had to devise its own methods of mechanization and technological improvement as it went along it could not have built up its industries so fast, even if its rate of saving had been the same. And, starting from close to zero, its *rate* of increase was necessarily greater in percentage terms than it could have been in a more advanced country.*

### *Where Does the Money Come From?*

The financial aspects of the saving and investment process may now be considered. The order of procedure, as we have seen, was, first, the decision to build the new factories and machines, then the "material plan," involving the engineering problem of putting labor to work on materials, and finally the Financial Plan, to fit the "material plan."

In essence the problem of financing capital goods construction was simply one of assuring that the added money laid out to pay the wages of the workers in capital construction did not overbalance the goods available for purchase. The mistake the planners made at first was in paying out far more money in wages than there were goods to buy at the prevailing prices.

Several alternatives were open. They could raise the prices of consumer goods, to absorb not only the cost of the labor that went into producing them, but the labor cost of the capital construction as well. If the whole industrial system had had only one bookkeeper this would have been simple, but since each enterprise kept its own accounts, the additional money that came in from consumers must be collected from the sales enterprises as a "sales tax." This came to be the method principally relied on, a "turnover tax" being levied on the wholesale price.

Another alternative was to lower wages, which would have been

* There are those who argue that since the industrial revolution was so long delayed in Russia it would have taken place with equal rapidity under any reasonably stable government, capitalist or otherwise. Brutzkus cites the prewar rate of expansion of coal and pig iron production to show that the rate achieved in the first Five Year Plan could have been achieved also under capitalism. But all of this is speculation. The facts are that the fourfold increase of industrial expansion under the two Five Year Plans has never been equaled in a capitalist country.

unpopular, or to take part of them back in taxation. If every worker had had 30 per cent of his wages taken away by an income tax the balance between purchasing power and consumer goods available could have been restored. This income tax could be disguised in various ways, and in effect the forced loans and the compulsory savings were a disguised income tax.

When I was in Moscow in 1931 an American friend of mine who was working in the telephone system described to me how one of the great public "loans" was raised. The Liberty Loan drives were amateurish by comparison. In his shop the workers were called together, and told that a shop in another city had subscribed 100 per cent to the loan, which meant that every worker had agreed to subscribe to the extent of at least one month's wages; the Moscow shop was "challenged" to do as well. (These "challenges," occasionally genuine, went by the name of "socialist competition.") After speeches urging that the "challenge" be taken up, a motion was put that every worker in the shop subscribe a month's wages. Voting was by show of hands, and no worker dared vote "No." The shop committee then went around getting signatures. At the end of the process, lo and behold, every worker in the shop had agreed to give up a month's wages. This was at the height of the inflation: while the bonds bore interest and were repayable in ten years, they were rapidly to lose most of their value by depreciation, so that the effect was the same as an income tax.

Savings were "encouraged" in the same way. Where the thousands of new savings banks were not getting their quota of savings, "socialist competition" would be resorted to, and workers coerced into making deposits. However, in a country of much petty thievery it was found to be increasingly a convenience to deposit surplus cash in these banks; in addition, certain payments, like that for rent, could be made out of these deposits; and these inducements, along with 8 per cent interest, probably meant that coercion was less and less necessary. Savings bank deposits by individuals were over 5.8 billion rubles in August, 1938.

Capitalism grew up through the accumulation of individual savings. But in the last generation corporate savings, the plowing back of profits into the business that produced them, has been increasingly important. In the Soviet plans it had been intended that enterprises would grow by plowing back their own profits, and that new enterprises would be financed out of additional profits passing through the government's hands or the investment banks. Actually costs rose so much more rapidly than prices in the first Five Year Plan that little in the way of profits appeared. After "control by the ruble" was established, and more rigid accounting required, profits began to show up. These profits found their way back into investment in various ways: a part was paid into the Treasury as if it had been a tax, for the Treasury financed most of the new construction; a part was paid to the Prombank or one of the other investment banks (also for new construction); a part remained with the enterprise, or with the Trust of which it was a unit; the remainder was spent, as we have seen, in improving local living or working conditions (workers' clubs, crêches, etc.), or in vocational training, or turned over as a bonus to the management. In addition to the profit item on any enterprise's books entries were made for depreciation and amortization, and these funds were plowed back into capital maintenance, replacements and repairs.

Profits, of course, are obtained by marking up prices above costs, so that all these bookkeeping entries merely involved further methods of adjustment to bring purchasing power into balance with consumer goods.

Three additional methods remain to be mentioned. The first are payments by workers to social insurance funds and to cooperatives, representing a further deduction from wages, though the investment made possible by these deductions was public investment in social services directly benefiting the workers. The second consisted of lotteries, which furnish an easier way of getting money than taxation. And finally there are exports: large amounts of consumer goods, chiefly grain, butter, and other foodstuffs, were exported in the first Five Year Plan to buy foreign machinery. Here was enforced abstinence in a very real sense: Soviet citizens gave up some of their food so it could be exchanged abroad for capital goods.

We may summarize what we have been saying by tabulating the monetary aspect of savings and investments in a typical year as follows:

In 1934 capital investment was about 24,000,000,000 rubles.

Some 80 per cent of this was advanced by the government directly, out of funds in the Treasury, and the other 20 per cent came out of profits plowed back directly or by way of the investment banks. How did the government get the money for its share, which we will call 19,200,000,000 rubles? A look at the budget figures for 1934 tells the story. The aggregate expenditures of the national and local governments amounted to 52,398,000,000 rubles. This seems to have been divided roughly in this way:

| | |
|---|---|
| Governmental expenses (administration, defense, education, etc.) | 20,141,000,000 |
| Capital investment | 19,200,000,000 |
| Payments to enterprises to cover operating deficits | 13,057,000,000 |
| Total expenditures | 52,398,000,000 |

The government's revenue comes into the Treasury without being specifically allocated to its own expenses or to investment; but here is the way the revenue was raised:

| | | |
|---|---|---|
| Turnover tax | | 30,242,000,000 |
| Direct payments by enterprises into Treasury (including profits, reserves, taxes, loans) | | 14,352,000,000 |
| Payments by individuals: | | |
| Individual taxes | 3,621,000,000 | |
| Public loans | 3,343,000,000 | |
| Net deposits in savings banks | 413,000,000 | |
| Social insurance funds | 696,000,000 | |
| Total payments by individuals | | 8,073,000,000 |
| Other receipts | | 2,401,000,000 |
| Total receipts | | 55,068,000,000 |
| Excess of receipts over expenditures | | 2,670,000,000 |

It will be seen that the turnover tax itself was more than sufficient to pay for all the investments. But it was not so allocated. And it would be purely arbitrary to designate the exact source of the funds for investment. From a broad point of view, if one assumes that the whole country was building itself up, all the expenditures from the budget may be thought of as investment. But enough has been said to indicate how funds were extracted from purchasers' pockets, so that a balance could be achieved between purchasing power and consumption goods.*

One sharp difference between the process of saving and investment under capitalism and the same process in the planned economy of the Soviet Union should by now be evident. According to orthodox capitalist theory, savings are accumulated in money form (in a stocking, or a savings bank, for instance), and when a sufficient pile has been accumulated it is invested, along with other similar accumulations, in building a new factory or in some other form of capital construction. Theoretically no investment is possible unless the money has been previously saved (and even then, of course, it will not be made unless there is an expectation of profit).†

In the Soviet economy, on the other hand, the investment is made first, and the money savings are accumulated afterward. We have seen that the first stage is an engineering blueprint of the new capital construction planned for the ensuing year, which is then translated into a Financial Plan, including long-term credit, short-term credit and cash. The long-term credit is the investment proper: funds are advanced from the Treasury or the investment banks as needed, without expectation of repayment, and these bookkeeping advances are balanced by current receipts from taxes, loans, etc.

Both the long-term and the short-term advances are the result of a direct creation of credit. They spring into being when somebody writes figures in a book with pen and ink. In the early years of the Plans little effort was made to write figures on the other side of the ledger. This meant that the printing presses were kept busy furnishing the cash whose payment was authorized by writing

* The amount that had to be extracted was unnecessarily increased by the more than 13 billion rubles advanced to enterprises to cover their deficits, most of which simply meant heavier labor costs than planned for. See above, page 106.

† In practice, payment of interest and repayment of principal on past loans as well as other income from past investment is constantly going into new investment in the present, so that there need be no waiting period. See below, pages 346-347.

down the credits. Later the various means of collecting cash outlined above permitted the figures for long-term credits to be balanced with cash receipts. And a strict accounting control over short-term credits assured their repayment when the enterprises to which they were advanced collected the price of their products.

Direct creation of credit by bookkeeping entry is a familiar device in capitalist banking practice. Some of our investment has even been financed in this way, and our short-term commercial credit may be considered largely of this nature. Various arbitrary rules have been developed in capitalist banking to make certain that the purchasing power resulting from these credits shall not exceed the total amount of goods for sale, at which point an inflationary price rise would become likely. Investment must be balanced by savings. Commercial credit must be balanced by being repaid.

The course of Soviet finance has followed familiar capitalist practice more and more closely. The only difference, and in a sense it is a crucial one, is that in the Soviet Union investment comes first, the credit being directly created without any mumbo-jumbo, as the Plans provide on the basis of supposed social need, and the saving is then compulsorily achieved afterward. In a capitalist system the amount of investment is, at least in theory, determined by the amount of previous voluntary saving, and it only takes place when an enterpriser sees a chance to make a profit by using the savings.

It scarcely needs to be pointed out again that the old criticism of socialism, that it could not save and accumulate capital, has been blasted by the experience of the Soviet Union, which has saved and accumulated capital at an unprecedented rate.

## *What Is Left of the Market?*

A capitalist system in orthodox theory is supposed to accumulate capital at a steady and rapid rate through voluntary saving. The balance between saving and investment is supposed to be maintained by means of the automatic market mechanism. A market is a place where prices are fixed. In the case of money lent for capital purposes, the price is the interest rate. If savings increase faster than the demand for funds for profitable investment, then the interest rate will fall off, for supply will have outrun demand. With this lower interest rate investment will be encouraged, and a new balance will be achieved. If there is a shortage of funds for investment the interest rate will rise. The interest rate also serves to allocate capital funds efficiently as between industries. This mechanism no longer works, for various reasons; but it is a good example of the market mechanism and it leads into a consideration of the function of the market mechanism in the Soviet economy.

The market plays almost no part in the Soviet Union in determining investment. The amount of saving is necessarily equal to the amount of investment, since it is made *after* investment *in order to* balance the outlay of money incurred. The amount of investment is determined as a proportion of the total economic activity: a certain portion of labor and resources is arbitrarily allocated to building up the capital equipment of the country, and that portion represents the saving and investment. The allocation of labor and resources as between particular enterprises is likewise largely arbitrary. Thus a tremendous amount of industrial development has been concentrated in the comparatively remote regions of the Urals and western Siberia, because of their military invulnerability, and with little regard to economic considerations.

However, the restoration of strict accounting methods and the emphasis on book profit, along with a price system that more accurately measures costs and reintroduces the criterion of profitability, has brought back an important part of the market mechanism even as regards investment. If a new plant cannot earn a profit it may now be adjudged to have been a bad investment (disregarding military or other extraneous considerations). Presumably, in planning future investment and capital construction, the Soviet planners will take profitability into account as a test of efficiency. They will estimate more and more accurately in advance whether or not a plant can meet this test. Likewise in the allocation of resources to investment their decisions will approximate those reached automatically by a market mechanism.

Take, for instance, the Dnieprostroy dam, the pride of Soviet construction. Only a part of its power is yet developed, and critics have pointed out that the same expenditure of labor and materials might have been made to much better advantage in other construction, say, for instance, in steam power plants nearer existing sources of raw materials. At the time the dam was built there was no accurate way of measuring whether or not its construction was economic or wasteful. With present methods, on the other hand, it might be possible to measure the relation of costs and earning capacity—that is, profitability—in advance.

The Soviet apologist will say that is unnecessary. The great dam stands, and some day its power will be fully employed. But this introduces the question of time. If the dam had been built by private initiative and financed by bonds it would have made a lot of difference if full operation and use of the power produced were to begin in five years' time or in twenty years: to pay interest on the bonds for twenty years with inadequate earnings would bankrupt the concern; or rather the dam would not have been built in such case. Interest is a measure of the desirability of present wealth as against future wealth. It is a further check against uneconomic expenditures under a market mechanism. It does not operate in the Soviet Union, for long-term investment credit pays no interest. The Soviet planners have only their own judgment to rely on in determining the relative value of present wealth over against future wealth. In a rough sort of way they will, of course, not make investments from which the return is too remote. But this is part of the whole problem of investment, and a more accurate criterion would be far less wasteful.

To a considerable extent this problem confronts a capitalist economy, too. Dam building in the United States is largely left to public enterprise today: the calculation of profitability or ability to earn interest is not necessarily decisive, for example, in the case of the TVA. The Panama Canal was finally built without regard to the market mechanism. Schools and highways and other public improvements are undertaken by social planners, with quite other considerations than those that govern private investment. The Soviet Union has merely applied the same tests of social desirability to all industrial construction. The mechanism of the market, as it affects the accountant's books, is merely one of the tests of social desirability. It can disregard that test whenever it wishes.

In one other respect the market mechanism may come to affect the process of saving and investment in the Soviet Union. In so far as the floating of bond issues and the accumulation of savings bank deposits become less coercive, the interest rate offered may become a partial measure of whether or not the Soviet citizen wants to save. Conceivably the Soviet Union might abandon compulsory saving entirely. Then the amount of saving would be determined not arbitrarily but automatically, as under a completely free capitalist system. Obviously saving would be inadequate if this method were adopted today. But when the equipment had been built up to something like the abundance level, a lower rate of saving would be safe, and the higher level of income would induce more saving. The question whether this eventuality would be desirable is no longer within the scope of economics. For it involves the question whether the ability to accumulate savings so that one can later live on them without working is in accord with the socialist goal. Presumably it is not—even though there were no private ownership of the means of production, but only ownership of government bonds, and even though the appearance of a privileged class were avoided by progressive income taxes and confiscatory inheritance taxes.

Whether or not the market mechanism reappears in whole or in part as regards savings and investment, there seems little question that it has come to stay as regards the distribution of consumption goods and of labor. Rationing has never been thought of as other than temporary in the Soviet Union. Freedom for the consumer to express his individual choice in making his purchases has been widespread since "derationing" in 1935 and 1936. All stores are "open" stores, and prices reflect market conditions, that is, they are fixed at a point where supply and demand balance. The choice of articles is still very limited, to be sure. There is little variety in the stores and quality is poor. But as between the goods offered there is freedom of choice.

An example will show how this mechanism may tend to work. If a particular make of shoe is uncomfortable and unpopular, the shoe trust will have to cut its price drastically to clear it off the shelves. The loss will show up on its books, and it will cease manufacture of so "unprofitable" a brand. On the other hand, a new sports model might be very popular. The shoe trust would be unable to keep the shelves in the shoe stores stocked. It would raise the price till a balance was achieved. At the high price its profits on that model would be considerable, indicating that manufacture should be expanded in the ensuing year's plan. In this way consumers may more and more come to dominate the plan. The planners will merely watch the indicators on their books, as an airplane pilot watches the indicators on his instrument board in making a blind landing.

The mechanism of the market operates in similar fashion in distributing workers to jobs. Forced labor has been a political expedient rather than an economic device, except perhaps in the case of especially disagreeable jobs like lumbering in Siberia or coal mining. For the most part the principle of freedom of occupational choice has been adhered to. The great extension of piece wages, and the wide range of wages between the lowest paid and the highest paid, are an application of the market principle.

The demand for highly skilled workers and for trained engineers and experienced managers is still so much greater than the supply in the Soviet Union that the market mechanism operates in a fashion tending to defeat the equalitarian ideals of socialism. Some critics have denounced these differentials as a proof that capitalism was returning. But there seems every reason to believe that with the vast widening of educational opportunity the scarcity of trained workers will decrease. Ultimately the market mechanism as applied to labor would tend, as has been frequently pointed out, to a complete equalitarianism, not an exact leveling of wages but an equalization according to the agreeableness or disagreeableness of the job.

Enough has been said in the historical chapter preceding this to indicate the wide degree to which the Soviet Union has turned back to the market mechanism. The market mechanism is one in which price is the balance wheel of supply and demand. Strict cost accounting enables individual enterprises, under socialism as under capitalism, to choose the most economical and efficient combination of materials and labor, for any combination that is less economic than the average will shortly show up as a loss, and greater efficiency will show up as a profit. To what degree the prices of raw materials in the Soviet Union are determined in this way is not clear, but it seems reasonable to assume that the trend has been the same as in the case of consumer goods and labor.

Later in this book I am going to discuss the way marginal utility theories have recently been adapted to a theoretical planned society. But it is worth emphasizing at this point what the history of the Soviet Union has proved as to the basic problem we are investigating in this book. Twice they abandoned the market mechanism in the belief that Marxism and socialist economics superseded it, and twice they had to return to it. The first time was in the NEP, the second after the early blunders of the Five Year Plans. The nearer they got to the free market of capitalist theory the more successful their planning became. As L. E. Hubbard puts it:

"Where the Soviet economists tried to disregard the fundamental laws of an organization based upon capitalist production and exchange, they but tended to demonstrate that these laws apply with equal force to a socialist economy. . . . By the beginning of the second Five Year Plan the administrative organization and labor discipline in Soviet enterprises differed little from private enterprise in capitalist states."

Does the Soviet Union, then, represent merely a new form of capitalism? We are finally brought back to our original problem. What does the Soviet Union prove as to the main issue of this book, the nature of "socialism" and its relation to freedom?

### *Is Capitalism Returning?*

As I have frequently emphasized, capitalism is too vague a term to be useful. Obviously the Soviet economy is not the same as the economy of the so-called capitalist world; it has had a most phenomenal growth while the outside world has been mired in depression. What then is the difference?

The difference is that in such a country as the United States the market mechanism is master, and in the Soviet Union it is servant. In this country no enterprise is undertaken, except in the special field of public works, unless under the market mechanism it promises to earn a profit. In the Soviet Union profitability is only one of the tests of whether or not an enterprise is to be undertaken: all economic enterprises are "public works." Here there is no production unless the purchasing power which happens to be available on the market is adequate to buy it. In the Soviet Union engineering blueprints determine production, and purchasing power is maintained at a level adequate to purchase all that can be produced: the market is merely a check and balance wheel. Here purchasing power is subject to terrific cyclical swings, and periodic depressions under the tyrannous whims of the market extend to the farthest corners of the economy. In the Soviet Union money and credit flow in as a lubricant of the process of production and distribution, and nothing worse than momentary and localized disequilibria have occurred to impair the continuous operation of the plant at capacity, with full employment.

Planning consists in using the market mechanism along with the engineer's blueprints. Unplanned capitalism means that the blueprints gather dust when the market says "No."

In conclusion, what can be said about freedom? It is frequently argued that planning destroys freedom. It is said that freedom of enterprise in a free market has developed under democracy, and is the condition of all other freedom.

It is true that a market where the consumer can spend his money in his own way, rather than having goods rationed out to him by a master, is a condition of freedom. It is true that a market for labor where a worker can choose his own occupation rather than being conscripted for labor service is a condition of freedom. It must be said, however, that the breakdown of the market mechanism where it has been allowed to run uncontrolled has almost nullified these freedoms—for those without jobs and without purchasing power. In the Soviet Union these freedoms seem to have been coming into their own.

As for the freedom to determine how much shall be saved and invested, that is meaningless in a society of rich and poor, and it is one of the chief causes of the breakdown of the system of "free enterprise." In the Soviet Union it is conceivable that compulsory saving will some day become unnecessary. And in a democracy which sought to plan, the rate of social saving could be determined without the arbitrary fiat of present Soviet planning. Dictatorship has at least had this justification in the Soviet Union, that without it productive capacity would have risen much more slowly.

In no other economic respect has the Soviet dictatorship been a necessary feature of the Five Year Plans. Wherever Soviet economists have learned to plan efficiently they have found the greater freedom of the market mechanism desirable. Efficient management has required discipline and concentration of authority rather than direct worker control; but the authority could have been responsible to democratic government as well as autocratic government.

The political absolutism of the Stalin regime is loathsome to me and to most Americans. It is a heritage from the Czars, from war and revolution, from Marxian and Leninist doctrine. The Bolsheviks have been able to go so far on the road to a socialist economy where the democratic socialist movements failed even to get started, because they had the ruthlessness to push ahead on a horribly costly experiment. No democracy would have been willing to pay that price. Yet if the democratic socialist movements had been able to discover in advance as much about economic planning as the Bolsheviks have learned at the price of incalculable suffering, they too might have succeeded.

In the last two years the demoralization that tends to grow on any absolute dictatorship has begun to threaten the positive achievements of the Soviet Union. The "blood purges" that have horrified the outside world since 1936 were ostensibly to get rid of wreckers and saboteurs. But the three years, 1934, 1935 and 1936, when the sabotage was supposed to have been at its height, were the most successful years in Soviet planning. And the two years since the shooting began have been years of stagnation. However much one believes or does not believe of the confessions of the accused, the statistics of industrial progress indicate that progress was halted *after* the "wreckers" were liquidated.*

* These official figures, the latest available, are revealing:

| | 1933 | 1934 | 1935 | 1936 | 1937 | 1938 (Oct.) |
|---|---|---|---|---|---|---|
| Index of Industrial Production (1929=100) | 198.4 | 238.3 | 293.4 | 382.3 | 424.0 | |
| Per cent gain over previous year | 8.2 | 20.1 | 23.1 | 30.3 | 10.9 | |
| Coal production (thousand tons per month) | 6,020 | 7,792 | 8,652 | 10,075 | 10,215 | 10,651 |
| Per cent gain over previous year | 12.3 | 29.4 | 11.0 | 16.5 | 1.4 | 0.5 |
| Pig iron production (thousand tons per month) | 597 | 867 | 1,042 | 1,193 | 1,210 | 1,283 |
| Per cent gain over previous year | 16.4 | 45.2 | 20.2 | 14.5 | 1.4 | 0.8 |

Managers and administrative heads of Soviet enterprises have been fearful of taking any initiative in these days of sudden arrests. The inert weight of bureaucracy, which can deaden the activities of any organization, large or small, is at its worst when official fear and favor become dominant forces, and the automatic incentives of a free market mechanism give way to the corrosive influence of boot-licking, patronage and vengefulness.

The hope of the Soviet future is that the new power politics has nothing immediately to gain by curtailing present progress. Yet when security and plenty are achieved they will prove poor soil for the rank weeds that have lately been growing in the Kremlin. The poison is still far from destroying the religious zeal that has been developed, thanks to an heroic revolutionary history, in millions of people, particularly the younger generation. Even Stalin, once his increasingly despotic regime has come to an end, will be remembered, like Peter the Great, for his building rather than his despotism. However one may abhor present-day Soviet politics, there is ground for having the highest hopes for a free and happy Russia.

But may we never have to take the same road in America!

# Chapter Seven

## THE FASCISTS APE THE COMMUNISTS

"BUT fascism *is* socialism. Fascism *is* communism."

This was Mussolini talking. He always liked to talk to foreigners, expounding his theories, pumping them with questions. It was startling, even overwhelming, after the long theatrical march up marble staircases, through innumerable antechambers, and across the ridiculous expanse of mosaic in the ballroom that served as his "private" office in the Palazzo Venezia, to have these flattering confidences and discussions. Perhaps it was because the "sawdust Caesar" could never unbend among his fellow-Italians, that he enjoyed talking to foreigners, and that I got the chance, fresh from the Soviet Union, to ask with considerable trepidation what was the relation of fascism to socialism and communism.

I had been told at the American Embassy that Il Duce would be interested in Russia, so I told him at once that I had only just come from there. He spent half an hour asking questions, obviously curious, almost giving the impression of ignorance. When I tactfully condemned the "fanaticism" of the Communists, I was immediately taken to task.

"Fanaticism is needed to accomplish anything. It is faith that moves mountains. After a job is finished, then one can afford to be liberal, then one can afford to look at both sides." A sudden shift: "What do they think of me in Russia?" No doubt I looked embarrassed, for he went on: "I know. They think me the tool of the capitalists, isn't that it? But if a capitalist doesn't please me, he has to go, like anybody else."

Mussolini, the old Socialist, who even continued to call his newspaper "Socialist" for several years after the party expelled him, still seems to have a guilty feeling about the cause he betrayed. At one other significant point too, in an interview that was otherwise bland enough, I caught a trace of defensiveness when he shouted at me with saucer-like eyes: "Italy will never permit her rights to be trampled on!" He seems still bothered by the feeling that Italy is a second-class nation.

The two points on which Mussolini is sensitive are his nationalism and his socialism. His chief imitator calls himself a National Socialist. I have not heard anyone reporting Hitler as declaring that National Socialism is "communism," though his whole propaganda machine keeps emphasizing that it is "socialism."

There is no doubt that the leaders of fascism everywhere claim to be replacing capitalism with a new economic system. But for some time the outside world was inclined to treat these claims as mere demagogy. Mussolini had been in power over ten years before his much vaunted "corporative state" began to take shape. But when Hitler took power in 1933 his pace was so much more rapid than Mussolini's that some observers, who had been inclined to be tolerant of Mussolini's "reforms," saw Nazism as the next thing to "bolshevism."

Hitler's methods made it virtually impossible for any observer to be objective. The labor movements abroad, and the Marxist groups which counted on labor to lead the march to socialism, saw their brothers in Germany slaughtered and jailed and the labor and socialist movements annihilated, and they jumped easily to the conclusion that fascism was merely "capitalism plus murder." Liberals and humanitarians found another all-embracing concept in such words as "brutal dictatorship," for Hitler's assault on parliamentary democracy, civil liberties, and the Jewish race could not be explained in economic terms, but only as a "reversion to barbarism."

In this book I am not prepared to say whether or not this latter judgment is correct. We still do not know enough about the nature of human culture to account accurately for the great historical cycles, or to say with any assurance how a civilization is capable of "reverting to barbarism." I am concerned more with an analysis of fascist economics, for the light it throws on my main problem of economic organization and freedom. So far as possible I want to be objective. It is particularly difficult since the redoubled Jewish pogroms of the fall of 1938. But a scientist should be able to study even a loathsome disease without turning away in disgust. And fascism has become the ardent faith of so many millions of otherwise normal human beings that even to call it a loathsome disease may be unjustified.

When I first went to fascist Italy I got the distinct impression that here was a somewhat shoddy imitation of the Soviet system I had just left. Its spirit was less vital, its building was picayune in comparison, its party, its secret police, its bayonets, all reminded me faintly of musty stage properties—yet it was nevertheless extraordinarily similar to the Soviet Union. I have since seen Nazi Germany at first hand, and received a further impression that the fascist phenomenon was of the same type as the Soviet phenomenon, though Germany's superior efficiency and technological advancement dispelled the impression of shoddiness.

By now it has been largely accepted, by most liberals and even by many of the Marxists, that the fascist economy is more collectivist than capitalist; and the disillusionment among many liberals as regards the Soviet Union since the Moscow trials has permitted many to accept the parallels between the two political systems. Moreover, there has come to be an increasing recognition of the fact that fascism has a mass base in the middle classes, and that so far as it represents a social movement, and not merely a seizure of power by a few individuals, it represents the "revolt of the middle classes" against the intolerable economic and social conditions of the post-war world, rather than a capitalist maneuver in the struggle between the capitalist class and the proletariat.*

The purposes of this inquiry, however, are neither political nor social but economic. I have gone back to the study of fascism, as I went back to the study of the Soviet Union, to see what I could learn about the nature of the economic problem and its solution.

* In my *Insurgent America* I analyzed fascism as a form of middle-class "revolt," and suggested that its collectivist features developed naturally from certain middle-class interests. The economic analysis of the present book may repeat some of the conclusions of the earlier one. But in the intervening years it has become obvious that the earlier estimate of fascism as a "static" economy, "freezing" the *status quo*, was not justified: fascism for better or worse is today the most "dynamic" force in the world. Neither politician nor political scientist can keep up with its swift internal and external moves.

If it be thought that this analysis is too objective, let me merely say that there can be no adequate defense against all that we fear from the successes of fascism unless we can make democracy produce better results in the economic sphere than fascism; and that a first necessity is to understand how the fascist economy works.

### *Sources of Fascist Planning*

Fascism did not spring full blown into existence on those days in October, 1922, and January, 1933, when Mussolini and Hitler respectively took power. Its sources, in many cases, can be traced far back in history. Even some of the impulse toward economic planning originated in pre-fascist eras, though in large part it developed spontaneously in the process of fascist evolution in pursuit of other than economic ends.

In this latter respect there is a sharp divergence between fascism and Russian communism. The Russian revolutionists were impregnated by the socialist doctrines of Marx from the very beginning, and while they took twenty years to learn the techniques of planning, the idea of planning was planted decades before. Fascism, on the other hand, made such a profession of preventing Marxian socialism that both its communist enemies and its Big Business campaign contributors leaped to the conclusion that it was the savior of capitalism and hence opposed to planning. Certainly the development of fascist planning has been far more from unconscious pragmatic needs than from any theory.

Yet fascist planning "is no accident," as the Marxists would say. Partly it arose from pre-war factors, partly as a product of depression, partly out of the political and social nature of fascism. We shall mention these briefly in turn.

Among the pre-war factors is of course the evolution of capitalism itself, from small business with emphasis on laissez faire, to trusts, cartels and other combinations which did a good deal of planning on their own hook, and established increasingly close contacts with government, till they became largely dependent on it.

Mussolini sketched this evolution himself in two remarkable speeches on November 14, 1933, and January 13, 1934, when the depression (which he called a "crisis of the system" rather than "*in*" it) was forcing a fuller implementation of the corporative structure. According to him the "dynamic" period of the individual capitalist, when a true freedom of enterprise flourished, began to give way about 1870 to a "static" period: first the joint stock company (the "corporation" in the American sense, as opposed to the "corporation" in the Italian sense of "guild") and then the trust and cartel began to undermine competition. Enterprise became dependent on the state for protection and on the banks for finance. This culminated in what Mussolini called the era of "decadence" after the war, when the "super-capitalism" of vast combinations required state intervention at every step.

The development of state and banker supported cartels went farther in Germany even than in Italy. Unlike the United States, where the "folklore" of laissez faire was so deeply ingrained that constant attempts were made to "exorcise" combinations through "anti-trust" laws, Germany encouraged these combinations.*

In any trade association, trust or cartel the familiar evidences of economic planning, price and production controls, appear, even though unrelated to the rest of the economy (and therefore, be it noted, increasingly compelling government intervention). On the other hand it is impossible to have an integrated planned economy without some such machinery to co-ordinate individual enterprises: it is significant that the Soviet planners used all the old terminology of capitalist combinations—"trusts," "combines," "syndicates"—in organizing their industries.

Fascism in both Italy and Germany found ready to hand a considerable number of these combinations. Many of them were dependent on government aid. It was natural that the industrialists who dominated them should hope for much from the strong and stable state that fascism promised, and should try with more or less success to turn fascism to the service of their own special interests and need for subsidies. It was natural on the other hand that the fascist governments should look on these cartels (usually

* Only once has America abandoned its traditional attitude: under the NRA the American government undertook for the first time to regulate and encourage combinations, as we shall see in a later section. Businesses which would not enter into agreements regarding prices, wages and the like, were called "chiselers." When the NRA was discredited the New Deal Administration swung back to an attack on "monopoly" and called for a restoration of price competition.

called "consortiums" in Italy) as public utilities or agencies of the state, particularly when the government encouraged or even compelled their formation.

This close interrelation of the cartels and fascism, each trying to use the other, has provided the chief justification for the Marxist's theory that fascism is a "tool of the capitalist class." I shall point out in a moment how far from the truth this is.

Another source of fascism, in part from the pre-war world, is Catholicism. The Catholic social doctrines expounded in the two encyclicals on the social order, "Rerum Novarum" and "Quadragesimo Anno," which will be more fully analyzed in a later section, indicated that the Popes had never become reconciled to laissez faire liberalism. The disciplined hierarchy of a fascist planned economy would always have been more congenial to the Church of Rome than competitive capitalism. The fact that fascism arose first in Italy, and that Rome is the capital city both for the Popes and for Mussolini, naturally fostered the coloration of fascist ideas by Catholic ideas. Mussolini derived the "corporation" from d'Annunzio, who got it from the medieval "guild," but the Popes have likewise looked back to the "corporation" as a model for a balanced and harmonious social order.

Since the attacks on the Catholic Church in Germany have grown to such intensity as to indicate Hitler's belief that there is not room in Germany for both the Roman faith and the National Socialist faith, the Church has become aware of the fact that fascism is more of an enemy than capitalist democracy. And the influence of Catholicism on fascism as well as its political alliance with it are probably at an end, even in Italy. The Pope is as much as ever a prisoner in the Vatican, in spite of Concordats, and the Blackshirt child, from his grace before meals to his bedtime prayer, worships God only through Mussolini His prophet. Yet there is no doubt that in determining the original direction of fascist economic development, the Catholic Church played a part in undermining capitalism.

To a certain degree there was a mating here of the Church and its arch-enemy, Marxism. Mussolini was a militant atheist, a militant republican, and a militant Marxist, before he became a fascist. The syndicalist movement, which was an always quarreling but nevertheless blood brother to Marxism, relying as it did on the same expectation that the workers would take over the factories as the essential step of "the revolution," was an even closer progenitor of Italian fascism. The first seizures of factories in Italy in 1920 were hailed by the fascists, though Mussolini later got more support by denouncing them. The chief framer of the labor aspects of the Italian corporative state, Edmondo Rossoni, was a former syndicalist (I.W.W.) organizer in America. The young middle-class Blackshirts who provided the mass support for fascism in its rise to power were motivated by a mystical combination of syndicalism and nationalism, which looked to the liberation of the world proletariat by way of the liberation of Italy, the proletarian country. Consequently there has always been a powerful element in the fascist movement which has thought of it as the Italian variant of the socialist revolution against capitalism. And as the inner requirements of the fascist regime gradually necessitated an increasing amount of economic planning, the socialist and syndicalist background readily facilitated a collective structure. "If the nineteenth century," Mussolini has said, "was a century of individualism—liberalism always signifying individualism—it may be expected that this will be the century of collectivism, and hence the century of the State." At another place he speaks of it as the "century of the left"; this in spite of the fact that when his followers were first elected to the Chamber of Deputies they took seats at the extreme right, to signify that they were "anti-parliamentarian, anti-democratic, and anti-socialist." *

Hitler's deputies likewise sat at the extreme right in the old Reichstag, though observers spoke of the political alignment as a complete circle in which the extreme left and the extreme right met. German fascism has always been strongly tinged with socialism. The name National Socialist was selected in 1919 at a time

* To what extent Italian fascism has developed along truly syndicalist lines is not altogether clear. On the one hand it is easy for a Marxist critic to point out that much of the syndicalist emphasis in the "corporative state" is make-believe. Trade union officials are usually party officials, and representatives of business interests are much more prominent in the party structure than representatives of the workers. On the other hand, a recent friendly survey concluded: "Italy is a trade union state in the making. . . . Morally the battle is won, and economically is being won, and politically the future is his" (the worker's). Quoted in the *People's Lobby Bulletin*, October, 1938, from *The Class Conflict in Italy* by Karl Walter.

when the socialist revolution required all parties that aimed to be mass parties to call themselves socialist. This was not objectionable, even to the military nationalists with whom the Nazis were frequently in alliance. Had not Bismarck put through much of Germany's socialistic legislation, in the days when he was building Germany to greatness? Had not Spengler, the romantic prophet of the will to power, exalted Prussianism as a form of socialism worthy of Germans, whereas Marxian egalitarianism was a coward's creed? It was natural that the Nazis fell heir to a vague concept of a special type of "German socialism."

This "German socialism" sounded phony to the orthodox Marxists, who knew there could be no "socialism" till the proletariat had liquidated the bourgeoisie. But for millions of more muddy-minded Germans it was easy to grasp the idea that "socialism" meant a "national community" (the heroic and mystical connotations of *Volksgemeinschaft* are untranslatable), in which all, rich and poor, employer-leader and employee-follower, worked together for the common good. The conservative ("liberal") American doctrine that government should keep its hands off business had never been strong in Germany. Interventionism was a heritage from feudalism with no such sharp break as occurred in the Anglo-Saxon world. "German socialism" was merely the ultimate expression of interventionism in a disciplined soldier-state where the national welfare was all the more exalted for being a comparatively fresh and shining symbol.

The fullest expression of this concept is furnished, interestingly enough, by Werner Sombart, the latter-day Marx, whose historical approach to economics differed from Marx's in its emphasis on psychological factors, but who was little less merciless in his analysis of capitalism. In his book *Deutscher Sozialismus*, written in 1934, he indicates his faith that the Nazis will bring "German socialism"—the ideal form of which he outlines as a planned economy with large areas of private enterprise—to ultimate fruition. He concedes that Germany is still behind Russia: "What is still lacking (except in Russia) is the unified plan. . . . As long as this unified plan is lacking, there is in fact no Socialism, whatever you may call it. Let us hope that this last step will be taken by us very soon."

Sombart and other German writers sympathetic with Nazism

have, like their Italian prototypes, played with the idea of the medieval guild. Gottfried Feder, author of the Nazis' "unchangeable" *25 Points*, included the corporative idea in that program. But in the complex structure of German business under the Nazis, with its incredible maze of vertical and horizontal organization, the "estates" (*Stände*) have remained as mythical as did the Italian "corporations" long after the announcement of the "corporative state." Only the "Food Estate" (*Reichsnährstand*), under Darré's opinionated leadership and the compulsions of autarchy, has materialized: within its all-embracing membership the whole production, processing and distribution of foodstuffs is almost as rigidly planned and controlled as in the Soviet Union.

Some Nazi theorists still see this *Stand* as the model for industrial organization too. But the strength of socialist ideas in Nazism depends only to a small degree on the nostalgia for the medieval guild. To a much greater extent Marxian socialist ideas permeated every cranny of Germany during the post-war years, when the battles between Marxian Social-Democrats and Marxian Communists almost drowned out the struggles of Big Business to retain its privileges. Millions of German workers and unemployed as well as middle-class paupers drifted back and forth in their allegiance, between Socialism, Communism, Nazism, carrying ideas from one camp to the other. Some of the more outspoken "Bolshevik Nazis," like the Strasser brothers, were liquidated, and the initial seizure of businesses in the first "bolshevist" wave following Hitler's victory was stopped to prevent a "Second Revolution," but the socialist ideas continued to spread. "National Socialism," recently declared the Nazi press chief, Otto Dietrich, "fulfills the century-old socialist yearning of all who work. . . . The capitalistic system is replaced by a new economic system." In addition, "National Socialism has removed all prerogatives of birth and class."

This can be squared with the continuance of a wealthy capitalist class, and with such a pledge as Hitler's to "the utmost furtherance of private initiative and recognition of the rights of property," only as we understand the nature of the planned economy that is evolving in the fascist countries. But before we go on to describe these methods we must include in the sources of fascist planning not only ideas prevalent long before fascism appeared, but also those arising out of war and depression and out of the inner development of the fascist movements themselves.

## *Out of War*

There is at least some explanation, if not justification, for Mussolini's boast that "War puts the stamp of nobility upon peoples," and Hitler's "Mankind has achieved greatness in everlasting battles," when one considers to what an extent both dictators owe their power to the World War. And the war stamped their regimes with a character quite hostile to pre-war capitalism.

So far as economic planning is concerned, the effect of the war was mostly indirect, through the train of social and economic changes it initiated. But in one respect the war directly fostered the planning habit. Each one of the major warring powers came to the point where it felt it necessary to marshal all the national strength for war effectiveness. Even the United States had its War Industries Board, its federal operation of railroads and shipping, and a host of other socialistic devices which were dropped like hot cakes when Big Business and Harding brought the country "back to normalcy." But in Europe, socialists organized governments after the war, the disorganization was such that there could be no thought of "normalcy," and the various schemes of war planning were not so swiftly forgotten. In Germany particularly, the rigid controls necessitated by the blockade—rationing of raw materials and consumer goods alike—remained as familiar ideas, even after their practice was abandoned. Walter Rathenau, who had headed the War Materials Section during the war and had worked out many of the schemes of raw material priorities and substitutes, price-fixing, requisitioning and the like, was one of the architects of Weimar, and went on to develop a theoretical planned economy of a guild socialist type, with an Economic Council as a national planning board on top. The Economic Council idea actually was tried in Germany as in other post-war countries, but it remained embryonic and functionless: one cannot plan unless one knows for what one is planning, and the end of the war left no planning goal. Yet under the Weimar regime governmental action in the economic sphere was on so extensive a scale that it is estimated one-third of all economic activities were carried on by public agencies.

It is true that this meant merely "interventionist" capitalism rather than socialist planning, but a rich background of experience and theory had been provided for future planners in the fascist states.

The indirect effect of the war was ultimately of much greater importance than its direct heritage of planning, however. The indirect effect was felt through two by-products of the war, nationalism and depression.

Nationalism is not something that can be isolated on a laboratory table. In the final analysis it is a complex psychological phenomenon which will not be understood until psychology is much further advanced as a science than it is today.

The war raised nationalism to the pinnacles of a religion, for which the whole people and all their institutions must be willing to sacrifice themselves; and it was a religion whose creed—Wilson's "self-determination of peoples"—could appeal alike to atavistic tribal racialisms and to the most refined idealism.

The nations that were to become fascist were among those in which nationalism was still in its youthful heat. Both Italy and Germany felt humiliated by the Peace of Versailles, Italy because her stronger allies took what seemed the lion's share of the spoils, Germany because she was shorn of vast territories and vast wealth. Mussolini and Hitler were able to give new pride and self-respect to millions of their countrymen—and let it never be forgotten that pride is often a more powerful motive than economic interest, Marxists to the contrary notwithstanding. The discouraged and frightened middle classes particularly were given a new faith. Surrounded by enemies they yet were made to feel strong enough to "take it." They put on the new creed of nationalism as if it were a suit of armor.

For them all the bonds of internationalism were loosened. The League of Nations was part of the Treaty of Versailles. Internationalism, whether of socialism and communism on the left or finance capitalism on the right, was alien and sinister. Even the international aspects of native capitalism—its foreign trade, its search for markets and sources of raw materials, its interest in foreign investments—were irretrievably weakened if not shattered by the impact of the war. Germany was no longer an imperialist power in the old capitalist sense. Italy never had been one except in a feeble, imitative fashion.

The development of the idea of national self-sufficiency—autarchy or *autarkie*—would have been a natural outgrowth of nationalism, even if it had not been given a potent boost by depression. Now the significant thing about autarchy for our purposes here is that it leads almost irresistibly toward economic planning of a more and more comprehensive sort. Tariffs and import quotas are implemented by foreign exchange controls, especially when depression enhances the difficulties of maintaining stability of a currency in relation to the rest of the world. The search for self-sufficiency leads to the development of substitute industries, which need to be constantly subsidized if not directly financed by the government. The shrinkage of foreign trade leads to a shortage of certain vital raw materials, which leads in turn to rationing of the available supplies. This process is exaggerated by the military aspects that necessarily accompany violent nationalism; fascist Italy and Germany have had to direct so much of the national effort into non-economic armament channels, which bore no relation to the market laws of supply and demand, that the evolution from one stage of planning to the next has naturally been hastened.*

Autarchy can hardly approach complete self-sufficiency, except perhaps in countries like the United States or the Soviet Union which include virtually all the essential resources. In a country like Germany it means the building up of stocks of certain foreign raw materials, and therefore, at least during such a transition period as Goering's Four Year Plan, perhaps an expansion of for-

* "Not by careful choice but by stumbling, the autarchical nation would be forced into a high degree of governmental direction and control of economic activity—since autarchy means developing processes at home to an extent they would not have reached otherwise, stopping the development of other processes before the point they would have reached otherwise, controlling the distribution of income so that products can be sold, and so on. Finally, in a world of self-contained nations, the problem of what is contained within the boundaries of each nation and its possessions becomes extremely intensified; the urge for additional territory is strengthened. If a nation wants not only peace but also a high standard of living under autarchy, it may first have to wage several 'successful' wars." *Report of the Committee on Economics and Peace of the National Peace Conference* (1938).

eign trade rather than its contraction. Imports must be paid for with exports. Exports are forced out on an unwilling world, but in a fashion that is much more like the "dumping" of goods "below cost" charged against the Soviet regime during the first hectic years of the Five Year Plan, than it is like the old-fashioned capitalist search for foreign markets. It is an export trade subsidized and promoted by a collectivist regime aiming to assure itself military strength and independence. If profits are made in the process by exporting firms and manufacturers, that is purely incidental.

Finally, this nationalistic economy in the fascist countries approaches the type of war socialism foreshadowed in the last war, but on a much higher plane, foreshadowing in its turn the completely regimented war economy, which in the next war is likely to force all countries into economic collectivism virtually as complete as that in the Soviet Union. War and the imminence of war are swift collectivizers. Italy has gone farther in the direction of planned control and socialization of her economy since the start of her Ethiopian war than in all the intervening years since Mussolini's "March on Rome." The driving force of Hitler's Four Year Plan may be Field Marshal Goering, but the guiding genius is Colonel Fritz Loeb, who has never had any career outside the army.

In his speech of March 23, 1936, when the imposition of sanctions had virtually put Italy at war with the world, Mussolini went over an "inventory of our resources," and outlined, more completely than any other national leader except Stalin has ever done, exactly what raw materials could be found and what substitutes could be developed. This required, he said, a complete regulation and control of the economy, especially rigid in the case of all heavy industries producing war materials. For the most he deprecated the idea of "taking over" any industry, for he is firmly wedded to the idea of "private initiative" as a motive force (like a carrot held before a donkey), but all these industries he nevertheless called "quasi public."

The Four Year Plan announced in November, 1936, likewise proceeds with an estimate of Germany's productive resources, and of how they could be expanded to fill the greatest proportion of her needs in time of war. Here as in Italy a good part of the effort is directed to shifting consumption habits away from those articles of which there are shortages. Domestic production of gasoline from coal is being rapidly pushed, and will probably provide for 85 per cent of her consumption needs by 1940. Stocks of vital raw materials are being built up; substitutes like aluminum and synthetic products to take the place of rubber and textile fibers devised; and preparation made for economic survival during a not-too-long war even if all imports are cut off. This program requires a growing mechanism for economic planning, including production and price controls, and allocation of raw materials and resources.

The Four Year Plan is merely an aspect of Germany's rearmament—which in this historical survey likewise may be considered as an indirect result of the last war and the nationalism it fostered. And rearmament has been the most potent incentive to economic planning.

A recent penetrating study of the effects of Germany's rearmament program puts the matter thus: *

> "The price for the enormous scale of rearmament is no less than the supersession of private initiative by state control. . . . The Nazi leaders have been convinced by experience of the necessity of transforming the German economy on socialist lines, whereas they assert their adherence to an economy based upon the rights of private property and the individual initiative of the entrepreneur. They denounce the theory and practice of Marxist Bolshevism with a fervor unknown in even the most orthodox countries, while their actions bear a greater resemblance every day to those carried out in Russia four to eight years ago. Are the leaders of National Socialist Germany deliberately playing a double game in their economic policy? A close analysis of the position does not support this view. The reason for the socialist tendencies in the economic policy of the Nazi regime lies, in fact, in the party's military program. . . . The present socialist tendencies in Germany, therefore, are not the result of some theory, as they are in Russia, but part of a vicious circle started by the largest

* This striking statement first appeared in the conservative London *Banker*, almost as a warning to British capitalists; it was later published in *Germany: The Last Four Years*, by "Germanicus" (1937).

armament program the world has yet seen. . . . State control of economic life in consequence is growing so rapidly that it represents in actual fact a far-reaching process of socialization."

*And Out of Depression*

If preparation for a new war to avenge the last war is a major reason for fascist planning, the depression, whose causes are also closely linked in with the World War, is its other chief indirect source.

Psychologically the depression heightened the nationalist psychosis, and made millions of sufferers eager for the security and discipline, the stability and order, which a totalitarian regime promises, in the economic as well as in the political sphere. The economic suffering of the later war years, culminating in the suffering of the blockade and the incredible experience of the post-war inflation, were hardly forgotten, in the fleeting glimpse of something like prosperity in the twenties, when the catastrophic unemployment and stagnation of business came down like a new vengeance. The middle-class-minded average German—whether of the industrial working class or the white collar and professional classes—craved security above all else. Only a strong government taking drastic measures in the economic field could give it to him.

In Italy, too, fascism was a depression product. Mussolini came into power in the earlier post-war depression, which in Italy was especially severe. But it was only with the depression of the early thirties that the corporative state really got under way. In his early years of rule Mussolini seemed afraid of upsetting the economic *status quo*.

He seems to have been impressed quite early—perhaps at the time of the occupation of the factories—with the importance of competent management of business enterprises. Like many an ambitious politician he concentrated on the techniques of political manipulation, and when he got to power he was as unsure of himself in the economic field as he was reckless and confident in the political. In the first years of Italian fascism he gave his Big Business backers a free hand. Fortunately for him his first years were years of rising prosperity all over the world. When he finally set himself the task of studying economics, particularly banking, one of his first concrete ventures, aside from issuing vague pronunciamentos about the new "corporative state," was a disastrously orthodox attempt to stabilize the lira at too high a gold value—which brought on the Great Depression in Italy two years earlier than in the rest of the world. Even by the end of 1933 his efforts to stem the depression were still so lacking in boldness that he was horrified by the radicalism of the NRA: it seemed to him communistic in its machinery and wild in its monetary aspects.

Nevertheless the emergency measures that were taken hastened the implementation of the corporative idea. The Istituto Mobiliare Italiano formed at the end of 1931, and the Istituto per la Ricostruzione Industriale a year later, were imitations of Hoover's Reconstruction Finance Corporation, and served to keep banks liquid and solvent and to refinance tottering industries; but in the hands of Mussolini they became instruments for government control of the enterprises whose securities and obligations were taken over. Other "institutes" and "agencies" (*ente*) were set up for special industries, shipping, textiles, etc., when they needed help, and these became the models for the permanent corporations when they were finally set up. As in the United States, capitalist businesses came to the government for rescue; but, unlike the United States, the government did not withdraw into the background when they were back on their feet.

Hitler was as willing as Mussolini to give business a free hand in the beginning of his regime, while he concentrated on what seemed to him more important matters. But Germany was in a far more catastrophic depression than Mussolini ever knew. Hitler had promised jobs to the unemployed, and he soon found that his rearmament program, which he was interested in for other reasons, could at the same time solve depression and unemployment, if boldly enough pursued. His first year's effort, however, was more concerned with public works than direct arms production, and his success in financing this three-billion-mark program out of a bankrupt treasury was such that it greatly encouraged the pace of the armament program which began in earnest in 1934.

The financial techniques devised, which resulted, in Germany as in Italy, in complete government control of money, credit and investment, are discussed in the next chapter. But it might be noted here that the depression out of which Hitler lifted Germany provided incentives to all sorts of government interventions with industry, which reinforced and in many cases were inseparable from the incentives of militant nationalism and autarchy. If the institutional results of emergency aid to business were less obvious in Germany than in Italy it was because all the machinery —cartels, subsidies, semi-public-semi-private agencies to assist particular industries—were already in existence before Hitler came to power.

### *In Whose Interest?*

All the urges to decisive governmental action in the economic sphere which we have been considering were reinforced by a feature of fascism that was of its very nature. Partly this may be thought of as the natural tendency of any bureaucracy to expand, but in a larger sense it is an aspect of the rise to power of a new social class.

The World War, everywhere but in the United States, brought the era of capitalist expansion and imperialism to an end and started a new era. It was an era of armies of unemployed, and of almost perpetual economic crisis demanding governmental action (and a consequent proliferation of governmental bureaucracy). More important, it was an era of increasing psychological and social, if not numerical, preponderance on the part of the new middle classes. This meant the decline in relative importance of both the old capitalist class and of the industrial proletariat. The new white collar and professional workers were engaged in furnishing services, and in distributing—rather than producing—goods. Some prophets, indeed, declared that the automatic machine would reduce the amount of industrial labor to be performed to such an extent that most of the work of the future would be in these fields rather than in production.

A part of the new class was parasitic: however hard they may have worked and however miserably they may have been paid, large numbers of workers in advertising, salesmanship, financing and marketing, were as socially useless as any political "tax-eater" and "hanger-on." But most of the new occupations in both private enterprise and in government—particularly those furnishing professional services like education, health, entertainment and the public services—were adding materially to human and cultural values. At the top of the new class was the salaried administrator, the trained manager and engineer in private business, the expert "public servant" in the government. Even in the case of the executive of a big corporation, his interest often tended to be concentrated on his job and his salary rather than the profits absentee owners might collect. At its worst the new class might be represented by the political job-holder on the public payroll, whose maximum effort was put forward as a ward-heeler, or a clock-watching clerk going through some socially valueless motions in a Wall Street office.

It was largely the discontented elements in this class which put fascism into power. And it is this class, with particular emphasis on the governmental bureaucracy—often in its most unattractive form—which now has the dominant interest not only in the continuance of fascism, but in the continuous expansion of its economic controls.

I remember a Fascist party headquarters in a North Italian town, where I was seeking an interview with the local Blackshirt leader. The hangers-on that swarmed in the anteroom, humble people seeking dispensations and favors, grafters seeking plums, ambitious youngsters seeking the road to success—reminded me of what I knew of Tammany Hall and its prototypes in every American city.

I was told in Italy, and I have since heard the same about Nazi Germany, that the graft and corruption are great. In so far as it may be large-scale graft in which private businesses are buying big favors, this suggests the heyday of American capitalism, when Lincoln Steffens found every government agency had its price; but there is probably this difference, that in American capitalism the capitalists did not bother to run their own government because they were too busy with other matters, whereas under fascism it is no longer the capitalists' government, and the only way they can get favorable consideration is by bribery. It might be thought that corruption of this kind, if it is as widespread as anti-fascists allege, would undermine the regime and make any economic planning impossible. But corruption tends to protective devices against itself: even the outright criminal racket of the American prohibition era imposed standards of honesty within its own ranks, and infringements were sternly punished, frequently with death; for even a superracketeer must have accurate bookkeeping and trustworthy agents.

So long as fascism retains the machinery of the profit system—and the reasons why it does so will occupy us in a moment—it will be subject to pressure from "special interests." One advantage of Mussolini's corporative system over Nazism is that it brings these pressures out into the open, legitimizes them in the "consortiums" and employers' "syndicates," and gives them full representation in the Council of Corporations, visualized as the new parliament; back-door methods are therefore unnecessary. In Germany, with its stronger tradition of an independent civil service, now unrelieved by any representative legislature, the Lobby has suddenly burst into full bloom. The only way businesses can escape the suffocating toils of red-tape regulation is by having constant attendance in the corridors of the government buildings where real power lies.

On occasion business men can themselves secure the key positions. Many prominent capitalists have at one time or another held important positions in fascist governments. One thinks immediately of Krupp and Thyssen and Schacht in Germany, of De Stefani, Volpi and Pirelli in Italy. Their prominence reinforced the theory that capitalists had initiated fascism merely for their own special interests, and that they held the real power. This theory was given particular credence by the disclosure that Thyssen, a potent steel magnate, contributed a million marks to Hitler's campaign expenses in 1930, three million in 1932, and four million in 1933, that he introduced Hitler to the biggest industrialists in Germany early in 1932 in an effort to cement an alliance, and that he became president of the Reichsverband der Industrie (the semi-official National Association of Manufacturers) on Hitler's accession to power.

But if Thyssen is the keystone of this theoretical structure it is a weak structure. As early as 1930 Hitler was getting 19½ million marks from his rank-and-file supporters (why he should choose to betray them rather than his wealthier contributors has never been explained). In 1932 few industrialists were convinced that Hitler was their man, most of them, including Krupp, remaining aloof till after the failure of the Papen and Schleicher governments at the end of that year. Other individuals and organizations who helped Hitler to power for one reason or other—notably the Stahlhelm, and Hugenberg's Nationalists—were quickly dispensed with. And Thyssen himself, after an apparently hurried trip to South America at the end of 1934, has never since had any significant influence.

The evidence has been piling up overwhelmingly in the last few years, for all who were willing to see it, that the influence of wealthy capitalists in fascism is of minor significance. Some wealthy men remain in positions of power, particularly in the more slow-moving Italian form of fascism. But fascist governments are not dependent on "campaign contributions." They are not dependent on bankers, financiers or private money markets. The economic interest of the remaining capitalist class is slight (income from property in Germany in 1937 was 3.8 billion marks) compared to the economic interest of a government bureaucracy which has at its command many times that amount (German government expenditures in the fiscal year 1937-38 were estimated at 25 billion marks). A capitalist class remains under fascism, and it is undoubtedly a privileged class. But it is a class largely shorn of its power, existing on sufferance, and existing only so long as it performs the functions assigned to it in the fascist scheme of things.

When I was last in Germany, in the fall of 1934, I had an introduction to a wealthy manufacturer who was more prosperous than in years, thanks to Hitler's rearmament policy. He invited me to dinner in a fashionable and expensive restaurant where it was obvious there were plenty of wealthy people still with money to spend. Naturally I tried to steer the conversation toward politics, but always without success; when finally I asked him outright what he thought of Hitler he begged me with terror in his voice not to ask such questions in a public place; afterwards, in his handsome American car, he permitted his venom against this "madman's regime" to explode. The fear and disillusionment of the business man has gone far since that year.

Against the theory that it was the middle classes who put Hitler into power and who profit from fascism, it is sometimes argued that the middle classes have suffered greatly. In spite of glittering promises to the small tradesmen and shopkeepers they have become terrorized and wretchedly paid functionaries. In so far as there is evidence of social leveling it is down to the manual worker. There is indeed good evidence that the Nazi regime has come to rely for its mass support on the proletariat more than on the middle classes. But this, while all perhaps true, overlooks the bureaucracy itself, in which power lies.

It has been estimated that there are five hundred thousand government employees in Germany concerned with business regulation. In a recent series of articles in the New York *Times*, Otto Tolischus, the most informative American newspaper correspondent in Germany, describes this bureaucracy. It consists, he says, of

> "intricate interlocking systems of authoritarian organization in which membership is compulsory for everybody, which fix prices, ration raw materials, regulate markets, control exports and imports, pass on plant extension, direct the disposal of profits, lay down rules for the conduct of business, collect subsidies and 'gifts,' determine wages and working hours, allot workers to their jobs and superintend the employer's attitude toward his workers. As a result it has become a common complaint among business men that they are little more than administrative officials, or, as the National Socialist says, 'work agents of the State.' "

The key to the process is, in Tolischus' words, that "government control feeds on itself."

An army, as a military bureaucracy, is in some degree a pattern for fascism. It is an organization where discipline and hierarchy, and the drawing of a sure and steady salary, are far more important than profits—or even graft. The army had a good deal to do with the arrival of fascism: in Italy it refused to stop the "March on Rome," and in Germany it was long considered to be the real power behind Hitler. But it is only as part of a more inclusive bureaucracy that the army is politically important.

Only a very flexible Marxist, one who can imagine a new economic class beyond the purview of Marx himself, in the guise of a government "salariat," rising in the dialectic of history to a new type of class rule, can grasp what this process means. If Marx was right in believing that capitalism builds socialism within its own shell, and that the bearers of the new social order are functionally dominant long before they emerge politically dominant, at which time the old "integument bursts asunder," then it is the middle-class fascists who have proved the theory rather than the proletarian communists.

The orthodox Marxist, knowing that the proletariat does not control fascism, necessarily looks for a capitalist control; failing to find it, he is either utterly baffled, or he imagines what he does not see. Yet, as some of the most extreme Marxists would in this case admit, the same type of class rule by a government bureaucracy has grown up in the Soviet Union. But the Bolshevik bureaucrats had to go a long way round, thanks perhaps to a misinterpretation of Marx, before they could painfully rebuild the vital parts of the economic structure they had smashed along with the "integument."

What I am most anxious to bring out in describing this new "ruling class" under fascism, is that it necessarily hastens the transition from a capitalist to a collectivist economy. There is no longer any dominant economic interest favoring the perpetuation of capitalist procedures. Power after all expands with its exercise. With the immense reserves of human labor released by the machine, there is always plenty of room for new jobs and new jobholders in the government services.

Fascism may start out with its leaders solely concerned with establishing their political power, ready and willing to let business continue to run its own affairs in the economic sphere. It might even start, under certain circumstances, as some of its enemies claim it did start, as a mere maneuver by the capitalists to maintain their power by the bludgeon. But, because of the dynamics of its inner development, as well as for all the other reasons we have found implicit in its origins in the post-war era, it will end up as a regimented collective economy.

# Chapter Eight

## THE FASCISTS PLAN WITHOUT PLANNING TO

THE year 1936 marked a turning point in the history of economic planning. In that year the Soviet planners abolished the closed store and restored the market mechanism in distribution, Mussolini put his corporative system to work under the impact of sanctions, and Hitler launched his Four Year Plan.

In the light of what was said in the last chapter about the origins and causes of socialist planning under fascism, it should be clear why it was an indirect, haphazard and often unconscious process, resulting more from pragmatic requirements as they arose than a preconceived belief in a full-fledged socialism, such as inspired Soviet progress. Yet, because of that very fact, the fascists, at least the German Nazis, seem to have learned much more quickly some of the essentials of effective planning than the Bolsheviks. The Bolsheviks, as we saw, started by destroying the whole capitalist structure root and branch—the banking, money and credit system, and the market and price mechanism for the allocation of distribution and the guidance of production—and having destroyed it they had painfully to rebuild a great part, without which their economic planning was all but impractical. The Fascists, on the other hand, tended naturally to conserve the old structure wherever they could.

It is undoubtedly true that in spite of avoiding many economic blunders the fascist powers are still far behind the communists in socialist techniques. Mussolini talked about his corporative system for a dozen years before the pressure to do something about it overcame his caution. And Hitler, after all, has been in power only six years, to the communists' twenty-one. Yet it is startling to see in how many respects fascist and communist economic practice has converged, particularly since 1936.

First let us have a look at fascist monetary methods.

### *How the Dictators Pay Their Bills*

Mussolini, as I have already suggested, was a timid conservative when it came to money matters, and his advisers were of the most orthodox. He maintained the gold standard—but he had to force a deflation of wages and prices, to keep even with the devaluating countries, a process which had the same effect as devaluation but was far more difficult. He balanced his budgets—till depression and war made it impossible. He tried to keep his imports below his exports—till the pursuit of glory in Ethiopia forced him to requisition all the foreign balances held by Italians to pay for foreign war materials. He gave the banks free rein—till they all began to fail.

By 1928, following the difficulties arising from stabilization of the lira, the Bank of Italy was given the sole right of issue. By 1934 all imports and foreign exchange were under direct government supervision. By 1935 all foreign securities and currency were confiscated, with government bonds given in return, export of Italian money or securities was prohibited, and government monopolies were set up to handle the importation of vital war materials like coal, tin, copper and nickel. In March, 1936, as one writer has put it, "the State took over the control and unification of the country's whole banking and financial system," with the Bank of Italy dominating the entire credit structure.

How has Mussolini paid his bills, in spite of frequent pronouncements of bankruptcy by his enemies abroad? So far as money to pay for imports is concerned, his method has necessarily been orthodox: he has paid value for value either in goods or gold. The required sums have been raised, aside from what his exports would bring, by requisitioning domestic gold and taking over all the foreign balances privately owned by Italian citizens. Having exhausted these amounts he is necessarily forced to limit his further imports to the barest necessities—which to him mean military necessities—

and develop makeshift substitutes, like synthetic fibers, at home where he can.

As for money to pay for his public works and his wars and his great bureaucratic army, he never tried the easy but ultimately rocky road of merely issuing money without regard to the supply of consumer goods available, as did the Bolsheviks. But he has used as many devices as they to keep the supply of currency in people's pockets from outstripping the goods available. Taxes are of course heavy. Control of credit agencies permits the marshaling of all savings, whether in savings banks or benevolent institutions or insurance companies, to take up the loans that have raised the internal national debt to well over 100 billion lire in recent years. Syndical dues, "voluntary" collections and dues of other kinds are an additional form of compulsory saving. As in Germany, profits are limited to 6 per cent, and all earnings above that are invested in government bonds.

The net effect of raising money for a swollen government budget, and at the same time giving direction to the new financing of productive enterprise to meet the needs of war efficiency and autarchy, is to put the whole process of investing savings in government hands to almost as great an extent as in the Soviet Union.

Let us see how the same financial problems have been solved in Germany. To raise foreign (gold) balances, to pay for imports essential to rearmament, Hitler's "financial wizard," Schacht, used methods that, however they might be denounced as "immoral" abroad, were nonetheless highly effective. Germany has had virtually no gold since some years before Hitler. With this as an excuse, the foreign debt has in one way or another been effectually repudiated. The Hoover Moratorium was extended through the perennially renewed "standstill agreements." Reparations were denounced. Interest payments on private and public securities held abroad were reduced towards zero. Few value payments were made abroad except for imports. To restrict imports to essentials, Schacht's "New Plan," in September, 1934, set up twenty-five boards to issue licenses for the major classes of imports. To promote exports for securing foreign balances a number of complex methods were tried, the most important of which was the Export Subsidy Plan of June, 1935. Under this Plan the Chambers of

Commerce and Industry are required to levy what amounts to a 2 to 5 per cent turnover tax on all their members, and the sums raised, amounting to over a billion marks in 1936, are passed on to the exporting firms as subsidies to enable them to sell cheaply abroad.*

The Nazis developed another method of stimulating exports by using various kinds of specially devalued marks as a bargain inducement to foreign buyers. Much of the debt owed by Germany and Germans to foreigners has not been repudiated outright but is payable only within Germany, in marks which cannot be taken out. These marks are put in all sorts of special funds, and are available at a discount to pay part of the price of exports. As one economist has said: "Today Germany's currency system offers a tragicomical variety of Free Marks, Blocked Marks, Security Marks, Emigrants Marks, Aski Marks, Clearing Marks and Register Marks —a maze from which no one will ultimately find his way."

When I went to Germany in 1934 I found it possible, as thousands of other tourists have been encouraged to do, to pay for a certain part of my expenses in these depreciated marks; they cost me twenty cents instead of the official gold rate of forty. Tourist expenditures are, of course, like exports, an important means of getting the foreign exchange necessary to obtain imports.

All these devices remind one of the Soviet Union. When a country with a controlled economy is desperately in need of certain imports, and has no gold or credit with which to buy them, it finds it worth while to export at almost any price—even a price that is nominally below cost. This export trade is far removed from the type of export trade promoted by capitalist firms for private profit, in the familiar pre-war phenomenon known as "imperialism." This is not to say that German exporting firms may not make a profit, which in contrast to the Soviet Union may accrue to private individuals, and that such private individuals may not put pressure

* This is not quite as clear a case of "dumping" as might appear. The Nazis, having maintained the nominal gold value of the mark, for perhaps the same reasons of false pride as Mussolini, were in the same hole as he when they tried to compete with the exporting nations that had devalued their currencies. Schacht's solution of the problem by export subsidies had the same effect as Mussolini's compulsory deflation in bringing prices down to the new world levels in terms of gold, but it was far less painful.

on the German authorities to procure some kind of subsidy that will enable them to export at a profit. But all indications point to the conclusion that the interests of capitalist exporters is of purely secondary importance, compared to the interests of the government and the army; this is in direct contrast to the days of prewar imperialist competition, when the capitalist interest tended to be paramount.

To turn now to methods of internal financing in the Nazi regime, we find them for the most part almost orthodox. The purchasing power that is paid out for armaments, road building, housing, labor camps, concentration camps, and political patronage on a huge scale, does not result in consumer goods, and it must therefore be once more withdrawn from circulation, if it is not to pile up faster than consumer goods are produced. Since, as in Russia, a deliberate attempt was made to keep the production of consumer goods low, and turn all excess productive capacity into armaments and capital goods, it was all the more essential to get that money back.

It might appear that Germany followed the orthodox method of borrowing pre-existing savings and then spending them, rather than the Soviet method of making the expenditures first by direct creation of credit and then recouping the money afterwards. But the practice was probably much more nearly like the Soviet method than Schacht would have liked to admit. As it was, his conservative upbringing made him describe his own methods as "economic insanity."

The table on the opposite page shows how a nation that was thought bankrupt was able to spend the equivalent of at least fifteen billion dollars on armament in five years.

These figures, of course, are for the most part guesses, for the Nazis have not told how much they were spending on armaments, nor how much they were "borrowing." Moreover, the totals are somewhat artificially balanced, through an arbitrary figure for "other" revenue which will be explained in a moment; and the estimates for the last fiscal year were made before the completion of that year. But I have no reason to doubt the reliability of the sources where the original guesses are to be found. Most of the figures appear in *Germany: The Last Four Years*, by "Germanicus," and were first published in the London *Banker*.

## ESTIMATED GERMAN GOVERNMENT FINANCES *

(*millions of reichsmarks*)

| *Fiscal Year:* | 1933-34 | 1934-35 | 1935-36 | 1936-37 | 1937-38 |
|---|---|---|---|---|---|
| *Expenditures* | | | | | |
| Armament | 3,000 | 5,500 | 10,000 | 12,600 | 16,000 |
| Other | 6,700 | 6,700 | 6,700 | 7,500 | 9,000 |
| Total | 9,700 | 12,200 | 16,700 | 20,100 | 25,000 |
| *Revenues* | | | | | |
| Taxes | 6,900 | 8,300 | 9,960 | 11,500 | 14,000 |
| Long Term Loans | 850 | 760 | 1,675 | 2,300 | 3,600 |
| Short Term Loans | 1,900 | 2,740 | 4,565 | 4,400 | 5,700 |
| Other | 50 | 400 | 500 | 1,900 | 1,700 |
| Total | 9,700 | 12,200 | 16,700 | 20,100 | 25,000 |

They are indeed staggering figures, reminding one strangely of the figures of the Soviet Five Year Plans. Yet there is one obvious difference, the enormous amount of revenue Germany has secured from "loans" as compared to the small amount of borrowing in the Soviet Union. How do the Nazis borrow so much?

Partly they do it by channeling the larger part of voluntary savings (which hardly exist in the poorer Soviet Union) directly into their own coffers. One method of short-term financing, that developed into the chief source of revenue for a while, was the "work-creation bill," which by 1938 had raised the floating short-term indebtedness to something like 20 or 25 billion marks. This was little more than a simple I O U which a recipient could take to his bank and discount like ordinary commercial paper. Yet it was not commercial paper, for it signified no goods later to be sold,

* It is not easy to translate the marks into dollars, for there are varying exchange rates, but it seems not unreasonable to reckon about three marks to the dollar, midway between the official gold rate and the discounted marks. This gives a figure of over five billion dollars for armament in the last fiscal year, far more than any of Germany's capitalist enemies can possibly afford. No wonder they backed down at Munich. And no wonder they have a panicky feeling that even their renewed armament pace cannot possibly keep up with German armament, much less catch up with it.

and thus no repayment could be expected: the short-term credit became "frozen," like much of the early short-term credit in the Soviet Union, and became in effect long-term credit, or investment.

Banking is by now completely under government control in Germany. The Nazis inherited a banking system already largely public: savings banks and investment banks particularly have long been so rigidly supervised as to be almost public institutions. By 1936, after three years of Nazi rule, less than a quarter of the total deposits in the country were in private joint-stock banks. The Reichsbank as the sole bank of issue is in effect a public agency. Its head is appointed by Hitler, and the fact that this head long was Hjalmar Schacht, a conservative capitalist, is not particularly significant. As it has been aptly put, "The Nazis had the sweeping élan of revolutionaries, but no experts. Dr. Schacht was given a free hand in dealing with foreign indebtedness, because here his views and those of the Nazis coincide. Otherwise he has had to follow the narrow path of Nazi policy determined by rearmament."

Having complete control of the banking system, it has been possible for the Nazis to get all the credit they need. A billion-and-a-half-mark long-term loan offered in October was immediately oversubscribed, though it was only the latest of several such loans made during the year. The short-term obligations can be forced not only on the banks but on insurance companies, and on all the institutions for small savings, and the latter need never fear being caught short of liquid funds, since the government treasury is always in effect behind them.

Taxes, as noted in the above table, have risen amazingly in the last few years. It is reported that corporation tax rates have gone up more rapidly than any others.

The "other" sources of funds by which huge government budgets have been "balanced" loom increasingly large in the table. Certain official reserve funds, as for unemployment insurance, were first liquidated, with scant regard for financial orthodoxy. Then the Winter Help campaigns were instituted to relieve distress, and they have remained as generous sources of getting "voluntary" contributions to help fill the Treasury for special purposes. There are other "voluntary" collections, too. Such, for instance, is the method by which the vast new factory for manufacturing a cheap car—the "*Volksauto*" or "Strength Through Joy" automobile—is being financed with public capital, by requiring virtually every worker to make a monthly contribution as an "advance payment" on a car that will supposedly be set aside for him in some unascertainable future. The government's revenues in the current fiscal year will also get the benefit of the vast robbery of the Jews that has been taking place in the guise of a "fine."

Another lucrative source of funds has been found in the sale of government owned shares of "private" corporations. During the pre-Hitler years the government frequently came to the rescue of banks and other businesses by buying their security holdings, until it was the majority stockholder in many businesses. In a regime where there is totalitarian control over businesses anyway, the Nazi government decided there was no reason to hold these securities, and it sold them back to private individuals. This has been cited by Marxists as proof that the Nazis were merely the servants of private enterprise, and that their "socialism" was a lie. For people who think of control only in terms of the increasingly antiquated concept of "ownership," the Nazis' sales of these businesses was a betrayal to capitalism. But as a more modern commentator has described the return of certain banks to private ownership, "Now that the control over the banks is complete and final the government is no longer interested in holding their shares." The effect of such sale is little different from the sale of government bonds: merely a transfer of some individual's savings to the government to help cover the government's expenses.

As noted a few pages back with regard to Italian fascism, the result of all this centralized government control over money, credit and banking, is to subject investment to whatever planning is desired. The Nazis have not abolished "unearned income," as Feder promised they would in one of his *25 Points*. They have found it much too useful a means of keeping down consumption and *channeling off a large proportion of the national income as savings,* for investment and nonproductive public expenditure.

Dividends, as in Italy, have been limited to 6 per cent, with 8 per cent possible in certain cases: any surpluses are taken by the government as a "loan." But all the remainder not taken in taxes or spent on consumption is invested substantially where the government plans require. With the rigid control over allocation of raw materials and capital goods, and with the innumerable regulations for carrying on business, it would be impossible for a business man to make headway against official wishes even if he could raise the money capital. But he can neither invest his own savings, nor others', as he chooses.*

Otto Tolischus, whose despatches to the New York *Times* throw more light on German economic development than any other current source, says of the private business man:

> "He cannot raise capital in the public capital market because that market is reserved for the government or government-fostered enterprises. On the contrary, he must often invest his own capital in such government-fostered undertakings. Thus the brown-coal industry had to raise 100,000,000 marks to promote synthetic oil production, the textile industry was forced to finance synthetic 'cellwood,' or viscose-production, and the iron manufacturing industry and the handicrafts were compelled to subscribe 130,000,000 marks for non-voting preferred shares in the State-owned Hermann Goering Iron Works at the rate of 50 marks of stock for each person they employed."

In building the new "substitute" industries for synthetic fibers, oil, rubber and other items required by the Four Year Plan, no regard is paid to what would be the dominant consideration under

*A writer in the London *Banker*, charging that the Four Year Plan is breaking down "the last dams of economic reason," declares that "the larger part of individual profits has found its way into the pockets of the State (in the form of taxes or loans), and the laying down of new plant (for armaments and substitutes) has swallowed up the remainder."

The confidential reports of the illegal German Social Democratic party, now published in Paris, stated not long ago that of 4,628,000,000 marks in new capital issues in 1937, only 591,000,000 marks were for private companies, and all of the latter were in accordance with the Four Year Plan. "These issues," ran the comment, "are serving military aims in the same way as the public loans. There is no scope in Nazi Germany for financing any industrial development independent of the aims of autarchy."

Recent corporation reports in Germany indicate, however, "that as a consequence of the withholding of profits from stockholders, and of the excessive writing down of assets, industry is in a great measure able to finance expansion out of current resources." New York *Times*, January 29, 1938.

capitalism—whether or not the new business can earn a profit. As subsidies are available to help such a plant to the point of production, so subsidies will be available to carry on production regardless of loss.

Who pays for it all? There are two simple rules, which it took the Soviet planners much longer to learn: 1. Keep the production of consumer goods down if you want to have adequate labor and resources to put into investment and non-productive public works. 2. Keep purchasing power in the hands of consumers down to your planned supply of consumer goods if you want to avoid inflation.

Borrowing, after all, whether short-term or long-term, is not inflationary in itself. If it represents a definite taking over of savings (whether those savings are voluntary or compulsory does not change the economic effect), then it is only a disguised form of taxation, with more or less reliable commitments to pay interest, and an illusory promise to return the principal amount at some future date. If it represents a direct creation of credit without an equivalent expansion of goods, as some of it undoubtedly does, then only is it inflationary. But so far the inflationary effect has been comparatively slight. Notes in circulation have doubled under Hitler, but so has industrial production. The national income increased 50 per cent between 1933 and 1937, and the index of consumer goods production showed a rise of 27 per cent. But the slight price rises that occurred would indicate that this was more properly a "reflationary" movement than an "inflationary" one. The cost of living is not above 1929 levels (unless poorer quality of goods is weighted very heavily). Prices, of course, are all rigidly controlled, but that in itself is no guarantee against an inflationary rise. On the whole it may be stated that so far there has been no dangerous inflation of the currency.*

It might be argued that Germany is now saddled with a crushing burden of debt, and a crushing burden of current government expenditure. A year ago the national income was estimated at 68

* Notes in circulation at the end of the year were reported as 5.0 billion in 1929, 3.6 in 1933, 5.5 in 1937, and 8.2 in 1938. The former figures are from the League of Nations *Monthly Bulletin of Statistics*, the last from the New York *Times* of January 26, 1939, giving the additional figure of 7.1 billion for January 24.

billion marks, as against a total governmental debt of 57 billion, and annual governmental expenditures (including those of government controlled organizations and local government as well as of the national government) amounting to 35 billion. But the service on the debt is less than a billion marks, many of the recent short-term loans paying no interest at all. And the cost of government after all merely measures part of the national income in process of circulation.*

## *Planning Production*

The Nazi leaders, for all their mental unbalance in other respects, have shown extraordinary sanity in their attitude toward money. The Soviet leaders, though properly stressing the need for production of real goods in the real world, started with such a complete disrespect for the imaginary world of money that they made all sorts of trouble for themselves. The Nazis, being always pragmatists without economic preconceptions, likewise put real production first, but—perhaps because they were able to use such men as Schacht—they always sensed the importance of a sound relation between the mental world of money and the real world of goods.

Schacht put it this way:

> "The whole secret of where the money for our great achievements like labor creation and rearmament comes from is merely a question of financial discipline. . . . We know there are boundaries for our financial policy set by the effects of credit expansion on the general economy. These boundaries are reached when the credit policy ceases to be guided solely by an *economically sound relation between money and the volume of goods.*" (My italics.)

* Remember the Soviet budget, estimated in 1934 to have amounted to 80 per cent of the national income. Obviously this was not a deduction from the national income, but merely an indication of the extent to which the total circulation of money was passing through government hands. An individual's wages, for instance, show up as government expenditures when the government is the employer, and consumer purchases show up as government income when the government is the actual seller or receives a sales tax.

Hitler, in two striking speeches in 1937, put the emphasis on production even more forcefully:

"Money is nothing. Production is everything. The problem of our living standard is a production problem, a problem of work, the organization of labor and the distribution of its results."

"We have given to the German currency that unique and only real coverage which is at the same time the indispensable condition of its stability, the stability of its purchasing power, namely, goods on the market. With every purchase we made we had to have the additional volume of products. This simple but true National Socialistic economy and currency policy has permitted us to increase our production to capacity and at the same time maintain the purchasing power of our reichsmark."

Mussolini, as I have suggested, was far more conservative in his monetary views. But in Italian fascism, too, there is a consistent emphasis on utilizing productive capacity to the full. The Labor Charter says: "From the national point of view the whole of production is a single process," which aims at "the welfare of individuals and the growth of the national power." "Property," said Mussolini on one occasion, "should be considered in its social function, not as passive ownership but as active ownership, which does not merely enjoy the fruits of wealth but develops, increases and multiplies them."

In a sense there is nothing unusual in this emphasis on increasing the production of wealth. All over the world today, perhaps, under the impact of Soviet planning, public emphasis has been put on making goods rather than "making money." If Italy were the only fascist country, we might be inclined to conclude that there was nothing peculiar in fascist economic methods, as compared to capitalist methods, beyond a greater degree of government interference. For there is no conclusive proof that the Italian economy has surmounted the ills of capitalism. But Germany does seem to have pushed production to the limits of her resources and her capacity, and to have given evidence of surmounting the economic maladjustments that lead to depression.

What then is the nature of this new fascist economy? Is it capitalist or is it socialist?

Obviously "private enterprise" and the "profit motive" are still the prevailing mode. There has been nothing comparable to the blueprinted production planning of the Soviet Five Year Plans. Neither Mussolini nor Hitler has indicated any intention to build a complete socialized planned economy. Mussolini, in fact, has declared himself against a "programmatic" economy. Both of them have extolled the virtues of individual business initiative under the spur of the profit motive, and both of them have protected and fostered this initiative as the major incentive to economic activity. As the Italian Labor Charter says: "The Corporative State regards private initiative in the field of production as the most effective and useful instrument of the national interest." In one of Hitler's first speeches after taking power, he attacked "economic bureaucracy" and called for "the utmost furtherance of private initiative and recognition of the rights of property."

Yet an American business man would be much mistaken if he thought such pronouncements meant the same as they do in the resolutions of the National Association of Manufacturers. The whole spirit of fascism is so permeated with the doctrine of the supremacy of the state, and all economic activity is so much under the direction of the state, that the business man in pursuit of profit has about as much independence as a squirrel in a revolving squirrel cage.

Even though Italian fascism was late in imposing the directives on business which were implicit in its social attitude, Mussolini declared "liberalism" ("liberalism always signifying individualism") dead almost as soon as he came to power. It is true that his corporations have developed mechanisms for directing production much more slowly than his magnificent pronouncements might have suggested; for a long time only one (for the "stage") was formed, and even when the structure became more complete the questions with which corporations concerned themselves—matters of rationalization, technological improvements, grading, and the like—were comparatively minor. Yet the whole tendency from the beginning has been toward the extension of the machinery for controlling economic processes.

German fascism has moved much more rapidly. And the machinery for economic controls is vast and complicated. The Nazis have even tried one huge experiment in the planning of production outside public works and armament, for, as we noted earlier, the Food Estate, or *Reichsnährstand*, reached out over all phases of the production and consumption of food. It is worth considering in a little detail.

The drastic decrees of the "blood and soil" policy established the peasant homestead as a sort of inalienable trust (the peasant can neither sell his farm nor mortgage it, nor, for the most part, leave it). But private property concepts are even more eliminated in the supervision that has been imposed on the whole process of producing and distributing agricultural products. All speculative markets and middlemen having been abolished, the Reich, as sole buyer, is in a position to dictate: its allocation of grain quotas and its grain collections remind one of the most radical phases of Soviet collectivization.

The results have been almost as disappointing as in the Soviet Union, if measured in terms of quantity of output. The Nazis claim to have reduced their dependence on foreign grown foodstuffs from 28 per cent of the total consumption in 1929 and 25 per cent in 1932 to 17 per cent in 1937. This meant chiefly a reduction in imported fodder, which has apparently somewhat impaired the quality of livestock. Grain harvests have been much more dependent on the weather than on Nazi decrees, and in general show little change from pre-Hitler figures. Food consumption figures are unreliable and inconclusive: they seem to indicate a slight rise in food consumption over 1932 and 1933, but not up to 1928 and 1929 levels. Talk of acute food shortages has, however, hardly been warranted. The rationing of fats, and the issuance of food tickets in certain instances, redeemable only at particular stores, seem to have been far more in an attempt to make more equitable the distribution of a supply that had always been short, that is, to keep the price low in spite of a rise in purchasing power, than because of serious shortages.

Nazi agricultural policy has in fact been markedly successful in regard to distribution, by contrast to its failures in the production field. It has given the farmers a much higher income without substantial price rises to consumers. The farmers' net income rose from 300 million marks in 1932 to 2,300 million in 1936: they received far better prices chiefly because of the virtual elimination of the middleman. Yet retail food prices, while showing some increase from the depression lows, have not risen to the 1928 levels, except in the case of sugar and beer. Even hostile critics have admitted that so far as there has been any decline in standards of food consumption under the Nazis it has been confined to the prosperous classes, whose ability to buy fancy imported foodstuffs, and butter in any quantity, has been limited.

Outside this far-reaching experiment in planning the production and consumption of foodstuffs in Germany, then, fascism has left the competitive system in operation as regards most of the economic activity concerned with the provision of consumer goods and services.

Yet it is possible that the inner drives of a bureaucratic planned economy will push fascism farther left in this respect, and that a detailed planning of consumer goods production and distribution will be attempted, as in Russia. There are already signs that the Nazi agricultural theorists are going to repeat some of the mistakes of over-drastic control committed in Soviet collectivization. The constant extension of new controls for the most minute regulation of the smallest phases of production, even of consumer goods, suggests a trend that is likely to prove more of an impediment to full utilization of resources than an aid. When quantity, quality, price, conditions of manufacture and distribution, labor conditions, use of raw materials, and access to new capital are all under official control, it might almost be better to have a single integrated blueprint on the Russian model. Yet if the recent shifts in the Soviet Union, towards greater freedom of management and greater freedom of the market in determining price, are an indication, then the extent to which the Fascists have retained these methods is to their advantage, and their present trend away from them may be a temporary phase.

A comparison of fascist and Soviet economics brings out remarkable parallels.

One major test of an economic system is whether or not it is liable to depression and unemployment. Mussolini's regime suffered severely from the depression which began there in 1927; but as I pointed out, fascist economics was only in its infancy at that time. The wars Italy has been fighting in Ethiopia and Spain would tend naturally to obscure normal domestic trends. And there is no doubt that the Italian economy is still in a more experimental stage than Germany's. So Italy presents no conclusive evidence. On the other hand, there is no doubt that Nazism has eliminated unemployment, and the most recent news is that labor shortages are being made up by the importing of Italian laborers. The recession of 1937 seems to have had little or no effect on Nazi progress.

The Soviet Union, interestingly enough, eliminated unemployment only when it undertook the vast capital expansion program of the first Five Year Plan. Under War Communism, as we noted, production almost stopped, and millions of jobless city workers went back to the land. In 1923-24, under the NEP, there was a serious depression with much unemployment; and as late as 1929, when the first Five Year Plan was not fully under way, there were a million and a half workers looking for work.

The elimination of depression and unemployment seems then to have little to do with whether ownership of the means of production is socialized or remains in private hands. What is crucial is whether there is adequate planning and control of new investment in capital construction—and from the point of view of eliminating unemployment it makes little difference what this construction consists of. It may be mines or steel mills or factories for the future production of consumer goods or of more capital goods; it may be "public works," useful or useless; or it may be mere instruments of war, and the expansion of plant for waging more effective war.

Another way to look at this test is whether or not the economy produces plenty. If one ignores the question "Plenty of what?" it may be said again that fascism like Sovietism can produce up to the limits of the productive capacity of the nation. It is true that in the early stages of fascism there were indications of "scarcity planning." One of the boasted accomplishments of the new Beet Sugar Corporation in Italy was a reduction in acreage; we are reminded of the New Deal, which, in spite of emphasis on the "more abundant life," applied planning methods most effectively in the AAA to limit production. Nazi planning, too, bore some of the earmarks of "scarcity planning" in its early stages, when the Nazis were still concerned more with trying to make jobs for idle workers and with "spreading the work" than with finding workers for jobs: labor-saving machinery was discouraged, and one decree even forbade the operation of labor-saving machinery whose use had been discontinued during the depression. But there has been no recent instance of this sort, and with the present shortage of labor the trend is undoubtedly the other way.

If the test of plenty is the level of consumer goods production then the Soviet Union and Nazi Germany must both be considered to have failed. But if plenty be taken to include armaments and capital construction, then both have succeeded. The 15 billion dollars' worth of armaments Germany has produced may be a grim comment on the moral level of our civilization, but it is certainly an economic triumph.

It is difficult to make a comparison between Germany's capital construction and that of the Soviet Union; for Germany was already a highly industrialized country when Hitler came to power, and the Soviet Union is still building its basic equipment. Moreover, the emphasis on substitute industries in Germany—for wood fiber textiles, extracting oil from coal, synthetic rubber—requires heavy investment with little to show for it except military self-sufficiency. The investment index was 34.4 in Germany in 1932, and 124.4 in 1937; the latter figure represents no marked advance over the 1929 base figure of 100, while Soviet investment has multiplied five or six times in the same years. One of the few bases of comparison is the production of coal and iron, in which, up to 1935, the Soviet Union was catching up to Germany, but in which Germany is now getting farther ahead once more. Here are the figures for average monthly production in some recent years in thousands of tons:

| | | 1929 | 1933 | 1935 | 1937 | 1938 (Oct.) |
|---|---|---|---|---|---|---|
| COAL | Germany | 13,620 | 9,141 | 11,918 | 15,376 | 15,638 |
| | U.S.S.R. | 3,472 | 6,020 | 8,652 | 10,215 | 10,651 |
| PIG IRON | Germany | 1,103 | 439 | 1,070 | 1,330 | 1,611 |
| | U.S.S.R. | 362 | 597 | 1,042 | 1,210 | 1,283 |

If we were justified in assuming that Soviet planning methods are capable of building up the productive plant to produce abundance, not only in raw materials and more factories, but in consumer satisfactions, then it seems a justifiable assumption that the Nazi economy could do so if it had the necessary resources.

In any case there is a basic parallel between the Nazi and the Soviet economy in their methods of channeling productive resources into investment and financing them. The difference between private ownership and public ownership, private enterprise and public enterprise, private investment and public investment, as distinguishing the fascist from the Soviet economy, appears to be largely verbal and legalistic. It has been said that under Nazism "private management is left intact, but it is permitted to function only in line with detailed government instructions." In view of the extent of these instructions the word "intact" is optimistic!

The role of the profit motive in the two systems is not on the whole very different. The chief distinction between the "private" profit of German industry and the profit which Soviet managers try to show on their books, is that in the former case the profit passes through the bank accounts of the "owners" before being taken by government agencies for new public investment, while Soviet profit passes directly through the Prombank and the Treasury into new public investment; and that in the former case a somewhat larger portion of the profit may be diverted into consumption, particularly of luxuries, than in the case of the Soviet managers and bureaucrats.

As for the role of the market and the "price system," we have seen that it was destroyed in the Soviet Union and has of late been more and more reinstated, though under complete public control; in the fascist countries it has functioned throughout the period of transition, but has come under almost equally complete public control. Moreover, if we are to trust the available figures on prices and currency in circulation, as well as Hitler's pronouncements on the function of money, we may say that the Nazis have learned how to keep a balance between the quantity of purchasing power and the available goods on the market, and how to use price controls to maintain that balance, much more quickly than did the Soviet planners.

A young Roman Blackshirt once told me that Mussolini could introduce communism in a single day, and since most of the machinery for communism was already available, the only people who would notice any difference would be a comparatively small number of still wealthy capitalists. The day has not yet arrived. But if the much more rapid evolution in Nazi Germany is an indication of direction, the day may be much closer than most observers have thought.

### *Fascism versus Democracy*

When Russian communism was in its most explosive stage immediately after the war, its armies threatening to overrun Europe, its brother movements in Germany and Hungary and elsewhere giving promise of being able to carry the "world revolution" through to completion, many people thought of it as the "enemy of civilization." Even the liberals who then bravely defended it because they understood that its brutalities were merely the expression of an upheaval against oppression, and knew that its faith was founded on the same scientific and humanistic tenets as liberalism itself, might have shared the conservatives' alarm if they could have known how its totalitarianism in politics and in thought would perpetuate itself.

Today fascism is in an explosive stage. Conservatives and liberals alike feel its menace. It has not even the mitigating background of communism. Even when left-wingers recognize that it is abolishing capitalism and building a collective economy, they can see it as nothing but the incarnation of evil because of its crimes. Whether or not the word socialism can be used of a society where there are none of the freedoms known in the democracies, and no indication that such freedoms are desired as an ultimate goal, certainly fascist economics can be nothing but repellent to the believer in a democratic planned economy, however much he may marvel at its efficiency.

This book is the story of my search for an understanding of the basic economic problems, and I have no intention of being diverted at this point into an analysis of fascism as a political and social phenomenon, or into an estimate of the extent to which it is in fact a menace to "civilization." But there are certain of its social and political aspects which have a bearing on its economic development, and which can be fully understood only in relation to its economic development. Our economic analysis should help us understand, even if it cannot make us more tolerant of, the fascists' emphasis on aggressive war, their glorification of dictatorship and "leadership," and their hounding of the Jews.

Autarchy or economic self-sufficiency was an obsession with German nationalists after the experience of the Allied blockade in the last war, and the tendencies of Italian fascism in the same direction were exaggerated by the imposition of sanctions during the Ethiopian conquest. Autarchy is a turning back to reliance on one's own resources, and has nothing in common with the imperialistic search for foreign markets and fields of investment that characterized pre-war capitalism, yet it may be equally imperialistic in its own way. It must seek to incorporate or control territories which may furnish the resources for self-sufficiency.

To be sure, the economic drive of "autarchic imperialism" is not the only reason for fascist belligerence. Italy's ventures in Ethiopia and Spain have been equally motivated by the desire for glory and power and prestige, nurtured by the neurotic nationalism of which fascism is as much a result as a cause. And the Nazis, especially Hitler, are so inspired with megalomania and the desire to avenge the humiliation of 1918, that romantic dreams of empire may have more effect than economic compulsions. But the economic compulsions are real nonetheless.

One of the early fallacies about fascist economics expounded by the Marxists, though now largely discredited, was that fascism was a final phase of capitalist imperialism. Today this interpretation is given fresh support by the Nazi demands for colonies, and by their energetic attempts to capture markets in South America and elsewhere. No evidence has been adduced to show that the initiative for this revived "imperialism" comes, as it did before 1914, from capitalist business men trying to make profits out of exporting goods which they cannot sell at home, or looking for opportunities to invest accumulated capital funds which they cannot invest at home. Once more this "imperialism" is to be explained in terms of an autarchic planned economy, seeking to assure for itself those raw materials which it cannot produce at home. There is no essential difference between the Nazis' interest in colonies and export markets, and the Soviet Union's interest in the far-flung possessions it inherited from Czarist imperialism, and its interest in foreign markets during the first Five Year Plan, when it was desperately trying to assure supplies of vital imports by "dumping" its products abroad.*

If fascism means military might and imperial conquest it also means absolutist dictatorship. And here again, though there are ideological and social causes for this emphasis, there is also an economic explanation. Laissez faire capitalism seemed the source of Germany's and Italy's economic woes. Germany in particular had seen Socialists and capitalists both unable to cope with depression and unemployment. Vigorous economic policies seemed called for, and it was the easier to impose rigid economic controls the more rigidly totalitarianized were all other features of the regime.

Here, once more, a parallel with Soviet experience can be drawn. The dictatorship was justified as necessary to achieve economic success. The new economic controls came most simply through dictatorial methods of a war character. The Nazis did not go so far in subjecting all economic activities to authoritarian direction as did the Soviet planners, but in at least one case, that of agriculture, they seemed likely to go to the Soviet extreme, and to be making the same mistake of destroying the effectiveness of the market mechanism. Everywhere economic activity has been hampered as much as it has been encouraged by an overelaboration of bureaucratic machinery and regulation. It is conceivable that there will be a return to a greater approximation of a free market in Germany as there has been in the Soviet Union.

When one comes to the more brutal aspects of the Nazi dictatorship—concentration camps, suppression of civil liberties, burning of books, purging of universities—the connection with economics is more remote. Yet many of the same features characterized the Russian Revolution, and indeed have characterized

* An editorial in the Nazi *Voelkischer Beobachter*, the day before the Munich settlement, sought to reassure British imperialism that it faced no rival in Nazi Germany. With all the smugness of an editorial in the Moscow *Pravda* it declared: "The goals of National Socialist world politics are not to subjugate any other people, but to give an example of how national economy can be made depression-proof. . . . We are not carrying through our Four Year Plan to effect any industrial offensive against any other people." See also Economics Minister Funk's statement of Germany's economic aims in central and southeastern Europe, as reported by Tolischus in the *Times*, October 18, 1938.

every revolution. Is fascism of its very nature brutal, or is the brutality symptomatic of a social revolution, which is basically economic? This cannot be answered with any assurance. Certainly an increasing number of observers are noting that fascism has not only the negative but the positive features of a social revolution—social equalitarianism, fanatical faith, dynamic enthusiasm in the younger generation, a widespread belief in a world mission. Yet the ideology of fascism, with its glorification of sheer animal strength, can make it unspeakably sadistic.

Most of all in its anti-Semitism do all the degenerate and psychopathic features of fascism come to the surface, and anything like a complete economic interpretation is out of the question. Yet it is probably true that many elements in the Nazi regime saw in anti-Semitism more a means of hastening the transition from capitalism to a planned economy than a mere outlet for bestiality. In Austria especially, the persecution of the Jews seems to have been utilized as the easiest method of destroying the power of private business, and the expropriation of Austrian Jewish property was touted throughout the Danubian region, particularly among the peasants, as proof that the Nazis were carrying through a social revolution. Those leaders of the Four Year Plan who may not be personally anti-Semitic no doubt condoned the similar and far more drastic expropriation of Jewish business properties in the pogroms of November, 1938, on the ground that it was essential for the "co-ordination" of the Nazi economy; and obviously the "fine" levied on the Jews following the wrecking of their shops, as if to fling Nazi cruelty in the face of the civilized world, was a convenient way of raising government revenue.

From all of this it would appear that what is most offensive in fascism to all those who believe in world peace and decency and who cherish democracy is at least partially explicable in terms of economic changes. The economic transition under way in the fascist countries is part of a profound social change, a transformation that can indeed be called revolutionary. Its violence, its menace to democracy, to civilization itself, may be the temporary aberration of this period of great strain. If our generation can survive this period perhaps what remains will not be merely a memory of terror.

# Chapter Nine

## MORE AUTHORITARIANS

IT IS easy to think of the struggle between communism and fascism as dominating the present-day world. The totalitarian regimes seem to be tearing at the remaining countries from left and right, inside and out, seeking to force them to conform to one or the other pattern. Spain was often cited as the pre-view in miniature of the titanic world struggle yet to come. Depending on the point of view, the outsider was likely to see one side or the other in Spain as fighting a defensive battle against the encroachments of a portentous international "ism." Supporters of the Loyalists tended to see the Civil War as a defense of democratic civilization against the "fascist international." Those who sided with Franco, chiefly Catholics, saw the struggle as a defense of Christian Spain against the depredations of the Communist International. Others again, more awed by the sheer horror of the contest itself, saw Spain as the first victim of a war between communism and fascism, in which democracy and humanity would be crushed regardless of the victor.

We have noted how complex are both types of regime, the communist and the fascist, defying the simple characterizations that are sought to be imposed on them. Yet as compared to the non-communist and non-fascist world they give a vivid impression of coherence and understandability. If it is wrong to give a snap label to Russia or Germany or Italy, how much more wrong is it to think of the world confronting them in the oversimplified terms of "democracy," "freedom," and "capitalism"?

If you have ever traveled in Russia or Germany you must have had somewhat the same sense of bewilderment that I have had in coming back to France or England or the United States: the "democratic" "capitalist" countries defy pigeonholing. The interests are so many, they are so out in the open, their voices—governmental, private, corporate—are so discordant, as compared to the stability of the monolithic state, where there is one authority, one interest, one party, one voice. Yet, even as you are acutely conscious of the differences between the totalitarian regimes and the democracies, so the next moment you are conscious of the similarities. Externally life is much the same everywhere. People walk the same streets, work at the same jobs, rely on the same street car and telephone and municipal services, eat, drink, sleep and laugh in much the same fashion.

From what I have seen of the world, East and West, I am convinced of the essential likeness of human beings. In their attitudes and habits and technical adjustment to their environment (always making allowances for primitive survivals) the Japanese and the Frenchman, the Russian and the American, are very much alike.

It is natural, therefore, that in their group relations and their social arrangements in this particular period of history they should follow similar patterns. In the previous few chapters of this book I have sought to show how the communists and the fascists are following closely parallel, or rather converging, lines in the development of new economic folkways. In this and the following chapter I am interested in showing how, beneath all the diversity of interest and institution in the rest of the world, there is discernible a common pattern of economic development, which, at least potentially, is not far from that of the authoritarian collective states.

An unprejudiced man from Mars would be astounded, not only at the similarity of the two new contending forces of fascism and communism for which no destructive sacrifices seem too costly to their adherents, but equally perhaps at the similarity of institutional arrangement in the other countries, where likewise people are willing to kill and be killed to preserve their own shibboleths. More concretely he would find that in every country, communist, fascist, democratic, or what not, there is the same rapid evolution of methods of group action, or collective action, in the matter of supplying goods and services. To risk, for once, a word I have been trying to avoid, it is possible to speak of the *universal growth of "socialism," regardless of the nominal form of government, and regardless of what class or interest happens to be dominant.*

It would throw this book out of proportion to enter into an extensive discussion of all the major economic changes of the post-war world in every country. The most that can be attempted is the citing of the major types of economic development, first authoritarian and then democratic, in the significant countries. Yet it will be noted that most of the pressures toward collective economic action are to be found in every part of the world today; and many of them have already been discussed among the sources of authoritarian collectivism in the Soviet Union and the fascist states.

### *Through War to Fascism in Japan*

War is the most rapid collectivizer in the modern world, as I have had occasion to point out more than once, particularly in the chapters on fascism. Nowhere has war socialism proceeded so rapidly as in Japan. Fascism has in fact come to Japan in spite of the failure of fascist groups to capture power directly as they did in Italy and Germany. Yet the extreme degree to which economic planning has been imposed—combining "the best features of communism and fascism" according to some Japanese leaders—suggests that the most effective method of destroying capitalism today is warfare.

Yet there was much in modern Japanese history to make its adoption of a fascist collectivism easy and natural.

My only visit to Japan was in the spring of 1931, before events began to happen with startling rapidity. I was completely charmed by the outward graces of this civilization that seemed to have taken all that was best from the West, and retained all of its own best. I was hardly equipped to realize how much instability this outward appearance hid.

Japan went through the whole evolutionary history of capitalism at breakneck speed. With virtually a feudal economy at the time of Perry's landing in 1854, all the symptoms of monopoly and banking capitalism and commercial imperialism developed in the space of two generations. As one observer has put it, Japanese capitalism became "rotten before it was ripe." At the time of the Manchurian "incident" in 1931, when the shift to fascism began, fifteen closely held monopolies controlled 70 per cent of Japan's industrial and commercial activity. The political institutions modeled on the "liberal democracy" of the West served in purer fashion than anywhere else the class interests of the few great capitalists: the rapacious exploitation of the many by the few, and an astonishing political venality and corruption, had spread over the whole surface of what was still in spirit a feudal social order.

In spite of a superficial flaring of communist revolt, particularly in the universities, discontent was primarily from the middle classes. In the Japanese social structure the capitalist class and the capitalist interest were concentrated in a tiny group, and the industrial proletariat was smaller than in any other important country, only 19.4 per cent of the population. In contrast was an unusually high proportion engaged in commerce (15.1 per cent) and in public service and the liberal professions (6.9 per cent), the bulk of the remainder being peasant farmers, debt-ridden, increasingly reduced to tenancy, and in the grip of economic and social forces they could not understand.

The peculiar feature of Japanese fascism is the role of the army. Inculcated with the traditions of the feudal "knights," the samurai, who had held money to be untouchably filthy, and drawn largely from the countryside rather than the city, the army had at neither top nor bottom any reason to love capitalism or the capitalists. Its older leaders, however, have been inclined to be tolerant of the capitalist interests that had obviously been responsible for Japan's meteoric rise to the rank of a first-class power, and have apparently felt these interests could be used further to increase Japan's greatness; the younger officers, closer to the poverty of the people and more reckless, have been ready to wipe the "corrupt politicians and self-seeking capitalists" off the map.

In September, 1931, came the Manchurian incident, in which the younger military first forced the hand of the politicians. Six months later occurred a wave of terrorism. Premier Inouye, son-in-law of the head of the Mitsubishi monopolies, and Baron Dan of Mitsui, head of the Mitsui clan and its even vaster interests, were among those assassinated in plots that were aimed at all the big banking and industrial leaders and their political connections. The Mitsubishi Bank was futilely bombed. The young military nationalists who were implicated were treated with extraordinary leniency by their military superiors. But the agrarian fascist leader, Tachibana, who had been urging a united front of peasants and army to establish a "national social planned economy" through the nationalization of banks and industries on a co-operative basis, received a long prison term for his alleged incitation of the plots. General Araki and the military leaders apparently hoped to use the revolt for their own purposes, which involved military aggrandizement without too great a break with capitalism.

In 1934, with the conquest of Manchuria achieved, the Press Bureau of the War Department issued an official pamphlet declaring:

> "The present economic system has been developed on the basis of individualism. It is desirable that the people should abandon their individualistic economic conceptions; instead they should recognize the importance of a collective economy. The state should rigidly control the entire national economy."

The military services were in fact carrying on a constant agitation for economic and social reform, stressing particularly the poverty of the peasantry. Individualist, "liberal" laissez faire ideas had never taken deep root in Japan. It was a short logical step from the paternalistic, military, feudal concepts, in a state where business and government had always been tied close together, even at the height of capitalist development, to concepts of a totalitarian collectivism. Japan's meager resources and crowded population but emphasized the trend. As General Isogai put it a few years ago: "Japan naturally requires a planned economy more comprehensive in scope than that required by any other country." The idea of a Five Year Plan on the Russian model was put forward as early as 1932.

The next stage in this curious transition to "military socialism" was the "incident" of February 26, 1936. Assassination of a new batch of "corrupt politicians and self-seeking capitalists" was attempted. Among those who fell was Finance Minister Takahashi, close to another of the great "monopoly" interests, that of Yasuda.

Among those who escaped was Prince Saionji, last of the "liberal" Elder Statesmen, uncle of the head of the Sumitomo family-combine. Leading figures in the three greatest business combines, Mitsui, Mitsubishi and Sumitomo, which together were supposed to control 25 per cent of Japan's business life (and which together were said to have made a profit of 34 million yen in the devaluation of the currency in 1931, thanks to their political ties), had now been subjected to murderous attack, and no man of wealth felt safe any longer. They were now more ready for a foreign war, as the only hope of diverting popular unrest, though they must have known that war would more swiftly complete the collectivizing of the economy.

Offensive war seemed a way out to all those concerned with the poverty of Japan and its people. The sinews of industry—coal and iron and oil—as well as other basic raw materials like cotton, were inadequate or entirely missing, even after the annexation of Manchuria.

A threefold solution began to present itself: development of home resources, trade, and conquest. The first meant the exploitation of Japan's existing resources to the limit, through industrialization, rationalization and the development of substitute industries. As early as 1934 an Oil Control had been set up, which among other purposes was to work on the problem of synthetic liquid fuel from low-grade coal deposits. Here as always a shortage of private capital, even under semi-compulsion, pointed to the use of public funds and government enterprise. The proposed Five Year Plan to expand productive capacity in every possible line finally blossomed early in 1937. Its emphasis on expansion programs ranging from twofold to sevenfold, particularly in the basic raw materials, and in the heavy industries and chemical industries, while not as ambitious and all-inclusive as Soviet Five Year Plans, was far more like them than like the Nazi Four Year Plan. Its 9 billion yen cost admittedly would far exceed the existing economy's "capital accumulating power."

The second phase of the Plan involved the complete rationalizing and controlling of Japan's foreign trade. Japan's demand for markets was far less motivated by hope of private profit than the requirements of a planned economy dependent on the outside world for vital materials.

A month after the proposal was announced came the "incident" at Marco Polo Bridge, once more due apparently to the younger military radicals who felt there could be no economic solution without the third item, conquest. By the end of a year of war, the planned collectivism of a war economy was in its advanced stages. The following list of agencies should show what sort of economy Japan now has:

National Planning Board. For co-ordination of industrial expansion, particularly new investment.

Price Policy Commission. For price controls. As yet there has been no serious price inflation.

Commodities Control Bureau. To allocate scarce goods for industrial and individual consumption.

Trade Control Commission. To license imports, to conform to the requirements of the war machine rather than consumer wants.

In addition there is rigid control of foreign exchange and of the stock exchange. The central bank and one-third of the commercial banks have long been publicly owned. For some time there have been special controls for various industries, shipping, automobiles, steel. All war industries are now under particularly stringent supervision. Raw materials and semi-finished goods are rationed. Mergers, new businesses, capital expansion, in any business, may be compelled or forbidden as the government chooses. Finally, the Industry Mobilization Bill, which the Diet rejected but which the military have been putting into effect nonetheless during recent months, permits government control over all production, prices, wages, profits and investments.*

There is evidence that the millionaire monopolists of Japan are

* It is significant in this connection that *Business Week*, which declared that the Japanese Five Year Plan would result in "almost as strict governmental regimentation as has the economic life of Germany, Italy and Russia," could think of nothing worse to say of the Industrial Mobilization Bill than that it was like the May Bill introduced in the American Congress. The May Bill, formerly the Sheppard-Hill Bill, and originally sponsored by the War Department and the American Legion, has been most violently denounced by the radicals, though its proposal for a war economy would carry the country farther from laissez faire capitalism than any specific proposal the radicals have put forward.

still in the picture and are still making handsome profits. But the totalitarian regime to which Japan has so swiftly succumbed seems to believe, as does the Nazi regime, that profit-taking capitalists are a useful device for allocating resources and labor to capital expansion and public enterprise. They might today be compared to the "tax farmers" of the Roman Empire or the French monarchy, who were permitted to grow rich in the process of filling the public coffers. In a poor country like Japan the abolition of the little group of capitalists would merely force the government to pay for its program of industrial expansion and war *entirely* out of taxation and credit manipulation and inflation—instead of only partly.

Moreover, the Japanese planners, no less than those in other countries, have found that direct state operation of enterprises is inefficient. They are now encouraging "private enterprise" in the development of Manchukuo and conquered China. But this seems to mean largely the use of the "business corporation" as a form (like the autonomous Soviet "trust") for securing concentration of responsibility and initiative.

So long as the controls over every economic process, particularly those concerned with the basic capital equipment, are all in public hands—and there is no reason to expect that they will ever again be relaxed—it is hardly possible to think of the capitalists retaining any other function than that of coupon-clippers for the government. The capitalist system in Japan, weak enough when the Chinese war started, was one of its first casualties.

### *Civil War Makes Strange Bed-Fellows in Spain*

Another war is just coming to a close in Spain. On both sides of the contest the brutal necessities of war tended to brush aside the ideologies of the contestants. After two years of fighting it is probable that economic processes on the two sides of the front line were not dissimilar.

On the Loyalist side a social upheaval from the bottom began in 1936, as both a cause and an effect of the rebellion. With a long anarcho-syndicalist tradition, tentatively allied with socialist and communist movements, the first months saw all the symptoms of a revolution that would destroy capitalism from the bottom up. Factories were seized and run by the workers, 60 per cent of the land was collectivized, the dictatorship of the proletariat was very nearly a fact.

That later the ultra-leftists complained the struggle had been reduced to a defense of bourgeois democracy was not due alone to political exigencies, though, in view of the necessity of winning middle-class support both at home and abroad, politics played a major part. Almost as important were the exigencies of war. Factories in the hands of self-disciplined workers may run efficiently after a generation of schooling, but war products had to be turned out instantly. Collectivized farms run by peasants hardly out of serfdom do not produce as much food as peasant homesteads, competing in the market. So private enterprise had to be encouraged, whether the revolutionists liked it or not. Yet so far as banking and investment are concerned, and the types of production planning and price controls familiar in the fascist regimes, here was collectivism—perhaps not the democratic "socialism" hoped for by some of the revolutionists, for the authoritarian disciplines required by war are the same everywhere—but a collectivist economy nonetheless.

I am here less concerned with Loyalist Spain, however. The shift to the left might have been expected, since a social revolution was under way and radicals were in large measure in command—though the subsequent shift to the right might have been unexpected, to anyone not familiar with the course of Soviet economics. I am more concerned with Franco Spain for the purposes of this inquiry. It has been so usual in liberal and radical circles in America to think of Franco as the archetype of reaction —not merely capitalist-imperialist reaction, but clerical and feudal medievalism, even Stone Age savagery—that it takes temerity to suggest that Franco is building the same kind of new economy as the Loyalists would have built had they won.

Here again the impact of war and the elements of fascism tended to drive the Rebels to the "left," even though it may be largely true that in the beginning they were supported and promoted by the most reactionary elements in Spain.*

* This chapter was drafted while the outcome of the war was still uncertain. At the moment of going to press Franco appears to have won. In his hour of triumph it may be that reaction will once more seem to be his guiding prin-

It was early apparent that the revolt had a vitality and a popular support which could not be accounted for if one thought of it as merely a grandees' counter-revolution. The army under any regime is a collectivist institution, as we have seen, a job-holding bureaucracy with its own class interests, a sort of "middle class." But more important was the mass organization of the Falange, which, with a membership variously estimated between a million and two million, drew its strength originally from the younger element of the professional and middle classes. Here again was the mass base for a war collectivism, making of the Franco movement essentially another example of fascism.

In the beginning the Franco revolt was an army revolt, financed by a few big capitalists, landowners and aristocrats, and supported by the Catholic Church and other reactionary elements. They found a middle-class fear of proletarian revolution already strong. As the revolt developed into a full-fledged war the reactionary elements were forced in a fascist direction for three reasons: they were dependent on Italy and Germany for material and technical aid; they required popular support, without which modern war cannot be fought; and they had to put their financial arrangements and their whole economy on a sounder base than that of the few private fortunes with which they started.

The resulting economic structure is a totalitarian state which bears considerable resemblance to both Italian and German fascism, draws rather more from Catholic social doctrine than Mussolini, but is necessarily shaped most markedly by the exigencies of war.

"Economically Spain is a gigantic syndicate of producers which we shall organize co-operatively by means of a system of syndicates according to branches of production." This is how certain un-

ciple: there is even talk of restoring the monarchy. Yet I am convinced that the forces of economic change that were let loose on both sides of the Civil War cannot be long suppressed. The end result, even with a Franco victory, is bound to be very similar to what it would have been if the Loyalists had won. This is not to say that for me or any other believer in democracy there could ever be any question of personal neutrality in the struggle. On the Loyalist side the social revolution was in the direct tradition of liberalism, humanism and democracy (in spite of some early and inevitable excesses); while on the Rebel side any constructive social change will be blind and brutal because largely inadvertent.

named Franco officials described the "national syndical state" to an interviewer. Since "the state must be a Catholic state, both from a social and cultural point of view," adherence may be assumed to the "corporative" principles of the Papal Encyclicals. A "Labor Charter" on the Italian model has been adopted, propounding the "right to work" as well as the "duty to work" and "abolishing" the class struggle. "We shall defend the tendency toward nationalization of banking services and of the great public services," is another statement in the same interview.

All this might be thought empty verbiage if it were not borne out by actual trends.

Licensing provisions for exports and the limitation of imports to needed war materials and an "exchange control committee" together imply the complete control of foreign trade, and have allegedly resulted in a pay-as-you-go financial policy which has required little inflation. The textile industry has been developed with public aid. There is an officially recognized monopoly for buying oil. Mining properties remain under private ownership, much of it foreign, but "all trading in mining property, bonds or shares" has been banned, to keep the industry "under the control of the highest authority." A "technical junta" of capitalists and government specialists integrates the whole economy for war purposes. Price controls seem to be widespread.

The press has become in effect a government agency, for, as it was officially stated, "Journalism must be rescued from servitude to capitalism or to revolution or to Marxism."

Collective controls are being increasingly imposed on agriculture. The National Wheat Service allots quotas of production to farmers, sets an official price and buys the entire production, thus claiming to eliminate low prices, overproduction and speculation. Land distribution has been promised, and some beginnings seem to have been made. Communal ownership in villages is to be "reconstructed." The peasant family homestead is declared the basis for a strong state, but it is to be highly organized under syndicates, communes and government agencies, to promote fertility, afforestation, more productive livestock and stable price levels.

All of these measures and pronouncements are necessarily suspect. There is still little accurate information about Franco Spain, and it is easy to mistake mere windy generalizations, intended to win popular support, for actual accomplishment. It does seem, however, as if the influence of reactionary elements in the rebellion has been steadily waning, while the "red or reddish" sentiment of the Falange, as one correspondent described it, has been on the increase. War, moreover, to repeat it again, is the most potent force toward totalitarianism. It is not possible to go backward. Spain, under Franco, will not be a pleasant place to live in. But it will never again be what it was before the republican-socialist revolution of 1931 or what it was before the enforced collectivism of a brutal civil war.

An able correspondent, Harold Callender of the New York *Times*, declared, after a survey of Franco Spain in the spring of 1938, that, even if Franco won, "It seems accurate to say—and conservatives have admitted it to this writer—that the Left will achieve its revolution after all."

The greatest tragedy of almost any war is that, no matter what the brutality of the killers and no matter what the idealism of the killed, it so often makes little difference who wins. Is all the pain then for nothing? Or is some of it the pain of birth?

### *The Backward Countries Look to the Left*

This is being written at a time when the agony of Spain and China seems likely to become the agony of all the world. Optimism about the future of civilization might be thought almost fatuous. Yet if the pattern of peace and plenty is to be fashioned out of a new ordering of economic arrangements, then it takes no fatuous optimist to see this pattern emerging out of the most unpromising situations.

Carry through a hypothesis. Imagine a country where a dictator, closely allied with the financial and business magnates, seizes power purely from motives of greed and personal aggrandizement. The last flickers of freedom and democracy are snuffed out. To enhance his power in the modern world that dictator must regiment his country along the lines of military collectivism we have been describing. More and more of the functions of the community will be taken over by the governmental apparatus. Resources, whether natural or industrial, will be developed at top speed, with the finances of the state taking a leading role. Since neither the country nor its government will be able to hold its own in the power politics of the twentieth century if the people are desperate with hunger and revolt, it will be to that dictator's interest to promote public health, social services, a high level of production and employment.*

This hypothesis cannot be made by a Marxist. For to a Marxist there are only two possible social forms today, a capitalist society ruled by a capitalist class, and a socialist society ruled by a working class. Since our hypothetical dictatorship is obviously not the latter, it must be the former. And since the "contradictions" of capitalism require scarcity and poverty and depression, it is inconceivable that a dictator could achieve any such results as those suggested. Yet the Marxists have been forced to postulate "Bonapartism," a temporary stage in which a political dictator rises superior to the class struggle, while the contestants in the class struggle lie exhausted. The classic case was Napoleon. What the Marxists cannot permit themselves to imagine is a condition where a Bonaparte permanently subordinates the power of the capitalist class.

Yet in many parts of the world this sort of development seems to be taking place. Turkey has long been a notable example. Greece is a recent addition to the totalitarian states. The other Balkan powers have many of the same features. And throughout Latin America there is a tendency to approximate that same pattern.

The potent forces that tend to accentuate the collectivist trend of fascism are all likely to be present in some degree in the countries of the little Napoleons. The emphasis on military strength in every country entails features of "war collectivism." The financial devices of taxation, central banking, and deficit financing have developed to a point where private banking and private finance, even that of foreign imperialisms, may be overshadowed by the power of the state. No longer need rulers beg the money lenders for gold, nor go to private capitalists, domestic and foreign, for permission to develop internal resources. Then again the widening range of governmental activity, military and civil, means a con-

* A partial example of this pattern in practice is furnished by Dictator Trujillo of the Dominican Republic, modernizer yet incredibly bloody tyrant.

stantly widening bureaucracy directly tied to the fortunes of the regime—a "class" whose economic interest is synonymous with the power of the dictator.

It must be admitted that no country is likely to exhibit this dominance of political dictatorship over capitalism in any pure form. Even dictators are human. They have their palaces and their estates, their friends and their mistresses. An inherent interest in strengthening and developing a regime through economic and social improvement may be all but blotted out by the corruption and inertia of the immediate circle around the dictator. Local or foreign capitalists may for a time use what appear to be puppet dictators. But there is nonetheless a continuing social pressure in the direction of collective economic planning and control, to which capitalist institutions are increasingly likely to fall victim.

Furthermore, at a time of heightened nationalism like the present, the weaker and less developed nations are bound to have a strong emotional bias against exploitation by a foreign imperialist power. Even more potent a force for collectivization than petty dictatorship is the revolt against imperialism in the remotest corners of the world. Capitalism developed so unevenly in the nineteenth century, with a few specially favored great powers pushing far ahead and dominating the development of capitalism in the more backward nations, that a vigorous native capitalism never had much of a chance.

Marxists have seen the revolt of subject peoples against their imperial masters as part of the world revolution of the proletariat. Yet the slogan "Down with foreign imperialism" is one capable of appealing to all classes in the backward country, except those who are mere hirelings of foreign business interests. And frequently enough, with the machinery for democracy as backward as the economic development, it is the dictator who takes fullest advantage of the situation.

The Turkey of Mustapha Kemal Ataturk was the best instance of this nationalistic revival under a domineering "strong man." After my first trip to the Soviet Union I stopped off for a few days in Turkey, and was astonished to see how far this little country had gone in imitation of its great and friendly neighbor to the north. I traveled by train from Istanbul to Ankara, and marveled at the paunchy business men lounging in the well-appointed dining car—I had not seen a business man in months—yet there was a certain resemblance between them and the younger and less paunchy but little less impressive "experts" I had seen in the "soft-class" cars in the Soviet Union. I learned that their capital was, as like as not, goverment capital, and the businesses they were building up in the new Turkey were under government tutelage. I heard the word "étatisme," or "statism," for the first time. It was clear that Ataturk, in telling English bankers and French investors who was master, had not substituted a home-grown variety of their economic system.

In every part of the world the same kind of development is taking place: backward nations fired by the new nationalism revolt against capitalism because they are revolting against imperialism.

In India the independence movement is becoming increasingly socialist in attitude, under the leadership of Jawaharlal Nehru, and the older native capitalist supporters of Gandhi are increasingly uneasy.

The patron saint of the Chinese revolution is Sun Yat-sen, who worked out a hybrid of liberalism and socialism a generation ago, and called for a semi-nationalized economy as the only way to escape the strangle-hold of the capitalist empires; his program fitted in with the later upsurge of agrarian communism. Whether conquered by Japan or not, China will never again offer an "open door" to exploitation by the arrogant business men who built their skyscrapers in Shanghai.

Latin America furnishes numerous instances of the same revolt against foreign imperialism. All elements conspire to somewhat the same end. The older type of dictator like Gomez, who was often a mere pawn in the hands of American and other business interests, is giving way to a newer, whose popular appeal rests on economic nationalism. Where there are democratic institutions leftist parties win; and since the young intellectuals of South America have always been more under Marxist influence than in this country, Marxist slogans may play a big part. European fascist agents today devote themselves to stirring up hatred against exploitation by the democratic capitalist powers. In the recent election in Chile the winning Popular Front was supported by socialist, communist and Nazi movements, on a joint anti-capitalist and anti-imperialist program. Even the native capitalist elements seem not averse to forms of "statism" in which their meager private capital may join with public capital in ousting the hated foreigner: the Finance Minister of a previous Chilean government, himself extremely wealthy by Chilean standards, set up virtually a government monopoly of the nitrate industry, a government oil company dominating one-third of the market, government direction of copper exports, a government controlled power system aiming at nationalization of all utilities, and extension of public ownership of the railroads.

The Vargas regime in Brazil appears to have as its goal a corporative system, drawing some of its inspiration from Nazi and Italian fascist influence and some from the Catholic model of the mother country, Portugal.

It is possible in one and the same regime to have several conflicting tendencies all matched with a degree of harmony. Mexico is in some respects closer to the Soviet Union than any other country. It has virtually only one party, the National Revolutionary party, which declares that the "ultimate aim of the revolution is to overthrow capitalism." It has launched a Six Year Plan for industrial and social development. It is expropriating the oil and other properties of foreign capitalists, as well as dividing the big landed estates. It is moving toward the nationalization of banking.* Yet there are plenty of indications of fascist tendencies even in the present ruling group.

Two years ago a lecture tour took me to San Antonio near the Mexican border. I was invited to dinner at the home of a wealthy émigré, who had fled Mexico, with his assets, at the time of Diaz' fall. Guests of honor were a rich Mexican business man from Mexico City and the governor of one of the northern provinces. There were a number of American guests as well, and I had to content myself with their conversation and that of the wife and daughter of the Mexican business man, whose identification of

* The financing of *ejidos* or peasant communes on the confiscated estates is dependent on the government co-operative and land banks. Now the Banco Obrero Fomento Industrial, the Workers' Bank for Industrial Advancement, is seeking to promote the establishment of co-operative industrial undertakings, marshaling the resources of existing co-operatives. But sooner or later it is always a temptation for a government to use its own powers to manufacture currency and credit money for financing enterprise. Though it takes time for any government to learn how to do this without inflation, in the process private capitalism is likely to suffer further.

themselves with the "whites" against the "reds," both in Spain and Mexico, was revealing enough. I gathered afterwards that the rather boisterous and good-natured conversation of the three principals bore at least a distant relation to efforts then (and probably still) being made to foment a revolt against Cárdenas' "red" regime. The governor of the northern province was apparently something of a key figure. He had virtually his own army, his own finances, and within his own frontiers was almost an absolute dictator. As he was described to me he was much more a bandit war lord than an official of a "socialist" government. But apparently nothing could tempt him from his loyalty to the Cárdenas regime. He would shrug his shoulders genially and ask what more he could want than he had. Yet his state was said to be one of the most progressive, with public works, roads, schools, land distribution and other features of the current social program, all being aggressively pushed under his firm hand. The only term I could find to describe him was a "feudal socialist." The hold of capitalism, whether native or foreign, on such a political phenomenon is necessarily uncertain. The trend to governmental control of economic processes is correspondingly rapid.

## *The Catholic Church Thinks of New Things*

Friends of the Mexican regime and of Loyalist Spain are wont to see the Catholic Church as a bulwark of reaction, and particularly, in a time like this when the issue appears to be between "capitalism" and "socialism," a bulwark of capitalism. Yet we have already noted that Catholic doctrine was one of the elements driving fascism to the left. And it appears the Church of Rome may become one of the important factors in the construction of a new socialist order rather than its enemy.

It must be remembered that the Catholic Church was molded under feudalism, and was never entirely reconciled to capitalism. Capitalism and democracy were born of Protestantism and they grew together in the period of the anti-clerical "Enlightenment." The capitalist's absorption in purely temporal wealth always conflicted with the Church's interest in a spiritual empire. The "economic man" of capitalist theory, weighing pleasures and pains in the present world, is a mortal enemy of man the "son of God," with his thoughts on the next world. The rise of capitalism threatened for a time the very existence of the Church.

But with the flexibility of an army long trained in strategy, the Church managed to adjust itself to capitalist economics. Yet it maintained its intransigent opposition to the "liberal" philosophy of capitalism. "Liberalism" to the Vatican meant freedom of thought run amok, trampling the teachings of the past, denying God, asserting the dominance of material self-interest.

The Catholic Church might indeed be expected to be far more ready for a collectivist or planned economy than the Protestant Churches. It is worldly-wise enough to know that a return to feudalism is impossible, and its intellectual leaders have sought to outline a "new" and "Christian social order." Yet necessarily it is an implacable foe of Marxism, which declared "religion the opium of the people," and it has shied from the word "socialism" as indelibly tainted with atheism.

The fountainhead of Catholic social doctrine is the encyclical "Rerum Novarum" enunciated by Leo XIII in 1891. Its principles were repeated and elaborated by Pius XI in "Quadragesimo Anno" in 1931. The Popes announce their respect for private property and inequalities of wealth—quite understandably in view of the Church's material and intellectual heritage—but insist that property is always subject to social obligations and liable to social controls. The "interventionist" state is accepted as a matter of course, in contrast to the liberalistic doctrine, so dear to American business, that the state should merely be an umpire, never interfering with economic activity except to see that the rules of the game are observed. The encouragement given by Rome to the unionization of workers and the emphasis on collective responsibility of industry and finance, have justified the development in many Catholic quarters of the syndicalist and corporative theories. Since in recent years and months the dangers of totalitarianism, even in a corporative system like Mussolini's, have become apparent, there has been an increasing emphasis on democracy. The corporative state envisioned by many Catholics is a democratic corporative state.*

* At a remarkable Catholic conference in Milwaukee in May, 1938, to formulate a "Christian social order," such a system was put forward as the realization of the "American" ideal. Self-governing industries and professions,

The constitution of Portugal is sometimes cited as coming closest to the Catholic ideal, and is therefore worth brief attention. To be sure, Portugal is under a dictatorship. But this is considered a temporary necessity, because of the troubled state of the world and of Portugal's immediate past, and Professor Salazar is considered an eminently desirable type of dictator, who governs as closely as possible according to Portugal's quite superior constitution. The Church in Portugal was not the dominant landholder as in Spain, its power was in eclipse in the first years of the republic after 1911, and in consequence it has apparently been able to play a not unprogressive role.

The present regime sprang out of a military revolt against the republic in 1926, and its origins were reactionary enough: democratic institutions were abolished, the railways were returned to private ownership, an income tax was abolished, and replaced with crushing sales taxes; the social services haltingly inaugurated under the republic were curtailed. Dr. Salazar, Professor of Financial Law at the University of Coimbra, was brought in as Finance Minister to balance the budget in 1928. In 1932 he became Prime Minister and virtual dictator. In 1933 the present constitution was adopted.

This constitution is important in so far as it represents a structure of which the Catholic Church approves, and regardless of the extent to which it may still be merely a pious aspiration.

The state is declared to be a "unitary and corporative republic founded on the equality of its citizens before the law, the free access of all classes to the benefits of civilization, and the participation of all structural elements of the nation in its administrative life and the enactment of its laws." Civil rights and free elections are guaranteed (but loopholes permit the suspension of the former, and a single official slate of candidates has circumvented the electoral rights). Besides a National Assembly there is a Corporative Chamber, purely advisory, and including administrative and cultural representation as well as economic.

"The economic organization of the nation must provide the

along with co-operatives, all emphasizing decentralized autonomy, were declared to provide an alternative to both fascism and communism. A meeting of American bishops, also last year, instructed priests to educate those in their charge in the meaning of democracy.

maximum production and wealth for the welfare of society, and create a collective existence from which the State shall derive power and the citizens justice. . . . It shall be the right and duty of the State to supervise the co-ordination and control of economic and social life with the following objects,"—including "a proper balance of the population, the professions, occupations, capital and labor," a supervision of investment, and maintenance of low prices and high wages, "by means of the improvement of technical methods, services and credit." At the same time private enterprise is to be encouraged and state interference permitted only "to secure greater social benefits." Finally "the State shall promote the formation and development of the national corporative economic system," requiring the co-operation of capital and labor, banning strikes and lockouts, and encouraging "community concerns and provident, co-operative and mutual benefit institutions."

Behind these vague but significant pronouncements there is some evidence of a trend not unlike those we have been describing elsewhere. In the banking field, though Portugal has always been a satellite of the Bank of England, most of the internal banking system is in public hands; a State Savings Bank not only marshals private saving but holds the commercial bank balances, government funds and pension funds, and thus in effect dominates investment. In 1935 a fifteen-year "Reconstruction" Plan was announced, with its chief emphasis on public works. Foreign trade is subject to various controls, the autarchic trend being observable in a campaign for self-sufficiency in wheat and rice, and the rationalization of exports through compulsory cartels for the port wine and sardine industries. In the attempt at rural improvement and the promotion of local community enterprises, "Workpeople's Halls" have been established in the villages as community centers, supposed to promote the social attitudes of a "great family."

Whether anything really significant in the way of new social institutions will emerge in Portugal is perhaps doubtful. But such slight indications as these of experiments with an ostensibly democratic corporative system throw some light on the present role and objectives of the Catholic Church.

# Chapter Ten

## DEMOCRACY STUMBLES INTO PLANNING

IT HAS been said that the American reading public is far more concerned over war in Europe than the European. Besides the full news in the daily press, a constant stream of books and magazine articles is published in America on the maneuvers of the European diplomatic and military game. In addition there have been numerous exhaustive studies of the Soviet Union and its economy, and a growing literature on the nature of fascism in Italy and Germany. Meanwhile the vitally important but more prosaic changes that have been taking place in the economic arrangements of the democratic states have been virtually unsung.

Until Marquis Childs' alluring picture of Sweden a couple of years ago, the average intelligent American was wholly ignorant of the brave efforts of the Scandinavian and other small countries to meet the pressing requirements of the post-war world. The far more significant experiments in Fabian and Tory Socialism in England and in the *économie dirigée* in France have yet to be fully told: there are still educated people in America who think the New Deal is a unique American aberration.

The reason this story has not been told probably lies in the fact that it was to no one's interest to tell it—perhaps even to no one's interest to understand it. On the continent of Europe the Marxian belief that only the industrial working class could lead an advance to a socialist society, an opinion shared in diluted form by the British Labour party, meant that when concrete steps were taken toward economic planning or collective controls, even under the initiative of a Social-Democratic or Labour party, their significance was not understood if they did not conform to preconceptions about the nature of socialism and the role of the working class. And when such steps were taken on the initiative of conservative groups, neither side was likely to boast.

It is true that in no European country was the fetish of the do-nothing state worshiped as in America. "Interventionism," as we saw in an earlier chapter, was common enough before the war; England and Germany in particular had extensive systems of social insurance, and wide public ownership of utilities and services. The war and the troublous times that followed the war, leading up to the Great Depression of the thirties, called urgently for governmental action in one sphere of economic activity after another. But almost no one, either in governmental or academic intellectual circles, attempted any convincing rationale of what was going on. Even today, with all the interim discussion of economic planning, socialism, communism, fascism, and the problems of capitalism, I know of no adequate attempt at a synthesis that could bring some sort of order out of that bewildering mass of facts.

This chapter does not pretend to any such adequacy. It is only intended to suggest a few of the typical instances of collectivism, which have been worked out in a process of trial and error, as a resultant of many conflicting class and group pressures in the disconcertingly complex democratic countries during this post-war period.

Various ways of classifying the phenomena might suggest themselves if one were to attempt a thorough study. One could proceed according to the various levels of governmental activity, from the mildest sort of general police regulation, such as parking ordinances, all the way to government operation of specific industries, like radio broadcasting. One might classify in terms of the class or group interest responsible for the initial pressure, or of the interest controlling the government at the time a step was taken—though it might be very difficult to sort out the interests behind the taking over of the English coal mines under a Tory government. One might classify by economic function, covering in turn devices at the consumer end such as co-operatives, then controls over finance, banking, money and investment, and finally legislation and organization affecting labor at the producer end; that would still leave problems of foreign trade, planning for conservation and utilization of natural resources, rationalization of industry, and so forth.

In this chapter I shall content myself with mention of a few highlights in Scandinavia, France and the British Empire.

### *The Middle Way: Co-operatives?*

Marquis Childs' book, *Sweden: the Middle Way*, described the Scandinavian pattern in a way particularly appealing to those middle-class circles which had been desperately seeking a "middle way" between communism and an apparently collapsing capitalism. The sub-title was unfortunate, however, for it misled readers (and I suspect perhaps the author, too) into believing Sweden had found a solution, an answer, a more or less Utopian social order, rather than having merely shown the ability to move forward along a democratic road toward a goal that was still not formulated, much less achieved.

The Scandinavian pattern comprises four elements: first, a strong, responsible, recognized labor movement, Marxian in ideas but fairly conservative in action; second, a strong left-wing political movement, committed in theory to labor action for socialism, but astute in its alliances with agricultural and other interests behind a reformist program, enabling it to win political dominance; third, a growing policy of state intervention in every phase of the economy when called for; fourth, an impressive co-operative movement.

The first two need not concern us here. It is worth noting, however, that the Scandinavian labor and socialist movements have apparently learned more about the importance of the middle classes from Hitler's conquests than have similar movements elsewhere. Though lip-service is still occasionally paid to the concept of proletarian socialism, in practice labor has admitted it cannot exercise effective power unless it joins with non-proletarian elements, and the notion of a complete theoretical socialism has been conveniently laid on the shelf.

As for state intervention in economic processes, the response to constantly changing pragmatic needs has been necessarily of no very coherent pattern. It does seem, however, as if Scandinavian leaders were coming closer to an understanding of the basic problems of enlarging productivity, promoting a steadily rising level of production, and maintaining a balance in foreign trade, investment and public works.

In Sweden the state owns (either outright, or through corporations with a dominant state interest) the forests, the mineral resources, many power sites and "yardstick" plants, as well as a dominating power "grid" of transmission lines in process of construction, the communications system, part of the railroad system, liquor and tobacco monopolies; it has made some impression on the housing shortage, chiefly by encouraging co-operative building societies; it has had a carefully planned public works program which it applies to smooth off depression and unemployment more successfully than elsewhere (its epoch-making budget policies in this connection are discussed in a later chapter); it is moving toward what has been called a "nationalization of consumption," involving free meals, clothes and shoes for children, free health services, and various subsidies, loans and privileges for large families, all with the purpose of combating an alarming decline in the birth rate; it has almost isolated agriculture from the disastrous play of the world market, monopolizing the home market for domestic production, and maintaining a stable price level, through such devices as crop loans to store surpluses.

Norway has been putting an increasing emphasis on expansion of the productive plant through subsidies, and government directed investment by means of a government controlled industrial bank. Shipbuilding, rayon manufacture, iron, steel and power are subject to nationalization under the present Labor party's program, though the alliance with the Farmers' party is slowing down this trend. The government is keeping up agricultural prices, and maintains an agricultural bank that has greatly decreased foreclosure of farms.

Denmark is almost wholly agricultural, and its national existence is consequently largely dependent on foreign trade, chiefly with England and Germany. The comparative well-being of the country in recent years has resulted from a state policy of financing the resettlement of the farmers on the former feudal estates, and of carefully conserving its resources and balancing its foreign trade. The Social Democrats here as in the two other countries are in the majority.

It is perhaps the co-operative movement of Scandinavia which has received most attention, and for the last two or three years a flood of summer tourists from America has been descending on the Scandinavian landscape, eager for a co-operative Utopia. As a matter of fact consumers' co-operatives have grown to much vaster proportions in England than in Scandinavia. But their advances into production in Sweden have been more spectacular, attacking as they did some of the most powerful private monopolies.

Marketing co-operatives, for collective bargaining in the sale of agricultural products, was the first step in the co-operative movement in Scandinavian countries (as in America). But when farmers get together to pool their sales it is natural to make the next step, to pooling their purchases. In Denmark a single national co-operative, including 90 per cent of the farm population, has carried the combination of marketing and consumer co-operation to its ultimate extreme.

One-third of the households of Sweden are enrolled in consumer co-operatives, and between 10 and 20 per cent of the retail trade is carried on in co-operative stores on a non-profit basis. A marked effect in lowering the general retail price level has been claimed. As the consumers' co-operative movement found its strength, it felt it had the financial resources and a sufficiently assured market, to engage in manufacture in certain selected fields where monopoly conditions maintained artificially high prices. Margarine, electric light bulbs, rubber goods, were some of the more dramatic. In 1934 only 2 per cent of all manufacturing was carried on in co-operative factories, however.

It might be well at this point to look at some of the larger aspects of the co-operative movement generally, and to consider the significance of this type of economic collectivism for the problem I have posed in this book. In Great Britain about half the households belong to co-operative societies, and their purchases in 1935 amounted to over a billion dollars, an estimated 12 per cent of the country's total retail trade. At the same time, productive enterprises carried on by the co-operative movement turned out goods valued at over 350 million dollars. In the United States the consumers' co-operative movement is younger and the competition of the chain grocery store has blocked its expansion into the area which has been most promising in Europe; its retail business has amounted to about half a billion dollars, a smaller percentage than in England, but nevertheless growing rapidly; it has only begun to venture into the production field.

Co-operative enthusiasts have sometimes expounded the theory that co-operation offers a means of completely transforming the economic system, of abolishing the capitalist system and production for profit in favor of a "co-operative commonwealth" with "production for use." There is no doubt that in a number of European countries and even in the United States the co-operative movement is today a formidable economic interest, and that it is almost certain to continue to grow unless submerged by totalitarianism as in Russia and Germany. It may be considered one of the most important elements in the world-wide evolution of new forms of group economic activity.

So far, however, the evidence does not justify the hope that a consumers' co-operative movement, even if it were to embrace the whole population, would ever absorb all distribution, or expand its productive activities till it embraced the larger part of economic activity in "production for use." In spite of the objections to extension of state activity expressed by some co-operators, it is fairly obvious that such services as power, transportation and communication could not be handled by consumers any better than by the state (which in such cases would be merely another name for the same people). Co-operative enterprise, moreover, can have little effect on the major problems of monetary and banking control, foreign trade and exchange, and public investment in the capital goods industries to overcome depression and unemployment. Co-operatives, even when they have extended into the manufacture of many consumer goods, can have little other effect on the national income and the flow of purchasing power than large "private" corporations with many stockholders: profits are less and are more widely dispersed, prices are lower, and the income of middlemen is largely eliminated (which, incidentally, may tend to increase unemployment and poverty in that occupational field). A legitimate doubt may be expressed, too, whether a so-called co-operative enterprise, when it has thousands of members over a wide geographical area and sells more or less standardized products, can function very differently from a capitalist undertaking, or offer any advantage over the higher type of private enterprise.

It may be doubted whether any real democratic control can be maintained in such a case.

Consumer co-operatives have, I think, a more important role to play during this present transitional period than in any ultimate new economic order. They provide a standing example of the ability of business enterprise to carry on without an enterpriser's profit motive. They provide a standing inspiration to those who want to see democracy function in the economic sphere. They can educate a growing public to the possibilities of group action in economic practices generally, and in every country they have therefore tended to strengthen the socialist political movements. But in a consciously controlled economy where prices were rationally determined, where there was no incentive to poor quality or to restriction of production, and where the economic mechanism was geared closely to individual consumer choices expressed through the market, true consumer co-operatives would find most of their functions gone.*

### *Blundering Progress in France*

France is in some respects the most backward of the great powers today. The Revolution of 1789 established the peasant on his land and consolidated the position of the petty bourgeois tradesman and rentier, all of which gave stability to the economic and social structure. Up to the war, social legislation and interferences with the free play of competition were far less than in Germany and England. But the war put a vast strain on the whole economy, production and transportation had to be maintained at a high level of efficiency, the rebuilding of ruined cities required government funds and government initiative, the financial shocks of the

* The destruction of the independence of the consumer co-operatives in the Soviet Union and the fascist states is partly due, no doubt, to the sheer pressure of totalitarianism, which cannot tolerate independent organizations. But partly it is due to the fact that their functions dwindle under economic planning. On the other hand, producer co-operatives and marketing co-operatives are likely to flourish in a planned economy. The Soviet collective farms and the artels of artisans are essentially producer co-operatives. And the more democratic a planned economy is the more producer co-operatives may flourish, as a means of integrating individual producers with the rest of the economy. Marketing co-operatives for farmers may provide a government with all the administrative machinery it needs for rationalizing agriculture.

war produced inflation and led to practices of monetary management and, more recently, the impact of the depression and the menace of war have speeded up the whole pace of governmental activity in the economic sphere.

In most of the period since the war, conservative business interests have been dominant in politics. Intervention was at the behest of the huge trusts dominating most industrial fields, and its aims were the safeguarding of the home market, the stabilizing of prices and competitive conditions, and the promoting of public works and public services which were too risky or unprofitable for private enterprise. With the coming into power of the People's Front under Léon Blum the process was hastened and given a more truly social emphasis, but the underlying trend was not greatly changed.

A National Economic Council was established in 1925. First proposed by the Confédération Générale de Travail (the "C.G.T." corresponds to the A. F. of L. in America) to provide an advisory planning board with representation from labor, consumers, government and business, Premier Poincaré was its first presiding officer, and it developed few functions beyond those of a technical fact-finding body; occasionally it has recommended rationalization (*i.e.*, elimination of competition!) in an industry.

Military interest probably predominated in the setting up of the National Liquid Fuel Office, which licenses oil importers and refiners on condition of their maintaining adequate reserves. Legislation forecasts a government oil monopoly, and there is a "mixed" (half-public, half-private) oil company, with government supervision of management, already doing a large part of the business. Considerations of defense also had much to do with the state domination of shipping: the government has for some time had control of the board of directors of the Compagnie Générale Transatlantique, the major shipping interest, in return for essential subsidies.

A general scheme of social insurance, covering sickness, childbirth, invalidity, old age and death, was enacted in 1930.

A vast system of import quotas and price controls has thrust the laissez faire world market into limbo so far as France is concerned. The inflationary and deflationary troubles of the post-war franc kept producing unexpected repercussions which required further adjustments. The farmer's vote being often of controlling importance, the ups and downs of currencies and world prices resulted in protective devices.

If control of foreign trade and control of prices are essential features of a planned economy, then France has gone a long way, though there has been little co-ordination of these controls. Three thousand items, including practically all agricultural products, have been on the import quota list. Some degree of price control has been imposed on coal, gas, oil, alcohol, electricity, iron and steel, aluminum, tinplate, chemicals, building materials, rail passenger and freight rates, and such agricultural products as wheat, bread, milk, butter and sugar. Most of these controls are less in the interest of consumers than of the producers concerned.

The Office du Blé, or Wheat Board, allocates marketing quotas to farmers, fixes minimum prices, and by handling much of the marketing itself has virtually eliminated the speculative grain market. All the parties at interest have a voice in regard to fixing prices. Under the Popular Front a complete socialization of grain marketing under co-operatives passed the Chamber but was stopped in the Senate.

The Office du Blé is one of a large number of autonomous boards, in form virtually private corporations, with the government in control and usually owning the stock. Among these are the Alsatian Potash Mines (controlling two-thirds of the industry), the State Railway, the National Liquid Fuel Office, the National Agricultural Credit Bank, the ports of Havre and Bordeaux and others, the Industrial Nitrates Office, the Caisse des Dépôts et Consignations (for investing savings bank funds), the National Factories of Sèvres and Gobelins making porcelain and tapestries. Recently the whole railway system was unified under the National Railways Company, of which the government owns a majority of the stock.

Rural electrification has gone forward under state initiative, 20,000 rural communes having been electrified by 1934, with a billion and a half francs of public funds expended between 1928 and 1932. The nation's forests are owned and managed by the state. Public works, with an emphasis on improving the "national equipment," have had a growing importance as a means of relieving unemployment, and 75 per cent of the social insurance funds may now be turned into that channel. A considerable housing program was started in 1928, and in the next five years 180,000 cheap dwellings were built, with the government lending up to 80 per cent of the cost, and granting tax remissions and other subsidies. The Paris Municipal Office alone found itself *managing* 16,000 dwellings.

Most of these measures in the way of public enterprise in the economic field were taken without active opposition from business interests, and many of them were at their behest. When the Blum government tackled the Bank of France and the munitions industries, the opposition to "socialism" became vocal. But even in these two cases it is probable that they could not have been accomplished if there had been no other incentive than a desire for "socialism": as a matter of fact, the Bank of France was ruled by so tight an oligarchy as to have won the enmity of a considerable part of the business world, and the munitions plants were of military concern.

The new banking legislation abolished the virtually hereditary "regents" of the Bank of France, and put it under the control of a Council of twenty, of which nine are government representatives, and the rest representatives of various economic interests: a government able to command the support of the farmers and the labor movement would thus have a majority. The central bank has thus become potentially a government organ. Actually its operation has not been greatly changed: the Blum government was unable to pursue any very daring financial policy; and under the Daladier regime the administration of the bank is probably not much different from what it was before the People's Front victory. Yet the center of gravity has definitely shifted to the government.

As for the munitions plants, only the airplane factories were taken over by Blum; nationalization was by means of a semi-public corporation, two-thirds owned by the state, which exchanged its securities for those of the old private companies. Since the Munich settlement and the more feverish demand for rearmament, the pressure for "war collectivism" has doubled. There has been talk of industrial mobilization and conscription, even of "totalitarian" economic planning, as the only hope for catching up with German armament.

France is in a highly fluid state, with no trends fixed. Sometimes reactionary forces are put in a radical light, as when the Daladier government broke the general strike which had been called to protest lengthening of the work week: the government temporarily "nationalized" the key industries and the public services, and it argued, with some justice, that the country must increase production rather than curtail it, whether it was to have peace or war. The labor forces, the military forces, and the capitalists are in a curious three-cornered battle, with the peasants and middle classes, as usual, holding the balance of power.

When Blum came in, a newly unified and rejuvenated labor movement, five million strong, much under Marxist influence, seemed to have the upper hand. The setting of a forty-hour week, the guarantee of two-week vacations with pay, with a new Department of Leisure to arrange cheap holiday excursions and cultural activities (reminiscent of the German *Kraft Durch Freude* and the Italian *Dopolavoro*)—these were high points of labor's social gains; but they may have less effect on the attainment of economic planning than such a measure as the Collective Contracts Act which followed the first big wave of strikes and the Matignon agreement. This measure sought to avoid labor disputes by providing for regularly negotiated labor contracts, covering industries as a whole, and binding on all members of the industry.*

It is probably the military interest which is dominant in the present emphasis on increased production. It seems as if, for the moment, the almost universal craving for military security had played into the hands of Big Business and had destroyed the People's Front and put labor definitely on the defensive. Yet there is no reason to suppose that the collectivist trend has been halted.

The emphasis on increased production and productivity is in fact more and more a popular demand, likely to have a distinctly progressive effect. Public works have long been considered as increasing the nation's productive equipment—"outillage"—rather than as mere emergency stop-gaps. Even war preparation, as we have seen, may be a means of approach to an "economy of

* This was partly in imitation of the NRA codes, for the People's Front in France consciously sought to bring "Le New Deal" to France. But it is outwardly more like Mussolini's "corporative" system.

abundance." But there is a growing search for a more intelligent approach.

Several minor political groups in the last few years have been laying stress on the necessity for abandoning the narrow concept of a worker-capitalist class struggle and developing a program of abundant production as the only means of assuring that the middle classes will not turn to fascism. Such was Bergéry's group around the newspaper *Flèche*, a left-wing offshoot of the Radical Socialists, and the Marquet-Déat defection from the Socialist party a few years before. A similar drift was indicated by the Charpentier-Duboin group, which drew some of its original inspiration from the American "technocracy" movement.

As a matter of fact, there is evidence in many of the smaller European countries of a search for a non-Marxian socialism which can win the middle classes by stressing increased production. The ideas of Henri de Man in Belgium, a dissident Socialist group in Holland, the "Folk-Socialists" who for a time were active among the German Social-Democrats in Prague, and who played with the idea of a coalition with the left-wing Nazis of Strasser's movement, the Social Democratic and Labor parties of Scandinavia—all these seem to portend a shift in socialist thinking.

### *Tory Socialists and Fabians*

The "inevitability of gradualism" was put forth as a doctrine most clearly in England. The trends we are discussing might be expected to show themselves likewise most clearly in that stronghold of classical capitalism. It was this country which furnished most of the material for Marx's thesis. It has dominated economic theory to such an extent that "capitalism" has been aptly defined as "what happened in England in the nineteenth century." England furnished models for much of the New Deal legislation, being always a few years ahead of American developments in such matters as unemployment insurance, old-age pensions and health insurance.

All the collectivist tendencies I have mentioned can be found in England in some degree. The growth of bureaucratic administrative interferences, thanks both to business requirements and to the reproductive powers of any bureaucracy, was denounced as "the new despotism" in the still hopeful days of the twenties. The requirements of military collectivism, first obvious during the World War of 1914-18, have exercised a continuing and increasing pressure, for rearmament has been not only a depression remedy, but in recent months an apparent condition for national survival. The growing preponderance of organized business and organized labor over free enterprise has fostered social insurances, and, under the application of the Trades Disputes Act, a semi-official system of collective labor contracts, which once more illustrate the "corporative" principle since they are framed industry by industry rather than enterprise by enterprise. The monetary and fiscal problems growing out of the war made the "world's banker" a pioneer in "managed money," to the horror of the orthodox capitalist theorists. England is the world's trader as well as the world's banker, and the dislocations in world trade—new economic nationalisms, autarchy, battles of foreign exchange—naturally called for the stabilizing hand of government: free trade was abandoned as a first step, and the Ottawa Conference to establish "empire preference" was a long second step towards a closed economic system, which by logic of events may in time demand a completely planned internal and external trade.*

But there are certain unique features of the English trends. For one thing there is the strange phenomenon known as "Tory socialism."

From the classic case of the Reform Bill of 1832, demanded by the Chartists and passed by the Tories, most of the steps to the left in England have been taken when conservatives were in power. The Labour party's program has repeatedly come nearer realization when it was out of power than when it was in. How can one explain a ruling class taking measures that tend to eliminate it?

A few years ago I spent a week-end at Cliveden, the Astors' estate overlooking the Thames. The great palace with its miles of wooded park, once the heritage of the Dukes of Buckingham, was more lavishly maintained, so I heard, than any other old estate in England in these evil days. Lord and Lady Astor had an American background and an American income; but they were nonetheless, with their seats in the House of Lords and the House of Com-

* The recent reciprocal trade treaty with America may turn out to be as much an instance of planning as of a return to freer trade.

mons, pretty close to the top of the English ruling class. Recently much has been said in liberal quarters about the reactionary influence on British policy of the "Cliveden set," and Prime Minister Chamberlain and Foreign Secretary Lord Halifax are constantly reported as plotting the betrayal of British democracy to the interests of the British ruling class at week-ends in Cliveden.

What I found there, at least in Lady Astor, was a person well aware of a rapidly changing world, highly humanitarian (in a social-worker sort of way), ready to consider any social changes no matter how drastic, and quite convinced she would remain on top whatever happened. She had been to the Soviet Union with Bernard Shaw, and came away with a certain hard-headed skepticism, but, so far as I could see, no fear or hatred. In the evening, after dinner, her son from Oxford, an ardent communist sympathizer, launched into a tirade against the iniquity of lavish wealth, and she attempted no other defense than one of good-natured evasion.

I am inclined to believe that with the urbane British aristocracy it is as with the Roman Church. That aristocracy survived the transition from feudalism to capitalism, shifting its interests from land to industrial capital, and flexibly adjusting itself, except for the brief unpleasantness of the Stuarts and Cromwell, to the requirements of a new economy. Where the stubborn and stupid French aristocracy lost their heads, the British retained theirs, and their supremacy. Consciously or unconsciously they must hope to do the same in the present transition. They are certain of their superiority—why should they not be top-dog in a collectivist era?

To be sure, this hypothesis would carry little weight if any step toward socialism always meant a corresponding diminution of their wealth and prerogatives. But from the day of the first protective tariff it has been obvious that every extension of state action may conceivably benefit some particular capitalist interest, and be invoked in its behalf, however it may strengthen the general trend toward collectivism.

Let us take a typical and significant instance of "Tory socialism," the Central Electricity Board. In 1926 the power industry was in a chaotic state. There were many hundreds of generating stations, either privately owned or municipally owned. There was no standard frequency. Manufacturers had been able to make far less use of electric power than in the United States, where the great holding company empires of Insull and the like were rapidly rationalizing the power industry and incidentally reaping a rich harvest. Village electrification offered a huge market whose initial capital cost was too great for private enterprise to risk. The Central Electricity Board was the result of extensive parliamentary investigation.

In form the C.E.B. is a corporation, with private capital raised by selling stock to the public. But the stock has no voting rights and the Board is appointed by the Minister of Transport. It is an autonomous business enterprise, charged with certain duties by the government which created it. It owns its own assets. The terms private ownership and public ownership are here valueless. The functions of the C.E.B. have been to build a "grid" of transmission lines crisscrossing the country, thus unifying the whole power system. Certain generating plants, private or public, are "selected." They must maintain a standard frequency, and sell all their power at a fixed price to the C.E.B. Distribution again is left in private hands, though rural electrification is publicly promoted. For the most part C.E.B. is merely a broker of electricity.

Admittedly this is only a partially unified power system. Complaints about the quality of service at the distribution end are resulting in increasing demands for a more complete socialization. But there has been no charge that C.E.B. itself, within its existing limits, has been other than a useful and impeccable public service. Its direction has been in the hands of a Board of eight members, now headed by Sir Archibald Page, appointed by the Minister of Transport. Titles seem to have counted neither as an asset nor a liability. The technical competence of the service and those responsible for it has counted for a great deal.

The British Broadcasting Corporation, the London Passenger Transport Board, the London Port Authority, and other autonomous public agencies are all similar in character to the C.E.B. They are not all instances of pure Tory socialism. In fact there is nothing pure about them. They fit no categories of capitalism and socialism. The London Passenger Transport Board, which runs the subways, trams, and buses of the two-thousand-square-mile London area, was the creation principally of Herbert Morrison, Socialist, Labour party chairman of the London County Council; but in the event he seems to have got as much support as opposition from private business interests.*

The group that has given greatest intellectual guidance to the left-wing movement in England is, of course, the Fabians. It is they who have filled the gap that the Marxists otherwise might have filled. Hence the despair of such a communist intellectual as John Strachey, who sees "British socialism" as hopelessly "unscientific" and therefore a betrayal of the workers. In one sense I would be inclined to agree that their approach has been unscientific: the Fabians have tended to see the key to successful "gradualism" in the mere extension of public ownership. The most concrete results here have been municipally owned utilities, and caustic critics have sneered at "gas and water socialism" as a weak substitute for the real thing. And when the Tory Baldwin government took the initiative towards public ownership of the coal industry in 1937 with the blessing of the existing owners of that bankrupt industry, it was easy to point to the fact that public ownership in itself puts scarcely a man to work or increases the national wealth one penny.

Yet the fact that the Fabians have consistently preached the possibility of a gradual and peaceful transition, by an "inevitable" pressure of events, has encouraged the hope that England will indeed accomplish the goal of a functional economy by a surer and less painful process than any other European country. Already, if we consider the scope of public and co-operative enterprise—I have not mentioned housing in this cursory survey—and the extent to which public controls on economic processes have been developed—I have not mentioned the English equivalents of the AAA—we must concede that the unrestricted profit motive is a thing of the past. With the structure of public business that has already been built, with the standards of government service and personnel that have been set up, with the precedents of graceful concession that Tory socialism has implied, the essential steps from England's long familiar New Deal to a full-production economy may be com-

* The London *Times*, primary organ of British Big Business and High Finance, led the defense of the measure against those who said it was "socialistic"; at the end of 1938 it was defending a measure to nationalize the air transport industry against a similar criticism.

paratively short and easy, shorter and easier than the present prevailing pessimism in that country would imply.

In the light of previous suggestions, and in anticipation of later sections of this book, it might be said that a public banking system and suitable controls over investment and foreign trade comprise the essential steps. As for banking, the Bank of England and the five great commercial banks are all privately owned. But in these days when government fiscal management tends to outweigh and dominate central and commercial banking, the process by which England's banks become "nationalized" may be hardly noticeable. It is possible that "The City," like "The Crown," will carry over as a picturesque anachronism into a socialist era. In regard to investment, the armaments program, with its incidental tendency to revivify "depressed areas," sets a precedent for governmentally directed investment that may some day mean an economy of abundance, not of guns but of butter. A managed foreign trade is another development that seems not far over the horizon. In the case of a country like England this is a particularly crucial step.

Marx and Engels had to concede the possibility of a democratic peaceful change to socialism in England, though some of their more recent disciples, lost in gloom, have said they doubted it. The Fabians, through their influence in the Labour party, have trained a generation of workers and middle-class people to take for granted the coming of a new social order, even though they may not have explained to them the technology of such a change. If capitalism is "what happened in England in the nineteenth century" it is not impossible that, whatever the word which popularizes the new social order, it may someday be defined as "What happened in England in the twentieth century."

Any such consideration of England as this must, however, take into account the fact that England is the hub of an empire and a "commonwealth of nations." In India the fact that the independence movement is so largely led by socialists must mean that its future relations to England can never be established on the old familiar lines of economic imperialism: what England gets in future out of investments in India and trade with India is likely to be determined increasingly by what planning boards and trade authorities decide, rather than by what the law of profit might dictate. Canada is economically dependent on the United States, and a generation behind the rest of the world in its economic evolution: at most it may contribute to a scheme of autarchic planning on an empire-wide basis, as suggested in the Ottawa agreements. On the other hand, Australia and New Zealand, with a history of labor governments, and much socialist influence, cannot help but react back on the mother country in so far as they experiment with new economic practices. "Corporative" principles of labor relations, rigid planning of production and marketing of the agricultural export items, public control of banking, and similar phases of the collectivist picture are particularly well developed in New Zealand, but they must necessarily remain limited so long as their relations with the outside world, and particularly the mother country, are determined by a still chaotic system of world trade and war fears.

### *Is America Behind or Ahead?*

My globe-circling search for facts, of which I have given the results in the last half-dozen chapters, was of a different kind from my first world tour (in the flesh), when I had no idea what to look for.

On my return to this country from the first tour, as I related in the beginning of this book, I was convinced that there was a sharp distinction between two possible economic and social systems, "capitalism" and "socialism." I saw America as definitely a land of "capitalism," with a "capitalist" government. Even when Hoover gave way to Roosevelt, I believed the New Deal was only another makeshift attempt to save a collapsing "capitalist" system. I was convinced that neither of the two old parties could accomplish the transition to "socialism," so a new party with a definite program of "socialization" was essential.

When I returned to America from my fact-finding search I saw this country rushing headlong on the road to collective economic controls, where most of the rest of the world, in various vehicles, had already gone. But the words "socialism" and "communism" and "capitalism" had lost their charm. Even "collectivism" was only a poor substitute. New procedures were being developed here, as abroad, which none of the old labels would fit. Yet I was more ready to sympathize with the conservatives who were howling "socialist" at everything the New Dealers attempted: previously I had thought them insincere, for it was clear that the New Dealers were really trying to save "capitalism," not destroy it, but now I realized that the ultimate result of all this "saving" would be as different from the old system as if a revolution were really taking place.*

At the same time it was clear that this swift development of public controls over economic procedures was inevitable. The pressures for governmental intervention were coming from all sides, from business and finance often as much as from the workers and farmers. It almost appeared that the leadership made little difference: much of the New Deal had actually been begun by Hoover, and it was conceivable that much of it would be carried on if conservative Republicans came back to power.

The especially swift pace of the New Deal, as compared to developments in the democratic countries abroad, was due neither to the "radicalism" nor to the "lust for power" of Mr. Roosevelt. Even making due allowances for his exceptional type of leadership, the fact was that the United States had fallen far behind European progress in new social controls during the glorious prosperity of the twenties: we didn't need them then, and when we did need them we needed them all at once.

When I looked over the New Deal measures I saw little that was unfamiliar in the light of European developments—except the difference of timing. I was still quite unprepared to give a rational explanation of what was happening. I still had no theory to explain the facts, or to determine just what were the essential differences between a laissez faire economy and an intelligent managed economy. But it was obvious that the same economic compulsions were at work everywhere, and that the same types of institutions were resulting. In some cases there were close parallels even to what was happening in the totalitarian regimes; but for the most part our progress was the same kind of pragmatic blundering to meet emergencies which had gone on in the democratic nations ever since the war.

* The English prototypes of the Liberty Leaguers cannot easily understand the frantic opposition to Roosevelt's measures, since their own Conservative governments have put through almost identical measures. But "Tory socialism" has the advantage of giving the Tories the illusion of controlling events.

The first emergency was that of hunger. Every community has always considered that it had a primary interest in the survival of its members, though this country so glorified "rugged individualism" and the laissez faire ideal in the nineteenth century that for a while during the depression we let people starve (we still do occasionally, but it has become exceptional). The New Deal leaped into the breach left by bankrupt cities and states, and fed the hungry—through FERA, PWA, CWA, WPA and other agencies. Other countries had social insurances to carry part of the burden of unemployment and poverty, but our burden was so much greater it could only be met by emergency forms of relief. With the Social Security Act, however, we made a beginning in catching up with similar systems abroad. And with the Wages and Hours Bill we finally achieved recognition of another principle, long accepted abroad, that to guarantee against hunger requires putting a floor under wages.

This fight against abject poverty carried two connotations in America which similar measures did not carry abroad. The first was that the much more vigorous American doctrine of laissez faire was now impossible to uphold if the government was to maintain a basic minimum standard of consumption. The "gentlemen in well-stocked clubs" had a right to be alarmed. Grant that government has an obligation to keep its citizens alive, and logic carries you to alarming conclusions. For in a land where "all men are created equal" and where the "American standard of living" is a national fetish, the people are not content with mere soup kitchens. You are well on the way to what the Swedes call the "nationalization of consumption"—and that, looked at from the proper perspective, is not very different from the old socialist doctrine of the "socialization of production." Inevitably the idea gained acceptance that the country owes every man, woman and child a living, and an ample living.

To be sure, the New Deal has not yet gone very far. It is not yet even able to guarantee its future citizens against undernourishment, as numerous official and unofficial reports have proved. Public opinion, when asked to express itself, still clings nostalgically to the notion that there is something sinful about relief and about accepting relief. The well-to-do, who feel (usually unjustifiably) that they pay for relief, have dinned into the public's ear, with a thousand effective tongues, that the country's "moral fiber" is weakened by the practice of assuring people a livelihood.* But in spite of these hangovers from an earlier period the idea is here to stay—and grow. And it is incompatible with a system of economic individualism.

The second connotation of unemployment relief in America grows in a sense out of the first. If private enterprise cannot assure everybody a job at a living wage, and must leave the support of millions to society, why should society waste all this potentially wealth-producing labor? Why should hard-working taxpayers support others in idleness—and demoralize them in the bargain? Americans feel particularly strongly that a man needs to work for his bread if he is to secure any nourishment from it; the notion has gained acceptance that a man is "entitled" to a job. So the government has turned to work relief. And from "leaf-raking" and "boondoggling" it has turned to building schools and parks and bridges, and improving the community services.

Public enterprise of this kind, however, is cumulative. It grows of its own inner drive. When Middletown gets a fine new schoolhouse out of WPA, nearby Centerville wants one, too. Moreover, public enterprise cannot be curtailed suddenly without at once affecting purchasing power, not only for the reliefer, but for several others besides who are furnishing materials, or are producing what the reliefer himself buys. Cut down work relief and depression returns. The economic mechanism comes to depend more and more on public business. The maintenance of a minimum standard of living ends by becoming a growing public sector of the economy. It makes little difference how those who worship folklore splutter and deplore, or those who put human welfare first applaud.

There were other emergencies besides hunger and unemployment, however. In spite of the old American timidity towards the "interventionist" state, there was no escape. Every interest was demanding rescue. Hoover sent the RFC to rescue the banks and the railroads. The AAA followed under Roosevelt, to rescue the farm-

* Curiously enough the well-to-do consider it their greatest privilege to do just that for their own children.

ers. Labor, small business, big business, all were asking help. Relief, recovery and reform were all mixed together in the rush of new institutions, which, while laughed at as "alphabet soup," were all welcomed by some powerful interest demanding some kind of protection from the ill winds of insecurity.

That government is "in business up to its neck" is now a matter of course. Most of its activities are familiar enough, either as outgrowths of earlier encroachments of our own government, or as part of the post-war European pattern.

One way to measure the growing role of government is to compare the governmental budget with the national income. In the socialist state of Soviet Russia the budget, on both income and outgo side, has been as much as 80 per cent of the national income. In Germany governmental expenditures are half as large as the national income. In the United States all public outlays, federal, state and local, rose from 10 per cent of the national income produced in 1915, and 14 per cent in 1929, to 34 per cent in 1932. It is now perhaps 25 per cent.* The problems which business has been unable to solve for itself and has left the government to solve run from railroad transportation to pants pressing. Public services to fill the gaps left by private enterprise extend from issuing bulletins on the proper pinning of diapers to throwing dams across the Tennessee River.

There are innumerable facets to this growing governmental activity, of course, but this is not the place to list them. There are some special procedures I wish to cite, however, resembling similar procedures abroad, which have a particular significance for our inquiry.

One is the growth of what in Italy, and in Catholic social doctrine, we have seen called "corporativism." This means essentially the attempt to *organize interests*, and bring them into co-operation

* Again let me make clear that these figures do not mean, as those who denounce the "tax-eaters" contend, that these amounts are *subtracted* from the national income, either here or in Russia. The fact that 30 per cent of the nation's business is done by large corporations does not mean that the people are 30 per cent poorer (though there is more truth in this statement than the preceding). The above figures merely signify that, measured in money terms, one-quarter of the nation's business is now public business. See above, pages 115, 159, 171-172.

where they conflict.* Business men have long practiced this in their trade associations. Any collective bargaining, whether of organized workers with employers, or of organized consumers (in co-operatives) with producers, is a step in this direction. The most ambitious attempt made in any democratic country was the NRA, in which the government directly fostered trade associations to represent industries, and trade unions to represent workers. Consumer representation was also sought. The NRA failed to achieve its aim because there had been no training or experience available to make representation of worker and consumer interest effective, and the trade associations had it all their own way in the "code authorities."

Under the present Wagner Labor Relations Act the effort is limited to collective bargaining between labor and individual businesses. But following the report of the President's Committee on British and Swedish labor relations in the summer of 1938, it is probable that collective bargaining by industry rather than by enterprise will be encouraged. And there has been continuing talk of a new NRA, in which the representation of ownership and management might be in a minority as opposed to the representation of the government, the consumers and labor.

The AAA was also an experiment in "corporativism." Far greater democracy was possible in organizing agriculture. Farmers are brought together county by county and product by product, to vote on the application of production and marketing quotas and to see to their enforcement. Unfortunately the consumer interest is again difficult to represent: no slum child can protest if the milk controls lessen his consumption of milk. But the New Deal agricultural organization is as democratic as present conditions allow.

A second significant new procedure is that of the autonomous public corporation, similar to those we noted in England. The usual form is that of a private corporation, but the capital is more likely to be raised from the government than from individuals. Sometimes, as in the case of the TVA, the organization is not called a corporation, but is still able to raise capital by borrowing

* "Corporativism" suggests neither dictatorship nor democracy. As we shall see later, it may be as important a technique of democracy as in Italy it is a technique of dictatorship. See below, pages 307 note, and 381.

from the public. On the financial pages of the paper you will find a listing of all sorts of securities of public corporations and authorities, which are traded in like government bonds and private securities. The HOLC, FDIC, and FFMC (Home Owners Loan Corporation, Federal Deposit Insurance Corporation and Federal Farm Mortgage Corporation) were all financed with private capital. In other cases one government agency will "own" all the stock of another, as in the familiar private holding company procedure; thus the HOLC subscribed to all the capital stock of the Federal Savings and Loan Insurance Corporation.

The question of "ownership" in all these cases is even more metaphysical than in the case of the American Tel. & Tel. and other big "private" corporations, which I discussed in an earlier chapter. The whole distinction between the words "public" and "private" is breaking down more and more. In the typical large corporation of private enterprise the capital is furnished by many stockholders and bondholders; the stockholders alone are considered "owners," but to all intents and purposes modern corporation law simply recognizes in the various types of "senior" and "junior" security holders, merely greater or less claim to the assets or earnings of the corporation. And this scattered ownership of claims stands over against a concentrated control of management. Very often this control is in the hands of bankers who represent "creditors" rather than "owners," that is, merely one particular set of claims as against another.

Now, the government may come into the picture with various types of claims. When it went into the banking business itself, with the RFC, it found itself in a position to dictate to corporations to which it had lent money, just as a private banker might do.* In the case of the autonomous public corporations it has complete control, even though all the capital may be raised "privately." In the case of the various regulatory bodies, such as the Federal Communications Commission, it represents the claim of

* When Stuart Chase examined the RFC's "portfolio" a few years ago he found two thousand small utilities, three insurance companies and a railroad, as well as scores of banks over which the RFC could exercise control. In the case of some of the banks the RFC was given special voting stock as security for its loan; but this would seem to be gilding the lily.

the public to good service and reasonable rates. It has been suggested that the government should represent all absent stockholders by holding their proxies at annual corporation meetings, and since usually only a small minority are personally present this would give the government complete control without any "ownership." The possibilities for a further breaking down of the distinction between "private" and "public" in the corporation field are numerous.

There is another area in which governmental influence on economic activity has grown mightily, as in Europe—the field of money and credit. Our money has become a "managed money" with its gold value subject to change in accordance with what seems the general economic interest.*

Currency is, however, of less importance in modern monetary systems than bank credit. The first move toward control of the volume of bank credit came in 1913 when Woodrow Wilson and Carter Glass established the Federal Reserve System as the equivalent of a central bank, or "banker's bank"; since then the orthodox method of influencing the volume of credit by means of the rediscount rate (which encourages or discourages borrowing by lowering or raising the interest rate) has been in use. But it is hardly effective any longer, so in recent years another method of affecting the volume of credit money has been tried: "open market operations" of Federal Reserve Banks in buying and selling government securities. Roosevelt's Banking Act of 1933 extended this practice, and also subjected the Board of Governors of the Federal Reserve System to definite public control, by requiring a majority of its membership to be political appointees. "Open market operations" have proved to be ineffective, too, at least in enlarging the volume of credit. But in spite of its failures the whole New Deal trend has been toward a greater control of the banking process. If and when the New Deal or a subsequent administration knows what

* Devaluation of the dollar actually had little effect, since every other country was doing the equivalent, and the only remaining significance of the gold base is for trade with other countries. But during the early stages of devaluation its effect on our foreign trade was such that the new Import-Export Bank had to license transactions: for a while we approached the planned barter trade of the authoritarian states.

it wants its banking system to do, the controls will be ready to hand.

The investing process is, as we have seen abroad, of central importance to the volume of purchasing power and the extent of economic activity. Here again our government has had no clear policy, but has nevertheless extended its influence and control for possible future use.* The Securities Exchange Act has begun transforming the exchanges from private gambling clubs, the turn of whose roulette wheels determined whether millions should go hungry or not, into public agencies for the utilization of savings; and it has subjected the issue of new securities to considerable supervision. Moreover, the requirement in the new Banking Act, that commercial and investment banking be separated, may have great significance. Far more important, however, to the investing process is the degree to which governmental spending has taken the place of private investment. And the recent shift to the term "governmental investment" is of the profoundest import.

Virtually all the New Deal depression measures, whether those controlling money and investment or controlling other phases of the economic system, parallel similar measures abroad. And most of the developments abroad find their prototypes here. Even the powerful stimulant to the development of collective economic controls that arms programs have provided abroad is now becoming evident here.

Yet still we have millions of unemployed. Still production lags behind the levels of ten years ago, while the totalitarian states zoom upward. Still we have chronic depression, though characterized by minor booms and "recessions." In spite of all the talk about putting the unemployed back to work and all the heroic effort that has gone into "restoring prosperity," the New Deal has not solved the basic economic problem.

Is the trouble after all that we still cling to a "capitalist system" and that the only remedy is "socialism"? Is the New Deal ham-

* Governmental control of investment is not entirely new in America. "Blue Sky" laws against issuing securities representing only imaginary assets, and regulations governing the proper investment of funds of insurance companies and savings banks, have long been common in the various states. And during the war a Capital Issues Committee was set up nationally to authorize the financing of new capital ventures. The New Deal has not yet gone so far as that.

strung because it is essentially a "capitalist" government—as the Marxists would say, the "executive committee of the ruling class"?

Yet clearly it is no such simple thing as that. If so, why are the wealthy its bitterest enemies? With as much heat and conviction as any Trotskyite, the "ruling class" denounces the New Deal, but declares it "socialism." Yet clearly it is no such simple thing as that, either. The European political labels do not fit. In Europe parties and governments are labeled "Conservative" or "Socialist Labor" or "Radical Socialist" or what not, though the actions they take seem to depend very little on their labels. The New Deal could be given neither a definite class label nor a definite program label. Its only theory is pragmatism—to "do what it takes," as Maury Maverick once put it. The only thing that can be truly said about its class backing is that it does not represent the wealthy class. It does indeed draw its strength from the unprivileged—the workers, the farmers, the unemployed, the Negroes—but in such a way as to make little less appeal to the un-class-conscious middle classes. If the New Deal is concerned with social change it is most certainly untouched by the European concept that social change must depend on the "proletariat." If it is "socialist" it is certainly uninfluenced by Marxian "socialism."

Is that then the reason why the New Deal has failed to solve the basic economic problem—because none but a working-class movement can impose an adequate program? If the New Deal is inadequate, what kind of program would be adequate?

My own search for an answer had led me to the point where I needed a theory. Facts were obviously not enough. I had always shied away from Marxism, feeling it was not relevant to America. Yet Marxism at least had a theory. And its devotees could cite that theory as explaining why neither the New Deal nor its European prototypes had been able to escape the dilemma of "poverty in the midst of plenty." I had to understand that theory before I could decide why it was irrelevant—if indeed it was. I had to know what it had to offer before I looked elsewhere; for I knew that there was no other economic theory that was as all-embracing and impressively complete as Marxism.

Part III of this book, which now follows, is an analysis of Marxist economic theory. The reader who is not interested in

Marxism, or in what I have to say on Marxism, will be able to pick up the thread without difficulty if he turns at once to Part IV. But in so far as this is a record of a personal inquiry, my excursion into Marxism is very definitely part of the story.

# *PART III*

# THROUGH MARXISM DARKLY

# *Chapter Eleven*

## BEARDING THE PROPHET

THE appeal of Marxism, as I have felt it, is the appeal of a religious faith. I should never have been drawn to it because of any intellectual qualities. In so far as it has an intellectual attraction I think it is largely the attraction that any comprehensive and final intellectual "system" has for the mind weary of uncertainties and inconsistencies. But that in itself is more an emotional than a strictly intellectual craving.

My own "personal history" coincided in a curious way with Vincent Sheean's, as we were both introduced to Marxism and felt its pulling power through contact with the same person. Sheean tells in his *Personal History* of meeting Michael Borodin in Hankow in 1927, when Borodin was virtual master of the Chinese revolution. Talking to Borodin was to Sheean like a great illumination. All the dark brutal facts of the world began to fit together in the Marxist pattern, as Borodin, fresh from Moscow as agent of the Communist International, elaborated the theories. The confused elements of economic and social development came into a comprehensible relation to each other: the tangle of trees became a forest; the forests and rivers and mountains and valleys could be seen as a whole, as on a map.

Sheean later tells of the dramatic escape of Madame Borodin from the clutches of the bandit war-lord of Peking, Chang Tsolin; during one stage of the escape Sheean was prepared to smuggle Madame Borodin out as his aunt. He also mentions, without detail, that when first captured the wife of the Communist leader had been saved from immediate execution through the intermediation of my father, who was then engaged on a one-man senatorial inquiry among the armies of China. My father had protested to the grim bandit chief that the summary strangulation of a political prisoner without trial, particularly a woman, would have a bad effect abroad, and, after a tense moment, when the interview nearly resulted in an additional execution, Chang agreed to give her a trial. Sheean tells how the trial judge was bribed, and ran away with his money even before Madame Borodin could escape from the city.

Now it happened, when I was in Moscow four years later, that Madame Borodin—or Comrade Borodiná, as she was more properly called—was the director of an Institute for Foreign Languages, where I applied for a temporary job teaching English (so that I would no longer be a "tourist" but a "worker"). She was most cordial, assigned me a job as a teacher of a class in English conversation for advanced students, and invited me home to meet her husband. There I came up against that same leonine personality which had so overwhelmed Sheean—also with lasting effect.

Though he was then reduced to minor officialdom, Borodin was as impressive, without putting on any airs, as if he had been still master of the fate of five hundred million Chinese. For a whole evening he talked about China and Russia and communism. I felt, as I had frequently felt since I first entered the Soviet Union, like an infidel from a distant country: I could observe and marvel at the faith of these devotees, but obviously the faith was not for me, a capitalist from the land of capitalism. Borodin caught me up on one of my deprecatory remarks, and said it would be quite possible for me to become a communist.

The more I thought about it afterwards, the more I was disquieted. I began to think about the whole communist belief in a new way. There was a "message" in it for me. It was as if I too were "called." I recognized all the symptoms of the religious impulse, which in my case had reached a high point at a student religious conference at Silver Bay in my freshman year in college. My intellectual skepticism had then supported my natural conservatism and prevented my giving way wholly to the strange emotional urge to "surrender to God." And in the same way my skepticism and conservatism fought now against an acceptance of this new faith—which can make the same appeal to surrender and sacrifice as the Christian faith.

A few months later I did go through a partial "conversion." I accepted the communist belief that the existing social order—the "capitalist system"—was in a process of decay and transition to a new and higher social order—"socialism"—and that individuals like myself should help to hasten the transition. For a while I was even willing to accept the full Marxist method: the "revolution" and the "dictatorship of the proletariat." But, as I related earlier, I could not muster real intellectual conviction for those new formulas, and I could not picture the America I knew ever repeating them with the simple fervor of the Russians. Added to my intellectual skepticism was the natural hesitancy of anyone with my background, not driven to any real revolt. After all, I was brought up on Prospect Hill, and the full Marxist creed (like the full Christian creed) seemed to require that the ragged slum-dwellers should rise in their wrath and "expropriate" the stately Prospect Hill mansion.

Often since then I have felt a lingering sense of guilt, like that perhaps of a heretic or apostate, when I have argued with a confirmed Marxist in all his strength of righteous conviction. I have the same sense of inferiority when I talk to a devout Christian, and he accuses me of lack of faith. More than once an ardent Marxist has ended an argument by saying: "You have no faith in the working class." And I realized that I had not, and that at heart perhaps I did not wish to have. But then, I would ask myself, should it be a matter of "faith," after all? And if my fear of a "dictatorship of the proletariat" is shared by a vital segment, perhaps a majority, of my fellow-Americans, if most of them fear, as I believe they do, an uprising of the "propertyless," that fact in itself is a valid argument against the Marxist theory. For if too few identify themselves with the "proletariat," then how can it ever establish its dictatorship? And so my skepticism has always come out on top.

I am moved to make this "confession," not for any personal reasons, and not because I want to suggest that my refusal to accept the whole Marxist belief may be unwarranted, but because it may help to indicate to what an extent the strength of Marxism in the world today is emotional. It follows that any purely rational criticism, such as I am undertaking in these pages, will be wholly unconvincing to anyone with the religious will to believe.

Marxists naturally resent the use of the word "religious" or "religion" in connection with their belief. They point out that Marx called religion the "opium of the people," and that their "science," which repudiates the supernatural, therefore cannot be called a "religion." The discussion hinges, of course, on the definition of the word "religion." The only question with which I am concerned is whether Marxism does or does not show the features associated with religions. From my own personal experience I have no doubt that it does.

Angelo Herndon's stirring autobiography, *Let Me Live*, gives the most revealing picture of the mind of a communist that I know. Both the strength and the limitations of Marxism are brought out. The ability of the Marxist movement to transform this Negro victim of abject poverty and brutal exploitation into an able and courageous leader is the kind of achievement generally associated only with religious conversion. But there is nothing to indicate that the new faith is better grounded in reality than the old. Herndon read Marx's *Capital* obviously in the same way he had previously read the Bible, with a will to believe, regardless of understanding. Devoutly religious people can go into raptures when they think they "understand" such a play upon words as: "In the beginning was the Word, and the Word was with God and the Word was God." When Herndon was being beaten into insensibility by officers of the law, a not infrequent occurrence in his amazingly heroic career, he saw visions of Marx and others of his saints as many a Christian martyr had before him, and they gave him renewed courage as they had to martyrs before. When he was sentenced virtually to death on a Georgia chain gang for organizing the unemployed, he seems never to have lost courage.

A mystical faith has immense power in changing human beings and hence in changing the world. But it need have no close relation to facts in order to have this effect. It is true that a faith which does seek a constant check against the facts in the real world, having little that could be called mystical about it, will not sustain anyone very effectively in martyrdom—any more than Galileo's faith that the world moved around the sun sustained him when he was told to recant. But I am convinced that if progress in mastering our environment is to continue, especially at this particularly difficult time, a healthy skepticism in checking belief against facts is more important—at least for "intellectuals"—than any emotional "surrender."

Yet one thing more should be said about the strength of a religion. Not only can it transform individuals and give them incredible personal qualities, but it can build a powerful movement. Here again communism has a close parallel to Christianity.

When I was in Germany in 1934 I established contact, through outside connections, with one of the Marxist groups working "underground" in Germany. For the most part they were ruthlessly honest—about their own limited strength, about the lack of revolutionary sentiment among the workers, about the success of Nazi propaganda. There were almost no discernible reasons why they should continue their frightfully dangerous and apparently hopeless struggle. But they had faith—a faith sufficiently powerful to inspire intellectual confidence, too—in the Marxist predictions. They had statistics to prove that real wages of the workers were going down. Was not the basic "contradiction" of capitalism—increasing ability to produce against decreasing ability to consume—still at its subtly destructive task? Fascism could not overcome that contradiction; depression, crisis, war, collapse, all were inevitable; the workers' day would come. Like Christians in the Roman catacombs, daily expecting to be torn in pieces in the arena or nailed to crosses, their magnificent faith sustained them. Whether there was warrant for their faith, or, as I came to believe, none, obviously made no difference to its effectiveness in sustaining that movement.

If a religious movement has a strength of its own, it also develops its own peculiar vices. The communist movement, where it rose from the status of a persecuted sect and now rules a vast country, has shown a tendency to institutionalize its beliefs as the Christians did in the Roman Church. Like the Roman Church the communist movement now has its orthodoxy, its priesthood, its heresies and their priesthoods, its scriptures, its martyrology, its belief in ineffable mysteries, its faith in the sure coming of the "kingdom."

But in becoming a faith, and in building a church, Marxism

has largely lost its potentialities for being a science or a "technology."

## *Marx and Marxism*

It is impossible to treat Marxism lightly. I have come from Marx with no small amount of respect for him, and for the set of beliefs he founded, even if I have felt the necessity of taking a definitely antagonistic position. For better or worse he is one of the great figures of history. He spent a lifetime of poverty and ill-health in a struggle for human betterment and in arduous intellectual effort. He was the founder of the most powerful religion of modern times. He made some great contributions to the understanding of social forces. He is far too big a man and historical figure for any single critic like myself to add or detract from his stature. Moreover, many of his followers have sufficiently emulated his industry and his endurance so that no one can lightly dismiss them and their work. And, finally, the fact that millions have been affected by him and the course of world history changed, is sufficient to call for a wholly respectful treatment.

I am not here concerned with Marx himself, however; rather I am concerned with Marxism, in fact only a part of Marxism, its economic theories. Marxism is a set of traditional beliefs. In certain superficial respects they are fluid and subject to change, but basically they are crystallized in a hard framework, tending to imprison men's minds rather than release them. It is that framework which needs critical analysis.*

It might seem that there is little need for criticism of Marxism in America. Certainly I do not share the absurd fears of those who see America threatened by a "communist menace." The average American is probably ignorant of any other Marx than the four Marx brothers; and the followers of Karl Marx have and are likely to have no considerable influence on American history. That in fact is my quarrel with them and with Marxism—their ineffectiveness. The system of beliefs I am calling Marxism is, it seems to me, a principal obstacle to intelligent action in this country. Thou-

* It has often been pointed out that Marx himself disclaimed being a "Marxist." In his own lifetime he could see the crystallization of ideas taking place. Yet his own polemical intolerance was partly to blame.

sands of earnest and able people, particularly young people, are being swept into the Marxist camp, and their intellectual capacities, which might be turned to effective purpose in molding the American scene, are virtually sterilized. If they escape both the ineffectuality of a permanent acceptance of Marxism and the disillusionment of a reaction against it, they are likely to revert to pure pragmatism—which rests on too dangerous a confession of ignorance.

Much of the intellectual appeal of Marxism to its present devotees is still emotional: as I suggested, it satisfies the intellectual craving for certainty and order in a bewildering environment. It has an immense prestige derived from a long history, a voluminous and comprehensive literature, and the official support of the Soviet Union.*

This prestige, particularly of Marxist economics, is comparatively recent in the English-speaking countries. Marx lived much of his life in England, and did most of his work on *Capital* in the British Museum. But English economists paid little attention to him. He wrote in German and a few German economists engaged in theoretical tilts with him in recondite publications. His first volume was translated into Russian, and certain sophisticated intellectuals in St. Petersburg dropped the cruder forms of mysticism with which they were occupying their leisure to discuss Marx: some of the young ones, eager for a faith in which they could become active, spread Marx's revolutionary political ideas, and hundreds of young aristocrats went to jail. But in England his book was not translated till long after his death, and then only in part. It was not till the Great Depression of the 1930's that many a young English intellectual became critical of economic institutions, and Marx alone seemed able to give some of them the emotional justification and rationalization for their discontent.

America was ahead of England in its respect for Marx, because many immigrants from Germany and Russia at the end of the

* It is perhaps unnecessary to point out to how small an extent this prestige value affects the validity of Marxism. The Catholic Church has today far more scriptural backing and an incomparably greater weight of tradition behind it, yet a non-Catholic does not therefore feel constrained to accept its doctrines. And the Soviet power no more proves the validity of Marxism than Hitler's Germany proves the theory of Aryan supremacy.

nineteenth century brought their Marxism with them. The second and third volumes of *Capital* were first translated and published in Chicago, though this was only thirty years ago. Marxist economics was not taken very seriously in this country, any more than in England, except by those who could read him in the original German or in the Russian translation; great universities set up their departments of economics without paying any attention to what he had written. A few labor unions, in which recent immigrants from eastern Europe had a large membership, like the "needle trades" unions, were centers of the Marxist faith, but even there a younger generation, American-born, soon began to overshadow the influence of the old Marxists. Marxist influence among American workers is waning at the very time when American intellectuals, like their English prototypes, are taking him up.

It is largely because of this new interest in Marxism among my own contemporaries that a searching test of its validity seems called for. For the last few years it has had a blighting effect on all social analysis.

In two of the three fields of Marxist thought there has already been a reaction. Marxism has three aspects, a philosophy, a political theory and an economic theory. Its philosophy and political theory have been under considerable attack, but its economics has been largely ignored—being nominally accepted even by many who have rejected Marxism as a political method. I am here concerned with Marxist economics, but a few words seem called for on the other aspects. Marxist thought is woven into a tight texture, with all parts more or less interdependent.

## *What Is Marxism?*

The Marxist philosophy of dialectic materialism and the economic interpretation of history have been under much recent discussion. Marx derived the concept of the dialectic from Hegel. Its unscientific character goes back to that curious mind which, as Chase and Hogben have recently told us, believed that there could be only seven planets (astromers using scientific methods have since discovered two more) because of the remarkable mystic properties of the number 7! Hegel, objecting to the static quality of formal logic, conceived of Truth or the "Absolute Idea" as emerging out of a "dialectic" conflict of opposites: thus a jury is supposed to get the facts (with equally little scientific justification) from the argument (*i.e.*, dialectic) of opposing counsel making conflicting assertions. Marx turned Hegel "right side up" by declaring the conflict one of materialist rather than idealist forces, and "dialectical materialism" became the philosophical formula which the Marxists have repeated ever since. As applied to history, the dialectic sees evolution proceeding by the "reciprocal interaction" of opposing forces, e.g., in "class struggle."

To a degree the dialectic may help in emphasizing the changing organic nature of human society. But other writers have dealt with social evolution without using such an abstract and metaphysical approach. At its best the dialectic is no more than a clumsy and oblique way of approaching science. At its worst it is a useless and pernicious form of magic. Much of the Marxist political and economic analysis is false because derived from the theological concept that the conflict of ideas and institutions is always in opposing *pairs*—dualism rather than pluralism. Just as society is thought of as divided into two warring camps, instead of as an intensely complex resultant of multiple group and individual interests, so the economic process is seen purely in terms of two conflicting claims on the social product, that of the laborers and that of the capitalists; and contemporary history is seen purely in terms of two economic systems, capitalism being identified with the capitalist class, and socialism with the working class. The confused realities of the present-day world are unintelligible to the simon-pure Marxist.

Similarly Marx's economic interpretation of history—the idea that man's economic arrangements condition his other social arrangements—is reared into a dogmatic abstraction till it may be as much a hindrance to understanding as an aid. The Marxist always has a weakness for making general and relative tendencies into absolute facts. It is probably true that among all the conflicting interests that shape human behavior in the group, the economic interest often tends to dominate. That is the kernel of one of Marx's greatest contributions to thought. But if the "economic interpretation" is made into a "law" it prevents a due understanding of all the other interests and forces that condition our social development.

The same hankering after absolute "laws" is apparent in the political aspects of Marxism. The heart of the political and social theory is that the working class has a special "historic mission" to bring the socialist society. The theory is a logical outgrowth of the dialectic in history, for the working class is in the present era the opponent of the capitalist class, which is dominant in a capitalist system. And the economics of capitalism, according to the Marxists, is such as to impoverish the working class until it is compelled to revolt. Actually in Marx's mind and in the minds of his followers the logical processes have probably been the other way round: the Marxists are emotionally aroused by the poverty and exploitation of the working class, and they derive their historical and economic theories as a rationalization of their *hope* that the workers *will* revolt. Hence they see society split up, in Marx's words, "into two great hostile camps, into two great classes directly facing each other: Bourgeoisie and Proletariat."

Since the rise of fascism as a revolt of the middle classes, there has been much analysis, even in Marxist circles, of the modern class structure of society. And there is a growing realization that it is far from the simple dualism of Marxist theory. The Marxist political and social "laws" are being subjected to as penetrating criticism as the philosophic "laws."

Only the economic "laws" have been left largely unchallenged in this present period of enhanced Marxist prestige. This is the more surprising since the whole concept of "laws" of economics, as applied by the classical or orthodox economists, has been riddled, often by the Marxists themselves.

It was natural that attempts should long have been made to establish economics as a science similar to the physical sciences, and even today conservatives think of the "law of supply and demand" of economics as similar to such "laws" of physics as the "law" of gravitation. The difficulty with any such concept is that economics is dependent on human behavior, and our knowledge of human psychology is still so primitive that prediction is often impossible. For instance, consider the crudity of the nineteenth-century psychological economists, who attempted a mathematical balancing of the "pain" of paying a certain price or making a certain effort, over against the "pleasure" to be derived from satisfying some want. It is true that much progress has been made along these lines, particularly with the development of the "marginal" concept and the elaboration of the science of statistics. But at best our economic "laws" merely indicate tendencies, in a rough sort of way.

The Marxists have appreciated the limited degree to which the generalizations of the orthodox economists were "laws," but they have gone right on expounding their own "laws." And these laws became so rigidly formulated early in the history of Marxism—thanks to its ecclesiastical character, as I noted above—that they are in some respects as outdated as medical treatment by bleeding.

The essentials of Marxist economic theory were published by Marx in the *Manifesto* in 1847, almost a hundred years ago. They were based on the unscientific approach of the dialectic, and as a rationalization of an emotional desire to end the injustice of economic exploitation. During the many years they were elaborated by Marx, he had virtually no statistical data with which to test his theoretical abstractions, in comparison to the voluminous data available today. He died over fifty years ago, leaving much of his work to be finished by Engels, but Engels was far more interested in the philosophical and political aspects of Marx's teaching than his economics, and he added little. Few of the followers of Marx have attempted to keep Marx's economics up to date, either as regards the discoveries of the theoretical economists of the "marginal utility" school (at least until the last decade), or as regards the rapidly changing world of business and industry in which they found themselves.

It is a testimonial to Marx's own genius that his work has stood up as well as it has, considering how it has been kept intact as a finished thesis instead of being constantly built upon (as all other scientific formulations have been in the past half-century). He did have amazing prescience. He foresaw much of the economic development of the succeeding years—the growth of big business, monopoly, banking, new credit mechanisms, economic imperialism. But he could not foresee how these changes would affect the basic operations of the system. And there were many changes which he did not foresee, or foresaw so dimly that his predictions were of no value—the growth of the new middle classes in distribution and the services, economic nationalism, "state capitalism," "deficit financing," and the whole mixture of "private" and "public" enterprise, "capitalism" and "collectivism," during the post-war era.

With Marx's natural limitations of time and place there can be no quarrel. But the general religious and philosophical cast he gave his movement seems to have prevented any of his followers from carrying on his work in the field of theory.

They have made virtually no progress in understanding "capitalism" or its "laws of motion." And because he discouraged the study of the economics of "socialism" as "Utopian," they have contributed little to an understanding of the economic requirements of our present era. Their intellectual failures have extended into other fields than economics. No Marxist as such has, so far as I know, contributed anything substantial to the natural or social sciences. I say this in no petty, caviling spirit. If the Marxists did not make such great pretensions it would not be necessary to go so far afield. But, claiming a uniquely valid approach to knowledge, the Marxists lay themselves open to the counter-charge that they have contributed pitifully little to an understanding of the modern world.*

The communists will point to the Soviet Union as the refutation of these charges, and to the work of Lenin and Stalin (or Trotsky) as proof of the value of the Marxist intellectual tools. These leaders—take your choice—were great revolutionists, great leaders of men, as Mirabeau and Danton were in another revolutionary period. But their intellectual contributions to a theoretical understanding of social forces are of little account. Where they followed Marx they merely repeated him. Where they produced

* The economists and political scientists who have made the most valuable contributions to current thought have not done so by using Marxist methods or tools. The Fabians in England, Wells, Shaw, the Webbs, and more recently Cole and Laski and others, have done far more intellectual spade work than any Marxists, and though some of them in the stress of the present critical period have gone over emotionally to the Marxist camp, they have not done their best work as Marxists. Likewise in America our chief dependence has been on the "institutional economists" of Veblen's school, rather than on the Marxists, for help in developing new economic procedures. So far as work bearing on the organization of a future society is concerned, many schools of thought have contributed more than the Marxian: the "Christian Socialists," the "guild Socialists," the syndicalists, the monetary and banking reformers, the sheer "Utopians" like Edward Bellamy will, I think, all be seen to have had a greater influence on the shaping of the institutions of the future than the followers of Marx.

original work (as in Lenin's analysis of the nature of a revolutionary political group in *What Is to Be Done?* or Stalin's solution of some of the problems of economic planning) they owed nothing to Marx. In action they went wrong when they tried to be Marxists, and they succeeded when they forgot their Marxism. The toll of human suffering and brutalization which Marxism has exacted in the Soviet Union is immeasurable. The clash between the requirements of practical necessity and the dogmas of the faith is probably a major reason for the recent purgings, for Stalin the ruthless man of action could not square his activities with the Marxist religion except by exterminating the purists in that faith.

In the rest of the world the Marxists have made an impressive showing because of their faith, and have failed when adequate understanding was called for. In particular, the Marxists have consistently been unable to understand fascism. They did not predict it. They misinterpreted it when it appeared. They have been unable to cope with it, and have succumbed miserably to it when conditions were ripe for its advent.

Outside of communist Russia and the fascist states there has been, as we have seen, a vast range of developments, transforming the economic system in the direction of collectivist controls. In certain countries Marxist parties (though of the "revisionist" and "opportunist" type denounced by Marx in his lifetime) have played an important part in these developments. But equal progress has been made by non-Marxist groups—co-operators, Farmer and Labor parties, "Tory socialists," military interests, Democrats, and by the subtle non-political pressure of consumers seeking public services. The world of today, outside of Soviet Russia, owes nothing substantial to Marxist economic theory.

Marxists will point to the depression period beginning in 1929 as proof of the validity of Marxism: did not they alone predict it? They will quote from the remarkable prophecies of the *Manifesto:*

> "In these crises a great part not only of the existing products but also of previously created productive forces are periodically destroyed. In these crises there breaks out an epidemic that, in all earlier epochs, would have seemed an absurdity—the epidemic of over-production. Society suddenly finds itself put back into a state of momentary barbarism: it

appears as if a famine, a universal war of devastation, had cut off the supply of every means of subsistence: industry and commerce seem to be destroyed; and why? Because there is too much civilization, too much means of subsistence, too much industry, too much commerce."

"Commercial crises, each time more threateningly, put on trial the existence of the entire bourgeois society. . . . Society can no longer live under this bourgeoisie."

Yet the Marxists' predictions impressed me more a few years ago, when with many others, Marxists and non-Marxists alike, I believed the end of capitalism imminent. But now that it has been once more "postponed" I realize that this is only the latest of a series of postponements going back ninety years to that paragraph in the *Manifesto*. If a doctor has predicted the death of a patient off and on for ninety years, then, even if the patient should die, how much credit can be given the doctor? And in this case the patient isn't dead yet.

Twenty-five years after the *Manifesto*, Marx was not quite so sanguine about the imminent breakdown of capitalism. In 1873 he went no farther than to speak of the "periodic cycles to which modern industry is subject, and the culminating point of these cycles, a universal crisis," but added ambiguously, "Such a crisis is once more approaching." In 1886 Engels believed a "permanent and chronic depression" had succeeded to the previous cycles, and declared: "We can almost calculate the moment when the unemployed, losing patience, will take their fate into their own hands." Again, in 1894, when Engels brought out Volume III of *Capital*, he asked in a footnote: "Is it possible that we are now in the preparatory stage of a new world crash of unparalleled vehemence? Many things seem to indicate this." * In the heyday of Social Democracy, 1900-14, the peaceful victory of socialism and the end of capitalism by democratic means were widely believed imminent. With the war and the Russian Revolution the end of capitalism was expected to come with the rapid spread of world revolution, but with the establishment of the post-war prosperity Marxists once more turned to hopeful predictions of the final eco-

* Actually world capitalism was at that moment moving into its greatest period of stable expansion.

nomic collapse. The Great Depression seemed to justify their hopes and gave them new prestige: they claimed that Marx's economics had permitted them alone to foresee this final crash.

Still the wish was father to the thought, and the final crisis and revolution have once more been postponed.

Marxism has been a great religion. It has offered hope and courage to the insecure and the oppressed. It has fired thousands and millions of people with the energy needed to overthrow outworn institutions. It has been a dynamic force in the modern world. But it is not a science. In the field of economic theory as in the field of social theory it may be worse than useless, for wrong prediction may be worse than no prediction.

## *Wading Into "Das Kapital"*

Offhand that record of ninety years' failure in prediction might lead one to consider there was no value in pursuing Marxist economics further. But at least the Marxists can claim that Marx understood the unstable nature of capitalism, which would lead to periodic crises, and that this was a greater achievement than his contemporaries, who considered capitalism as stable and eternal. Moreover the Marxists will point to the fact that the last depression was of unparalleled severity, that our whole civilization has been imperiled by its repercussions, and that there is evidence that any permanent and real recovery is now out of the question, all of which bears out the Marxist analysis of inherent contradictions in capitalism which would lead to its ultimate downfall.

Moreover, no one is justified in passing off the Marxist economics as of no account, unless perhaps a purely academic theorist. Such an economist may rightly feel that Marx's theories are mere curiosities in the long history of economic thought. But being a political and social force gives Marxism and its economics the right to demand a thorough analysis, even if it had no other claim.

To understand Marxist economics is a painful and laborious, and on the whole quite unrewarding, undertaking. Having a New England conscience I have not felt I could depend on secondary sources and on word-of-mouth discussion, though I am inclined to believe no one could make much out of the Marxist writings without a good antecedent dose of both. I breathed an atmosphere of Marxism (official, uncritical, diluted, of course) in the Soviet Union; fortunately I also ran into a young English university man who was in the process of conversion from Fabianism to communism, and with him I carried on endless discussions and later a massive correspondence. It is by such personal contacts that most Marxists are made, I am certain. Then on my return to America I took a concentrated course in Marxism from one of the profoundest (if in recent years most dissident) Communists I have known. But finally, after skirting a good deal of secondary Marxist writing, I tackled the "Bible" itself, the three theoretical volumes of *Capital*, in 2,500 pages, and have by now driven myself through most of them twice. I will not deny that I consider this something of an heroic achievement.

What Marx attempted in *Capital* was a comprehensive analysis of the way the economic system of his time worked—it is in the Preface to the First Edition that he speaks of "the economic law of motion of modern society"—with the specific purpose of finding the "tendencies which work out with an iron necessity towards an inevitable goal." The goal was of course the collapse of capitalism and the seizure of power by the proletariat. The proof which is attempted in *Capital*, and which Marxist enthusiasts believe achieved, is that the inner contradictions of capitalism tend to aggravate themselves, producing ever more serious crises, until the system becomes wholly unworkable.

The real significance of *Capital* then should be that it provides an adequate understanding of the business cycle, and a proof that depressions will get worse till they end in collapse. The fact that the prediction has been constantly projected into a new future, the collapse not having materialized, should at once suggest that the proof is faulty. Actually the proof is never made. At least I have been unable to find it. Let me summarize the argument as it is built up.

In the first volume a contemporary (and long since discarded) theory of value as arising from labor time is expounded, and various definitions, of commodities, money, capital, are laid down. Then Marx derived, in his own original way, the concept of surplus value, by which he sought to explain the difference between the value of the worker's labor power as expressed in his wages, and the value of what his labor produced as expressed in the price of the product. This surplus value was produced by the worker but it did not belong to him; instead the capitalist took it, in this way "exploiting" the labor of the worker. The bulk of Volume I is devoted to showing the extent and method of that exploitation. It is this picture of the callous cruelty of the profit motive in the first half of the nineteenth century—long hours, starvation wages, child labor, abject poverty, unemployment—which has made this volume the classic indictment of the capitalist system.

The volume concludes with an explanation of how the surplus value piles up in the accumulations of the capitalists, thus resulting in an ever more rapid industrialization—but an industrialization which contains within itself the seeds of its own destruction. For, as Marx puts it, in the "general law of capitalist accumulation": "As capital accumulates the condition of the worker necessarily grows worse." Underpaid and unemployed workers cannot buy the goods that can be produced. Crises of overproduction recur with increasing severity. The volume ends with a magnificent peroration depicting the rising crescendo of conflicting tendencies and conflicting interests which finally "sound the knell of capitalist private property."

There is here no theory of crisis beyond a bald statement of recurrent overproduction in the face of inadequate purchasing power; and no proof that the crisis will get worse, beyond the simple demonstration that capitalism tends to grow at an accelerating pace. For the full theory and the proof Marxists rely on the succeeding volumes of *Capital*, published by Engels after Marx's death.

Briefly summarized, Volume II goes back to describe the process by which money and commodities circulate throughout the economy in a vast harmonious balance. The production and distribution of capital goods and consumer goods are seen as all part of a single process, out of which the capitalists are able to draw surplus value and reinvest it so as to produce an ascending spiral of economic activity. Unfortunately the harmonious balance is far from perfect. The planless "anarchy" of the whole economy brings about constant maladjustments, dislocations and disequilibria which may culminate in a depression.

This volume is the least valuable of the three. It does add to the concept of the economic system as a living "organism," in contrast to the dry and static analysis of prices and the effect of supply and demand on prices, on which contemporary economists were concentrating. And it describes the various types of disequilibria, though without explaining how they may contribute to depression or may on the other hand be automatically counterbalanced. We still have no adequate theory of the business cycle, or proof that the disequilibria will ultimately be fatal to the system.

The thousand pages of Volume III are the chief reliance of the Marxists for this basic proof. A large part of the volume, however, is devoted to filling in certain gaps in the original exposition, and trying to meet certain inherent defects in the argument. Thus there is an extensive exposition of how surplus value shows up in the form of profit, interest and rent. Marx distinguishes the profit of enterprise from the "wages of management," and shows how profit is figured on the total capital invested, on a yearly basis, in a way to disguise the "rate of surplus value" or exploitation of labor. Hundreds of pages are taken up with inconclusive jottings and quotations dealing with questions of banking, paper money and credit money (questions which were naturally upsetting to a believer in money as a "form" of value, derived necessarily from labor, and therefore based necessarily on gold). Another large section is taken up with explaining the apparent absurdity that, if surplus value is derived from labor, then the more a manufacturer sticks to hand methods and avoids labor-saving machinery the more profit he ought to make.

This part of the argument leads to the gist of Volume III, where the "law of motion" of capitalism is at last elaborated. It is to any single capitalist's advantage to introduce labor-saving machinery, because in this way he obtains a temporary competitive advantage on the market, being able to sell his own products at a market price above their true value (measured in labor). But competition soon flattens out his advantage. Competition likewise tends to equalize the rate of profit as between different lines of production which are more mechanized or less mechanized. So far as prices tended to be the expression of value, they would tend to net an exaggerated profit in the least mechanized industries where (as in the case just mentioned of the least mechanized plant in any particular industry) most of the capital invested can be used to exploit labor. Marx shows that prices here, too, may fluctuate far from value, and they will find an equilibrium at a point where an average rate of profit is earned. On the other hand, looking at the whole capitalist system, mechanization will indeed mean that more and more capital must be invested in machinery, and less and less in labor, which alone produces the surplus value. Hence Marx deduces the "law of the falling tendency of the rate of profit."

Here Marx felt he was close to the self-destructive dynamics of capitalism. Mechanization will produce more and more unemployment. The falling rate of profit will force an ever keener competition between capitalists, forcing them to reduce the wages of the workers still employed. At the same time the increasing productivity of the whole system will make possible ever greater aggregations of wealth and a consequent expansion of industry. The contradictions and instabilities will get worse and worse—until the final social and economic cataclysm predicted in Volume I.*

In the overpoweringly voluminous form presented, the "proof" seems irrefutable. Actually the conclusions are not proved, they are merely asserted. And the incidental light that is shed on the workings of our economy is far overshadowed by the vast jungle of involved and largely useless verbiage.

In one respect Marx was at a special disadvantage. He had had no adequate training in mathematics or accounting. Endless pages of bewildering figures in *Capital* attest to this failing. At one point in Volume II his editor, Engels, is driven to despair of Marx: "The handling of figures in arithmetic gave him a great deal of trouble," he interpolates, "and he lacked especially the practice of commercial calculation. Consequently Marx entangled himself to such an extent in his computation of turnovers that the result, so far as he completed his work, contained various errors and contradictions." Engels tried to correct and simplify, but the result is anything but lucid or convincing.

Engels gave him credit for knowing his algebra, but I am unable to do the same. Take these basic formulas of the capitalist process:

* It may be noted in passing that nowhere in this theoretical presentation is there room for a consideration of the nature of a socialist economy, or of the stages of transition following the final breakdown of capitalism. Whether or not a reader of *Capital* is better able to understand our present economic system, he will have no idea of how to build a better system.

$$C = c + v + s$$

$$M - C\begin{cases} L \\ \\ Pm \end{cases} \ldots P \ldots C' \begin{bmatrix} C \\ + \\ m \end{bmatrix} - M' \begin{bmatrix} M \\ + \\ c \end{bmatrix}$$

The first one means that the value of any commodity (C meaning commodity) is made up of three parts, the constant capital (c) which is the value of the raw materials and equipment going into the product, the variable capital (v) which is the value of the labor power expressed in wages, and the surplus value (s) which goes to the capitalist, and which he either spends or invests. The second formula is intended to show that capital in the form of money (M) is laid out by the capitalist in commodities (C), consisting of labor power (L) paid for in wages, and means of production (Pm), and that these then enter into the productive process ( . . . P . . . ) and emerge as an increased value of commodities (C′ or C prime or C + c) which are then sold for more money than was put in (M′ or M prime or M + m). The small c in the second formula is not the same as that in the first formula: instead it corresponds to the surplus value (s) in the first formula, being the commodity form of that surplus value, while m is its money form.

The second formula is carried another stage in the following:

$$P \ldots C' \begin{cases} C - \\ - M' \\ c - \end{cases} \begin{cases} M - C\begin{cases} L \\ \\ Pm \end{cases} \ldots P\,(P') \\ \\ m - c \end{cases}$$

This may seem unfair to both the printer and the reader. Actually the idea is not complicated. Marx is simply elaborating the second half of the second formula above, and showing how part of the capitalist's surplus value in money (m) is spent on commodities for his own use (the final c) and part is reinvested in the productive process, which is then carried along on an expanded scale (P′ or P prime).

It is hardly Marx's fault that in the English language, in which he was not writing, "commodities," "capital," and "constant capital" (to say nothing of "circulating capital," which includes the "variable capital" and the part of the "constant capital" which is not "fixed") all begin with a c. But it makes what is already a difficult use of algebraic symbols into something frequently unintelligible.

Algebraic symbols and mathematical formulas to describe human events are always dangerous. They give a fictitious reality to what is only a mental concept, which may have most unfortunate results. We shall see in a moment how another formula using the sign of equality (=) started Marx off on a basic fallacy in the exposition of the labor theory of value in the first pages of *Capital*.

With the preliminary sketch of his economic theory and its covering formulas as I have presented them in the last few pages, it should now be possible to look at his concepts one by one, particularly in the light of the historical changes that have taken place since Marx wrote. Even if Marx's mathematics were not all they should be, there is one limitation for which he deserves no blame: the fact that he lived over half a century ago, and that the "capitalism" he was describing is not our economic system.

# Chapter Twelve

## CAPITALISM ACCORDING TO MARX

THE impression made on me by reading Marx must have been made on many another reader. One moves in a strange and incomprehensible world of fantasy. One longs for some reference (or "referent") that will connect with one's own real experience. Finally, after sufficient discipline, the various abstractions begin to take on some reality of their own. But still one suspects that it is merely the illusion of reality.

The same difficulty arises, to be sure, in any technical or scientific writing. A textbook on physics requires the same initial effort. But there at least the abstract concepts are all shorthand methods of describing facts in the real world, and are derived from experiments which can be duplicated. Much of economic theory—and not alone the Marxian—is never capable of similar operational tests.

Perhaps this is due to the fact that economics deals with the infinitely complex interrelations of infinitely complex human individuals, and one can bring the apparent chaos into some sort of simple order only by artificial analyses—"other things remaining the same"—which are never capable of strict verification.

The economists on that account have always had a field day. They can spin theories with an abandon no worker in the natural sciences would be permitted for a moment. Even the most intelligent modern critic of Marxism, von Mises, is as guilty as Marx of spinning theory without factual verification. "We shall do better to leave statistics on both sides," he says, in attacking Marx's theories of the concentration of capital. "For it must not be forgotten that there is a theory underlying every statistical demonstration." True enough, but it is hardly an excuse for an argument, whether Marx's or von Mises', which includes scarcely a single statistical fact from the real world.

The propensity to march boldly off into the unknown afflicts all economists. The intricacies of language and reasoning in which they so often become involved are like those of the Ptolemaic astronomers. Having started with a false assumption taken without verification, that the world was the center of the universe, the Ptolemaic cycles and epicycles, which proliferated beyond the mental grasp of ordinary mortals, could go on indefinitely. The Copernican conception of the solar system brought a new simplicity and comprehensibility. It seems reasonable to suppose that if modern economists can keep their attention focused on real people, and real operations in the furnishing of real goods and real services, they can save much of the mental strain required by the older economists—and be far closer to the "truth." Considerable progress has been made in this direction by the historical and institutional economists, and by the more recent marginal or equilibrium economists.*

Marx was in a sense the first of the historical school. But having reached a final formulation, as he thought, of the historical process, and of its then stage, he was incapable of keeping up with changes and developments in his own time, much less of an unseen future. As von Mises says justifiably enough (at least so far as economic theory was concerned), Marx's *Capital* was out of date virtually before it was published. For socialist economists to think the last word on the capitalist system was said by Marx is little more logical than to depend wholly on Adam Smith.

In the following analysis of various Marxist concepts I shall attempt to show both how the concepts, even at the time they were enunciated, could not have withstood factual tests, and also, what is more important, how a rapidly changing world has often invalidated what at the time seemed to have sufficient factual basis to be thought permanently true.

* Thorstein Veblen, John R. Commons, John Maynard Keynes, Alvin H. Hansen, Paul H. Douglas, Edward Chamberlin and the Brookings Institution economists are some of the economists who have seemed to me closest to "reality."

### *Value and Surplus Value*

The first and basic concept of Marxist economics is the labor theory of value. It was, of course, not Marx's invention. It was as much a current axiom among contemporary economists as, say, the gold standard in pre-depression America. The more orthodox schools of economic thought were already abandoning it during Marx's lifetime, though he appears to have been unaware of this, and would undoubtedly have objected violently to its abandonment. Such an enlightened modern Marxist as G. D. H. Cole declares that it is not an essential part of the Marxist system. But the orthodox Marxists (who are never such because of Marx's economics, but rather because of his political and social theories) have clung to it: John Strachey considers that there can be no economics without a theory of value which provides a common measuring rod, and that the labor theory of value is indispensable.

My own view is that the Marxist theory of value, being the basis for the theory of surplus value, is rather fundamental to the whole Marxist economics, and that the weaknesses of this foundation make the whole superstructure shaky.

It has often been pointed out how Marx's dissatisfaction with an apparent dilemma in the current value theory led him to "surplus value" and hence to the whole development of the argument of *Capital.* The then current concept that the value of any commodity is derived from the labor going into its production ran into this difficulty: if the labor cost of a pair of shoes is one dollar (including the labor that went into the leather, nails, etc.), then the value of the shoes should be one dollar. How can a manufacturer make any profit in that case, except by cheating his customer and selling the shoes for more than their value? Marx answers this dilemma by explaining that a worker is paid, not according to the value of the product of his labor, but according to the value of his own "labor power." This is itself a commodity determined by the value of the goods—food, clothing, shelter—necessary to maintain and reproduce the laborer. The value of the shoes, therefore, consists not only of the dollar which goes to the workers as the value of their "labor power," but an additional amount, which their "labor" has created, and which Marx called "surplus value." This, in the capitalist system, is appropriated by the capitalist, and forms the basis of the unjust exploitation which marks that system.

There is one important point at which this argument touches on reality. It is true that, except under the unfavorable conditions of primitive savagery, men can produce more than they themselves require, for current consumption in their own maintenance and the raising of a family. Speaking of ancient Egypt, Marx says: "The smaller the number of natural wants and the greater the natural fertility of the soil, the smaller the amount of necessary labor required for the maintenance and reproduction of the producer." (I, 556.) * The "surplus labor," as Marx calls it, can be used, and has almost always been used, in two ways: first, to produce tools or permanent improvements or cultural works, which in the long run may benefit all the social group; and second, to furnish luxury goods and services, usually for an exploiting class. The Pharaohs used the surplus labor of the peasants partly to build irrigation works, keep the peace, and maintain a high culture, and partly to build pyramids and minister to the Pharaohs' vanity and love of luxury. Even in a society without exploiting classes, the surplus labor would still go in two directions, first to increase the productive and cultural level, second for luxuries, entertainment, and the like. And it is important to note that luxuries (like electric light or gas) have a way of becoming habitual and customary until they join the ranks of the necessities for everybody—and then the labor necessary to produce them ceases to be what we have called "surplus labor," for it is part of the labor required to maintain the workers at the customary level of subsistence.

If one chooses to designate what workers produce with their "surplus labor" by the term "surplus value," one is still on fairly solid ground. In a slave system, as in the pre-Civil War South, a small amount of slave labor went to feeding and maintaining the slaves and the rest to feeding and maintaining their masters. In a feudal system, as in medieval Europe, a serf worked part of the time on his own land, to maintain himself, and part of the time on

* In this and the following chapter all references to Marx's *Capital* will be given in the text by volume and page. All other references will continue to be found in the Bibliographical Notes.

his lord's land. In a capitalist system, where a comparative few can live in luxury on the labor of others, it is possible to speak of a capitalist class appropriating the surplus value produced by a working class. And it is not hard to see that a situation where one group can hire the wage labor of another group facilitates all the injustices and brutalities of our present system.

Marx was so obsessed by these injustices and brutalities that he tended to think of the surplus value as little better than robbery. He contrasts "the producer's labor for others and his labor on his own behalf": he calls the former "unpaid labor for some other person." By continually harping on this "unpaid labor" he gives the impression that this is the chief evil of the capitalist system, and that in a free social order the worker would get the full product of his toil. Yet it is easy for a conservative to argue that a ruling class performs a necessary managerial and organizing function—whether it is a slave-owning, feudal or capitalist ruling class—and in so far as it directs the surplus labor into productive channels, the ruling class thereby performs the essential social function of "saving and investment."

At one point late in life Marx attacked a socialist appeal he considered demagogic in demanding the "equitable division" of the "whole proceeds of labor," and he listed six items that would be deducted from what the worker received under socialism: "replacement of the means of production used up," new investment, insurance reserves, administration, social services, and maintenance of those unable to work. These items are necessary under any system. The general assumption, therefore, which runs throughout *Capital,* that the surplus value is all "unpaid labor," by means of which the worker is unjustly exploited, is such a half-truth, even by Marx's own admissions, as to make the concept of surplus value itself highly misleading.

I have been giving the concept of surplus value the benefit of the doubt here, by showing where it might connect with the real world. But as Marx develops it out of his theory of value it is a pure abstraction—like the traditional shadow of a nonexistent black cat in a dark room.

The dark room we find on the third page of *Capital*. The paragraph is worth quoting in full:

"Let us take two commodities, such as wheat and iron. Whatever the ratio of exchange may be, it can always be represented by an equation in which a given quantity of wheat is equated with some quantity or other of iron. For instance, our equation may read, one quarter of wheat = x cwt. of iron. What does this equation mean? It tells us that in two different things, namely in one-quarter of wheat and in x cwt. of iron, there exists in equal quantities something common to both. They are, therefore, equal to a third something, which differs in essence from them both. Each of them, in so far as it is exchange value, must be reducible to the third."

What Marx is apparently thinking of is a primitive market where two men work out an exchange by barter. The use of the sign of equality is like turning off all illumination on that barter transaction. Clearly no exchange would take place if the owner of the wheat did not value the iron more than his wheat, and the man with the iron did not value the wheat more than his iron. Marx admits elsewhere that the "use-value" differs for each person (I, 62-63). But he is interested not in "use-value" nor in "exchange value" but in a "third something." Still, what right has he to use the sign of equality? If he wants an algebraic picture of his barter exchange he should have used something like this: one-quarter of wheat $\leftrightarrows$ x cwt. of iron. The arrows indicate something dynamic, what has aptly been called a "transaction," rather than a static relation. If you use a different method of shorthand, then you need no new concept, the "third something" which Marx calls "value." The black cat is nonexistent.

Still the layman may argue that commodities obviously do have value, and that a certain amount of wheat has a value equal to a certain amount of iron. What the layman will be thinking of is the price, as an expression of value. A bushel of wheat may be sold for a dollar, and a certain amount of iron for a dollar, and therefore the bushel of wheat and that amount of iron have an equal value. Marx uses the same logic. The difference is that the layman is using value and price synonymously, and when he says the two commodities have an equal value he means they have an equal price: you can sell them for the same amount of money. But Marx knew that the labor theory of value would not explain prices; though he started by defining price as the "money form of value" he immediately had to admit that the price might differ from the value, and, while in Volume I he tended to think of the "difference as accidental" (I, 79, 153n), by the time he got to Volume III he had to confess that it would be merely accidental if the price did happen to be the same as the value (III, 190, 244). No, Marx is not concerned with anything so real as the price—what he is after is the "internal and disguised essence" (III, 245).

Let us take another tack to show how nonexistent this "essence" is. You as a layman might think some of the value of the "quarter of wheat" Marx mentioned would come from the fertility of the soil on which it was grown. But you would be wrong; the value of the wheat comes only from the labor that went into producing it. Marx admits that part of the "use-value" or "material wealth" is "supplied by nature without the help of man" (I, 12); but just plain "value"—the "something," the "essence"—is derived solely from labor (I, 13).

It is not, however, the labor of the farmer who produced this particular quarter of wheat that Marx is concerned with. Nothing so simple and real as that. For obviously that particular farmer may have been inefficient or slow, or again he may have been using the very latest modern machinery, for which he was trained in an agricultural college. What Marx is interested in is "abstract human labor," a "mere jelly of undifferentiated human labor," "generalized human labor," "simple labor" (I, 6, 13). If a man's labor is highly skilled, because, let us say, of a high degree of technical training, it "counts as multiplied simple labor, so that a smaller quantity of skilled labor is equal to a larger quantity of simple labor" (I, 13). Marx never tells us how many times you should "multiply." So even if all wheat farmers begin to go to agricultural colleges, we will still have no idea of how many hours of labor represent the value of the wheat.

A few years ago an extraordinary illustrated edition of Marx's *Capital* was issued. The drawings were by Hugo Gellert, an ardent Marxist, and many of them were of astonishing beauty, almost religious in feeling. In illustrating the labor theory of value Gellert pictured the working hands that had produced a garment, not as something outside the garment, but mysteriously "congealed" (Marx's term: I, 8) within it. The effect, like a doubly exposed photographic plate, was as if a religious artist were to depict a soul. The "value," which is the "essence" of a commodity, is as mystical as any soul.

Moreover, since Marx conceives of value as embodied in commodities or goods, he apparently does not consider that the effort involved in the furnishing of services—the work done by a doctor, for instance, in furnishing professional services—is value-producing labor, subject to any of the general laws he works out in *Capital* (III, 448). Services which have to do directly with the physical processes of production, like managerial supervision or transportation, he admitted were legitimate forms of labor and added to the value of a product (II, 169; III, 456). But he ignored the professions, and he was baffled by the white-collar occupations. One suspects that the vast overgrown processes of distribution in the present-day world, merchandising, selling, accounting, financing, are not a proper part of the capitalist system he is describing.* Marx says of "the merchant" that he "parasitically thrusts himself in" between the buyer and seller of commodities (I, 151). The whole of Chapter 6 in Volume II is devoted to analyzing the "expenses of circulation." Marx has the greatest difficulty trying to decide whether workers in this field add to value or not. At one point, for instance, he says that such expenses as storage "enter in part into the value of commodities, in other words they increase the price of commodities," and a few pages later he reverts to a strict construction and says they "do not add anything to the value" (II, 157, 165). Storage and bookkeeping are "legitimate" though "dead" expenses. Salesmanship does not seem to be even "legitimate."

All of this serves to emphasize the artificiality of the labor theory of value. At least half of the working population of America at the last census was engaged in occupations which Marx would not have considered labor (creating values) at all. Where will they be in the class struggle?

Just as it is true that all work does not create value, so it is possible for a thing to have a price without having any value. I mentioned the fertility of land, as an example; so likewise, says

* All of Part IV in Volume III, devoted to "Merchant's Capital," is full of doubts and contradictions on this point. Compare III, 329-330, with 386.

Marx, a man's honor may have its price, but it will have no value (I, 79, 80).*

We come, therefore, to this definition of the value of a commodity according to Marx, that it represents the amount of time of undifferentiated abstract human labor socially necessary for its production under average conditions. That is the nonexistent black cat. It may seem, offhand, to be no more abstract a concept than any scientific concept derived for purposes of analysis, and it may seem unfair to quote Marx's symbolic terms out of their context, when he was using them admittedly only for purposes of a special analysis. Such an abstraction might even be accepted, for what it is worth, to describe the labor cost as one of the elements going into the determination of price. But from the theory of value Marx derives the theory of surplus value, and that in turn links up with his whole social theory, of the historic mission of the working class, so that the theory of value becomes the justification for certain very concrete *predictions* of human behavior, and for the expectation of a revolution—which is a very real event in a very real world, and not a matter merely of abstract analysis. Let us turn back to the concept of surplus value, which, following Cole, we were willing to accept as valid even if the theory of value is not. As Marx uses it, is it not merely the shadow of our nonexistent black cat?

Marx says that the product of all the labor beyond what men need for bare maintenance is appropriated by the capitalists as "surplus value." But what is maintenance? At what standard is the worker to maintain himself? Luxuries, as we noted, have a way of becoming necessities. Marx believed that the workers must remain at the poverty level under capitalism. Yet he attacked the "iron law of wages," which some of his contemporaries like Malthus expounded: for if workers could never rise above a bare subsistence level, what would be the use of trade union activity? He admitted that standards of living change with time and place, and that the workers share in the general advance of technology (I, 159, 567, 610, 665, 682).

But see how this works hob with his theory. The value of a

* Marx runs into new trouble when he comes to consider interest as the "price of capital," for obviously this is not the "value" of the capital (III, 417-419, 448-449).

commodity is measured by the abstract labor in it, but the worker is only paid for his "labor power," whose value is the value of the food, clothing and shelter that went into producing it—*i.e.*, the maintenance of the worker and his family (I, 187). But if this is a variable quantity, varying with the customary standard of living which a worker will consider a minimum, as well as with the effectiveness of collective bargaining, how can one differentiate with any accuracy between the worker's share and the surplus value, or deduce any laws of motion from the ratio between one and the other? And if the values of the food, clothing and shelter are themselves abstract and indeterminate (not their prices, remember) the surplus value will be more than ever indeterminate.

True, there is a struggle on the part of the industrial working class to get higher wages—to secure a larger share of the total social product it produces. But if this is looked at as a class struggle between those who produce value and those who appropriate surplus value, most of the white collar and professional workers, the independent business men, and all farmers who employ hired men, as well as the workers in governmental administration, must be put on the side of those who appropriate surplus value. Under a socialist system, too, there would be a conflict between productive workers in industry on the one hand, and all those whose income depended on any of the six functions the expenditures for which Marx himself admitted would have to be deducted from the producers' income. Can one predict a revolution arising from the appropriation of surplus value?

Surplus value is a still potent concept in the real world because of one ingredient only—the part which the capitalist spends on his own extravagant luxuries. It serves to typify the unjust exploitative features of the capitalist system, by which the idle rich live on the backs of the toiling masses. Yet Marx professes to be quite unconcerned with that, in the formulation of his theory.

### *The Rich Grow Richer*

If the capitalists consumed all the surplus value in riotous living there would be no revolution, according to Marx. For the distinguishing feature of capitalism, and the feature that is responsible for its laws of motion, is that it snowballs up through the accumulations of the capitalists until it falls apart. Properly to perform his historical functions the capitalist should frugally save and reinvest every penny. "The capitalist," says Marx, is nothing but "personified capital endowed with will and consciousness" (I, 138). And "capital," as Marx loosely conceives of it (he never attempts a clear-cut definition), is value—alternately in the form of commodities and money—which "has acquired the occult quality of being able to add value to itself" (I, 140).

In Marx's day it was usual for economists to think of capital in the crude way the man in the street today (the "investor") is still likely to think of it, as money that is put to "work," invested to yield an increment.

It must be said that Marx came nearer an engineering concept of capital than the classical economists, for he emphasized that capital by itself can produce nothing, all production being a result of labor applied to materials. But if we carry engineering concepts all the way through, and apply the term not to money but to the physical tools of production—"the concrete material instruments which aid man in the processes of production," as the Brookings Institution defines it in one of its studies—a quite different impression of "capitalism" emerges.

A growing part of this capital in modern society is social capital: it belongs to society, it is publicly owned—such as highways, for instance. As this kind of capital is "accumulated" it adds to the wealth of the whole community. It is not difficult to say the same of the "accumulation" of "private" capital: in so far as this capital represents more machines, more factories, more power to produce, the whole community is enriched.

This is the line of argument which capitalists have used to justify the capitalist system as against the Marxist criticism. The capitalists claim to serve the important function of accumulating capital, and thereby enhancing the productive capacity of the whole community. If they did not "save," if they consumed all their income in extravagant living, then perhaps they might be condemned. But since Marx is not concerned with their own consumption, and since he admits that under the capitalist system the productive capacity of society has vastly increased—which has obviously been due to the existence of a wealthy class able to "save" in large amounts—what then, asks the capitalist, is wrong with the capitalist system?

Marx's answer, as I summarized it a few pages back, is that this process of accelerating accumulation ultimately brings about the self-destruction of capitalism, regardless of whether this is desirable or undesirable: all the disequilibria that develop in the increasingly hectic course of capitalist growth, are exaggerated (as in a defective automobile which must constantly increase its speed till its defects result in a smash-up); at the same time wealth tends to concentrate in a shrinking group of capitalists, while poverty spreads among the masses, until a social breaking point is reached. The first tendency involves a theory of the business cycle. Let me postpone it for a moment while I consider the second problem, the concentration of capital.

There is so much truth in Marx's picture of the accumulation of wealth that it has always seemed easy for latter-day Marxists to point to the fulfillment of Marx's predictions. Billionaires like Ford, Rockefeller and Mellon, billion-dollar businesses like the American Telephone and Telegraph Company, and General Motors, over against millions of unemployed and more millions of miserably underpaid workers, are the living proof of Marx's "absolute general law of capitalist accumulation." *

Why then has the revolution not arrived? Because, briefly, Marx's picture is only half-true. Let me list some of its inaccuracies:

*"Large-scale production is more economical."* This is partly true. It serves to explain why huge factories in many lines of produc-

* "The greater the social wealth, the amount of capital at work, the extent and energy of its growth, and the greater, therefore, the absolute size of the proletariat and the productivity of its labor, the larger is the industrial reserve army. The available labor power has its extent promoted by the same causes as those which promote the expansive force of capital. Consequently, the relative magnitude of the industrial reserve army increases as wealth increases. But the larger the reserve army as compared with the active labor army, the larger is the mass of the consolidated surplus population, whose poverty is in inverse ratio to its torment of labor. Finally the larger the Lazarus stratum of the working class and the larger the industrial reserve army, the larger, too, is the army of those who are officially accounted paupers. *This is the absolute general law of capitalist accumulation.* Like all other laws it is modified in its actual working by numerous considerations, with the analysis of which we are not here concerned." (I, 712.)

tion have tended to take the place of small workshops. The big capitalists, says Marx, have an advantage over small producers and drive them out of the field (I, 688-692). But this is partly wrong, too. A "law of diminishing returns" quickly makes itself felt in most types of agriculture, so that there is no economic incentive to large-scale capitalist agriculture as Marx believed there was. The farmers in every advanced country have remained petty entrepreneurs rather than become wage-workers, even though there is a tendency under certain conditions for tenancy to replace farm ownership.* In industry, too, and even more in commercial trade, and in the provision of services, small-scale operation often has high survival value. According to a recent survey by the Twentieth Century Fund, only 30 per cent of the total economic activity of the United States is carried on by "Big Business," the rest being in the hands of individual enterprises, partnerships, and small corporations. Ever since a fluid source of power was made available in the widespread industrial use of electricity, the tendency toward large-scale industry seems to have been halted, if not reversed. All of these exceptions to Marx's law have perpetuated and even enlarged the middle classes, between the big capitalists and the industrial wage-earners.

"*Private ownership of business enterprises tends to concentrate in fewer and fewer hands.*" As contrasted to the Jeffersonian ideal in which every citizen is an owner of productive property—preferably a farmer—there is sufficient evidence of the concentration of wealth today to seem a proof of Marx's contention. But again it is a half-truth. Even if small business had not survived as it has, the growth of the big corporation since Marx's day has tended to diffuse ownership. Marx saw that the corporation would facilitate the accumulation of capital, but he failed to see that it would soften the impact of the class struggle. The 5 million stockholders in America in 1929, the 30 million savings bank depositors, the 65 million insurance policy holders (savings banks and insurance companies, especially in the "mutual" or co-operative form, dilute the ownership of corporate securities), all tended to remove the possibility that America's worst depression would result in the rev-

* But when American farmers become tenants of banks and insurance companies as "owners" this does not mean the introduction of mass production methods as a general rule.

olutionary rise of the "propertyless proletariat." The fact that the *control* of the vast corporate structure of America may have been largely in the hands of a little handful of powerful individuals—"the sixty families," the "Wall Street bankers," the "economic royalists," or what you will—did not materially alter the social consequences of the diffusion of ownership.

*"The difference between rich and poor tends to widen."* Obviously there is a greater difference between the average wage-worker in the United States earning one thousand dollars a year and a multimillionaire's income, than between the wage-worker and the capitalist in Marx's day. But once again the generalization is a half-truth. Marx admitted that occasionally wages might rise, though he considered that profits would always increase faster, and that any rise in wages was necessarily temporary. It is hard to reach a clear-cut conclusion here: on the one hand modern apologists for capitalism in America point to the high and ever-rising standard of living, and the apologists for Marx point to the wide extent of extreme poverty.

Indexes of real wages are never reliable, for the elements of a standard of living change: many an American worker is no better fed and clothed than his prototype in Marx's day, but he has a car and a radio. Is he poorer or not? In all advanced capitalist countries there have been many developments that have tended to mitigate the extremes of wealth and poverty: trade unions, social services, and various social welfare schemes at the bottom, and income and inheritance taxes at the top. The Great Depression reduced new millions to dire poverty and seemed to give new force to the Marxist predictions. But by and large it must be said that Marx's "general law of capitalist accumulation," in prophesying the sharp division of the population into a few rich and an "army of paupers," was only partly sound: it ignored the middle classes, and the higher paid workers. Moreover, it rested fundamentally on the idea of technological unemployment, which I shall take up in a moment under the analysis of Marx's theory of crisis.

There were two economic phenomena rising to prominence in Marx's time, which he treated largely as aspects of the increasingly rapid accumulation of capital; these were the growth of monopoly, and the growth of bank credit. Trusts and cartels and other monopolistic practices may be more or less able to escape from the competition of the market, and therefore to follow different "laws" of motion. These "laws" have only recently been investigated, and in certain respects the "monopolies" turn out to be stabilizing factors in the economy rather than factors hastening its decline. Engels, and Lenin after him, were inclined to feel monopolies were a stage already halfway out of the capitalist system on the way to socialism. Marxist economics is likewise little able to make sense out of the vast credit system, as we shall see in a later section.

### *The Contradictions of Capitalism*

In trying to understand Marx's theory of the business cycle whose fluctuations will finally prove fatal to capitalism, it is important to bear in mind both the helpful and the confusing aspects of the dialectical method. In so far as "dialectics" enables the economist to think of the economic system as a vast complex of conflicting tendencies, a changing, growing, evolving organism, it permits a more intelligent understanding of cyclical disturbances than any simple theory based on one factor alone. In so far as it is crudely dualistic, always looking for tendencies in opposing pairs as a law of nature, it may be highly misleading.

One of Marx's justest claims to fame was his recognition of the fact that the various causes of maladjustment in capitalism are so inherent in the system that crises are a normal feature of the system. The "classical economists" have always tended, as apologists for the system, to consider a balanced equilibrium as the normal state, and a boom or depression as abnormal. They have concentrated on the factors in the system which tended toward balance. Marx concentrated on the factors which tended toward unbalance.

Scattered through the three volumes of *Capital* are numerous references to possible dislocations. Marxists point to these as showing Marx's profound understanding of the workings of capitalism. Thus Marx cites the delicacy of balance between the "departments" of economic activity, capital goods industries, consumer goods industries, luxury goods industries (II, 472-476). He mentions the ten-year replacement cycle of machinery (II, 210, 545), and the problem of premature obsolescence (III, 135). Fluctuations of prices, panics on the securities and money markets, credit inflation and deflation, fluctuations of foreign exchange and trade, and problems of the flow of gold, are discussed at various stages of his exposition (III, 140, 575-580), though they are treated as secondary symptoms of crises rather than as prime factors, and are never brought into a coherent pattern.

All of these various minor elements in the instability of capitalism together form a formidable array of defects. The picture of capitalism that emerges, especially with the constant emphasis on the progressive acceleration of all the tendencies in a vast interdependent world network, where a disruption of normal processes at one point will immediately spread to the farthest corner, is a picture of all-embracing anarchy. One wonders how there could ever be any smooth functioning. There is no explanation of how the various automatic adjustments of the price and market mechanism tend to restore equilibrium, once it has been upset by any of the instabilities. This explanation was offered by the economists who followed Marx; though the picture of ideal equilibrium they drew was imaginary, it was no more false than the picture of ideal anarchy Marx drew. The scattering explanations of this anarchy to be found in *Capital* constitute not even an adequate description of a crisis—much less a theory of crisis.

But we have yet to consider the main "contradiction" of capitalism, the disparity between power to produce and power to consume. This is the key to the Marxist theory of crisis. For a crisis to Marx was always necessarily a "glut"—overproduction in the face of underconsumption (I, 486; II, 87; III, 302).* Is Marx's contribution to economic thought here an adequate explanation of the dynamics of capitalism? Remember that he is not merely interested in the nature of crises; he is interested in showing that they will get progressively worse until the final collapse.

How then does Marx explain this lagging of consumption? and how does he explain the worsening of this condition till the final

* Marx mentions much extraneous material, on where and how the falling off of consumption first shows itself. With the development of the banking and credit system, and the complexities of the distributive process, the first sign of trouble is likely to be when wholesalers' inventories begin to pile up, and the banks begin to call loans. A scramble for liquidity will ensue; the more complex the credit structure, the worse the crash (I, 120; II, 87; III, 359, 522-32, 567-69, 575). Yet this is only the outward manifestation of the inability of consumption to keep up with production.

collapse? We have seen that his attempted proof rests on the "general law of the accumulation of capital" which declared that poverty would grow as wealth grew, and on the "law of the falling rate of profit," which reinforces and aggravates the working of the other "law." The "febrile impetus" of the greed for profit, becoming ever more hectic, results in the capitalists producing more and more, while the workers are able to consume less and less (I, 486, 567; III, 287).

Marx seems to have been much impressed by what has in recent years been popularized as "technological unemployment." Machines, for the introduction of which Marx shows there is a constant incentive under capitalism, throw workers out of work.* Since 1929 the spectacle of wealthy America swamped by millions of unemployed seems to have given a new justification to Marxism. Is our unemployment not the living proof of Marx's law? Marx's reasons for believing the "industrial reserve army" a necessary part of capitalism are, however, not convincing. He appreciates how the industrial revolution is making possible a more rapid growth of population than ever before in history (I, 676). Over against this he shows that, with the development of industry, the investment in machinery and equipment and means of production is constantly going ahead at a faster rate than the investment in labor (I, 694-695, 713). The means of production represent "past" or "dead" labor (I, 189): the "living" labor is a constantly smaller

* "The characteristic course of modern industry," Marx summarizes, "its decennial cycles (interrupted by intercurrent oscillations) of periods of average activity, production at high pressure, crisis, and stagnation, depends on the continuous formation, the greater or less absorption, and the reconstruction, of the industrial reserve army, composed of the surplus population. In their turn the vicissitudes of the industrial cycle swell the numbers of the surplus population and become one of the most energetic agents of the reproduction of this surplus. . . . This supply of available human material is dependent upon the simple fact that some of the workers are continually being 'set at liberty' by methods which reduce the number of employed workers relatively to the increase in the amount of production. Thus the whole movement of modern industry is characterized by the continuous transformation of part of the working population into unemployed." (I, 698-699.) In addition Marx argued that it was to the advantage of the capitalists always to have a large "industrial reserve army" available for starting new enterprises and to keep wages down, but obviously this advantage is not one of the causes of unemployment. (I, 706.) See also I, 329-333.

proportion of the total outlay (I, 687). The major reason for growth of unemployment seems to be conceived as a difference in rates of growth, the increase in jobs always lagging behind the increase in population and the increase in production (I, 702, 703).

It might seem as if the facts bore out Marx's contention. Machines do throw men out of work. There has always been in every advanced industrial country a "reserve army" of unemployed. But until the post-war world, sixty years after Marx worked out his theory, it had not grown to unmanageable proportions. Actually this tendency is merely one of many, and to lift it to the status of a "general law" was unwarranted. Apologists for capitalism are just as accurate and just as inaccurate as Marx when they deny "technological unemployment" by insisting that workers thrown out of work by machines will find new employment, either in making those machines, or because of increased production, or because of new industries. There are two conflicting tendencies at work, one creating jobs, the other "saving labor" (I, 469-471, 482). Over the past century they have generally counterbalanced each other. Sometimes one tendency gets ahead of the other, and causes a temporary maladjustment. Sometimes it is the other way round. Marx himself cites occasions when there may be a shortage of labor (I, 676, 682; III, 256, 295). The various elements of unbalance and disequilibrium which he mentions, and which later economists have described at much greater length, all may produce temporary unemployment during the period of maladjustment. Unemployment is indeed always latent. But there is no *proof,* in Marx's *Capital,* that unemployment must constantly rise.

The argument that the larger the proportion of any investment going into machines and means of production, the smaller the proportion going to labor, reminds one of the fallacy in Major Douglas's "social credit" argument. After all, the money laid out for means of production is not removed from circulation; it does not go to "dead" labor, but to "living" workers in the capital goods industries. The increasing "roundaboutness" of production does not produce unemployment, even if it were to be extended indefinitely: the increasing production of means of production, to produce means of production, to produce means of production, might be compatible with full employment.

Furthermore, there is an immense mitigating factor, which has tended to counterbalance technological unemployment: the opening up of jobs outside production in a vast growth of the distributive mechanism, of the service trades and professions, and of governmental activities.

So far as one can test the Marxist theory here against figures, the events have turned out contrary to the theory. A constantly larger part of the American population became employed workers until 1929, and it was not until 1920 that a decline began even among the industrial workers.

But, says the Marxist, unemployment is merely a "tendency," and "relative" at that. The tendency has been effective in keeping wages low and the working population too poor to buy its own products. The essential kernel of the theory is the poverty of the workers. Is that not sound?

There is no doubt of poverty, even under the American standard of living. Capitalism has been a system of exploitation, where a powerful and privileged few have made fabulous fortunes out of the toil of millions who have always remained near the pauper level. But the fact of poverty is not denied even by the orthodox and conservative, and it is exposed with as much vehemence by non-Marxist liberals and radicals as by Marx. We are concerned with the explanation of that poverty and its implication for the Marxist theory of crisis and collapse. We still have no explanation for the inadequacy of purchasing power.

Marx's followers have often attempted an explanation crudely in this way: Since the worker is paid for only part of the value of his product, obviously he cannot buy it all back. Hence surpluses of unsold products are constantly piling up. Marx would never have admitted that this was his argument. For he shows how all the elements of cost enter into circulation (II, 373-399). The capitalist's share is either spent on his own consumption, or reinvested. The share going to raw materials and equipment flows into the capital goods "department," where again part of it goes to workers and part to capitalists. Marx does not consider that hoarding or failures in the money system are of any significance here—though he well might have.

Nevertheless, I cannot help suspecting that when Marx started his economic thinking he was influenced by this crude conception: that the worker could not buy back the full product of his toil, and that this was the reason for the chronic threat of overproduction. He was profoundly stirred by the poverty of the working class; as a revolutionary, he felt it an emotional necessity to consider this poverty an essential "contradiction," which would bring the downfall of the capitalist system. Hence a fallacious theory underlay the whole of *Capital*, even though when he came to the detailed analysis of "Capitalistic Circulation," in Volume II, he had to admit that there was no necessary stoppage of the flow of money and goods.

What then is left of the "general law of capitalist accumulation"? It is true that in the course of capitalist development the rich grow richer and the poor grow relatively poorer. But this is in itself neither a cause of capitalist depressions, nor a reason why they get worse and worse. Capitalism went on from triumph to triumph after Marx wrote his law. It may even be argued with justice, as I have said, that it was the great disparity of wealth which permitted the unprecedentedly rapid development of our productive powers under capitalism—a development from which the working class has during most of the history of capitalism derived a constantly rising standard of living.

If it is not true that there is an inherent shortage of purchasing power in relation to production, then all that can be said of Marx's theory of crisis is this: there are many factors leading to disequilibrium in our economic system, and in the growing complexity of capitalism some of these factors may become increasingly upsetting. Given these disequilibria, oscillations are bound to occur in economic activity, that is, business cycles, showing up at a certain stage in each cycle as a temporary overproduction with relation to effective demand, and producing a crisis, with consequent unemployment. The depression of 1929 did seem to be worse than any previous one; but it came two generations after Marx's predictions. If there are certain factors tending to exaggerate the oscillations, we cannot find them in Marx, and clearly there have been others tending to lessen them.

But the Marxist can still rely on the "law of the falling tendency of the rate of profit." This, as we saw, depends on the increasing mechanization and "roundaboutness" of production: since the capitalist can only extract surplus value (*i.e.*, make a profit) out of exploiting labor, then the smaller the proportion of his total expense that goes to labor, the smaller must be the ratio between the profit and the total outlay. Marx conceives that a capitalist cannot make a profit on the part of his outlay which goes for machinery or raw materials, since he buys these at their "value." Hence, the more advanced capitalism becomes, the less profit any capitalist can make on his capital, and since the rate of profit tends to level off to an average over the whole system, then the average rate of profit tends to fall. In the long run this deals the death blow to capitalism.

There are two theoretical objections to this argument. First, it could be counteracted by simply increasing the "rate of exploitation," that is, the ratio of the profit to the labor cost, so that the rate of profit on the total outlay would remain the same. Marx gives no indication of what governs the "rate of exploitation"; he gives no reason why it should not rise as rapidly as or more rapidly than the change in the "composition of capital."

Secondly, the argument ignores the fact that the producer of the machinery or raw materials is himself making a profit. Each producer may have a greater capital outlay, and it might even look to him as though his rate of profit on the total were small, because so much of it would be eaten by fixed charges such as interest on borrowed capital. But Marx is using profit in the inclusive sense, covering all property income including interest, so this cannot be the cause of his concern. Moreover, he is not concerned with any individual capitalist's profit but with the total property income of the capitalist class throughout the capitalist system. The "roundaboutness" of production, its increasing mechanization, the fact that in any particular enterprise the larger part of the outlay is for equipment and raw materials representing "past" labor rather than "living" labor, none of this in the aggregate of the whole productive system means a fall in the overall rate of profit.

In the years since Marx's death there have been ups and downs in the rate of profit under the impact of various forces, but on the whole it appears that there is no factual proof for an actual long-time fall in the rate of profit.*

* Between 1909 and 1929 the proportion of the national income going to property holders remained steady. It was 14.7 per cent in 1909, reached a high of 16.0 per cent in 1911, a low of 12.2 per cent in 1918, and was at 14.9

It has sometimes been argued that there is an observable long-time fall in the interest rate, which proves Marx's thesis. But since interest is only part of Marx's profit, and the rate of interest is in Marx's view not affected by the "rate of exploitation" but is merely the competitive price on the market for the loan of money capital, it is hard to see how this is any proof.

Lewis Corey, perhaps America's leading Marxist scholar, believes that the present low interest rate, accompanying a super-abundance of savings seeking investment, over against a "secular" fall of the prospects of profit, bears out Marx's thesis, and that Keynes's "general theory" explaining the present stagnation is in effect a reassertion of that thesis. For Marx saw as one of the dynamic elements of capitalism a tendency to the overaccumulation of capital, and described the phenomenon of excess capital as a phase of a depression; only by a destruction of some of the excess capital in the deflationary period, or its export, could it be brought back into relation with the possibilities of profitable investment (III, 294-300). But Keynes's theory is an explanation of the modern "secular" trend, not of the depressions of the past; and he believes the interest rate has not fallen enough, not that it has fallen too far; so that there is no close relation between Keynes and Marx.

In conclusion, then, there are two principal laws expounded in Marx's *Capital*, the "law of capitalist accumulation," and the "law of the falling tendency of the rate of profit." Neither of them offers an explanation of capitalist crises, and neither of them offers any conclusive proof that capitalism must destroy itself of its own inner contradictions.

per cent in 1929. In the depression it rose somewhat, to 17.3 per cent in 1932, when the national income fell unprecedentedly. In 1935 it was 14.6 per cent. While this does not exactly express the rate of profit, it should be a fair indication of it.

# Chapter Thirteen

## THE WORLD MOVES ON

### *Imperialism and War*

CLEARLY if the Marxist "contradiction" between increasing production and increasing poverty is sound, the grand and final crash of the system would not be long in coming. But Marx saw a mitigating factor. The "contradiction" within any country could be relieved by going abroad. Higher rates of profit could be made by exploiting the more primitive conditions in the backward countries (III, 278-280). The primitive plain robbery and cheating of colonial nations ("primary accumulation") is followed by their exploitation as markets for the goods which cannot be sold at home (I, 832-833, 848-858; III, 300). Surplus capital can be invested abroad. It is as if the youth of capitalism could be recaptured for a time (II, 392).

Engels, in an interesting footnote to Marx's discussion of crises in Volume III, which he added during his editing of the manuscript in the early nineties, forecasts the theory of imperialist war as the inevitable result of the search for foreign markets (III, 574n). Lenin elaborated the theory in his famous pamphlet on "Imperialism."

According to Lenin, the progressive accumulation of capital required by Marx's laws results increasingly in a concentration of economic power in the hands of bankers and monopolists, and competition for profit takes on increasingly the aspect of competition between nations controlled by these super-capitalists. The competition for markets, raw materials, and opportunities for investment, becomes a world struggle between a few great powers.

Writing in the midst of the Great War, Lenin was able constantly to test his theories against facts.

In addition to predicting that the imperialist struggle would at last bring the capitalist contradictions to a head, Lenin was able to cite a new reason why the final collapse had been so long postponed: the workers in the leading capitalist countries had been sharing in the benefits of the exploitation of foreign workers, and thus had been "corrupted" into a sort of new middle class.

Marxists today lean heavily on the theory of imperialism. Part of the current explanation of fascism by the Marxist groups is that fascism is merely an exaggerated form of the imperialist phase of monopoly capitalism; the warlikeness of the fascist countries is simply due to the fact that the powerful capitalists, who are thought to control the fascist countries, are compelled to seek foreign markets and fields for investment more urgently than ever; for the inherent contradiction of inadequate consumption at home in the face of growing productivity is aggravated now that the power of the workers to fight for higher wages is entirely crushed.

There is no doubt that capitalists have long sought for competitive advantages abroad, and that the explosion of 1914 was caused by commercial rivalry as much as by any other one factor. But this rivalry can be accounted for without postulating the Marxist theories of inherent "contradictions."

The United States grew to the position of dominant capitalist power without depending on foreign trade or foreign investments. Our brief experiment in colonial expansion after 1898 is already being abandoned, as we prepare for final withdrawal from the Philippines.* Our domestic economy has never been heavily dependent on foreign trade, and since the Great Depression we have come to accept the loss of many of our foreign markets, for cotton and wheat, for instance, as permanent. Foreign investment at its peak in 1928 was less than one-sixth of all investment; and almost half of this consisted of loans to foreign governments rather than investment in production. The much more preponderant foreign investment of English capitalism, which has always been the model

* Non-economic political and military reasons have recently indicated a possible reversal of our Philippine decision.

for Marxist theorists, is not the compulsory expression of a "general law." America, the most advanced capitalist country, has been least dependent for its development on imperialism.

All the evidence today points to the diminishing importance of capitalist imperialism rather than its enhancement. Foreign trade has been stagnant and foreign investment virtually nonexistent since 1929. The growth of autarchy in the fascist countries is merely the latest phase of a development of national self-sufficiency that has been going on in every country for at least a generation. In fact, from the installation of the first British loom in India, the financing of foreign industries went on in a way that would ultimately eliminate those countries as markets for finished goods. Fascist autarchy has gone so far in developing a new economic system that the capitalist "laws" would not be likely to apply even if they once were valid.

Of the Marxist analysis of imperialism and war, then, we can say that while it stuck to facts it was helpful and illuminating. But as a theory growing out of the general "law of motion" of capitalism it is inaccurate and misleading. There are indeed certain tendencies in capitalism leading to imperialism, and these bore a frightful fruit in 1914; but these tendencies are in no sense a "law," and in the last decade they have been reversed.

It is significant that the chief economic drives toward war today—the desire for raw materials (the incentive to export being reduced merely to the need to pay for imports), the desire for land for surplus population and for the rounded resources of a self-sufficient economy—are wholly compatible with economic collectivism, and can be considered without reference to the dynamics of capitalism as conceived by the Marxists.

## *Money and Credit*

I have previously mentioned the difficulties Marx had in dealing with all monetary and credit problems because of the labor theory of value. Since money was a "form of value" it had to be conceived of as metal, which derived its value from the labor required to mine it (I, 81-93). The circulation of commodities was conceived of by Marx as a process of the constant "metamorphosis of capital" from its "money form" to its "commodity form" and back again (II, 31-71). But it became clear to Marx that in practice most of this "circulation" was carried on by means of pieces of paper—bank notes and credit (I, 109). These he thought of as "symbols of value," which circulated in place of the real metal that would otherwise be necessary; because this permitted "economies" in the use of metallic money, a tremendous growth in the productive system was possible, regardless of whether or not enough gold was being mined to take care of the need for an increased circulating medium (II, 128, 397-399, 412; III, 515, 612).

In describing the processes of the business and financial world, Marx was on sound enough ground, though he showed his lack of assurance by relying chiefly on quotations. He was as much disconcerted as his contemporaries over such verbal questions as whether or not credit money is "capital," whether a share of stock or a government bond is "actual capital" or "fictitious capital," and whether a deposit in a bank counts twice as "money capital," once for the depositor and once for the bank. He devotes over two hundred pages of Volume III to puzzling over monetary and credit problems (III, 469-496).

Many of Marx's arguments, and suggestions about possible dislocations in the circulation of money and goods, go back to the original fallacy, that money must be mined gold and therefore limited in amount; credit, being originally a claim on someone else's money, is felt likewise to be limited (I, 691; III, 231, 591, 673, 696). They all ignore the fact that modern money is anything but a fixed quantity, and that the credit system is so flexible that it is capable of counterbalancing any of the disequilibria.

It has been shown, in the Brookings Institution's survey of the "Formation of Capital," that, in our financial system, there need not be any close relation between saving and investment. A large part of investment may come from new money—bank credit—and a large part of savings may go into speculation or other wholly nonproductive channels rather than investment. In the last few years we have seen an immense amount of public investment financed in a sense by direct creation of credit—by the issue of government bonds to banks which then enter "deposits" to the government's account. Capital then need no longer be formed by the accumulation of capitalists out of surplus value.

Marx himself realized that new investment could be financed

out of credit. And he saw that various forms of "money capital"—stocks, bonds, bank deposits—seemed to exist as a duplication of the "actual capital" (such as a factory plant). He had to speak of "fictitious capital" and "illusory capital" to save the logic of his previous analysis (III, 547-553). But therewith another prop for his "general law of capitalist accumulation" is gone. Regardless of whether one uses the slippery word "capital" for the machinery and instruments of production in the real world, or for the paper which is issued in the imaginary world in connection with their creation, it is clear that "capital" may on occasion be "accumulated" without either impoverishing the worker or enriching the capitalist.

Marx sensed this but could not admit it. He asks himself over and over again just what is the correspondence between the "actual capital" and the "fictitious capital," with the evident intention of showing that the latter is merely the reflection of the "actual capital" and therefore subject to its "laws" (III, 559, 580). But he never gets nearer an answer than by asserting that the "fictitious capital" is an anticipation of future income (III, 549). During six agonizing chapters his editor Engels had "real difficulty." As he puts it in his Preface, "The task before me was not only the arrangement of the references, but also a connecting of the line of reasoning" (III, 14). The critical reader may doubt that Engels succeeded. What chiefly emerges is that Marx vented his dissatisfaction with his own difficulties by ridiculing the "great confusion" of his contemporaries.

The fact is that the credit system, with its immense complication of all economic processes, could not be made to fit in with Marx's "laws." He virtually admits as much, on several occasions. It was "beyond the scope of our plan" (III, 469, 520, 522). But he had gone much too far to turn back.

### *Private Property and a New Social Order*

Marx and the Marxists have devoted all their intellectual energies to showing why the capitalist system must break down, and to preparing the working class to take over the "social ownership" of the means of production. They give few hints as to the nature of the system that will replace capitalism, and fewer still as to the nature of the economic transition from one system to the other.

Marxism therefore adds to its failure to understand the present system a failure to understand the nature of the steps that should be taken to institute a new system. We have seen how the Soviet leaders, in attempting a transition in practice, made a long series of incredibly costly mistakes, having only a few hints in Marx's writings to rely on, and those misleading.

A brief analysis of the various statements and hints in the Marxist writings will indicate how useless they are for our purposes.

Since to the Marxist the basic characteristic of the capitalist system is the private ownership of the means of production, over against "socialized production" (by the exploited workers in the factory), the basic change will be the "socialization" of the means of production. But in the modern corporation the ownership is fully as "socialized" in the sense used there as the production.

It should be apparent from our whole analysis of the Marxist theory that no basic *economic* fault has been proved in the fact that the capitalist class takes an undue share of the social product because of its "private ownership": if the capitalist spends his income on riotous living that may be socially and aesthetically undesirable, and if the share he spends in that way is so large a share of the total national income that it actually lowers the standard of living of the rest, it can be morally condemned; likewise if he invests his income it may be that his choice of an investment is socially undesirable, from a moral, or aesthetic point of view.* But the private ownership of the means of production and the private appropriation of an undue part of the social product by the capitalist have not been shown by Marx to lead to the economic difficulties of the modern world. So that social ownership is a quite inadequate guide to the construction of a workable system.

A general term frequently used by Marx and his followers is the "anarchy" of the capitalist system (III, 221). It is assumed that the new system will be planned. But the anarchy of the capitalist system is only relative. Even under the terrific dislocations of the last few years the vast majority of the population of the capitalist

* The capitalist may choose neither to spend his income nor invest it but to "hoard" it. But the economic effects of this important decision Marx does not consider.

countries have gone about their daily business in orderly fashion, buying, selling, consuming, working, in an intricate and marvelously efficient division of function. There has been want and unemployment and waste; but nothing approaching the anarchy that reigned for a while in Soviet Russia after the Revolution, when industrial production collapsed. And, if it is decided that planning is necessary in order to attain a maximum economic efficiency, with the fullest satisfaction of all human wants, how much planning will be required? The Marxists do not tell us. The comparative achievements of Russia and Germany suggest that overall production planning is probably unnecessary and unsound. The Marxist economists, however, throw no light on this problem.

The Marxists followed the Utopian Socialists in conceiving of socialism as an ideal social order. Ideally money is not necessary to an economic system, where the goal is "from each according to his ability to each according to his needs"; at most, Marx suggested in *Capital*, certificates of labor performed would be sufficient to entitle a worker to take his share of the social produce (I, 52; II, 413). Some of the more enthusiastic Bolsheviks, thinking the millennium had come, tried to abolish money and to introduce labor certificates early in the revolutionary period, with the disastrous results I have described.*

One difficulty with basing money on labor units arises from the inequality of the labor of an unskilled laborer and, say, an orchestra conductor. Another is suggested by the discrepancy between the amount of labor certificates issued and the consumer goods they are supposed to buy, since so large a part of labor must go into capital construction, public services, and other lines not productive of consumer goods. The labor unit could be used arbitrarily as a standard, as so many grains of gold may be used; but this is not what some of the Marxists have meant when they called

* In a real world where wealth is only produced with effort, and hence there is a scarcity of good things in relation to wants, some sort of rationing is imperative. To depend on good behavior—on good manners—to prevent anyone taking more than his share (except where it is something like water or use of a highway of which it is hardly possible to take more than one's share) would obviously be to expect "cloud cuckoo land" overnight. So some kind of money is essential.

for a direct relation between the labor time going into goods and the labor certificates issued to workers.

Another of Marx's few references to the future socialist society concerns the relation of capital goods to consumer goods. Having shown that one of the causes of crisis is maladjustment between the two "departments" of production, it is natural to consider one of the features of a planned society the maintenance of a proper balance, and the building up of reserves of certain raw materials needed in capital replacement so that a sudden lump requirement will not disrupt the even flow of production (II, 546). This is a sensible observation, but not particularly helpful. In fact Marx is so much struck by the nice balance that can theoretically be maintained under capitalism, between the various phases of production, that he suggests the flow of production would be "*just as regularly*" maintained "if production were socialized" (II, 493, italics mine). Here again there is little to assist the revolutionist in constructing a new economic system, though a "gradualist" might point to this as a hint that the key to the problem is merely the maintenance of a proper rate of investment.

Yet the Marxist is bound to be obsessed with the notion that since the prime evil of capitalism is the exploitation of the worker by the capitalist, therefore the key to the millennium is simply a system in which profit is eliminated. At one point in *Capital* Marx even suggested that when the workers own the means of production they will receive the surplus value or profit along with their wages (III, 207). Later, however, as I have related, Marx himself castigated those who thought the worker should get the "full proceeds" of his labor, by showing that all sorts of deductions, for maintenance and expansion of plant, social services, administration and the like, must be made. Essentially the problem here is the disposal of what in a social sense is truly "surplus labor"; that is, first, who gets the benefit of the labor available for the production of luxuries, and, second, who decides on the amount of saving and the direction of new investment? In a social sense it is of vast importance whether only a select few enjoy the luxuries and amenities of civilization, or whether through a wide extension of social services and a rise in the general standard of living these are made available to all. In a social sense, too, it makes a great difference how new investment is directed, whether by speculators into some new gadget industry, or by military bureaucrats into new munitions factories, or by democratic processes into plants for prefabricated housing. But in an economic sense these questions are irrelevant. And to suggest that in the new social order profit will be eliminated may be quite misleading if it suggests that the worker will get the full product of his toil.

The capitalist system is often referred to as a profit system, and the distinction from socialism is said to be that production is for profit instead of being for use. Marx uses the term profit in a general sense as synonymous with surplus value, except that the rate of profit is the ratio of the surplus value to *all* the costs of production (the "cost price" or "advanced total capital") while the rate of surplus value (also called the rate of exploitation) is the ratio of the surplus value to the cost of the labor (III, 55). Then again Marx considers that the surplus value is divided among different groups of exploiters, interest to the money capitalist, rent to the landowner, commercial profit to the merchant, profit of enterprise to the industrial capitalist (this in turn being distinguished from the wages of management). Taxation and governmental expenditures apparently also come out of the surplus value. Profit then is used both in a general sense and in various restricted senses.

Since Marx never described how a socialist system of "production for use" would work, the contrasting term, "production for profit," is not clear enough to be useful. In the early stage of socialism or communism (sometimes called "socialism in a strict sense" to distinguish it from "communism") Marx envisioned workers still motivated by monetary considerations, and the Soviet economists have adequate scriptural justification for their wide wage differentials and for piece wages. The term "profit motive" then is not helpful. On the other hand, if production for profit is taken to mean production for surplus value, it might be argued that this too is still a characteristic of the Soviet economy, for the chief effort has been new investment in capital equipment.

The Marxist stresses that it is "private" profit arising from the "private" ownership of the means of production that must be abolished. But enough has been said to indicate that this furnishes no adequate clue to the nature of the economic changes to be sought as a means of transition to socialism. On the one hand it would be possible to "socialize" profit or ownership of the means of production or both and still have no idea what institutions to put in their place. On the other hand it might be possible to achieve full employment and a high standard of living—the essential economic goal—without touching private ownership and private profit. In addition, as I have pointed out earlier, the very meaning of the word "private" is being lost.

The failure of Marx and his followers to pose and answer the question around which this book is built—"how to get from where to where"—is one of the reasons the world is so badly bungled today. A whole series of false approaches, all more or less under the influence of Marxism, have been made. In western Europe and America, where one would expect the "law of motion" of capitalism to make itself most promisingly felt, fifty years of trial and error have netted the radicals little that the conservatives could not themselves be induced to grant, under the pressure of spontaneous forces.

Social Democratic and Labor politics bogged down for various reasons. Reliance was placed on the labor movement to lead the march to a new social order, where in the nature of things labor unions were committed to bettering their position within the *status quo* and to attaining vested interests in collective bargaining and social legislation. More important from the economic point of view, these political efforts sought the elimination of private ownership and private profit, and, not being revolutionary, this meant by gradual encroachment; but, as I have suggested throughout this analysis, neither the extension of public ownership over a widening sphere of enterprises nor attempts to eliminate or socialize profit by public or co-operative ownership could have much effect, in themselves, on the basic working of the system.

The syndicalist movement which sought the direct and revolutionary expropriation of the factories by the workers was a reaction to the slowness and stodginess of labor politics. But it never developed, whether in the American I.W.W. or the Latin anarchist efforts, into more than a romantic social movement with neither economic understanding nor economic potentialities.

The attempts of the "revisionists" to bring Marxism into accord with the concepts of liberal democracy, relying on gradual change to socialism by legislative enactment through parliamentary democracy, fared no better. Still tied to the "proletariat," a sufficient popular majority to permit a program to be put over was always out of the question; and the nature of the program that was to be put over was never adequately formulated.

Only the Russian Communists have secured a position where they could turn Marxist talk into Marxist action. How they happened to win that position is a matter of political history rather than economic theory. But, as we have seen, their Marxist economics was a hindrance rather than a help, once power was secured; and the Russian people are still paying the appalling price of Marx's failure to elaborate a technique of transition.

Today what have the Marxists to offer? They have learned nothing, and the weight of the Marxist tradition seems to hang like a ball and chain on the radical movement the world around. In the multifarious movements that take their inspiration directly or indirectly from the Marxist system of thought, two general branches are observable, centering in the Labor and Socialist or Second International and the Communist or Third International. The former is still groping with revisionist, reformist concepts of nationalizing particular industries, eliminating profit, expanding social services, but without a coherent program for a transition to a new social order, and with a still recurring profession of faith in "the revolution." The Comintern, under the dominating considerations of *Realpolitik* as the Soviet government sees it, has postponed "the revolution" in other countries, and though with some emphasis on immediate reforms, is essentially concerned today with defending the *status quo* from the demonic assaults of "fascism." Neither in the theoretical literature nor in the political platforms of either major faction is there an effective attack on the essential economic problems of the day. Their own sense of failure is evidenced by the black mood of pessimism that has settled over all Marxist elements, except those communists who are sustained by what amounts to a purely emotional faith.

# *PART IV*

# A THEORY TO EXPLAIN THE FACTS

# Chapter Fourteen

## CLEARING THE GROUND

AT this point let me sum up the results of my investigation as far as it has gone.

The world I have pictured is a world that seems to be going through an unusually acute, painful and rapid change in the direction of more comprehensive and effective collective controls. During the nineteenth century and the first years of the present century direct governmental controls over business practices were few; yet even laissez faire was a governmental policy, permitting more or less automatic processes within a definite framework of public law. Towards the end of the period governmental functions and state intervention were rapidly expanding. The Great War and its political and economic aftermath gave such increased emphasis to governmental action as to initiate a profound change in our economic system.

In analyzing today's world I have come to the conclusion that a common pattern of economic behavior is emerging in all countries, regardless of "system"—regardless, that is, of whether the country is "communist," "fascist" or "democratic" ("capitalist"). The main features of these collective interferences with automatic economic practices we might list as follows:

1. Guaranteeing all members of the community (whether conceived as a national, racial, or class community) a certain minimum standard of consumption, either out of humanitarian considerations, or because of political pressures, or for military reasons.

2. Management of the currency, and control of the central credit institutions, in the attempt to gear purchasing power to productive capacity and assure an adequate supply of money for capacity operation.

3. Public direction of investment, either through governmental expenditures or a channeling of private investment, or both.

4. Prices and production controls limited to checks on the automatic mechanism of the market.

5. Organization and co-ordination of group interests—"corporativism."

6. Decline in the significance of rather than destruction of "private property" (apart from tangible possessions).

7. Retention of profit as an incentive to individual activity and as a bookkeeping check on efficiency.

8. Retention of private ownership and private enterprise outside of the Soviet Union, except in the fields of social services and armament.

That will do for the moment, though it makes no pretense at finality. As between the Soviet Union, Germany, and the other countries discussed, one or more of these points may be emphasized or minimized, but for the most part they apply generally.

I might stop here and leave you to draw your own conclusions, to formulate your own theory on the basis of these facts. Most Americans, still clinging to what they were taught in school about the virtues of "free" economy, easily accept the conclusion that any governmental interference imperils democracy; their theory, expressed by such conservative-liberals as Walter Lippmann, is that we shall succumb to dictatorship unless the present trend can somehow be reversed. The only other view that at present has an intelligent following is the Marxist view that capitalism is in decay, and that the phenomena we have listed are signs of a chaotic struggle between the workers seeking to set up socialism and the capitalist class seeking to perpetuate its power.

Since the Marxists alone have a consistent theory capable of appealing to any considerable number of forward-searching minds, it was necessary to devote the preceding section of this book to an analysis of Marxist economics. My own conclusion, which my readers may or may not share, was that Marxist economics is of little or no use in understanding or guiding present-day developments.

I had to continue my search, to discover what meaning there might be in this bewildering array of facts; I had to work out a theory for myself.

A theory is a mental picture, a logical construct, having a pattern corresponding to certain facts in the objective world. If we are going to make the best use of our brains we must understand not merely the facts, but the patterns of which they are parts; and our mental patterns must correspond with the patterns in the real world if we are to act intelligently. Today most writing about political and economic developments suffers not from over-theorizing but from under-theorizing. Perhaps the chief reason for the low estate of theory is that in the social sciences so much theorizing has been done in a vacuum. Most economic theory of the classical (now the marginal or equilibrium) school has until recently avoided facts like the plague, and hence it has been of little value as a guide to action for either business man or statesman. Marxist theory is based on factual material mostly of the mid-nineteenth century: inconvenient modern facts are ignored or explained away.

On the other hand, economic theorizing is useless if it does not lead to the formulation of *policies*, which can be *applied in action*. And as soon as you begin to think in terms of action you are necessarily out of the field of pure "economics." You are dealing with living human beings. You have got to ask: What makes them act the way they do? You have got to set up standards and goals: What is the good life toward which action is to be directed?

And so, though this is a book on "economics," I must engage in another digression, into the field of philosophy and sociology. I am bound to ask myself: What values am I seeking, and what is the nature of the historical process within which I imagine my economic theories to operate?

### *Philosophic Approach: Scientific Humanism*

In my own personal development I have long felt a conflict between two ways of looking at the world: one might be called the soft-hearted and the other the hard-boiled approach. I suppose this may be merely a personal aspect of the great conflict between the natural requirements of the group, or even of the species, seeking survival, and of the individual seeking survival.

Being a member of a large family I early became aware of the necessity of compromising my own instinctive wants in consideration of others'. Without sympathy, that is, without the ability to put yourself in the other person's place, the harmony of any social group, family or nation, is impossible. Then, with an overdose of New England divines in my bloodstream, I went through a childhood phase of pious altruism which was probably as noxious to those around me as pure grabbiness might have been—a phase which brought soft-heartedness close to soft-headedness.

Having attended a church school where certain routines of piety were part of the curriculum may have further delayed the reaction back to sheer hedonism, which so often takes place in adolescence. At any rate, as I became increasingly aware of the standards of the business world, and its arrogant glorification of the profit motive, I was no longer impressionable enough to be able to accept it as part of the normal order of things. As I have previously related, I was given primer lessons in the profit system by my father; I was instructed to save rather than spend; I heard with a shock the use of the term "worth" to describe a man's wealth; I was taught respect for bankers and men of great wealth. But it did not sink in very deep—why should it when I already had, as a matter of course, all that money would buy? At the most I was only able to accept the doubtful reconciliation involved in the word "philanthropist."

The first mature synthesis of the demands of individualism and society I found in Henry Adams' great autobiography. His term "benevolent anarchism" appealed to me greatly. The world's apparent disorder and cruelty, for which none of the philosophical theories I had encountered gave an adequate explanation, arose from a complexity of natural phenomena beyond the reach of any human formulas, hence apparently "anarchic." At the same time, the necessary though irrational assertion of human dignity required an attitude of good will, "benevolence."

This individualistic synthesis of the soft-hearted and hard-boiled might not have resulted in any active social philosophy without an aesthetic sense keenly developed by the Utopian surroundings in which, at home, school and college, I had spent my formative years. In my last year in law school I gave up a small amount of time to a free "legal aid" service; and the tales of utter squalor that poured from bruised lips at those sessions in the grim old New Haven City Hall sent me scurrying back, with a feeling of nausea in the pit of my stomach, to the peace of Yale's Gothic quadrangles.

Before long I found the old conflict assuming a new form, as disturbing as ever. It was most strikingly set forth by the first ardent Communist I ever met. I was on the Turk-Sib Railroad, crawling over the bleak Kirghiz steppes, so far in the interior of Asia that I felt as if I were lost on another planet. The friendly young party member, who had been delegated to some difficult political job in Alma-Ata, thousands of miles from his wife and child in Moscow, explained to me with the aid of my pocket dictionary why a good Bolshevik must be "hard." The word came out several times, "*hard,*" "*hard,*" "*hard.*" Personal sufferings were nothing. The individual must sink himself in the mass. The mass was everything. The trouble with "liberals" and "reformers" was their "softness": like true "bourgeois" they worried over the possibility that someone might get hurt in the Revolution. I had no answer for him. I found his penetrating zealot's gaze as uncomfortable as a cultured Roman might have found that of a Christian evangelist, telling of the hell that awaited him if he did not repent. In this case the hard-boiled attitude was no more satisfactory for being associated with an altruistic social philosophy rather than with hedonism.

It was some time before I came to another partial solution. I became convinced in spite of what the zealots were then saying that individualism and socialism were not opposites but complements. I became convinced that the greatest expansion of the individual personality was only possible in a widened community responsibility.

Yet this still provided no workable social creed. For how was the "revolution" to be achieved? The criticism of the liberal reformers seemed justified. After generations of "reform" the capitalist world seemed to be sinking ever deeper in misery and cruelty. Perhaps a dictatorship, if not of the proletariat, then of some more enlightened elite, was necessary. Since conditions made it impossible to lead men, by sweet reasonableness, to freedom, they must be coerced to freedom. Perhaps even the dictatorship of the mind, represented by the dogmatic absolutes of Marxism, was necessary after all. Such dictatorships would be temporary, as surgery or other unpleasant but necessary use of violence is temporary.

I suppose the Moscow trials definitely ended for me, as for many another, the possibility of espousing the Marxist revolution. The whole question of ends and means was brought too brutally to light. The rationalized coercions of communism were too much like the irrational coercions of the fascist dictatorships. If I could forgive the corruption revealed by the Moscow trials as the outcome of dictatorship (corruption regardless of whether accusers or accused were the more guilty) I must forgive Hitler's purges. If, looking back at the destruction of the liberal intellectuals and of the kulak class in the light of the new reign of terror, I must forgive these means, as honestly (though probably erroneously) believed necessary to achieve a worthy goal, then I must forgive anti-Semitism, believed with equal sincerity to be a necessary instrument of policy.

Instead I came to feel that absolutism was what was most to be feared. The absolutism of a political dictatorship and the absolutism of a dogmatic creed, however pseudo-scientific the creed, and however humane the political goal, alike seemed to threaten the most fundamental values of civilization.

Capitalism, I was by that time convinced, "could not be saved and was not worth saving." The basic question before humanity was whether we could achieve the necessary collective integration without succumbing to absolutism. If either the fascist or the communist absolutism conquered the world, then, regardless of the integration that might be achieved, individual freedom and the scientific method (by which alone individual freedom can now be reconciled to social integration) would be lost. Moreover, before either one of these absolutes conquered, their wars might set back human development for centuries.

By this route I was gradually driven to this belief: that the scientific method, used to enhance human worth through social action, provides the only adequate basis for a social philosophy.

It was perhaps only a happy accident that the magazine of

which I had been an editor for the last few years was called *Common Sense*. But the words fitted the same early inclination that attracted me to Henry Adams' "benevolent anarchism." The modern emphasis on relativity in the sciences seemed to give further support to my antipathy for absolute categories and formulas. The more recent emphasis on semantics, with its warning of the "tyranny of words," strengthened my confidence in a combination of straight common-sense logic and good will.

Lancelot Hogben has been dramatizing this "scientific humanism" more cogently perhaps than anyone else.* John Dewey's "instrumentalism," logic used purposefully, as a means of inquiry to determine humane action, seems the philosopher's expression of the same idea. If America has any special contribution to make to the history of philosophy, thanks to her origins and the development of her uniquely pragmatic attitudes, it will be in this general direction.

But I am not a philosopher. I leave to professionals the further elucidation or criticism of this attitude to the world. At least this brief mention may help you understand how I have determined the values which I think an economic program should serve.

First of those values is the human individual. His worth and dignity cannot be abrogated because he belongs to a particular class, or race, or other abstract category. His stature depends on freedom to develop in his own way, and on his relations with his fellows in group activities. Only when environmental limitations are minimized, in conditions of material "abundance," can the higher forms of human development become generally possible. This is the task of economics, or, as we may once more learn to call it, political economy. On these assumptions war, whether international or civil, is obviously a paramount evil. And means and ends are all part of a process which may enhance or debase the social totality we call civilization.

* In his recent book, *Science for the Citizen*, he defines the concept thus: "The social contract of scientific humanism is the recognition that the sufficient basis for rational co-operation between citizens is scientific investigation of the common needs of mankind, a scientific inventory of resources available for satisfying them, and a realistic survey of how modern social institutions contribute to or militate against the use of such resources for the satisfaction of fundamental human needs" (page 1075).

### *Sociological Approach: Dynamic Trial and Error*

Marx saw historical change coming about through the conflict of certain group interests. If he had left it at that, a concept of an organic society in process of evolution, and had not tried to apply the Hegelian word-magic of the "dialectic," I would have less quarrel with him. As I pointed out, he saw the conflict all in terms of two groups, the workers and the capitalists, and he defined the groups only in terms of their economic interests. Hence "the class struggle" (note the "the"). Hence the "historic mission" of the workers who received wages, as against the property-owners who received profits.

The "middle classes" are upsetting all predictions based on Marx's class struggle. The very term "class" may be misleading, for no "class," whether capitalist, proletarian or "middle," is sufficiently clear-cut or self-conscious to act as a predictable political force. Even from the standpoint of economic interest alone, it is probably sounder to think of innumerable conflicting and interpenetrating groups, rather than "classes"; such "groups" are labor unions, industries, co-operatives, local or regional economic areas, private or public bureaucracies, economic units for various purposes as small as the family, as comprehensive as the nation or even the world.

But beyond the economic interest are many other interests, real or imaginary. In the long run it may be that the economic interest has more often been decisive than any other single interest. But pride, glory, lust for power, superstition, and noble idealism have all played their pre-eminent roles. Bertrand Russell has recently pictured history as primarily molded by the lust for power. Harold Lasswell has analyzed other more subtle incentives to social change, such as vanity, pride of place, the desire for security. Thurman Arnold's *Folklore of Capitalism* was a brilliantly revealing book in its exposure of the magical formulas and foibles which so often lead groups to a course of action directly counter to their economic interest.

These writers represent part of a present trend to link up the so-called social sciences. Anthropology, sociology, economics, history, psychology, and, extending into the natural sciences, human biology, all are becoming available to the intelligent layman in a co-ordinated fashion, thus making it easier than ever before to understand the complex ways of our human species. The concepts of organic evolution developed by Darwin are being applied increasingly to the social organism.

Human life is a process, ever in flux, changing, evolving. The method is almost as haphazard and irrational as the method of the jungle. Rather than a reasoned progress we see an evolution proceeding by trial and error, by social mutations which are harmful or helpful. Conceivably a social mutation might be lethal; such would be one leading to ever bigger and more disastrous wars, so that the species would die out. But for the most part the harmful mutations are suppressed in time without fatal damage, and those conducive to survival continue. History certainly warrants the optimistic belief in evolutionary "progress." Even its great cycles tend to have the spiral form.

Yet only too obviously "progress" is blundering at best. Men's passions and superstitions, their ignorance and lack of discipline, often stimulate and may long perpetuate modes of action contrary to their best interests. A strike between a steel corporation and a labor union may result in a collective agreement stabilizing their relations in a way beneficial to both, but it is almost as likely to lead to stupid violence and a lengthening chain of reactionary social consequences. Social and international peace are obviously desirable but war hangs on.

Brooks Adams pointed out a generation ago the danger that our capacity for administration might not be able to keep up with the requirements of a complexly interrelated civilization of two billion persons equipped with machines. Administration is management, collective organization of human beings. A temporary solution may be the dictator. But dictators are no more infallible than anyone else. The problem of the twentieth century is pre-eminently one of devising methods of administration that will give full scope to the individual through democratic methods, and still function with the requisite degree of efficiency.

## *Group Organization*

All social problems then are problems of individuals in groups: how they function as groups, how the interests of the individual and the group harmonize or conflict, how different groups may be adjusted to each other.

In place of Marx's dialectical theory of historical materialism we might attempt to phrase a formula like this: All history is a history of dynamic social evolution proceeding through the conflicts and adjustments of individual and group interests. Since survival of the species in the natural environment is an all-pervading and underlying interest, the economic interest is often the determining one in this social evolution—but not always.*

The social organism has often been compared to a human organism. It is an intricate complex of more or less harmoniously related cells, tissues, structures and organs. In its most inclusive sense it is the whole body of human beings on the planet through historical time. One feature of its evolution has been the growing size and organizational complexity of the various human groups.

Looking back over my own history I can see many analogies to social institutions in human history. The simplest form of group activity is the mass. Two people are stronger than one. I recall vividly my surprise the first time I was sent out with a big group of boys at school to move a grandstand near the playing field: it was a heavy plank structure, but fifty boys could lift it with one hand apiece.

Division of labor is the next feature of group activity. Football and baseball give every American boy a sense of the power of teamplay, with strength depending less on weight of numbers than effective co-ordination of various assigned tasks.

In the course of centuries these two principles, weight of numbers and co-ordination of different activities, have built up a social structure of inconceivable complexity. With every increase of complexity comes the need for greater integration. Conflicts must be resolved in terms of new and higher unities. Discipline, balance,

* Some of the more modern Marxists have attempted to revitalize the "dialectic" concept along these lines. But since Marx considered the economic interest as *necessarily* the determining one, and considered economic "classes" as the only important groups, and narrowed them to two, his formulation is so artificially narrow as to be worse than useless. Unable to understand the social mutations of the post-war years, Marxists find current events "meaningless," and take refuge in the thought that human nature has "degenerated" so that it cannot fulfill its historic role.

harmony, become ever more necessary and ever more difficult of achievement. New administrative techniques are constantly called for.

Here again a family experience is illustrative. Children never like to go to bed when they should. My father worked out a scheme—an administrative technique—that largely eliminated the arguing and wheedling and disciplining which make many a family evening hideous. He set official bedtimes fifteen minutes apart according to age. Each older boy in turn would see that the next younger went to bed on time, so that he could enjoy his privileged quarter-hour. It worked like a charm—most of the time.

Administrative techniques become more and more differentiated as the social group grows in size and comes into relation with an increasing number of other groups. The threefold division of our American government—legislative to make policy, executive to carry it out, and judicial to settle disputes—is one method of division of governmental or administrative function in a large national state. (Administration in the narrow sense, conceived of as subsidiary to the executive department, is currently under attack because it still entails legislative and judicial functions: government obviously cannot be put in water-tight compartments.)

Institutions are the patterns of group action. They are the more or less permanent forms of organization within which groups of various kinds function. Some of these institutions we call governmental and others private. But this again is a distinction hard to maintain. Government, like administration, is a vague word that will not keep in bounds. Every group requires government. Every group must be administered. We have chosen to call certain functions political; they may be local, state, regional, federal, or even, conceivably, international; and we attach the word "government" especially to them. But anyone who has had experience both in such organizations and in business or social organizations, corporations, clubs, churches, schools, knows that each one involves similar problems of government.

Any observer of the world about him must recognize that all these organizations knit and intertwine in a most intricate fashion. John Citizen finds the conflicting loyalties of his family, his neighbors, his church, his trade union, his business, his race, his school district, his town, his state, his party, his country, often quite bewildering; and when all those contacts are multiplied by a hundred million other John Citizens, the sociologist who tries to unravel the tangle is hardly to be blamed if he tries to find some simplifying formula.

A group or organization or institution exists for some function. It requires government or administration—a guiding control to assure that it performs its function as efficiently as possible, and to resolve the conflicts that arise between its individual members, between any member and itself, and between itself and any other group.

## *The Individual and the Group*

I am primarily concerned here with exploring the possibility of individual freedom in the group. I said that philosophically the worth of the individual human being is pre-eminent; yet groups to which the individual is subordinate are the essence of social growth. What are the conditions that will assure that the group liberates and develops the individual rather than limiting him? The old liberalistic formula, individual *versus* group, freedom *versus* control, will not do. The notion of absolute anarchism, in which there is complete absence of coercion and all group activity is on a basis of purely voluntary co-operation, is as unreal on the one hand as is the notion of absolute despotism on the other.

There are, I think, three possible ways of conserving freedom within the group.

The first is to seek to have power in as many members of the group as possible. The many should govern the few rather than the few the many. Rule by the majority is preferable to monarchy or oligarchy. Yet it is clear that coercion remains coercion even when imposed by majority vote. The individuals constituting the minority are as much imposed upon as if they constituted a majority, and they may feel the tyranny of the dominant number as irksome as that of an arbitrary despot. Freedom means more than counting noses. Moreover, there are many types of group organization, even in a "democracy," in which it is difficult if not impossible to apply the principle of majority rule. An army in wartime, a ship at sea, a railroad system, all require hierarchical and expert direction, unhampered by majority votes.

A second approach might ask the question whether or not membership in the group is voluntary. The manufacturer considers that the absolute discipline maintained in his factory is compatible with democracy because no worker is compelled to seek employment there. Before the Great War army discipline was justified in the democratic countries on the ground that service was voluntary: a volunteer freely gave up his freedom when he enlisted. With conscription universally applied in wartime that argument no longer holds. Membership in economic organizations, factories, businesses, farms, is all held to be voluntary, yet in practice we all know that the old-time freedom to work at what one chooses is largely gone. Moreover, membership in many groups, regional, racial, national, is an accident of birth, from which there may be no withdrawal. The question whether membership in a group is voluntary may then be of limited importance.

A third consideration—in the long run more important for our purposes—is whether the group control functions automatically or by coercion. Look at the instance I gave a moment ago of the bedtimes automatically enforced in a large family. Before the technique was developed my father would order us to bed, and we each felt the humiliation and pain of being little boys given commands by a physical superior, without recourse. When the automatic mechanism was developed the ultimate authority could doze if he liked. The technique was at once more efficient and more respectful of the individual.

In that example the ultimate coercive authority remained. Yet as I grew up I found coercion eliminated in one field after another and replaced by self-discipline and habit. That was what freedom meant. In so far as society grows up in the ways of freedom it will be by developing purely automatic controls over its group activities, with coercion wholly absent.

Yet there are limitations on the extent to which any such pure automatism can prevail. An ultimate authority with power to give orders and see that they are carried out, coercing recalcitrant individuals into line, is necessary in most social groups. No automatic mechanism can lay down policies, can make rules, can organize. Even to create and install an automatic mechanism, such as a traffic light on the corner, requires preliminary orders from somewhere. These orders often require technical skill; and their administration often requires hierarchic organization and discipline. Under any economic democracy conceivable, trains must run on schedules worked out by traffic experts, and orders must be relayed down from traffic manager to train dispatcher to locomotive engineer. In times of emergency or danger the need for swift and sure action must often take precedence over individual "rights." So long as we have factories and assembly lines we shall have regimentation.

Yet experts are arrogant, hierarchies tend to grow rigid, "emergencies" have a way of perpetuating themselves. The habitual and self-correcting and automatic must always be sought even if it cannot always be found.

Let me cite a few examples of these automatic social controls:

From my seventeenth-floor New York office I can look down on a busy street intersection. The sidewalks are jammed with people. I watch one person from above and see him thread his way through the throng. He will be followed by one, two, three or four people, finding the path he breaks through easy to pursue; for a moment a pattern emerges, with a line of people going in one direction without blocking a line going in the other. But almost at once the pattern is lost, and the crowd is merely an aggregation of atoms, each following its own erratic path. A highly complex group activity is going on, the moving of thousands of people from one place to the other, and efficiency might be served by more coercive rules. But obviously the automatic process by which each individual is his own policeman is preferable. Only when a parade or other emergency on the avenue arises is it necessary to put up ropes and give orders to "keep moving" in this or that direction.

I go out to buy a sandwich for lunch, choosing my favorite restaurant, and selecting the item I want at the price I want to pay. In so doing I am playing an important part in many economic processes, all carried on in complex interrelated groups. I am a consumer entering the market, in this case primarily a consumer of foodstuffs. Conceivably it might be more efficient for me to be fed as I used to be at boarding school: there a bell would ring, I would file in to my assigned place in the crowded dining hall, and a substantial meal, worked out according to the best dietetic standards, would be placed before me. That is the way it is done, with variations, in most families, in jails, and in the army. It has its advantages and disadvantages. Yet free consumer's choice, operating in the automatic mechanism of distribution and production we call the market, is an element of freedom no one would be willing to give up.

To feed and otherwise provide for a population involves many enterprises and many individual jobs. Conceivably those jobs might be filled by a dictator assigning each person to the job he was best fitted to fill. Within any single enterprise the management does just that. But the distribution of workers between all the available jobs is left to the automatic mechanism of the labor market. That is an essential condition of freedom for most of us. Yet in wartime we are conscripted. In Europe there is compulsory military service even in peacetime, and labor service for millions. Moreover, an increasing number of coercive rules have been imposed on conditions of labor in this country. The freedom of the individual worker seeking work from a large corporation may be so illusory that it becomes necessary to assure "collective bargaining" through a union, perhaps even under a "closed shop" agreement.

During 1938 a nationwide railroad strike was threatened in protest against a proposed 15 per cent wage cut. A generation ago the cut would have been imposed, the strike called, the nation's traffic disrupted, there might have been riots and bloodshed and widespread suffering. On the other hand, under a dictatorship the railroads would not have been able to impose a wage cut except as the government might decree, and if decreed the workers would have had to accept it without a protest—for the trains must "run on time." But the dispute was settled here by a slow and more or less automatic process laid down in a federal law, the Railway Labor Act. First collective bargaining, then attempted mediation, then a fact-finding commission with publicity for its findings. The whole issue was aired. The railroads were persuaded to withdraw their threatened wage cut in return for promise of government financial aid. The "corporative" mechanism within which the interests of the workers, the management, the owners, the creditors, the consuming public, the government, all found expression and within which their conflicts were resolved, proved its worth. The process was throughout more automatic than coercive.

Take an even more complex group enterprise, the TVA. It involves innumerable conflicts of interest, which are worked out in various ways no one could have predicted when the enterprise was started. It involves a gigantic public investment, conflicting at many points with private investment. The ordinary automatic controls of the market are in many instances absent. In other instances they may crop up unexpectedly: when a dam or a piece of road or a building is to be built the authorities are much more likely to turn the job over to a private contractor bidding competitively, and carrying on his own activities within the market mechanism, than to attempt the job on a pure engineering basis themselves.

I have cited five examples because they illustrate the chief aspects of economic automatism as a method of economic government.* It would be easy to think of countless others, where group activities are carried on efficiently and conflicts resolved with a maximum degree of freedom.

After all, the automatic group mechanism is the way of nature. Nature gives no vocal orders. Its "tropisms" direct life to survival, plants to the sunshine, animals to their sustenance and their matings, with no iron bars or coercive instruments.

As individuals we cannot evade controls and directives if we would live and work together. But discipline can become self-discipline, and self-discipline can become an irkless habit. Conflicts can be harmonious rather than dissonant. Courtesy is the civilized alternative to coercion. Freedom becomes the natural prerogative of man's mature estate.

And if this is true of individuals it is true of groups. The natural resolution of forces involved in a balance of conflicting pressures may be worked out by a conscious bargaining process or in an unconscious automatic synthesis. It is always likely to be more a rough approximation than a perfect balance. Representative legislatures, subject to the various lobbying pressures of

* I might call these five: freedom of locomotion, freedom of consumer choice, freedom of occupation, automatic adjustment of group conflicts, and flexibility in public enterprise.

special interest groups, are one solution. The syndicalists have thought the occupational and functional groupings of productive workers (after the elimination of private property) could provide all the needed social organization, without other government. The guild socialists refined this concept and visualized a government by functional rather than territorial representation. The medieval guild or "corporation" has also given direction to Catholic social teaching, and has been elaborated in Italian fascist theory, as previously noted.*

Co-operation and compromise, in reasonable adjustments, is the way of life, rather than coercion of the weaker by the stronger.

### *The Individual and the State*

In any social order there is one level of group organization which is supreme over all others, with power of life and death. At various times it has been the family, or the clan, or the tribe. But with the coming of civilization the state is the supreme coercive authority.

More than any other group, the state always aroused the fear and suspicion of the individualist. Its supreme coercive authority has always been abused. Yet without it there could have been no civilization. The great empires of antiquity were slave empires. But under them tools were invented, sciences were formulated, roads were built, commerce and exchange stimulated the development of new products and new ideas, the means by which man could conquer his environment and know himself were enlarged. When the empires fell apart, due to administrative failings, there was a reversion to more primitive ways, the arts and sciences were forgotten, the roads fell into disrepair so that fertilizing contacts ceased, and man slipped back for a while toward his animal ancestors.

The present authoritarian collectivisms, fascist and communist,

* See above, page 226. The "corporative" idea is not a fascist invention. Where every group interest is democratically represented, in a structure which provides for the automatic harmonizing of conflicts, such a "corporative" system would be conducive to the fullest freedom. The early Soviet leaders, who looked forward to a rapid achievement of democracy, conceived of the structure of "soviets" or councils also in this way.

are not altogether new, in so far as they represent a high degree of coercive discipline over comparatively large areas. What is new about them is, first, that modern applied science has greatly increased the complexity of the interrelations of the national group, carrying the disciplines into collective economic activity at every level, from growing crops and making shoes to maintaining an air-mail service; and, second, that the democratic ideal of equal rights to all members of the community (whether conceived as a class community or as a racial community) has become so deeply ingrained in modern times that the leaders wear simple army blouses instead of silks and ermines, and all group activities are given at least the outward trappings of equalitarianism rather than slavery.

It is natural, in modern or ancient times, for the state to take on the mystical trappings of absolutism. Even in our own liberal tradition the state has been idealized, and the government of the state has acquired an almost supernatural aura.

I remember the awe with which I first went to Washington to see the "government." I was taken to the Capitol and was duly impressed by its great bronze doors, flanked by nobly-proportioned brass spittoons, and guarded by antiquated political pensioners who couldn't qualify as policemen in a small town. The Senate and House Chambers, even in the midst of busy sessions, don't show a fraction of the dignity and earnestness of a high school debating society, and when I was introduced to the august law-makers of the nation in the Capitol corridors, I found them indistinguishable from the gaping tourists. I gave up the idea that this was the "government" and considered that it lay in the White House. One day my father was invited to bring his family to an informal showing of a movie at the White House. We felt very small when he told us that the President was the most powerful ruler in the world. When we found ourselves at the appointed time in the East Room it was with a sense of imminent majesty that we heard the major domo sonorously announce: "The President of the United States." A little squinty man shuffled in, gave us a sidelong glance and plumped in a big armchair. I sat directly behind him during the showing of the movie, near enough to touch his unprepossessing scalp, and was more than ever in doubt as to what was the "government." Gradually I accepted a hazy notion that it was the pretentious marble buildings of Washington. This is still the way I visualize those vague words "government" and "state." But, for anything like a scientific conception, one must think of a complex network of human relations, which permit certain individuals in Washington to give certain final decisive orders under certain specially important circumstances. When a President signs a tariff law, for instance, customs officials in the customs houses follow a new pattern of procedure, and indirectly the amount of food and clothing consumed by every person in America may be altered.

The nineteenth-century liberal who thinks of the state as the necessary enemy of the individual, and the Marxist who thinks of it as the mere coercive instrument of the ruling class which will "wither away" when classes are abolished, are both reacting against the state. But neither of them expresses its final reality. It is far too complex a group institution to be characterized in a phrase. In an earlier chapter I sketched some of the history of the capitalist state, and indicated how it is subject to all the pressures of all the subordinate social groups within it. And as I have been trying to emphasize in this chapter, all groups have much the same problem in governing themselves. The state is merely group action on a high level. Nowhere is the problem of democracy or of individualism a simple one.

Many modern liberals have felt the lapse from the pre-war internationalism as heightening the danger of domination by the state. But this, too, is an oversimplification.

Increasingly up to 1914 "free enterprise" developed its own international apparatus of world finance and world trade, and the national states, without giving up any of their sovereignty, found it expedient to observe certain world-wide rules of "international law" and mercantile practice, and to agree on other joint commercial and financial procedures.

The internationalism by common consent that existed prior to 1914 fitted in with the desires of the dominant economic groups in each country: it was an era of industrial expansion and commercial imperialism. The fact that this purely voluntary internationalism has been shrinking is quite compatible with the fact that at the same time the role of government within the national states has vastly increased. In so far as the elaboration of group activity represents civilized progress, the present era of nationalism need not mean retrogression, as so many present-day Jeremiahs are wont to believe. The national collective controls of different kinds over agriculture, for instance, including collectivization in the Soviet Union, the "blood and soil" direction of German farming, and Secretary Wallace's AAA experiments, however differing in technique and desirability, all represent great advances in the direction of planned group control of the natural environment, as compared to the free play of the world market in agricultural products in the pre-war era, though the earlier method gave the appearance of integration on a world-wide scale and the newer seems a restriction to national fields.

It now seems more than likely that a high order of group integration will be achieved in the important national states long before any great degree of international planning and control is achieved. This runs counter to two older ideals, that of the nineteenth-century liberals who conceived of world-wide peace and harmony built on the international commerce of private enterprisers, and that of the Marxian Socialists who tried to cement the international solidarity of the working class as a prerequisite to the achievement of socialism, whether in one country or on a world scale. The whole trend today in every country is toward the building of what might have been called "national socialism" if Hitler had not already patented the term to fit his own neuroses. Self-sufficient economic nationalism or "autarchy" has been the practical tendency since the war, in spite of the almost universal denunciation of serious thinkers on both left and right.

## *Alarm for Freedom*

How then shall the necessities of group action, especially in the modern state, be reconciled with individual freedom? The conflicts arising today within and between groups are so confusing as to seem quite baffling and discouraging. The loudspeakers blare one or another alarmist interpretation till the rational man almost despairs of making order out of the chaos.

I was brought up to believe that progress consisted in the gradual winning of liberty from tyrants. The American Revolution was the crowning achievement in that battle. Today I hear many deeply worried voices bewailing the resurgence of tyranny. Democracy, they say, is in retreat before returning despotism. The alarmists see an insidious encroachment on our hard-won individual freedoms even in America, the land of liberty.

Liberals of my father's conservative school are prone to view history as a cyclic alternation of despotism and liberty. The wicked despot becomes intolerable and is overthrown by the people. But in the heyday of democracy the people become indolent and lose their vigilance. Tyranny returns. At first it is a benevolent tyranny, but it becomes wicked in the end, and the cycle then repeats itself. Many sincere conservatives see the New Deal as a returning despotism.

A more modern type of liberal sees the issue as one between a privileged few and an exploited many. He believes that an aristocracy of wealth and economic power has been taking the place of the ousted feudal aristocracy of land and birth. He calls for an unremitting defense of civil rights against greedy and selfish interests seeking to turn government to their own ends. He would defend the little man against plutocracy and monopoly.

Still another set of spokesmen declare that we are at a crossroads, one way leading to freedom for individual economic enterprise, the other to totalitarian dictatorship. In the conflict between "business and government" they loudly insist business must be left "free."

Marxists in turn see the conflict explicitly between the workers on the one hand, and the capitalists who exploit their labor through private ownership of the means of production on the other. The capitalists control the "state apparatus" (government), and in spite of democratic forms dominate the toiling masses as ruthlessly as any ruling class in an era of slavery or feudalism.

Other voices again call to battle in an even more pressing cause, that of a decent world organization against the ruthless aggression of fascism. A peaceful world order, subject to international law, recognizing moral principles as supreme, must in their opinion take the place of the present reign of international anarchy based on force. But the fascist leaders on the opposite side call loudly for "freedom" and "justice" in a world in which they claim to be "have not" nations.

All these contradictory voices are obviously concerned with the conflicts of interest with and between groups. The issues are real issues. They are the problems of government, the problems of administering our joint human affairs on this crowded planet, the problems of reconciling freedom and organization. Yet the very divergence of these attitudes, even when they all profess devotion to "liberty," suggests that there is little common agreement on the nature of the problem. All see one aspect of a larger whole, and then seek by oversimplification to bring order out of their mental chaos.

Democracy is not a form of government. It is an attitude toward other people which determines social arrangements, including both political and economic institutions. If you respect human personality as you know it in yourself, and have a sufficiently sympathetic identification of yourself with others whom you encounter, as well as with those you know to exist but don't encounter, you will want others to be as well off materially as yourself, and have the same opportunities and freedoms. Any concept of human dignity requires that every man have the fullest possible share in determining his own destiny. Because a man's destiny is shaped by his many relations with others, in groups, then the democratic ideal is to be sought in every one of those groups, his home and family group, his neighborhood group, his club, church, union, professional or trade association, and his working group both narrowly conceived, as a shop, office or single business unit, and broadly conceived, as an industry or occupation. The political groups, local or more inclusive, are usually far less important in everyday life than those others. But since the state has the final monopoly on force—the policeman's club, the electric chair, the bayonet—and membership in it is more compulsory than in the other groups, democratic procedures in the state take on a special importance.

Economic planning, like any other group function, can be undertaken either by authoritarian methods, by bosses or dictators, or by democratic methods. The fact that expertness and discipline are necessary leads many persons, particularly conservatives with axes to grind, to the conclusion that democracy is incompatible with group action in the economic field. Yet the functions of the state, including the democratic state, require expertness and discipline. Because we do not subject every operation in the building of a highway system to majority vote, and because individual enterprise no longer builds private toll roads, we do not assume that democracy has been destroyed on the highways.

Does the spread of collective controls mean that liberty and democracy are being crushed by a new despotism? Is economic planning incompatible with democracy, as Walter Lippmann would say? The answer cannot be a simple yes or no. Much may depend on the types of group control employed, and their method of application. The questions should be: Are group decisions taken by majority vote when they can be? Is participation in any group activity voluntary or compulsory? Do the directives function automatically, or coercively and arbitrarily?

Again, is fascism a world threat to democracy? But fascism is not a simple abstraction; nor is democracy. In practice which is the freer, the unemployed Englishman in a "depressed area" whose life is lived within the confines of a pauper's dole, or the employed Nazi worker taken on a conducted *Kraft Durch Freude* holiday tour? The Nazi may need a ration card to secure butter, the former may be free to buy it without a card—if his dole can be stretched so far. The jobless Englishman may be able to vote, once every few years, for a slate of candidates he had no voice in selecting. The German may vote too, with no alternative slate, and the necessity of voting "Ja." The Englishman can swear at his government with impunity. The German cannot; but he may be restrained by no more terrible a sanction than that his children have been taught to believe it is shamefully bad form to criticize the "leader."

The Marxist points an accusing finger at the German factory where the "leadership principle" has been applied in such a way as to compel the subjection of the worker to the boss in even more brutal fashion than under pure capitalism. He will point with pride to the Soviet Union, where the workers "own" the factories. But I have seen Soviet workers like dumb cattle in the vast confinement of a factory, and felt their slavery to routine and noise and dirt and rigid discipline (always a soldier with a bayonet stood symbolic at the door) no less than that of American workers in an American factory. In a sense industrial slavery can in the long run be mitigated only by the advance of the automatic machine. But I have seen workers in this capitalist country with the pride of workmanship, with the pride of sharing in a business that aroused their loyalty, with the pride of responsible participation in a union. In the intricacies of modern industrial civilization freedom is not merely dependent on the outcome of a struggle between the workers and the bosses. "Industrial democracy" is not merely a matter of collective bargaining. If economic democracy is to be constructed it will have to take into account all the ramifications of group activity in the economic process—collective bargaining, personnel management, the union, the corporation, the "syndical" or "corporative" organization of industries, the co-operative, the pressure group representing a special interest, the interrelation of all political and social institutions. No simple formula will do.

Then again there are those who see civilization most threatened by war. The highest present form of group activity, the national state, must sooner or later give way to a more inclusive organization to resolve international conflicts. We have only begun to work out the techniques of international organization, but automatic and voluntary mechanisms seem to work best. Our world postal mechanism works with automatic smoothness. Scientists share their discoveries for the most part regardless of national boundaries. Voluntary pooling of statistical information in the League of Nations and the International Labor Office is less dramatic but may be no less important than attempts to impose "sanctions." Perhaps the same principles of freedom in group action which we have discussed in other connections apply here. Certainly coercive controls can be only a last and desperate resort. We want no super-state resting on mere force.*

A long-range historical and anthropological view shows men in different geographical areas evolving different types of group action, handicapped and motivated quite as much by their inherited folklore as by their economic environment. It is difficult not to pass judgment on the wickedness of Hitler or the Nazis or Germany, holding the nation itself to a kind of personal accountability. But since the method appropriate to deal with the situation is a war by the complex national group called the United States against the com-

* A few additional suggestions regarding the possible future of international organizations appear in the last chapter.

plex national group called Germany, which involves mutual slaughter and destruction, something more nearly approaching scientific objectivity may be preferable. The old concept of "sin" has largely been abandoned in our relations with Tom, Dick and Harry in our immediate neighborhood; why then should we go on using it in our more distant relations with Hans and Fritz and Adolf? Germany and the other aggressive nations are not "mad dogs" to be crushed, but large groups of bewildered human beings, with bewildered leaders, trying to adjust themselves to the exigencies of the modern environment. The same is true of the more fortunate aggregations, such as that we call the United States.

Here, as in all the other "burning issues," where alarmists see the world "at a crossroads," with "democracy" or "civilization" at stake, the philosophical and sociological approach I have outlined seems to call for objectivity. Human beings are so complex, and the groups and institutions through which the human family organizes itself are so complex, that all rigid and simple formulas must fail. Flexibility and tolerance seem required by the "scientific humanism," which I suggested as the only adequate approach to our social problems.

Man, in all his blundering and perplexity today, is seeking to fashion new group patterns, which may make possible a final conquest of his material environment. This is in the last analysis an economic problem, though it was necessary in this chapter first to decide what human ends economic procedures should serve. In particular I had to clear the ground of the argument that freedom depends upon economic individualism, for the greatest mental barrier to economic progress in America is the fear that any economic controls will mean a loss of freedom. Now I am ready to go ahead with my exploration of the economic problem proper.

# Chapter Fifteen

## GOODS AND PURCHASING POWER

MY exploration of economic theory has necessarily been an unorthodox one. Instead of the academic approach, which is always likely to build theory as a justification of the *status quo,* and explains depressions and other difficulties as variations from "normal" due to outside interferences, I came to economics with little textbook background, but with a conviction that the present economic system was incapable of producing the abundance that was physically possible. From my first acquaintance with the Soviet Union and depression-ridden Europe, and from my subsequent study of the new economic techniques in the process of development in every country, I was convinced that the economic problem was essentially one of making goods and services available in the "real world," and that one of the major sources of difficulty in the old economic procedures was that they depended for their functioning on unreal, or imaginary, or "paper" factors.

### *The Promise of Plenty*

My concern with "real wealth"—and "abundance"—went back, after all, to the background I described in Part I. Brought up in an abundant household where there was always enough of everything, educated in the Utopian surroundings of a private school and a munificently endowed university, brought into contact with economic realities at a time when the "capitalist" part of the world was suffering from "overproduction" and the "socialist" part was bending every effort to increase the budget of goods and services made available—it was natural for me to thrust monetary problems impatiently aside.

Shortly after my return to this country in 1932 the "technocracy" craze swept the country. I saw Howard Scott's fabulous charts. The graphs of electric power installations, the engineering rigmarole of "balanced load factors," talk of "ergs" and "productive capacity" and the floods of goods with which technicians could smother the country, all confirmed my growing conviction that, given efficient engineering of the whole productive process, abundance for all was near at hand. In my own brief factory experience I had seen the wonders of automatic machinery, and had sensed both their promise of plenty and their menace of technological unemployment.

The daily news lent further support to this emphasis on goods. There was talk of plowing under cotton, burning wheat, and shortly of slaughtering little pigs, all because an incredibly rich country had "too much," while its citizens went without.

From this point of view the monetary and banking systems were relics of an age of witchcraft, cluttering up a "power age." Bassett Jones showed, in a widely discussed little book, how the curve of increase of productivity could not possibly keep pace with the curve of compound interest which it was supposed to maintain. The "technocrats" pointed to the mounting load of debt as the major cause of the breakdown of a marvelous productive machine. The three hundred billion dollar debt burden would soon bring about the "collapse" of the "price system." Then the engineers would take charge. And soon they would be turning out an incredible flow of wealth—the equivalent of twenty thousand dollars a year in goods and services (whether this was per individual or per family was never quite clear), according to Howard Scott.

The discrediting of Scott led to a split and later disintegration of the "movement" that had grown up. The public's daydream was shattered by newspapers suddenly fearful of the implications of this new fad, though the dream of plenty once glimpsed refused entirely to fade. ("Thirty dollars every Thursday" was only its latest version.) One of the rocks on which "technocracy" split was the measurement of productive capacity. Howard Scott's blueprints of the future turned out to be largely imaginary, and his promised annual income meaningless. The sounder elements in the so-called Continental Committee on Technocracy, under Harold Loeb's leadership, were able with a grant of CWA funds to carry through a competent statistical survey. It made several important discoveries.*

Productive capacity, particularly in processing plants (such as flour mills, for instance), is so far beyond any possibility of full utilization that the only way to measure what our economic resources are capable of producing is to start with an inquiry into consumer need: how much flour *should* we produce fully to meet the need? Actually we now eat more bread than dieticians would say is good for us. A perfect national "budget" would probably include less bread and more dairy products. Our fields and farms are ample for handling any increased demand if the whole population were placed on a "liberal diet." Thus, the income of the country could not be multiplied by ten or twenty, as the wilder "technocrats" had said, because in the case of food we could not consume any but a slight increase in quantity (though we could eat a more healthy diet). The survey also measured possible consumption of clothes and other products, working back and forth between measurable consumer need and such limited factors as raw materials and labor. It drew a blueprint of the flow of certain desired goods from source to consumer, as an engineer-dictator might. It set a standard family budget, translated it into a national budget, and found that our plant was more than adequate to fill it. Only in one case was our plant inadequate—it would take ten years of concentrated effort to build adequate housing. By that time we would have achieved what Stuart Chase was calling the "economy of abundance."

The dollar equivalent of the Loeb budget was disappointing to me and other enthusiasts—$4,370 (of the 1929 general price level) per family per year. But this was to be compared with the 1929 median family income of $1,700. Only 10 per cent of the population had been enjoying the Loeb standard in that year of prosperity. Moreover, this standard was a minimum. If the determined

* The results were published in two volumes, *The Report of the National Survey of Potential Product Capacity* and *The Chart of Plenty*. They are summarized in Mordecai Ezekiel's *$2,500 a Year* and in John Strachey's *Theory and Practice of Socialism*, as well as in Harold Loeb's *Production For Use*.

quantity were to be consumed at all it could not be maldistributed. As Loeb put it, "You cannot maldistribute abundance." No one can sleep in more than one bed at a time, or consume more than a certain quota of milk. The appurtenances of opulent living at higher income levels, as I had personally known them, came from domestic servants; servants cannot be measured in engineering terms like goods, though the amenities and the civilized arts of living which in the past they have made possible could be increasingly made universal by the extension of "social services," even if "domestic servants" became obsolete under conditions of universal abundance.*

How was the budget to be distributed? To say our plant could turn out plenty of goods and services for all consumer needs was not a sufficient answer to the problem I was probing. The Continental Committee, with which I became associated, issued some pamphlets with solutions which seem to me as searching and original as any of this period, though now somewhat outdated. To assure the distribution of the "budget," said the *Plan of Plenty*, it was only necessary to issue tickets in exact equivalence to the

* I have long found the distinction between goods and services a little confusing. Any estimate of total national income, present or potential, must, of course, include services as well as goods. For on the money side, evidently, the income of doctors, barbers, teachers and janitors is part of the total monetary income; and the services they perform are part of the total "production" of the country. The production of goods and the "production" of services both require labor, but in other respects there are important differences: it is possible to produce more goods than can be sold, but not services, for they are used as performed: there can be no "overproduction" of haircuts or dental fillings. Yet there can be unused "capacity" in the sense of idle or inadequately occupied barbers and dentists. The Loeb Survey found that even with the production of goods at the abundance budget, the labor force would still be adequate to supply the necessary services at a greatly expanded rate: we have enough doctors, for instance, to meet the nation's fullest health needs if fully occupied, though there would have to be an increased number of professional workers trained for some other fields, like adult education. This interesting implication, then, can be drawn from the Loeb Survey: with the fulfilling of the "goods" budget by increasingly automatic machinery, more and more workers will be made available for "services"; while our capacity to consume goods is in many fields limited, our capacity to consume services is almost unlimited; hence the increase in standards of living beyond the $4,370 per year level will depend more on the multiplication of services than of goods. All of us might eventually get as much "service" as the millionaire does today!

ultimate products. The goods could be priced in any arbitrary unit —current dollar prices would do (Scott's "ergs" were rejected as a needless complication). If every ticket issued against goods were canceled when the goods were purchased there could be none of the evils of the "price" or market "system"—no overproduction or underconsumption, no hoarding, no maladjustments of supply and demand. Build the economic system like a theater, with a known capacity to meet a known demand, then issue tickets for each place for each performance, and there would always be an exact equivalence of production and need.

A helpful concept emphasized by the "technocrats" was the distinction between real wealth and token wealth. By the use of simple scientific measurements and engineering procedures real wealth in goods and services could be produced in abundance. The existing productive plant which the "capitalist system" had built for us was ample. But along with it went an archaic system of token wealth—money—unsuited to the real distributive function to be performed. The obvious answer seemed to be to throw our existing monetary system on the scrap heap—debts, currency, certificates of ownership, and the like—and devise a simple workable alternative on the analogy of theater tickets.

Another helpful concept was that of "nonproduction." Veblen, the spiritual father of the "technocrats," had called it "sabotage." Private business, unable to market its potential products in the price system, only produced what it could sell. It ran its plant at a fraction of capacity. According to the National Survey of Potential Product Capacity our national plant turned out 94 billion dollars' worth of goods and services in 1929 as against a potential budget of 135 billion: in that peak of prosperity, then, "nonproduction" amounted to 41 billion. In the depression years since, the total wealth "nonproduced" has amounted to hundreds of billions.

The Brookings Survey of productive capacity lent greater weight to the picture of horrendous waste, though its figures were more conservative. Using a different method of measurement, predicated on the continuance of existing procedures (a "business" rather than an "engineering" survey) and the maintenance of existing rates of capital construction, it found a 20 per cent unused capacity in 1929, about half as much as the Loeb Survey, but striking enough nonetheless.

My own hunch was that even the Loeb Survey was over-conservative. If one considered the additional wastes, as Stuart Chase had done—the production of "illth," of useless shoddy products forced on the market by advertising pressure, the wastes of duplication and competitive salesmanship and lack of planning, as well as unnecessary cross-hauling of people and materials—and if one added all this to the sum of "nonproduction" as it should be added, then the margin between what Americans enjoyed and what they could enjoy became staggering.

Yet one hardly needed to look so far afield for "nonproduction." The army of the unemployed grew during those years after 1929 from three to fifteen million men and women—wanting to produce wealth, wanting to consume it, denied both. Whatever might be the subtler forms of "nonproduction" in time of "prosperity," it was as glaring as daylight in time of depression.

I was aware, with many a fellow-American (though in my case with no physical suffering), of the great and challenging absurdity of our times—"want in the midst of plenty."

Unlike most of my fellow-Americans I waited hopefully, not for the return of prosperity, but for the final "collapse of the system." It seemed that it must come. I lectured about it. The discrepancy between what was and what might be was too great. The debt burden and all its interferences with the productive system were cumulative maladjustments which would inexorably lead to the final crash. I waited with bated breath. Meanwhile the recovery of the years 1933-37 became a statistical fact not to be blinked. I was puzzled. Along with my fellow-radicals, Marxist and non-Marxist, I persuaded myself that this was a false recovery, and that the final crash was only a little postponed.

It seemed important to devise methods of transition that could hasten the change and ease its pains. I worked out a "Plan of Transition" modeled on Bellamy's books and on Upton Sinclair's "Epic Plan." It proposed to take the nation's "nonproducers," the unemployed, and put them to work on the nation's unused capacity, so that they might produce for their own use, using the ticket method of distributing purchasing power. Here would be the new system in miniature, a closed system working within the old and gradually taking over its functions, a co-operative commonwealth growing to maturity while the old system died.

It was a good scheme. But little attention was paid to it. The world is not much affected by social blueprints except when demagogues make use of them. The idea of replacing the "price system" with another "system" cut out of whole cloth hardly conforms to the exigencies of the real world. I found I would have to push my inquiry farther.

Yet there was no doubt in my mind about the validity of what I had so far learned. Modern technology does contain the promise of "plenty for all." Some flaw does lead to nonproduction, to say nothing of cyclical depressions. A fatal discrepancy does exist between real wealth and token wealth, for purchasing power is quite inadequate to buy the wealth that our productive mechanism is capable of turning out. But why?

### *Abolish the Market?*

Having begun my economic analysis from the point of view of goods in the real world, I thought of the goal as "production for use"—directed by some super-planning board of engineers to meet the obvious needs of all the people. "Production for use" was to be contrasted with what? with production for profit, as the Marxists said? But I had already discarded the Marxist interpretation, and, as I related earlier, it seemed to me clearer to contrast production for use with production for sale, with production for the market.

In what way was the market—the price system—at fault? The machines were capable of turning out plenty of everything. But instead of obeying a super-planner's orders geared to need, they obeyed the fitful and obviously inadequate demands of the consumer's market. Only as much was produced as could be sold at certain prices in the market. Purchasing power was the resultant of a thousand haphazard accidents, arising in the banking system, the stock market, psychology, the general price level, the fortuitous operation of the capital goods industries. These forces interacted in a wholly unpredictable fashion. The purchasing power that emerged bore no necessary relation to the goods and services that could be made available or that people needed.

I came to the conclusion that it was necessary to do away with the market. The market was a place for buying and selling. I had a prejudice against the process of selling anyway. There seemed to me nothing more degrading and corrupting than most salesmanship: as I had found in my brief experience as a salesman, you must puff up your own wares, often without any regard to your real opinion of them; you must try to get as much from your victim as possible and give as little as possible in return; salesmanship seemed to me the antithesis of the Christian ethic, family or group or community spirit; in its final form of modern advertising, whether on billboards or in magazines or over the radio, it represented the ultimate triumph of vulgarity. If selling on the market could be done away with, life could take on a new beauty and nobility.

And if there was really plenty for all, why keep the market? The only excuse for the market was as a means of distributing scarce goods. If goods were abundant instead of scarce, why was the market necessary? A city's water system designed to meet the needs of all its citizens in the fullest measure does not try to sell its water to the highest bidder. Perhaps the secret of the breakdown of the "capitalist system" lay precisely there: prices tended to fall to zero under conditions of abundance, threatening to bankrupt every business.

In calling for the abolition of the market and of money, except in the form of tickets or tokens corresponding to real wealth available, I was unconsciously following much early socialist thinking. Though I did not take up the idea of "labor certificates," I was retracing much the same ground as the first Soviet planners.

One of the errors I made was in assuming that abundance was already a fact, or that it was an *absolute* abundance. The fact that goods and services can be made available to the limits of human wants does not mean that they are like the fruits in the fabulous isle, which drop into the mouths of the reclining natives at meal time. They all require some expenditure of effort or labor. And since the natural incentives to labor—pleasure in exercise, joy in creation, satisfaction in mental activity, ambition, emulation—fall far short of the effort needed to produce the desired abundance, the effect is the same as if the goods were naturally scarce. Moreover, certain raw materials, like timber and oil, are absolutely scarce.

We are in fact a long way from conditions of absolute abundance. It is quite conceivable, indeed, that a day will come, as visualized by William Morris in *News from Nowhere,* when the amount of labor required is less than the amount people find pleasure in performing, and then all goods can be as free as air. Some such idea seems also to be back of the Marxists' concept of pure "communism." But because of the shortage of voluntary labor in relation to needed labor, and the shortage of certain raw materials, all goods and services still tend to be relatively scarce.

*The market is a natural automatic device for rationing anything scarce.* A hungry pack of animals, finding a single small carcass, will fight for the pieces, and the stronger will get the larger share. Human societies have often developed authoritarian systems where a leader, exercising discipline, will ration scarce food in orderly fashion; this method is still used in armies, and is likely to be invoked in any emergency when the market breaks down. But the automatic mechanism of a price or market system, operating through money, provides a method of rationing without either bloodshed or surrender of freedom. It may permit inequitable results, but as a method it is certainly preferable to authoritarian rationing.

So I had to give up my first simple approach. Potential plenty does not make the "price system" obsolete. I had to find out more of its workings before I could predict its "collapse." Apparently it had greater organic vitality than I realized. Moreover, I had just been discovering that the Soviet Union was restoring the market. And I came upon the classic debates on socialist economics, which ended with a reassertion of the market. On the one hand the Austrian economists, von Mises, Hayek, and their ex-Russian ally, Brutzkus, were arguing that socialism made economic calculation impossible by abolishing the market mechanism or price system. The new school of "market socialists," on the other hand, including Taylor, Lange, Landauer, Lerner, Heimann, and a growing number of others, were demonstrating that the market mechanism could and should be used in a planned economy.*

* "Market socialism" is discussed below, pages 365-367.

The "price system" or "market mechanism" is an automatic device by which the supply and demand of scarce goods are equated at a price. It necessarily involves a system of money, for, except in conditions of primitive barter, demand means buyers coming into the market with purchasing power in their pockets in the form of money.

Why is purchasing power inadequate? I was brought back to the monetary approach of virtually every economist, reformer and amateur thinker. Though I had always had enough money in my pocket for my wants, most people have not. To them the economic problem is one of getting enough money.

### *Maldistribution?*

The first explanation occurring to the poor man is that he is poor because someone else is rich. Something must be wrong with the system by which money is distributed, for he has not enough and others have too much.

I had started from the other end: something is wrong with the productive system, because obviously not enough is produced. Perhaps I was biased because I did not like to think that the fault lay in the fact that I had too much money. As a matter of fact I did not have too much. And if I was to be leveled down to an average amount, corresponding to an equal division of the annual income, I knew I should not have enough. I knew that from an engineering point of view our resources were adequate to turn out a vast sufficiency of everything needful, as much for everybody as I had for myself. I knew that if enough were produced, "maldistribution" would be as meaningless as at a bountifully provided Thanksgiving dinner. In fact the margin of productive capacity over consumptive capacity was so great that society could easily afford the continuance of a class of idle and luxurious rich if it chose. I had a number of friends in this class, and I was not anxious to see them suffer, if it was not necessary. I was predisposed against the theory of "maldistribution," just as most people who think about economics are predisposed in its favor.

Now, however, I felt bound to examine the theory. First of all it was necessary to see just how distribution of purchasing power takes place.

Clearly there were two main streams: money income received in return for labor, as wages and salaries, and money income received in return for ownership of property. I was in the latter category, and my conscience had long told me that something was wrong. Was it that it was unjust for a privileged few to be relieved of the necessity of working for their own living, and thus to be supported by others? Or was it that most recipients of property income had larger incomes than those who earned their keep? Clearly there might be injustice either way. But I was not now concerned with injustice, as a reformer, but with the failure of the mechanism, as an economist. What was the nature of these types of income?

Property income is chiefly derived from three sources, rent from the ownership of land and buildings, interest from the ownership of money lent, and profit from the ownership of a going enterprise.

Profit in turn could, I found, be considered under various headings. If it is just the difference between what the enterpriser pays out to others and what he receives in return for his products—that is, what he has left over for himself—it might be considered merely his own wages. The farmer generally has so little left for himself that it amounts to less than a living wage. And many a small business man finds that what is left to him as the "wages of management" is less than what he has to pay his hired employees. Surely there is no injustice there. Then, too, the small enterpriser, whether farmer or little business man, usually invests his own savings, and if he cannot make the normal interest on this "capital" (as has been the case with farmers, again, for the last twenty years) his investment is obviously a poor risk. It seemed legitimate to argue that part of the total profit is a compensation for risk: in fact the classical economist justifies profit largely as a necessary compensation for taking the risk. Yet the margin of income over outgo may include unexpected amounts too, larger than sufficient to induce the original risk; this is sometimes included under the term "windfall" profit.

Profit is obviously a many-sided concept, even when limited to the enterpriser's share. But what of the profits paid out in dividends? I owned stock in a number of corporations. Was I paid for taking a risk? I did not feel I had shown any particular courage in buying the stock. And if the stock went up in value and I sold it, was that a "profit" compensating me for risk?

Much of the fruitless argument about the "profit system" is due to the fact that the arguers are using the word in different senses. In the term "profit motive" it is even used to cover all incentive to secure money, including wages and salaries. But even as an economic term it is vague.

Marx, as we saw, used it broadly to include all property income as distinguished from labor income; since the workers produced all the wealth any income which went merely to owners of property was, he felt, robbed from the workers. Marxists have therefore sought to abolish all property income, or to socialize it.

Believers in the consumers' co-operative movement sought to return profits to the consumers, by giving them ownership of businesses. Other reformers have merely wanted to limit excess profits, as by taxation, believing that they are the chief cause of maldistribution.

On the other hand, the followers of Henry George see another special item of property income as evil: rent. Profit, they say, is a legitimate reward for risk and enterprise. Even interest is justifiable since a man ought to be given a reward for saving. But rent is a return for ownership of land, which is a natural endowment, not created by the owner or any other man, its value arising from society itself. A single tax on rent alone will end the wrongful distribution of income, said George.

Still others have seen interest on money lent as a special evil. As "usury" it was held sinful by the Hebrew Prophets and by the medieval Church. Why should the man who had money make an additional gain by lending it to the man who had none?

It seemed to me that these criticisms of maldistribution sprang from ethical considerations rather than economic considerations. There is something indecent about the spectacle of Dives, the idler, feasting in luxury while Lazarus, who does the world's work, picks up the crumbs. There is something profoundly hideous, to me as to any imaginative person, in the contrast of slum hovels and palace towers as they are juxtaposed in our big cities. In 1932 the spectacle of men, women and children scavenging on garbage dumps and living in cardboard and tin "Hoovervilles," while a favored few enjoyed yachts and Rolls-Royces, brought public opinion to the breaking point: a whole set of new institutions began to be developed as the social conscience became aroused.

But maldistribution, however offensive, could not in itself explain what was wrong with the economic system. The world had always seen extremes of wealth and poverty. To give everybody an equal income was no way out. It has always been easy for defenders of the *status quo* to say that if you divided everything up equally you would only succeed in making everybody poor; and human nature being what it is, riches and poverty would soon return, unless a rigid dictatorship were maintained.

Moreover, it has always been easy for capitalist economists to argue against those who would do away with property income on the ground that it resulted in a shortage of purchasing power. Property income, they could demonstrate, is spent as well as labor income: whether spent on luxuries or invested in new capital goods it returns at once to circulation as part of the general spending stream. In addition, it is an essential part of the automatic mechanism of the market. It regulates the proportion of savings to consumption, for the greater part of savings comes from the large incomes derived from property: if it were not for the wealthy, says the apologist for inequality, there would be no adequate saving, for the poor consume all their income, and the failure to save would lead to the stagnation if not rapid impoverishment of the community.

At this point, however, I knew that the apologists were out of bounds. It is possible for society as a whole to save, as the Soviet regime has demonstrated by saving and investing in new capital goods at a more rapid rate than ever achieved under capitalism. Theoretically, an absolute dictator could decree that half the labor force shall be engaged in capital construction and only half in consumer goods production, thus compelling a "saving" of half the national income.

In addition, as I found before long, it is possible for savings to be too large for profitable investment. This is in fact the one economic objection to the maldistribution of income: with too many large incomes derived from property, the automatic regulators of savings and investment may break down, and the whole community suffer. But that had not been a serious factor until 1929. What had created the new conditions?

However, before continuing that line of inquiry, my pursuit of the elusive concept of inadequate purchasing power brought me up against another current theory.

### *Too Little Money?*

When a wheat farmer sells his crop and discovers he cannot get as much money for it as he spent in producing it, he jumps easily to the conclusion that there is not enough money. He may blame the grain "speculators" or the banks or Wall Street; the accumulation of vast hoards of money anywhere will diminish the supply for the rest of the community. The farmer calls for more and "cheaper" money, "cheaper" money being money he can "buy" more cheaply with his grain—in other words, higher prices for his grain. The grain belt has been the center of agitation for paper money inflation since the days of the "Greenbackers" after the Civil War.

Here again the apologists for the *status quo* have several quick comebacks. Currency is involved in only a small proportion of purchases and sales, credit money or "check-book" money being much more generally used as a medium of exchange. Moreover, the quantity of money outstanding is only one side of the problem: velocity is equally important. If one conceives of purchasing power as "flowing" or "circulating," then the velocity or turnover of a dollar bill is just as important as the number of dollar bills, and merely to increase the number may have no effect, for it may reduce the velocity in proportion. On the other hand, if it causes a fear of further inflation it may so increase the velocity that prices will sky-rocket, and a "runaway" inflation may ensue.

A more accurate way to conceive the process than as a "flow" with a "velocity," especially with a system of credit money, is as a series of *transactions:* in a system of commercial credit each of these transactions calls forth its own "money." There cannot then be any shortage of "money." There is always just enough money to complete every transaction: if more is interjected into the system this too may either lie idle or it may result in a general price rise, from which no one will benefit except the speculator; and speculation may soon push the rise in prices out of control.

When this argument is put, the crude inflationist or amateur economist is driven into a corner. Yet his often irrational hunch, that what is needed is more money, may not be as far wrong as appears. Scary talk about inflation is today almost always a bogeyman to frighten those who would upset the *status quo*. Yet radicals, too, have been guilty of this kind of talk.

At the same time the radicals have their own reasons for believing there is not enough money. They consider crises and depressions inevitable. Periodically more goods are produced than there is money with which to buy them. When business becomes generally aware that this has happened, industries halt or slow down production, men are unemployed, purchasing power is still further decreased, and we go skidding down the toboggan slide into a depression. Most Marxist thought, as I have emphasized, has concentrated on this theory of glut, linking it to the apparent fact that profit and property income tend to pile up wealth in the hands of the rich while taking it away from the poor.

As we saw, Marx did not reconcile this apparent discrepancy betweeen goods and purchasing power with the classic doctrine, first enunciated by Say, and carefully explained by Marx himself, that the right amount of money is always available to circulate commodities. In whatever form payments are made during the production of goods, whether as wages, rent, interest or profits, they do not leave the economic system: they necessarily find their way into somebody's hands, and in any period of time their total equals the total prices of all the goods produced. As it is sometimes put: supply creates its own demand. According to this law purchasing power must necessarily equal the goods and services available, for they are different aspects of the same thing: the producers and the consumers are the same people, and the total income they receive represents the total payments made in producing the goods. In a developed credit system, as I mentioned a moment ago, this balance is facilitated by the fact that each transaction can create its own money.

The debate between the orthodox economists and the unorthodox who insist there is a shortage of purchasing power has been a fascinating one, with the orthodox economists until recently consistently winning the theoretical argument, and the unorthodox consistently coming back to the facts of the real world—"poverty in the midst of potential plenty."

The Douglas Social Credit theory is one of the most popular current versions of the theory of a lack of purchasing power. Using a mysterious and vague "A plus B theorem," the advocates of Social Credit claim that only part of the cost of an article—the "A" part—goes to consumers as labor or property income, and that the rest, "B," goes to other enterprises (as for the purchase of raw materials) and is therefore not available as consumer purchasing power. Major Douglas and his followers argue that the "B" part must be made up by the government in some way, if purchasing power is to be adequate to balance the goods produced. Actually no discrepancy exists, for the "B" payments become available for purchasing when they too land up eventually in some consumer's pocket—the employee of a capital goods plant, for instance.

Other variants of the underconsumption theory are Foster and Catchings' profits-lag explanation, and the oversaving argument of John A. Hobson.

It is hardly possible for the layman to thread his way through all these theories and their answers. Unfortunately the layman is likely to find one which fits his peculiar bent, and he is likely thereupon to become an addict of a sectarian little faith, which is not so much an incorrect explanation of facts as a very limited and partial explanation of an extremely complex whole.*

Starting with a natural prejudice against any purely monetary explanation of economic failure, I was not inclined to adopt any of these theories. Yet it was clear that, in spite of the orthodox defenders, there are two ways in which purchasing power may indeed be inadequate.

* In this field as in the political and social field generally I have often been baffled by the plausibility of apparently contradictory interpretations. When I was in Russia, for instance, and ever since, I have heard people whose integrity I trusted describe the Soviet system either as a glorious liberation or as utter slavery, and proceed to cite plenty of evidence for their contention. I have learned that in such cases usually both are right; but because each interprets his partial picture as applicable to the whole it is biased and inaccurate. Likewise I have found so much truth in almost every economic theory I have read, that I have come to take the position increasingly that they are all correct—so far as they go. Our economic system is large enough and complex enough to lend justice to almost every explanation, only condemning their common failing, that of oversimplification.

In the first place, there is undoubtedly a recurrent tendency for gluts to occur—that is, a shortage of purchasing power in the face of goods and services actually offered for sale at a particular time. This "overproduction" or "underconsumption" appears when the equilibrium assumed by orthodox theory is upset. But I came to the conclusion, which I shall elaborate in a moment, that there are innumerable forces which may upset that equilibrium. A glut is most apparent at the beginning of a depression, but more as effect than cause; for a depression is merely the cumulative effect of many possible disequilibria.

But even in 1929, before the Great Depression, as I mentioned above, we were "nonproducing" a vast amount of wealth. There is a second kind of shortage of money. The trouble with our economic system is not merely that it has depressions, but that even in times of prosperity it leaves millions unnecessarily unemployed and the whole of society poorer than it should be: in other words, there is a *chronic shortage of purchasing power*, not in relation to actual production, but *in relation to potential production*. Keynes's great contribution to economic thought is his discovery of the tendencies which lead to what now appears to be a permanent equilibrium far short of full employment.

The way these tendencies originate might be put in oversimplified everyday language (as contrasted with Mr. Keynes's overcomplex one-man-specialist's language) by saying that savings tend to get ahead of investment. It is all right from an economic point of view for a rich man to receive a large income from property so long as he either spends it on his own extravagances or invests it. But if savings tend to outstrip the opportunities for profitable investment, then they represent what amount to hoardings, or withdrawals from purchasing power.

Orthodox economic theory on savings and investment runs along some such line of reasoning as this: When you receive a pay check or dividend check or other form of income you can either spend the money on immediate consumption or save it. But you will not (unless you are one of a negligible number of misers) hoard the money permanently in a sock or strong-box. You will invest it. Investment means the building of new productive machinery—capital construction, means of production—to make possible increased production, which will enable you to earn a profit on your investment. You may of course merely buy a security, and if it is an outstanding security—one listed on the Stock Exchange, for instance—you yourself do not make a true investment. But somewhere along the line, in the broker's office, or in the hands of some recipient of the money you saved and spent on the security, there will be a new investment: your money, instead of having been spent on consumption goods, has been spent on capital goods. Obviously it returns eventually to the spending stream. There is no shortage of money because you "saved" yours instead of "spending" it.*

But suppose that when you save there does not happen to be some enterpriser ready to build a new factory, or otherwise immeately prepared to make use of your money for new capital construction? Suppose in effect that savings tend to outstrip investment? Will this not mean that money lies idle for a time, if not in a strong-box then in a bank balance? And will this not mean that somewhere there are goods on store shelves for which there is no corresponding purchasing power?

The orthodox economist would of course grant that there may be a time lag between saving and investment, though under "normal" circumstances there would be a constant piling up of savings in the banks and a constant flow into new investment, with no serious gap. If saving tends to outstrip investment then the in-

* I have been much baffled from time to time by the confusion of various words in this field: savings, investment, capital, capital goods, capital construction, means of production, durable goods, semi-durable goods. What, for instance, is steel manufacture? Some of the steel goes into consumer goods, like hardware. Some into semi-durable goods like automobiles. Some into durable goods like houses. Some into new capital plant like a factory. But what about an apartment house, or a hotel? Are they capital, means of production, or durable consumer goods? Obviously no strict definitions are possible. The productive process must be thought of as a continuous process of building factories and machines, extracting raw materials, processing them, turning out all kinds of goods, some of which may be immediately consumed, others used for further production, others consumed slowly by a process of wear and tear.

In any case money is laid out in the various stages of the productive process, whether because of long-term investment or of short-term loans, and always finds its way back into the pockets of consumers. And the total prices of all the goods turned out should, in the long run, balance the total incomes paid out.

terest rate will drop; at the lower rate new opportunities for profitable investment will appear and the unbalance will be rectified. If the unbalance has gone so far as to cause unemployment, other automatic tendencies will come into play. The existence of large numbers of unemployed will depress wages, until there is an inducement for enterprisers to employ all the workers once more, in building new factories and expanding capital plant, and thus investment will once more come into balance with saving. It is natural, therefore, for orthodox economists to object to trade unionism, minimum wage laws, work relief, and similar interferences with the automatic mechanism which keep wages from falling far enough to make new investment once more profitable. In the same way, if the orthodox economist is logical, he must argue against any such measures as Hoover took to prevent "deflation" of the capital structure by bankruptcies and reorganizations; for this opens new opportunities for investment and thus provides another method of getting savings and investment back into balance.

Yet the fact is that none of these adjustments may work. The interest rate may not come down sufficiently. Wages and capital structures are artificially held up. A depression once started may go to disastrous lengths before recovery sets in. There may in fact develop a condition of permanent underinvestment. In any case there seems to be a tendency for purchasing power to lag, because savings are "hoarded" rather than invested.

Because of the curious nature of modern check-book money this question of "hoardings" is an extremely difficult one, and economists may come to different conclusions depending on their definitions. Even the same economist, like Keynes, may first say that savings tend to get ahead of investments, and then, by defining the two words savings and investment to mean the same thing, he will reach another type of conclusion. From an accounting point of view savings are always balanced against new assets somewhere, and thus may be called investments, even though the assets are merely in the form of unsold goods on some shop's shelves.* Cer-

* A good deal of saving today is done by corporations. In their case any funds accumulated as reserves or sinking funds are entered both as assets and liabilities, so that the saving might be thought of as taking the form of

tainly if one thinks of "hoardings" in concrete terms as a pile of coins in a strong-box, it is easy to conceive of them as being "withdrawn from circulation." But "idle bank balances" are merely bookkeepers' entries. They may even be changing title rapidly, if there is a wave of gambling, or of speculation on the Stock Exchange: then many "idle" bank balances will be shuttled back and forth between speculators and brokers, and if prices are being bid upwards more and more money may be absorbed.

Then, too, it may be argued that no real "hoarding" takes place, because the banks in which the "idle deposits" lie are constantly making loans and investments, and the only question may be of a difference in rate between the appearance of deposits arising from savings and deposits arising from loans. "Hoarding" then becomes merely a question of "velocity."

Whatever the terminology used to explain the phenomenon, there is no doubt that the effect of oversaving by the rich in relation to the possibilities of profitable investment is *as if* there were a shortage of purchasing power due to "hoarding" at the top. This "as if" shortage takes two forms, one cyclic, the other chronic. The cyclic form is our old friend "depression": at some point when the credit structure seems overexpanded "confidence" falls, the savings of the wealthy have been accumulating but new investment slows down, the capital goods industries operate at a fraction of capacity, the consumer goods industries then slack off, too, and of course unemployment snowballs up. The other form of shortage is a latter-day tendency of capitalism, which involves chronic unemployment. It has been best explained by Keynes, as we shall see in the next chapter.

Before going on, however, I should mention one further problem as regards a possible shortage of money. Will not an expanding economy outstrip its money supply?

We may grant that in any period of time there should be an amount of purchasing power coming into the market from wages, rent, interest, and profits paid to individuals as a result of current and past productive activities, exactly equal to the total prices of all the goods and services currently offered on the market (for the

an investment in cash, though the "cash" is merely a bank deposit. In any case the "liquidity preference" (to use Keynes's term) of big corporations is one of the chief causes of a shortage of purchasing power.

prices are fixed at the point where the cost or supply curve crosses the demand curve, to use a modern intellectual device). Nevertheless, a growing economy will require a constantly growing money supply.

The classical economists (including Marx) measured very accurately the amount of money that would always be needed. The demands of a growing population and increasing productivity would, they believed, automatically bring out the necessary amount of additional money by spurring the production of gold, which, in their opinion, gave value to money. Actually the supply of gold was fitful, growing by spurts as new gold fields were discovered. In between spurts, prices tended to fall and thus restore the balance between goods and purchasing power. What was far more important, new credit devices were invented to permit a given amount of gold to support more money. There were few real shortages of money.

In recent years it is being discovered that the value of paper money and credit money can be maintained, regardless of whether there are fourteen billion dollars of useless metal stored in a Fort Knox vault, as in the United States today, or virtually none in any vault, as in Germany. But the necessity of a constant increase in the amount of money remains.* Even if we achieved a stable full-production economy, with a stable population, the gradual increase in productivity due to invention would require either a constant fall in prices, or, if prices are to be held steady, a constant injection of new money. Only it is much easier to get the money now than when it had to be dug out of the earth.

## *Equilibrium*

A balance sheet is one of the great feats of the human imagination. I have always felt a sense of awe when I looked at one. How was it possible that a business should be so well run that its assets and liabilities exactly equaled each other, down to the last penny? Actually, of course, a balance sheet is a bookkeeping device, and a

* Harold Loeb has suggested that the maintenance of high prices by widespread monopoly practices, regardless of increased productivity, has exaggerated the lag in effective monetary demand, and thus contributed to chronic depression.

surplus or deficit to balance the two columns is merely a resultant of many more or less arbitrary items. The device is a convenient simplification undertaken for certain specific purposes. Its magical effect is, however, much the same, on a smaller scale, as that of the theories of general economic equilibrium.

The real world of economics is one of two billion individuals, working, loafing, spending, keeping money in their pockets, making magical marks on pieces of paper. There is no moment of time at which they all stand still to be counted. There is no moment of time at which their activities all stop so that a balance sheet can be drawn up—even in one country, even in one business enterprise.

An economic equilibrium, then, is not a static equilibrium, but an equilibrium of activities, a moving or dynamic equilibrium. The classical economist may try to conceive an equilibrium between getting and spending, between production and consumption, between supply and demand. A perfect equilibrium, in his eyes, might be one in which the flow of purchasing power paid out to individuals in the process of production, whether as wages, interest, rent or profits, will, in a period of time, balance the flow of payments made by individuals for goods—consumer goods if they are spending for consumption, capital goods if they are saving and investing. The perfect equilibrium will be one in which everyone is employed, and all resources are used in such a way as to maximize the consumer satisfactions resulting from production.

But consider some of the variables we have already mentioned, a growing population, increasing productivity, the prospects of profit (which may be governed by wholly unpredictable psychological attitudes), the interest rate—to say nothing of the weather, which may greatly affect farm purchasing power. In addition, remember that money is not merely currency, which people may keep in their pockets a longer or shorter time between occasions when it passes from hand to hand, but checks also, which flash on and off in various bank balances like electric signals: this means great variability both of "quantity" and "velocity" of money.

The most important element in maintaining an equilibrium at full employment is, of course, investment. Think how this complicates the balance. There must be just enough saving, and it must find just enough enterprisers starting new capital construction to absorb just the right number of workers. The interest rate, the prospects of profit, the number of wealthy people getting more income than they can spend on consumption, the rates of wages, the prices of consumer goods, raw materials, and capital goods, will all play a part. In a perfect theoretical world, such as the economists dream of, where there is perfect flexibility to adjust all these elements to each other, the market mechanism works wonderfully. But in the real world it meets difficulties at every turn.

It would be bad enough if we were dealing with a static economy. But the equilibrium we are looking for must be an equilibrium between rates of change as well as between all the other variables. For every new investment is likely to mean increased production and increased purchasing power. And some investments mean increased employment in new industries while other investments, as in labor-saving machinery, may mean less employment. To be sure, if the economy reached a saturation point, where all had as much as they wanted for the work they were willing to perform, and there were no new inventions, saving and investment would cover mere replacement of existing equipment, and the conditions for a static economy would have arrived. So would the "economy of abundance." But we are far from that point.

I mentioned Bassett Jones's demonstration that the mere compounding of interest tends to shoot ahead of any possible expansion of productivity. Actually the amount of interest paid has been a fairly stable part of the total income, simply because of bankruptcies, foreclosures, and the dropping of interest rates; but it is clear what a strain the constant piling up of debt puts on the system. It is one of the elements demanding expansion, and penalizing us all when expansion is not forthcoming.

Consider the fact that this is a rich country, with a considerable number of rich people often saving far more than they can spend. The richer a country grows the more saving there is, and it may become ever more difficult for new investment to keep up, and for equilibrium to be maintained.

What a precarious thing that equilibrium is may be seen from a glance at the last great period of American prosperity. Vast new industries came into the picture, the automobile (and all its subsidiary industries like oil, tires, gas stations, etc.), the radio, the airplane. The country's wealth grew by leaps and bounds, and with it the incomes that the millionaires could not spend on consumption. The Stock Exchange, Coral Gables and other gambling establishments were choked with funds. Fortunately the money that was hoarded there was counterbalanced for the time being by new bank credit, and a certain amount kept coming back for consumer goods in the guise of "capital gains." We lent billions of dollars of our savings to foreign countries—which merely meant that instead of spending the money on goods for ourselves we spent it on goods for foreigners, and took their IOU's (mostly worthless) in return. The process of getting rid of the savings that we were constantly making in excess of opportunities for legitimate and profitable investment might have gone on through various make-believe dodges indefinitely; but there comes a time when even capitalist make-believe becomes too obvious.*

To restore equilibrium today in America at a prosperity level, eliminating all unemployment, would, if left to private investment alone, require all the new industries of the twenties three or four times over. Something more than "confidence" seems to be required, if savings are not to pile up faster than they can be absorbed.

### *Where Does the Money Come From?*

So far I have been explaining where my search for an explanation of inadequate purchasing power led me. Purchasing power is money coming into the market. Now the question has arisen, Where does the money come from in the first place?

As I have snaked my way through the tangled jungle of economic theory, and found others struggling in its matted underbrush, I have been more and more impressed by the peculiar difficulties of the concept of money. Its difficulties are not limited to the economic jungle. More than any other concept it has ensnared the politician and the voter.

Look back once again to the Greenbackers, and to the Populists

* According to the Brookings Institution, total savings in 1929 were close to $20,000,000,000, of which $15,000,000,000 was seeking investment in securities, while the issue of new securities for productive purposes (capital construction) amounted only to $5,000,000,000.

of the nineties and Bryan's "cross of gold" speech (three parts hocus pocus, one part sound hunch), and the great 16 to 1 silver "heresy." Consider the noble emotions the thought of the gold standard can still arouse in old-timers. Consider the amount of heat generated since March 4, 1933, by arguments about inflation. Consider the magic formulas of devaluation and reflation. Think of the gigantic errors of judgment in the political manipulation of money in the last twenty years, the catastrophic inflations that took place, and the catastrophic inflations that failed to take place as predicted.

Coming to the consideration of economic problems from a non-monetary approach, I have never been able to take monetary arguments altogether seriously, as I have said. I have watched violent discussions over the gold standard and inflation and budget-balancing with tolerant condescension. Yet for all the advantage it gave me, I was probably wrong. Man does not live by bread alone. The real world of materials and machines and human skills will always be seen through the distorting vision of human eye and brain. The make-believe world, of which money is a part, is inescapable. It can indeed fall so out of relation to the real world as to cause terrible suffering. But it can also facilitate processes and make the impossible possible.

I have already explained how I came back to a belief in the market, and money is essential to the market. Not till the still rather distant day of sheer joy in work and universally free and abundant goods will money disappear.

For my purposes here, no new definition of money and no new monetary theory are required. I shall confine myself to a few observations bearing on governmental policy, which, after all, is the main theme of this book.

Almost every layman has had drilled into him by this time the still difficult concept of how credit or check-book money can be "created" by a banker. There may be argument over definitions—whether or not the "deposit" a banker enters to a borrower's account is "money"—but there is no argument over the process. Because the law requires that a banker shall not make such loans out of thin air beyond a certain point (a bookkeeping relation between the deposits arising from loans and certain items considered as "reserves"), it is still possible to maintain the fiction that the banker is the owner of a scarce commodity, gold, and that he loans it out, getting interest as a reward for abstaining from spending it on his own consumption. But he does create new purchasing power nevertheless.

The banker serves a number of useful social functions. He provides a safe place for people to keep their money, either in a strong-box or in a deposit account. He furnishes the great convenience of a checking account, and does the principal bookkeeping of a complex economic system, which functions in most transactions by check. He uses his business judgment to decide when commercial loans are justified as good business risks. He provides a mechanism for the accumulation of small savings. There is no reason to suppose that in these respects he does not do an excellent job, or that any great improvements would be expected, say, by having the government take over these functions.

But the banker is also a credit factory for manufacturing credit money. This is a purely mechanical process, involving mere book entries which any government clerk could make as well. Yet it gives the banker a vast power for good or ill; usually exercised for neither, only for general muddlement.

In the case of simple business loans, or short-term commercial credit, it is hard for him to abuse his power, except when too great timidity prevents his exercising it; for such credit is created against the production or distribution of actual goods. But the banker may make loans for quite other purposes, for capital expansion, for speculation, to finance building construction, and so on. And if he can create money he can also destroy it, by calling his loans, usually just at a time when he will do most havoc.

Actually the bankers have in times of depression done this part of their job, the creation of credit money, so badly that governments have taken it over to an increasing extent. Governments still pretend, however, that the bankers are doing it. Perhaps they are afraid of hurting the bankers' feelings. Perhaps they do not themselves understand what they are doing.

Thus the government prints a thousand-dollar bond, and sends it by registered mail to a bank that is "buying" the bond (*i.e.*, "lending" the government the money); the bank enters a "deposit" to the government's account; the government can then draw checks on the bank; the bank's power to lend to others is no whit reduced by its "loan" to the government, for it can always use the bond to increase its "cash" reserves. It might seem as if the bank were merely carrying on its usual practice of creating check-book money, for which it gets its usual rake-off in the shape of interest; but actually the government initiated the creation of the money by printing the bond, and there is no more reason why it should pay the bank interest than if it had printed currency in the first place. If either practice is inflationary they are both inflationary. If either of them is not inflationary, then neither is inflationary. The only difference between printing "fiat money" in the one case and printing a bond in the other, is that in the latter case there is an obligation to pay interest, which may or not involve difficulties, while in the former case there is none. Printing bonds is supposed to exercise a restraining influence on the indefinite continuance of this inflationary practice.*

Today the whole question, how much purchasing power is coming into the market to buy goods and services, depends on the important decisions of banks and governments. The banks are haphazard, moved by conflicting incentives, so uncorrelated that they may be all reducing purchasing power when it most needs to be expanded, and expanding it when it most needs to be reduced. Governments, on the other hand, can act with an eye to general policies, long-range planning, the needs of the whole community. They are, as we have seen in preceding chapters, taking over more and more banking processes, and they thereby determine the amount of credit money. *Government fiscal policy is becoming the final determinant of economic activity.*

What then are the possibilities of maintaining equilibrium by government spending, in place of private investment? How far can government spending go without danger of inflation?

* It may of course be argued that when a bank buys a bond it is investing some of the savings deposited with it, and hence no new money is created, either by the government or by the bank. The fact that the bank's power to lend is not necessarily reduced by the "loan" to the government suggests, however, that the effect may be the same as if new money were created. The miracle of German rearmament and other "deficit financing" indicates how far this process can go without inflation, so long as private savings are not being otherwise invested. The problem of inflation in this connection is considered on the pages immediately following, and on pages 384-385.

### *Government Spending and Inflation*

Inflation—like its respectable cousins, deflation and reflation—is among the trickiest words in economics. It usually means that new money (currency or credit money) is being issued faster than new goods and services are being made available on the market, and consequently that prices are rising.

In view of all the other difficulties of maintaining equilibrium it is obviously desirable to have reasonably stable prices (though it may be argued that a slowly rising price level may be conducive to a more optimistic prospect for profits). If for any reason consumers have more money to spend than there are goods available, prices will tend to rise. If prices begin to rise very rapidly, consumers will try to get rid of money as soon as possible. We may say its "velocity" has risen, or that the rate of transactions has gone up, or that "liquidity preference" as regards money has sunk towards zero. The process is cumulative, and if not stopped in time it becomes an inflation of the spectacular type. If prices are falling, the "velocity" of money falls; people hang on to it, in hopes of buying more cheaply later; "liquidity preference" is high. Both the upswing and the downswing may be aggravated by speculation.

A mere increase in government spending, however, need not bring about an inflationary rise in prices. In spite of dire prophecies, the payment of the soldiers' bonus in America in 1936 had no such ill effect: in fact it was the greatest single factor in bringing about the partial recovery that culminated at the end of that year. There were great reserves of productive capacity, and the increase in purchasing power merely set our productive mechanism to work at a higher rate. For some years our government has been spending three or four billion dollars a year more than it took in, with apparently little effect on the price level. Conservative fears of inflation never materialized. There was always a sufficiency of goods on the market to absorb the new purchasing power.

Let us suppose that a government decided it would throw caution to the winds and spend whatever was necessary to bring production up to capacity, and then, when every worker was employed, call a halt. Let us suppose further that it uses its power to print money, and its power through a controlled banking system to create credit money, with complete recklessness, in its enthusiasm for a spending policy. What will happen? Most of the money in a depression-ridden country like ours will go to unemployed workers and impoverished farmers, who will immediately spend it, and business will pick up to take care of the increased demand. But what will happen to the new money? It will not be canceled when exchanged for some new article called forth from the reserve productive capacity—as a technocratic ticket might be. It will enter permanently into the country's money supply. Sooner or later it will show up as some property owner's income, as rent, interest or profit, and with income as unevenly distributed as it is in this country, that person is likely to have so large an income that he will save a large part of it. But private investment is hardly likely to pick up so long as the process of reckless unplanned government spending continues—for who can have any "confidence" in the future? Hence there will be huge hoardings of idle money, and the government will find that it is pumping in money at one end only to have it pumped out at the other. If full employment is approached the day is likely to come when some of the hoarders begin to get frightened; they will begin buying commodities, and once prices have started to rise, the billions of hoarded wealth will suddenly appear on the market all at once. Runaway inflation will follow.

Let us suppose, on the other hand, that a government tried to get out of depression by spending only what it could get by taxation and borrowing. It is careful not to print any new currency or to force bonds on the banks, but, if it borrows, to borrow no more than actual savings. If it starts from a depression level, when savings are few and tax sources are dried up, it may be unable to secure enough funds to spend on any lavish scale. Further collapse may be halted—if it does not try to balance its budget and depend wholly on taxation—but if there is no new money injected into the system it will be unable to produce prosperity. It will have a much heavier national debt to show at the end of that period, with no increase in the national income. But there will have been no inflation.

Finally, let us suppose that a government applies a judicious mixture. It finances a heavy spending program from three sources

—new credit money ("reflation"), borrowing, and taxation. If it is generous enough in its spending, and reckless enough in its "reflation" during the initial period, production and consumption will increase, as in our first case. But as property income begins to grow, taxation will bear down on it more and more heavily, and the borrowings from the banks—which may at first have amounted to credit inflation—will now absorb real savings. The danger of hoarding will be correspondingly less.

This is substantially what Germany did to get out of the depression, though she spent the extra money largely on armament rather than relief or useful public works. The half-hearted spending of the preceding example might correspond roughly to the experience of England and the United States. Be it noted that there is little difference in immediate economic effect between financing a spending program by taxing the wealthy and by borrowing their savings. England tried the former method, having accustomed her wealthy class during the war years to heavy income taxes, and having a national debt already so heavy that she did not want to increase it. In America an equally heavy taxation program would have further discouraged business, and there seemed no reason why we should not add to a national debt so much lighter than England's. The net effect in both cases has been much the same—some recovery, but nothing permanent, and no complete absorption of the unemployed.*

Now let me look back to the Soviet Five Year Plans. An important difference between the Soviet Union and all other coun-

* In spite of the constant Jeremiads about inflation, because of the extent to which government spending in the United States was financed by borrowing rather than by taxation, the difference from the English procedure seems to amount simply to this, that our annual budget now carries a slightly larger interest charge than it did. But because the interest rate has been falling the total interest charge has not gone up by anything like the same proportion as the debt itself: between 1934 and 1936 the national debt rose by 6½ billion dollars while the annual interest charge rose only from 842 million to 845 million. But the alarmists cry out, think what will happen when the government has to pay back the principal! Yet why should the government not continue simply to refund (each time perhaps at a lower interest rate) as it has in the past? And why should a large outstanding interest-bearing debt be any more dangerous when it is owed by a government which has supreme financial powers including the power to tax, than when it is owed by private businesses?

tries, including Germany, was that there were no recipients of property income. Hence there were no hoardings. The extra money paid out beyond the limits of productive capacity did not accumulate in anyone's bank balances, it accumulated in the pockets of ordinary consumers, and they lined up in queues before the empty shops trying to spend it. There was an almost immediate inflationary effect, though for a while it was disguised, and Soviet apologists could point to prices in the closed stores to prove there was none; but finally queues and closed stores were abolished, and prices found a new level five times above their earlier level. None the less, the Soviet spending policy—a vast public investment financed in part by printing press money—absorbed all the unemployed, and resulted in the rapid expansion of the country's productive capacity.

You will remember that in the Soviet Union the planners found it astonishingly easy to create credit—to write down in the State Bank so and so many billion rubles to the credit of the various industries. But you will also remember that the industries needed cash to pay their workers. In the case of short-term or commercial credit actually issued for the production and distribution of goods the State Bank got its money back; but much short-term credit was diverted to cover unexpected costs or to capital construction, and in the case of the long-term or investment credit it soon became obvious that the new industries would not be able to repay a substantial amount, and the State Bank ceased to expect repayment of either interest or principal. When inflation was halted, investment came wholly from taxes and other state collections, and short-term credit was held to strict repayment.

With this in mind, what are the limits to governmental spending in such a country as America? What is there about private investment that delights the conservative economist, while public investment horrifies him?

Investment means the channeling of purchasing power to pay for the construction of capital goods. These capital goods cannot "pay for themselves" in the future. They are necessarily fully paid for as built, for the workers who build them receive their wages in cash at once. If the money is secured by a bond issue, this long-term credit is repayable as to principal and interest by a kind of tax on consumers. If it is private investment, say in a railroad, the tax is a rate somewhat higher than operating costs. If it is public investment, as in a highway, the tax is directly levied on sales of gasoline. In either case the tax is a *later* withdrawal of purchasing power, and hence it cannot pay for past construction, it can only pay for *subsequent* construction. The Soviet Union was starting virtually from scratch at the beginning of the Five Year Plans, so no repayments of past loans were being made to cover the present investment expenditures, and even when a trickle of interest started coming in it was only a drop in the bucket. From a monetary point of view the Soviet Union was investing more than it was saving, and the result was inflation. It was finally able to achieve a balance even without requiring repayment of investment loans; for repayment has little to do with the matter of balance, the whole question being one of various kinds of taxation to get back funds in the present as fast as they are paid out.*

In a capitalist system repayment of past loans with interest on those outstanding is merely one of the sources which may balance the total amount currently spent on investment. For some years now these sources have produced more savings than the amount invested. If the government were to take the savings by taxation or borrowing and force them into investment a balance could be achieved. Failing that, it must pump new money into the system to balance the hoardings withdrawn, or contemplate continually mounting unemployment.

The word investment when applied to government spending is somewhat confusing. In the case of private enterprise, if a business man builds an Empire State Building which remains more than half empty, and the investors lose their shirts, it may be considered bad business judgment, but it is none the less investment. If the government builds a battleship, which is never expected to produce income, the conservative may think the term investment misapplied, for the battleship makes no pretense at being self-liquidating or income-producing, yet the effect is much the same. If the government spends billions on relief, this is even less likely

* The non-repayable government investment might be compared to a capitalist's investment in common stock: he owns an "equity" but there is no obligation to repay. He may have borrowed the money to pay for the stock out of thin air or he may have used his savings. In either case he looks forward to having an income-producing asset.

to be considered investment, since no tangible asset results, though such spending represents an attempt to conserve our most valuable asset, our working population. In either case the economic effect is the same as private investment: the discrepancy between savings and investment is made up by government spending.

The term "state capitalism" has found increasing use in recent years. It might well be used to describe the tendency for the state to assume full responsibility for the maintenance of economic equilibrium, by becoming the chief investor. Its preponderant influence over the amount of currency and credit gives it the key position. It can inject new money into the system up to the point necessary to maintain full production. And it can assure a balance between saving and investment either by issuing new money, as old money is hoarded, or by bringing the hoardings out, taxing them or borrowing them. But whether or not the government is radical or conservative, whether or not it "owns" the banks or leaves them in "private" hands, and whether or not the system may be called "socialist" or "capitalist," the problem of equilibrium between goods and money is much the same.*

* An economist recently described aspects of the failure to maintain equilibrium in these words: "The outcome has been on the one hand that enormous growth of plant and equipment which has been described often enough, and on the other, as an accompaniment and a counterpart, reflecting the cost of the process, a steady accumulation all along the line of lags, disproportions, shortages and shortcomings, unfinished construction, unused capacity, wear of plant and equipment, and depletion of resources." Most of this would be equally applicable to the United States in the years 1929 to 1933 or to the Soviet Union in the same years. It was written of the latter.

# *Chapter Sixteen*

## FROM AUTOMATISM TO CONTROLS AND BACK

LET me look back at the ground covered in the previous chapter. I started out with the realization that if an economic system were to make full use of modern technology it could end poverty. But it must maintain full employment of its labor and resources. This means that no one who wants work should be unable to find it, and that resources should be used in such a way as to maximize the satisfactions to be derived from them without waste. If such conditions of "full production" are maintained we could have universal abundance instead of poverty.

So I took the position that to achieve this goal a system of planned "production for use" was required instead of production for sale on the market. But I discovered that the market was coming back into favor in "socialist" Russia, as well as in contemporary socialist theory, and that Germany had been able to achieve "full production" without abandoning the market. If the market system could be made to work, it offered the increased freedom of any automatic device. And naturally the transition stages would be easier.

But was there not an inherent defect in the market system, at least under capitalism? Depressions occurred, when goods could not be sold. And in the best of times purchasing power ran far short of being able to buy what could be produced. Maldistribution of income between rich and poor, though ethically and aesthetically offensive, did not stand examination as an intrinsic fault. Nor was it a case of too little money, for the money supply is flexible enough to meet any demand. The trouble appeared to be in the changing rates of "flow" of savings and investments, and of new money and credit, which caused periodic or chronic depression.

The problem of a market system emerged as a problem in the maintenance of equilibrium under conditions of constant change and growth, that is, a problem of dynamic equilibrium. I found both socialist and capitalist economists had arrived at this same conclusion.

Finally I explored some of the monetary factors involved in this delicate equilibrium, and the dominant position of any government. The government can inject new money into the system to counterbalance the savings not being privately invested. But this may further discourage private investment. It is not inflationary, however, in any immediate sense; for serious inflation cannot occur till money is being issued faster than plants can increase their production of goods. Or again the government can take private savings, by taxation or borrowing, and make sure that they are invested—which is not inflationary at all.

I could not help wondering how the system had been able to work as well as it had in the days before governmental interferences. The equilibrium required was so complex that it seemed nothing short of a first-class miracle that it had ever worked, or that it could ever be made to work. And if it had ceased to work what could take its place but some superhuman intelligence with vast powers?

I found myself looking on the laissez faire system with new respect, almost with awe. I realized why economists who studied the system were so impressed by the niceties of its mechanism that, following Adam Smith, they felt there must be an "unseen hand" at work. Some felt it must be the hand of God. Most of them preferred to consider it the hand of "Nature"; the explanations they propounded were considered "laws of nature," like gravitation. They pointed to the fact that the mastery of the material environment proceeded at a vastly more rapid pace under capitalism than under the previous authoritarian systems of slavery and feudalism. And they were quite right in emphasizing that it is a "natural" order of things: no theorist invented "capitalism"; it grew naturally (as did slavery and feudalism); it was a product of historical evolution. This fact alone gives it a sanction; it also explains the apparent miracle.* Trial and error have weeded out certain economic processes not conducive to survival and encouraged others.

### *How Laissez Faire Was Supposed to Work*

Remember that the market or price system is a method of rationing what is scarce, and that the heart of the mechanism is a price which adjusts supply and demand to each other. If oranges are a drug on the market the price comes down till demand is big enough to take the supply. If there is shift in demand to pineapples the price of pineapples goes up.

All commodities are subject to this "law," for that is what a commodity is; even though the Clayton Act declared that "labor is not a commodity" the price of labor does tend to behave in similar fashion: if there are too many workers looking for the same jobs the prices paid for doing those jobs, the wages, will come down, and vice versa.

Now one of the wonderful things about the price system is that it makes possible the measurement of all economic goods against each other. A manufacturer can decide on the basis of comparative prices of the things he needs—his costs—which combination will be most economical. He can choose between various raw materials, steel or aluminum. He can measure human labor against a new labor-saving machine.

But there a new marvel appears; for he has to buy the new machine, whereas he can hire the worker by the day. In buying the machine he is buying something that will provide benefits into the future. But since he will have to borrow the money to buy it, he will spread paying for it over a period into the future. In deciding whether to buy the machine he has to take into account its value over a period of future time as against the added costs

* For the human organism is likewise a miracle. The extraordinary checks and balances which maintain a constant temperature and humidity, automatically repair damages, facilitate reproduction, maintain an even flow of various vital fluids, co-ordinate the tissues and organs with a network of nerves—all this amazing equilibrium of life processes is a miracle only to be explained as a product of evolution. But we may thank God that none of our anthropoid ancestors thought the last word had been said.

he has undertaken. How can future costs and benefits be measured against present ones? Once again the price system provides an answer, for interest is a mechanism for measuring values at various times in the future. Suppose the machine costs $100,000. If the manufacturer borrows the money from a wealthy friend, that friend must weigh his interest against the satisfaction of spending his money immediately, say on a private yacht. Thus interest brings all sorts of present and future considerations into relation to each other at a present moment.*

Thus the market is a mechanism for rationing not only consumer goods and jobs, but all the so-called "factors of production" which a producer must take into account—raw materials, plant and machinery, land, labor. By going into the market for these things, with borrowed money, the producer selects between various alternatives those which seem to promise the greatest net profit.

As a magazine publisher (even if not in a profit-making field) I could tell you something about the kind of choices you would have to make as between various alternatives, if you wanted to publish a magazine. You would have to select a printer, and choose between various qualities and prices. If you want a convenient, spacious office you will have to pay accordingly. How much could you pay for articles, and illustrations? What kind of paper will you use? The demand for shiny coated paper has risen greatly since the style of magazines has become more lavish, and consequently the price has gone up. In each case you must choose between different qualities of goods at different prices. And in every decision you will be part of a vast network of decisions on the part of millions of people, directing productive effort into millions of different channels.

The theorists of the marginal utility school worked out abstract

*There has been considerable discussion about the role of interest in the Soviet Union. Savings banks pay interest as an inducement to savings, though this is one of the most dubious roles of interest in a capitalist country. Short-term credit is advanced at interest, as a means of speeding the productive and distributive processes. But since money is advanced for investment purposes without interest, its most important function is missing. In a rough sort of way the Soviet planners must decide between future and present satisfactions; but it has been pointed out that the Dnieprostroy dam would never have been built when it was, before its power could be fully used, if interest on borrowed money had been reckoned into its cost.

laws to show how supply and demand, cost and price, worked against each other in a wondrous equilibrium. Everyone was trying to maximize his own satisfactions and minimize his own outlay, and whether he was a consumer or a producer, the available amounts of scarce goods were rationed in the most economical way. All elements in the whole economic system found their own proper level, assuming a theoretically pure market, with everything flexible enough to find its proper adjustment. The result of competition between individuals trying to get as much as possible for as little as possible was, according to the theorists, that *society as a whole* got as much as possible for as little as possible.

If there were too much of anything, thus upsetting the balance, its price would drop—wages in the case of labor, interest in the case of money to lend, rent in the case of land. If there were too little, higher prices would bring out a larger supply, or cut down the demand, restoring a balance. All resources would be used and all labor employed; for if any were not, the price would fall just the right amount to bring it into use.

No wonder people worshiped Adam Smith and his "unseen hand." No wonder people still marvel at the beauty of the system of free enterprise, and hold up their hands in horror at the thought of ignorant workers, or socialist planners, trying to replace this amazing automatic mechanism with their own arbitrary and blundering decrees.

To be sure, no one claimed the system worked perfectly. When the equilibrium was upset the counterbalancing factors might set in too strongly and swing the pendulum over to the other extreme. Differing rates of readjustment complicated the problem further—workers could not move to a new location to open up a new industry as rapidly as money could be made available. The equilibrium was never more than approximate, with countless minor oscillations and larger cyclical swings. Yet on the whole the system worked.

And it is incorrect to think of it as having "collapsed" or "broken down." It still works, though with ever greater discrepancies between the actual and the ideal. Even at the depth of the Great Depression the majority of the population were little or no worse fed, clothed and housed, than in 1929; * essential services

* The index of consumer goods production was 75.9 in 1932 (1929 = 100).

were never discontinued; the miracle of the price system was still wondrously at work.

However, the system ran into cumulative trouble, as everybody knows. The condition of its adequate functioning was flexibility, particularly flexibility of price. If any rigidities developed it meant that the automatic restoration of equilibrium would be hampered: the longer the delay the more drastic would be the necessary readjustments. Some readjustments might become quite impossible. Others would take so long and be so drastic as to involve increasingly serious depression cycles.

Three rigidities seem to me to stand out preponderantly. The first is the rigidity of price obtaining when there is some control over supply. Any monopolistic tendencies will mean rigid prices (even trade unions can control the supply of labor and by threatening to strike keep wages more or less stable). The second is the rigidity of the interest rate, which for peculiar reasons cannot fall below a certain point. The third is the rigidity due to governmental interferences: governments, for instance, set floors below which wages cannot fall, by offering relief to the unemployed or by passing minimum wage laws; they fix prices, as of power and transportation; they create uncertainties in the minds of business men.*

A great flood of light has been shed in the last few years on these rigidities. So far as government interferences are concerned, all the business community and its apologists have been hammer-

* Other rigidities might be mentioned, though they are not, it seems to me, of as crucial importance as those mentioned. There have always been "sticky" features of the system: such, for instance, as the slowness with which workers may move to a new location or become trained for a new skill. Another "sticky" feature is that as certain businesses have grown to giant size, like the automobile industry, because of such technological requirements for cheap mass production as the assembly line, for instance, the possibility of new enterprisers entering the field to break a monopoly advantage disappears. Among monopoly advantages, moreover, which governments have fostered, are patents and protective tariffs. These latter have loomed particularly large in the minds of liberal economists, especially when influenced by the preponderance of foreign trade in the English economy: they had come to believe that the market should be world wide, and of course tariffs and the more modern quotas make its automatic functioning virtually impossible. Economists of the same school have also tended to emphasize the international gold standard as a necessary feature of an automatic world market, and have seen its restoration as the first condition to recovery.

ing away to make the public aware of their unfortunate effect. But in large part they are due to efforts to cope with the difficulties arising from the first two causes. The new light that has been thrown on these two is due largely to three economists: Joan Robinson in England and Edward Chamberlin in America simultaneously worked out the new theoretical explanation of "monopolistic" or "imperfect competition," and John Maynard Keynes developed his "general theory of employment, interest and money," which I have already frequently mentioned. Before the work of these economists no adequate appreciation of what was wrong with our economic system was possible, for all economic theories were based on certain subtle fallacies.

### *The Trouble With Monopoly*

It is easy to see how a monopoly makes for rigid prices. But virtually all previous economists, while admitting the existence of some monopoly, considered the system as a whole freely competitive. Now it has become clear that there is an element of monopoly in virtually all economic activity, and that in effect there is no such thing as pure competition; neither is there any pure monopoly.

At one extreme, even when supply is controlled entirely by one monopolistic enterprise, as is virtually the case with aluminum in America, there is competition with other similar products. If the price of aluminum is set too high, demand will shift to other products, and less profit will be made. Actually competition is still at work. The monopolist will tend to seek a price where most profit will be made—a price higher than the price orthodox theory allowed for under pure price competition, and consequently a price that will result in a smaller amount produced and sold, but a competitive price nevertheless. A special difficulty arises, however, in finding that perfect monopolistic price. Since there is only one producer (in our assumed case) he can tell at what point his profits will be greatest only by trial and error, and if he is earning what seems to him a satisfactory profit he is unlikely to experiment further. It might be that a whole new market for his product would be opened up by a slight drop in price, but if he is not sufficiently intelligent or daring he will keep his price where it is. In time of depression he will simply close down, or operate at a fraction of capacity.

At the other extreme even small business has monopolistic elements. Each corner drug store has a monopoly on its particular location, and on such intangibles as the personality of its proprietor. Most mass production articles sold on its counters have trade names, good will, standard prices—all of them signs of monopoly. Monopolistic features are ever-present in our economy. They all tend to raise prices toward the perfect monopoly prices that would prevail in any field if there were a single monopolist there, but few reach that happy state.

Two objections may be raised to monopoly prices. The first is that they are too high, the second that they are too rigid. Let us consider them in turn.

There is nothing about a high monopoly price that necessarily interferes with the free functioning of the market mechanism. It is true that at the higher price demand will be less, and therefore production will be less—in the case of that particular commodity. But if the extra profits which the monopolist makes find prompt investment, this will not mean that the system as a whole is producing less. It is obvious that the greatest expansion of our system in the last generation has been in the fields of big business where monopoly practices were most frequent.

For example, look at the automobile industry. By now it is largely dominated by the "Big Four." There are several price fields, and each turns out a car for that field—low price, medium price, high price, with gradations in between. It might be argued that each price is too high for what the consumer receives, and that if the price were lower more would be sold. But this would have an effect on the actual number produced only in the lowest price field, for all other buyers can already buy a cheaper car if they wish. And if it is argued that the present system results in taxing all the consumers for the benefit of the stockholders it might be replied that it was only because this possibility existed that the great automobile industry was developed so rapidly. Moreover, the big company can design and produce a special product to meet a waiting demand in a particular price field, and continue to improve it, in a way that would have been impossible under the necessarily smaller scale of price competition, with its smaller attraction to investors, and its more primitive technological methods.

The mere fact that monopoly prices are higher than those prevailing under free price competition does not seem to be a serious cause of difficulty. Such prices do, of course, add to the total amount of profits that can be made, and if there is a tendency for savings to get ahead of investment, monopoly prices will aggravate the tendency. But they do not cause it. Then, too, it may be argued that monopoly prices do not fall as costs are cut due to technological improvements. But this is a question of rigidity, the second difficulty we mentioned.

Rigidity in turn may be looked at from two different angles. On the one hand there is the rigidity due to the simple fact that the price is controlled or "administered," and hence not subject to the minor fluctuations of the market. It might seem offhand as though any element which made for greater stability in our highly unstable economic system would be to the good. Certainly those who are able to take advantage of stable prices seem to be better off than those who are dependent on highly variable prices: for years our government has been trying to give the farmers relief from the calamitous variations of the grain market. But the economist of free competition argues that the trouble with the farmer is that he sells in a free market and buys in an "administered" market. One of the chief objections to the administered price is this, that it does not behave in the same way as the freely competitive price. Why not have all prices similarly administered, then, so that they may all react in the same way? The laissez faire economist will insist once more that the whole market mechanism depends on the adjustment of prices to the varying pressures of supply and demand, and that complete flexibility of price is essential to its smooth working.

What is wrong is not that prices are administered but that they are administered unintelligently. Even the most orthodox economist would probably have to admit that railroad rates must be an administered price: they cannot be permitted to vary from day to day, or no business man would be able to calculate ahead. They must be set, for comparatively long periods. In the last few years we have seen passenger fares change several times. We have seen them lowered by the Interstate Commerce Commission at a time when the railroad system as a whole was close to bankruptcy, and most railroad executives groaned that lower rates would finish them off; instead such a large new demand was opened up that profits rose instead of falling. Later the rates were raised, and profits fell. The theorists of monopolistic competition could calculate, if all facts were known (and of course the more prices are administered the more facts will be known), at just what rate the railroads would make the largest profit. This represents a different kind of adjustment between supply and demand, from the old adjustment of price competition, but it is no less an adjustment. In the case of the railroads as in hundreds of other industries there can be no restoration of pure price competition. Monopoly is here to stay, whether we like it or not.

The trouble with monopoly prices is that they are so often stupidly "administered." Big businesses tend to be slow and bureaucratic, conservative and cautious. They may cling to a price which has made them profits in the past without realizing that many surrounding conditions have changed. They may feel that with the growing rigidity of other administered prices—wages fixed in union contracts through collective bargaining, interest on outstanding bonds and other debts, freight rates, power rates, prices of raw materials like steel—they cannot afford to experiment with their own prices. Moreover, they can never be sure what their competitors may do—remember that the administered prices of "monopolistic competition" are still competitive. The Anti-Trust Laws may be ineffective but they provide a standing threat against combination to share knowledge of the factors that should determine intelligent prices and to permit agreement on prices.

With our long-standing prejudice against monopoly we have penalized business men for getting together to share information, and tried to compel them to work in the dark.

So we have a system that is "half-slave and half-free"—some of its prices are determined by free competition on a highly unstable and unpredictable market, and the others are more or less administered in such a generally inefficient and blundering sort of way that they make conditions on the market worse rather than better.

### *Failure of the Investment Market*

Monopoly has always attracted the special attention of governments, and many of the rigidities in our system are the result of government attempts to cope with monopoly, or government responses to its pressure. But somehow we managed to get along through booms and slumps, in spite of monopolistic features, and in spite of growing intervention by governments.

Now, however, something new seems to have developed. Chronic depression, with several million permanently unemployed, has been widespread in Europe since the war, and in this country, on an even grander scale, since 1929. Apparently this final disease of laissez faire is a result of the second rigidity I mentioned above, the rigidity of the interest rate, first expounded by John Maynard Keynes.

I have all the sensations of walking over a treacherous swamp at night when I read Keynes; but I am inclined to believe the fault is less Keynes's or mine than simply that the swamp is really treacherous. It involves some of the most subtle of psychological problems.

The situation which needs explaining here is why investment has been increasingly lagging behind savings; and why the resultant poverty is greatest in the richest countries, England and America. I have mentioned the fact that in the rich countries there are more rich people, and they naturally save more than is possible in the poor countries. Under laissez faire theory the interest rate which enterprisers will pay to the lenders of this money will drop, if the supply of investment funds is higher than the demand for them, until finally a point will be reached at which all the funds will be profitably invested. But for various psychological reasons which Keynes elaborately hints at, the interest rate will not drop below 2 or 2½ per cent. Potential lenders will prefer "liquidity"—they will let their money lie idle rather than invest it at lower rates. And the prospect of profits above the given interest rate is not sufficient to induce promoters and enterprisers to borrow. Stagnation, bankruptcy and unemployment finally lower the whole system to a point at which a balance is achieved between savings, investment, and the consequent distribution of purchasing power.

But since even this equilibrium depends on psychological factors—what Keynes calls the "propensity to consume," "liquidity preference," and "the marginal efficiency of capital," all of which are tied in with what the business man calls "confidence"—it is an equilibrium likely to be freshly upset by every political gust.

The laissez faire economist argues that confidence cannot be restored till the government keeps its meddling hands off. Unfortunately the government is the only agency able and willing to borrow, lend, spend and invest, regardless of the interest rate. When investors hang on to their money, the government is forced to step in and make up some of the lag in purchasing power. It feeds the unemployed, and runs to the rescue of any other group when the chronic burden of depression seems too heavy, meanwhile spending lavishly on public works—all of which drives "confidence" still lower.

Finally, all these government interferences introduce new rigidities. Prices are held up, wages are held up, capital structures are held up. And a system which depends for its proper functioning on a greater and greater degree of flexibility in every part, finds instead an increasing ossification going on in its entire structure.

### *From Interventionism to Totalitarian Planning*

The post-war world I described in earlier chapters is one in which these subtle diseases of the nineteenth-century laissez faire economic system have been coming to a head. The gradual extension of government control over all phases of economic life, up to complete economic planning under a dictatorship, was not intended by anybody, except in the Soviet Union. It represented the natural response of the social organism to the evolutionary breakdown of the automatic price system.

But the interference of government was much older than the present breakdown. In earlier chapters I have described how laissez faire itself was a positive governmental policy, carried on through a framework of enabling legislation, corporation laws and the like, rather than a natural state of freedom. I have described how liberalism became more and more transformed from a principle of freedom of enterprise to a principle of governmental intervention, for humanitarian or other reasons. The laissez faire system always left such glaring social wrongs to be righted—read Marx's description of child labor in early nineteenth-century England for the most revolting picture—that new state interventions were being adopted even before the old mercantilist interferences were abandoned.

Protective tariffs, taxation policies, and government fiscal activities had a part in introducing rigidities at an early stage. All social and labor legislation—minimum wage laws, maximum hour laws, unemployment insurance and relief, social security and insurance schemes, the recognition of unions for collective bargaining—constitute interferences with the competitive system, especially as they tend to make wages more stable or higher than pure competition would make them. Railroad and utility regulation always involved further fixing of prices.

Every depression has induced additional government intervention, to rescue banker or business man, farmer or unemployed worker. Recovery measures are inevitably thought of as reforms, however much conservatives may insist they should be separately considered. For what is the use of recovery if you fall into the same slough of depression for the same reasons after a few years?

In so far as the competitive system tended to become world wide and international, the interferences of governments for reasons of pride and political power were even more drastic.

Finally, with the difficult post-war period, interferences with the free functioning of the competitive system became the general rule. "We are all Socialists now," said a prominent English Tory, though with his tongue in his cheek.

The three central problems governments faced were the maintenance of purchasing power, the maintenance of investment, and monopolistic price practices.

The first problem is to assure a constant supply of purchasing power, adequate but not more than adequate to buy what can be produced. For this purpose governments take decisive control over currency and credit. They try to force hoardings out by taxes, loans, threats and cajolings. They assure that new money flows into the system when the stream of purchasing power otherwise seems likely to dry up entirely. In so far as they are unwilling to tackle the problem of investment, they use many alternative devices for increasing consumer spending, to counterbalance idle savings, assisted by all the new types of "social dividends"—pensions, insurance payments, childhood and motherhood allowances, as well as direct relief—which have been developed to ease the hardships of the competitive system.

The second problem, and an essential aspect of the maintenance of purchasing power, is the investment process. Various techniques have been used to boost and maintain a steady rate of investment. Money is made available by the governments for investment loans at low interest rates, or without interest. Public expenditures for expanding public services, and for public works in the stricter sense, run ever farther ahead of "private" investment. Private savings are corralled by borrowings or taxes or collections, and invested where governments decide, especially in armaments production.

The market method of competition for profit is everywhere retained, but it is generally "monopolistic competition." Free price competition is by now practically extinct. Complete control of supply and complete information regarding the prices and production schedules of all other producers of the same commodity provide a more workable form of "monopolistic competition" than that in which there is partial price competition by a large number of producers competing more or less blindly. Instead of fighting against the "trust," the "open price" agreement, and other kinds of "administered" prices, governments have been encouraging cartels and trade associations as methods of "rationalizing" industries, stabilizing prices, eliminating the uncertainties arising from varying degrees of monopolistic control. The organization of each industry, virtually as a publicly sponsored monopoly, with power to fix prices and allocate production, has gone farthest in the fascist states, though even there the door is kept open for new enterprises, and it is held that inefficient enterprises must be left to eliminate themselves.

The interventionist state has been becoming, in a blind blundering sort of way, more and more a collectivist state. Look back at Part II of this book.

In Germany, where the situation was complicated by powerful socialist and communist movements, and by a hyper-sensitive nationalism, a curious coalition of Jew-hating neurotics, patrioteers, scheming supermonopolists, army officers, desperate unemployed, and harassed shopkeepers got control of the government, intent on more drastic measures. The result might have been only more of the same makeshifts, as in early Italian fascism, if their one common denominator, a desire to avenge the Versailles *Diktat*, had not started them towards a totalitarianized economy for war purposes. They abandoned mere rescue work, the helter-skelter pattern of the old interventionism, and began to reconstruct their economy for better waging of war.

The path which the fascist nations took for these limited purposes had already been charted by the Soviet Union in a conscious effort to arrive at "socialism." But it was much the same path, involving expansion of the productive plant, full employment, full utilization of all the territory's resources, no further scruples over using the government's power over money and credit to fill all gaps in the spending-saving-investing stream, whenever they appeared.

Today the fear of fascist aggression seems to be compelling the other great powers to take the same path. The press of the democracies is filled with rumors of "registration" or "conscription" of business, expansion and mobilization of the war industries, nationalization of munitions plants—all in imitation of what the Germans significantly call *Wehrwirtschaft* or "defense economy."

It is hardly likely that either the democracies or the fascist powers will go as far as complete production planning. They may have "three year plans" and "four year plans" and "six year plans" and "ten year plans." But they will never attempt to do what the first two Soviet "five year plans" attempted: the advance blueprinting of every shovelful of coal to be produced over a period of years, and of the route that coal would follow, until it would appear ultimately as so many ton-miles of transportation or so many kilowatts of energy, to be turned into the production of so many pairs of shoes. I have already described the unnecessary difficulties in which the Soviet planners found themselves involved when they tried this method—thanks to the inadequate and misleading hints about a hypothetical "socialism," which was all the guidance Marx had given them. The other economies had no such incentive. The attempt to blueprint all production in advance is never likely to be tried again but to remain one of the greatest unsuccessful experiments ever tried by man.

### From Totalitarian Planning to Strategic Planning

The Soviet enthusiasts were forced to go back to the old automatism of the market because of grim necessity, as we have seen. The fascists, with their ties to big and little business, had never been inclined to abandon any of those automatic controls that would still serve. The democratic states had the same reason for caution as the fascists; in addition the whole strength of the democratic tradition reinforced the desire to make the automatic devices work, and avoid authoritarian and arbitrary controls.

At the same time there has been a growing search among economists for some method of partial planning—strategic planning it has been called—which, without introducing any new types of drastic governmental control, would co-ordinate existing controls at strategic points in such a way as to produce the desired economic result. It would use the existing governmental powers, not for haphazard rescue missions, but in a coherent policy capable of attaining full employment and an economy of abundance.

While the Marxists, forced to postpone indefinitely their hopes of "the socialist revolution," have been fighting a rearguard action against the often imaginary legions of fascism, a few non-Marxist groups have been doing pioneer theoretical work in strategic planning. The two most important groups in America have been able to test their theories in close contact with the real world: the National Economic and Social Planning Association in Washington, which publishes *Plan Age*, has had first-hand contact with the New Deal experiments; and the New School for Social Research "University in Exile," which publishes *Social Research*, has had bitter first-hand knowledge of the European world of affairs. Valuable work is also being done elsewhere. Much factual data from which new institutional procedures can be devised is being assembled by the Brookings Institution and the Twentieth Century Fund. An increasing number of economists in the universities and in the academic journals are tackling fundamental problems.

It is true that reformers, cranks and thwarted geniuses have for generations worked out proposals for remedying the defects of the economic system by a few strategic changes. Almost all these innumerable schemes had elements of true understanding lacking in their critics of right and left. The critics on the right insisted the system could straighten out its own troubles if not interfered with, and the critics on the left insisted that the whole system must be scrapped and that no mere tinkering would do. The new crop of strategic planners will meet with the same charges, particularly the dogmatic blasts of the extreme left.

I know, because "I have been there myself." Many is the writer or the proposal I have blasted in the last half-dozen years because he or it attempted to "patch up the old system" rather than institute a new one.

Yet the theoretical and practical failure of previous attempts at reform is no reason for scorning the trial and error method. The experience of the Soviet Union, unavailable to previous generations of "reformers," indicates that the difference between "socialism" and capitalist reform along lines of "state capitalism" may not be so great. The experience of the rest of the world since 1929, and particularly since 1933, has given theory and practice a whole new set of materials to work with. And finally the epoch-making work of some of the newer economic theorists is at last bringing our past experience into focus.

Perhaps now for the first time we know enough to make our capitalist system work. Perhaps, in making it work, we shall find we have accomplished the much-disputed transition to "socialism."

For the most advanced theorists of "socialism" have been discovering that in certain respects the closer a "socialist" system approximates the working of a laissez faire market the more efficient it will be. The "market socialists" have been paralleling in the theoretical sphere some of the discoveries of the Soviet Union in practice.

Their theories grew out of the challenge of certain Austrian economists, headed by von Mises, after the war, when socialist experiments were beginning in many countries. Von Mises pointed to the fact that the market mechanism not only permitted the consumer to exercise the final choice as to what would be produced, and gave the worker a chance to choose his job, but that it enabled producers to choose, as we have seen, between various "factors of production" to maximize the product with a minimum of cost. Socialist planning, he said, with no price system, would have no means of "rational calculation." It could not use its resources efficiently, and even if made to work by dictatorship, it could not produce a high standard of living.

Oskar Lange, one of the later "market Socialists," declared that von Mises had so ably stated the challenge to socialism, making socialists for the first time aware of their problem, that he should be honored with a special monument in the future socialist society. Socialist replies to his challenge took two forms.

On the one hand there were those who pointed to the failures of capitalism. Its market mechanism had so far broken down that it was wasting its resources at a greater rate than the most blundering socialist planners could be expected to do (though early Russian experience proved the reverse). Moreover, inequalities of wealth so affected the choice of the consumer in the market, that prices became quite unreliable measures of relative value, and made the claim to democracy in the market absurd; and advertising created fictitious wants, so that there could be no assurance that what consumers bought was what would really maximize their satisfactions.

On the other hand, the "market socialists" pointed out that a socialist society could make the market work, where capitalism could not. The manager of a publicly owned enterprise could fix his prices, if so instructed, according to the same formula as a private business man. The balance between supply and demand could be achieved by a trial and error method of price-fixing, as it is today, thus having all the advantages capitalism offers in "rational calculation"; and since all producing units would be operated according to the same price formula, a socialist society would not get into all the trouble capitalism is in today.

Of course, as some of these economists pointed out, there would be no need to operate the whole system by the market mechanism. Social policy might be expected to override certain consumer wants, like that for heroin, and to stimulate others, like that for a healthful family diet. Direct government expenditures, central planning of investment, expansion of free goods and social services, would mean that resemblance to the old laissez faire system would gradually fade.

But by and large the "market socialists" visualized a system in which consumers, spending their money where and how they chose, and workers seeking congenial work, would determine in the aggregate what goods and services were produced. It would be the task of industry and agriculture and the service trades to anticipate consumer wants. The prices of the various factors of production would represent true "opportunity cost": the cost of giving up an alternative in the market. Wages would represent the true economic contribution of labor, weighed against the alternative of further mechanization; they would counterbalance attractiveness or unpleasantness of various occupations, and, with opportunity open to all, would tend toward equality.

The "market socialists" assumed that all industry would be publicly owned, and most of their discussions of the working of a socialist economy were purely theoretical analyses of what could be done "after the revolution." Some of their critics have raised the question, why have a revolution if the end result is merely a restoration of the market system? They might logically reply that one procedure they took from the original market system can no longer be carried on without a revolution, and that is pure "price competition," for our big businesses cannot be split up into little competing units. But under "market socialism" the producers are managers of state owned plants, and they can be directed to follow one price policy as well as another. The rule the "market socialists" would have them follow is to produce until marginal cost equals marginal demand—which means the same price as that achieved under pure price competition.

Suppose, however, they followed the rule of maximizing profit —which means the same price as a single monopolist, or "pure monopolistic competition." That might be equally feasible. The only question then would arise as to the use of the profits. If they were used for social services, in lieu of taxes, there might be no appreciable difference from the net social product of the previous assumption.

But in that case why would it be necessary to socialize all industry? Give every private enterpriser the chance to levy an "intelligent" or "pure" monopoly price, and he would be doing what a "socialist" manager would be doing, under the second assumption. The only question will be, again, what happens to the profits? The matter of price policies will have been solved, and only the monetary problems relating to the equilibrium between savings and investment will remain.

Once again it appears that the question of ownership may be irrelevant. At the end of my search of economic theory I find less justification than ever for the belief that there is a world of difference—a whole revolutionary world of difference—between "capitalism" and "socialism."

Three modern schools of economic thought brought me to that conclusion. First John Maynard Keynes modernized the old theory that depressions are due to a failure of investment to keep up with savings, by showing that, especially in rich countries, a peculiarity of the interest rate will perpetuate inadequate investment, hence unemployment and depression will be chronic; by suggesting that investment be "socialized," he provides the key to a solution of the savings-investment relation, and hence of the relation of purchasing power to full production. Secondly, the economists of "monopolistic competition" have worked out the laws that govern prices in a modern economy; it seems possible to draw the conclusions from them that since prices are bound to be administered they should all be administered with the same facilities for intelligent adaptation to the new conditions, and that if the savings-investment problem has been otherwise attended to there need be no fear even of "pure monopolistic competition" in every field.

And finally I have suggested that the "market socialists" point the way to a synthesis of "capitalism" and "socialism" if one assumes universal monopoly prices.

It now remains to be seen how these theoretical conclusions might be applied to the practical problems of American political economy—economics in action.

# *PART V*

# EXPERIMENT IN POLITICAL ECONOMY

# Chapter Seventeen

## THE JOB TO BE DONE

IT HAS always been one of the major functions of academic circles to rationalize and apologize for the *status quo*. In the days of mercantilism, when sovereigns took a vigorous and forthright hand in building up the wealth of nations, a vigorous and forthright set of thinkers developed the science of "political economy." As the practice and theory of laissez faire developed, a pale asceticism seized the academicians, and for a century and a half they worked on a disembodied science of "economics," which sought the natural laws of economic activities in a vacuum where no sovereign would dare interfere.

Today we are returning to positive government action—to "political economy." Not that the government ever abdicated. As I have pointed out more than once, governments undertook to do what the dominant economic interests wanted them to, and for the most part this consisted of setting up and maintaining a structure within which profit could be pursued *ad lib*. It was a policy that fitted the new democratic temper, and for a while it did give far greater scope for freedom than any previous policy. Now governments are once more exerting their powers directly; but if we would not lose liberties already won the new structure will likewise be one permitting a maximum degree of automatism in its functioning. This difference from the old automatism there will be: that government will not simply set up the mechanism and then step aside, waiting for breakdowns, confining itself to intermittent repair work. Instead it will have to furnish a continuing guidance.

Yet even that concept is not quite adequate, suggesting as it does a *deus ex machina*, a power outside the mechanism, a separation of politics and economics. For if a workable integration of the complex tissues and organs of our social structure is to be maintained, there can be no valid distinction between what is governmental and what is non-governmental. We must conceive of a social organism in which every individual and every group is constantly finding adjustment to every other.

Political economy, in other words, will operate at every level, from the individual consumer or worker making his free choices and co-operating in group activities, all the way to world problems of raw materials and populations. For, unless civilized man is due for permanent extinction, the ultimate unit of management will be the world.

Yet we happen to be at a period in history when the greatest concentration of power is to be found in the national state. A realistic political economy, for some time to come, will think in terms of national organization. And my particular concern here, while in the larger sense aiming to be human and therefore universal, is necessarily with the United States. Likewise, my concern is with governmental policies, rather than with group and individual activity at the lower levels. However important, I cannot go into such problems as labor policy, the development of the co-operative movement, spheres of functional autonomy like group medicine.

At the same time, if I am to follow the philosophical bias outlined earlier, it is obviously out of the question to glorify the state as the over-riding end and purpose of human existence. Political economists both of the older and the newer mercantilism have tended to worship the state, whose aggrandizement they were seeking to foster. A democratic approach such as mine must think first and last of the human individuals concerned. Whether workers or capitalists, Americans or aliens, Jews or Gentiles—they ought never to serve merely as means to a higher end, or as enemies to be liquidated. No group, not even the national state, has any divine right to ignore the lesser individual or the lesser group, no matter how arrogantly it speaks for the majority.

Political economy is essentially national housekeeping. As such it is primarily concerned with what we shall eat and what we shall wear and how we shall be housed. But even within the limits of the economic field it obviously makes a lot of difference whether one takes the humanistic attitude toward individuals as citizens, or looks on them as soldiers to be fed and given uniforms.

Yet there is little room for argument over specific economic goals. Whether one thinks of the aggrandizement of the state or the welfare of its citizens, whether one thinks of power to make war or the cultivation of the arts of peace, the objectives of political economy are likely to be the same. First and most important will be *plenty*. Here the humanist and democrat will think in terms of consumer goods and services, including those social amenities supplied free to all, and the fascist will think of guns and monuments. But they will both seek abundance. The second economic good is *stability*. There can be no difference of opinion here, either. Violent fluctuations, cyclic or haphazard, speculative booms and slumps, with all they mean in insecurity and suffering and waste, find no apologists. Yet probably all would agree that stability must not mean stagnation, and therefore *growth* is a third desideratum. Even if the time should come when man grew so accustomed to abundance that he ceased to want additional material goods, and the incentive to further expansion of the national income lapsed, still invention should not stop. Quantitatively our wants are finite. But there need be no limits to quality, variety, curiosity, interest. And so long as the desire for leisure outruns the desire for labor, inventors will seek labor-saving devices.

Until comparatively recently, the principles of laissez faire seemed to serve these economic goals with remarkable success. But during the last quarter-century the realities of poverty, instability, and even stagnation, have forced governments more and more to intervene directly. The world has entered upon a period of critical change, occasionally marked by revolution.

## *Nature of the Transition*

There has been an inability, in high places and low, to recognize the nature of the change, even in the exceptional cases where it was being consciously sought. There has been a general recognition of the fact that we are in a period of transition; but neither those who feared it nor those who longed for it have been clear as to its nature. A transition from what to what? From capitalism to socialism? from an unplanned economy to a planned economy? from production for profit to production for use?

These and other terms may have occasional value. Yet they are all colored by misapprehensions. It is perhaps unfortunate that there are no better terms. The new economy that is evolving is less a planned economy than a guided or managed or directed economy. For, as I have been analyzing the process, it emerges as a process of establishing *strategic directives for a mechanism that still is essentially automatic*. Instead of leaving the car to careen madly down the street driverless, we are putting a driver at the controls; but it is the same marvelous mechanism.

The best shorthand description of the transition is from production for sale to production for use. But even this is inadequate. So long as the mechanism of the market remains, goods will be for sale; but under the guiding directives we are setting up, the market becomes a tool for the economic process of production and distribution rather than its blind master. It is likewise true that under the old system goods were made for sale to *consumers*, and hence for ultimate use; but the use was incidental, and of no concern to the producer except as it induced the sale. In the new system guidance will be ever present to assure that the economic process results in the maximum satisfaction in use, and thus the element of sale will become incidental.

Since both elements, sale and use, are present in both systems, the transition becomes primarily a shift in emphasis.

Furthermore, since the transition is to so large an extent an unconscious one, an evolutionary mutation being developed in the social organism in response to new pressures and conflicts, the task of statesmanship is perhaps more one of understanding and assisting than of creation. We can have little effect if we get out of the main stream of history. There is plenty of scope for originality and creativeness, but we can seldom compel events to conform to a preconceived pattern.

Thus American Socialists, Communists, and independent intellectual radicals, with in many respects a better understanding of current historical trends than those in political power, have permitted themselves to get off into an eddy, where they go round and round insisting that events must take a certain course; meanwhile the New Deal, with few theorists but a number of good politicians and pragmatic "brain-trusters," has swept along on the powerful currents of the time, to a point far beyond them.

I have done my share of drawing up platforms and programs and plans for vast movements that were never heard of outside my ivory tower, while the traffic roared by below. It now seems to me more realistic to admit that the most any one of us can do is to deflect the course of events a shade from the direction they are taking anyway. It is most important, therefore, to understand what that course is. The program I am outlining here is largely a program that I think will be carried through regardless of any preaching, by myself or anyone else.

This is not, however, a counsel of passivity—any more than was the perhaps analogous appeal of Marx to the workers, that they should fulfill their "historic mission." Even less is it a denial of the possibilities of a rational solution of human problems. It is the essence of intelligence to know the limits of the practical and the possible.

The political economist, then, in so far as he wants to do more than merely analyze, will hope to influence events in this way: that steps which will be taken anyway may be more intelligently taken because more conscious, better understood, therefore better adapted to serve the ultimate purposes.

## *Rules for the Transition*

People like myself get impatient with the slowness of desirable change. We see fellow human beings hungry and cold because economic institutions work badly, and we want to see those institutions changed at once.

I discovered a few years ago that starting an enterprise as inconsequential as a magazine is frightfully difficult. I had to learn all sorts of things, about financing, about printing, about paper, about organizing. Organizing, that was the key word. It meant establishing new sets of relations between a lot of individuals, editors, authors, clerks, subscribers. Some people start magazines every year, and it is as easy for them as walking to the streetcar stop in the morning. But when you are learning to walk it is horribly difficult.

I discovered that the whole country was not waiting for what I had to say. I found a vast amount of what some highbrows have labeled "cultural lag." It is almost as difficult for people to work out a new line of thought as it is to start a functioning organization like a magazine. The inertia, the stickiness, of human habits of thought and human habits of acting together is an appalling obstacle to progress.

After several years of publishing the magazine I have found that a good part of the time now it virtually publishes itself. It has become a "going concern." The human relations between the various individuals involved have been worked out, systematized, and become habitual. Many of the procedures that involved painful mental effort on the part of the person responsible are now automatic. At the same time the editorial results, in getting across ideas, are far better, as we have found how to adapt new ideas to old ones, to graft them on to habitual attitudes, to take account of the difficult process of thinking, even in the case of the reasonably advanced thinkers who make up our subscribers.

Revolution has a great appeal. Social dynamite that blasts through inertia gets things done in a hurry. It wrenches people loose from their cherished ways of doing things. It may be a painful process and a destructive one. Dynamite may blow up the just as well as the unjust. But it does clear the ground for the building of new social habits.

A few years ago I liked to call myself a revolutionist. It was fashionable in many quarters to think and talk in terms of "revolution." Since it was a virtue to be "left," then the further "left" you were, the greater your virtue.

I still believe the changes we are passing through are "revolutionary" in a broad historic sense. But I have too healthy a respect for human inertia and for the human feelings that are hurt when it is rudely disturbed, I have too much respect for the difficulty of establishing "going concerns" and for the importance of keeping them going when they perform important functions like feeding cities, I have too much respect for the value of automatic adjustments, to want to see the whole job of starting up a new economic system dumped all at once in anyone's lap. A revolution in the sense conceived, let us say by some of our extreme left-wingers, is a horribly wasteful and painful process. In addition it only becomes possible when a great number of the existing going concerns in essential fields cease to function. In view of the inertia of social habits this is likely to happen only under most frightful dislocations, as after a disastrous war. No sane person can wish to see such dislocations occur.

In the last few years we have learned a good deal about violent social change. Like modern warfare, modern revolution has no glamour. With a better perspective on the Russian Revolution we see it not merely as an enterprise of Homeric proportions but as a period of total breakdown, starvation, suffering, brutality, and finally a glorification of sheer totalitarian power. In Spain we have seen at a less distance what can happen if social change degenerates into civil war: from the romantic excitement of the first month, when boys and girls took their muskets into the hills, it turned into a murderous war of attrition, with all the latest machinery for death, and with foreign intervention a matter of course, in view of the international stakes involved.

Moreover, even if violent revolution were not a grim prospect, it has come to seem remote and unreal in this country. Not even the Communists any longer write about Soviet America. After almost a decade of economic dislocation and discontent, there is, at the moment of writing, not a single movement or a single leader that can be taken seriously as the potential heart of insurrection.

We have learned much about the adaptability and flexibility of a society as democratic as ours. The old Marxist cliché to the effect that "no ruling class gives up without a struggle" is now unconsciously recognized as meaningless, at most a tautology: of course there is struggle, but it need never come within the remotest approach to a violent civil war.

Also we have learned much about the adaptability and flexibility of our economic system. It is not a rigid mechanism, driving itself by its own inexorable laws to a smash-up, but a human organism capable of gradual but profound adjustments, so that it may in a comparatively brief history change to something entirely different from what it was.

This is not to say that its toughness and resiliency are unlimited. It is at best a somewhat fragile structure of delicate balances. We have seen too many instances (in central and eastern Europe since 1918) of what suffering may result from a complete loss of confidence in the paper symbols by which the system normally functions, to want to take any chances of runaway inflation or a collapse of credit. The real world in which we get food to eat and clothing to wear is dominated by the unreal make-believe world of credit. Remember August, 1937, when production began a vast and swift decline because of events largely in the mental world. Remember that money is no longer gold, but bank "deposits," "check-book money."

Nowhere is the structure of promises to pay so intricately elaborated as in the United States. To be sure, nothing that has happened yet, even in the banking crisis of 1933 and the subsequent devaluation, has done more than cause a quiver at the top of that structure, and far more drastic operations could be performed without cause for alarm. But it is not difficult to conceive the kind of calamitous panic that might seize our financial and savings and insurance institutions if an administration were to be elected on as drastic and naïve a program of socialization as is sometimes drafted by minor left-wing groups. (On that very account it would never be elected.) Such vast edifices as the Bank of Manhattan Company Building on Wall Street, or the Stock Exchange, or the Metropolitan Life Building on Madison Square, or the "Pit" in Chicago, will not collapse in the real world without a good deal of very real dynamite, but the vast paper structures they represent may collapse with only a little social dynamite, and with a terrible toll in human suffering.

Economic reformers deal so much in abstractions that they may become somewhat dehumanized. They should be careful never to be glib about the possibilities of pain. And they should never forget that their own special interest in efficient production of food and clothes is only a part of human life. It is important to keep in mind the unstatistical values that people get out of going their own way, out of doing things for themselves. Freedom of individual choice, democracy in all possible group decisions, automatic rather than authoritarian controls, these all caution us to avoid dictatorship and bureaucracy like twin plagues.

Finally, if the essential differences between the existing economic system and a workable "economy of abundance" are as slight as this whole study seems to indicate, then it is a special folly to draft programs that involve unnecessary stresses or strains.

We have enough limiting factors now to permit us to formulate a set of rules for the transition. These are purely arbitrary, and you might formulate them into five or into a hundred, but ten is a convenient number to make our problem concrete.

### DON'TS FOR SOCIAL PLANNERS

1. Don't let "going concerns" run down: keep the wheels turning.

2. Don't try to change non-essentials: the essential changes are drastic enough to satisfy any would-be revolutionist.

3. Don't scrap any existing institution or social habit you can use: a slight change of direction may be all that is necessary.

4. Don't let the credit structure with its paper values collapse: otherwise you can't observe rules 1 to 3.

5. Don't attack any cherished social myth unnecessarily, while you are building new ones.

6. Don't set yourself or your word magic up on any pedestal: we're all in this together, and the more of us who can take an active part in working our way out, the better for all concerned. This means: no dictators, no orthodoxy.

7. Don't centralize any power or any function unless vital: automatic controls and decentralized administration are always to be preferred.

8. Don't bother with "ownership." The controls you want are almost never dependent on it.

9. Don't aim at the politically impossible: proposals are no good if they can't be passed as legislation and applied.

10. Don't try to do piecemeal what must be done in a lump: you can't jump over a ditch by a series of short tentative jumps; all non-essential steps, however, can be postponed and taken one at a time.

This final Don't should be a warning against many familiar types of social reform. The "Social Democratic" movement, for instance, agreeing with most of the other Don'ts and agreeing in general on the importance of economic planning, has visualized the transition as one of gradually subjecting one industry after another to public ownership. But because the essential hurdle was never faced, capacity production ("for use") as contrasted with irregular and inadequate production ("for the market"), the tentative experiments with "socialization" never even approached the objective of an economy of abundance. The British Labour party, the German Social Democrats, the French Socialists, have all muffed opportunities, not merely because they were not given sufficient power, but because they really did not know what to do.

The same is true of the co-operative movement, which has observed all the Don'ts of caution, but not the final Don't of boldness. It has aimed to chisel away the profit of business men for the benefit of consumers. But it has no way of assuring that producers will produce at capacity or that consumers will have purchasing power up to their capacity to consume; "production for use" has remained a mirage for them, too.

The monetary reformers of various kinds contented themselves with adjustments to hold up purchasing power, but they ignored the investment problem and assumed that production could take care of itself without other controls. Their proposals might be great improvements, but they could not achieve stability and abundance.

### *Outlines of a Program*

I have said there was agreement on the general economic goals of abundance and stability as well as growth. And I have told how I came to believe that the specific economic problems to be solved revolve around the few closely related questions of prices, purchasing power, investment, and government fiscal policies. Let me examine these problems more closely.

One cause of trouble is that varying degrees of monopolistic control over supply and price make for varying degrees of adaptability to the ups and downs of the business cycle. But one of our purposes is to eliminate the business cycle, which will mean more stable prices; it is obviously better then to give all prices the stability obtainable when they are monopolistically administered than to try to give them all the high variability of, say, agricultural prices. Since a high degree of "monopolistic competition" is inevitable anyway, and since the difficulty of adjustment between administered prices and free prices is a major cause of disequilibrium, is it not better that all prices be administered to the same degree? But if "monopolistic competition" is to become the rule it is essential that it be as intelligent as possible: this means full information at all times regarding the state of the market, experimentation in the opening up of new markets at lower prices, perhaps government "yardsticks" or other checks to make sure that prices never become rigid.

Such a price policy will make possible a consistent labor and management policy. No longer need there be demands for lower wages because prices are falling. Furthermore, organized industries are easier to bargain with than fly-by-night sweatshops. Then again, since the maintenance of purchasing power is a conscious objective, minimum wages established by legislation (and by "yardstick" in public employment) will continue as essential features of our program. In addition, recognition of the functional purpose of group pressures as an essential feature of a free society will mean the permanent establishment of a democratic system of organization, in which the various interests in industry—labor, management, and the consuming public—will have continuing representation.

I know no better word to describe this democratic organization of industry (it was crudely attempted in the NRA) than "corporative," despite the unpleasant fascist connotations. If you will think of it in the more familiar American terms of a democratic, representative, federal structure, rather than a blind for dictatorship, it may serve my purpose.

One of the chief economic advantages of such a structure for purposes of stability is that for the first time it will become possible to plan for a steady rate of capital expansion in each industry and in all industry. The main economic problem is, after all, to maintain the proper volume of investment.

Keynes's conclusion that investment must be "socialized" needs definition and elaboration. There are two aspects of investment, private investment and public investment. There seems no reason to believe that private investment will ever again rise to sufficient volume to absorb all savings and maintain full employment, but it is certainly desirable to stimulate it as far as it will go, and keep it reasonably steady.

Besides the long-range planning made possible by more comprehensive industrial organization, perhaps the best method of controlling private investment would be through controlling investment banking. Conceivably private investment banking might be so hedged about with regulations, and subject to such continual governmental supervision and integration, that it need not be nationalized. But with the present meagerness of the business of floating securities it might be easier for the government to set up its own investment banking system now, before the business became once more lucrative with returning prosperity, and thus to make it essentially a public function.

As well as floating securities, such a public investment banking system should handle all long-term or capital loans. At present it is difficult for small and medium-sized corporations to get new funds for capital expansion, as compared to big corporations. And if there is to be adequate control of all new investment it must cover long-term loans as well as new securities. Only thus can the interest rate be brought low enough to encourage business men to borrow.

Moreover, public control of investment banking will end the control of industry by private investment bankers. Bankers have become watchdogs, if not masters, of the industries they have helped finance. A public system of investment banking would permit a growing supervision of "private" business corporations in the public interest, and would facilitate inter-industry coordination. And just as private banking encouraged private holding companies, as well as investment trusts, through which investors could lessen their risk while relinquishing the last elements of control, so a public system might lead to public administration of and responsibility for private savings. From this it is only a short step to the financing of all such investment as is derived from private savings, by means of the sale of government securities.

So much for private investment. Public spending must take up all the slack left by inadequate private investment.

Much light has been thrown on this problem recently by the experience of Sweden in using its budget as the decisive factor in general economic stability. It conceives of government expenditures under three heads. The first constitutes all regular governmental expenses, administration, defense, etc., which should be covered by current taxation. The second includes those revenue-producing public investments which may be expected to pay for themselves in whole or in part, such as housing, power plants, toll bridges, and the like; these are just as legitimately financed by borrowing as if they were private ventures; when set up as public corporations, with financial autonomy, able to sell their own securities on the market, the analogy to private business is complete. The third type of government expenditure is for public works such as highways, which, while not revenue-producing, constitute permanent assets; the assumption is that they add to the nation's wealth and to its productive capacity, and hence to the taxable national income of future years; therefore it is considered legitimate to finance these also by borrowings, for future tax revenues will be able to carry the added burden.

This highly sensible approach to public spending seems to have been accepted by the American New Deal: its assumptions run all through President Roosevelt's messages to Congress at the beginning of 1939. It seems to have been developed in Sweden originally more out of pragmatic than theoretical considerations, and to have been accompanied by the belief that "deficits" in lean years would be counter-balanced by surpluses in prosperous years, rather than by the belief that government investment must be continuing and permanent. But it is equally applicable to the latter policy.

The basic principle of public investment must be the assurance of jobs to everyone seeking employment, for there is no better measure of "full production" than "full employment." But the termination of unemployment "relief" should not mean that other direct money payments to individuals would cease. Both to iron out temporary maladjustments (chiefly by means of unemployment insurance payments), and as a permanent aspect of public investment, the direct payment of "social dividends" in the shape of pensions, insurances, and other supplements to earned income should continue. These payments serve the same purpose in maintaining purchasing power as investment in tangible assets.

It might be asked at this point how much spending a government must engage in, through these various types of public investment, to maintain full employment. No simple answer can be given. Obviously the richer the country, the greater the savings, and therefore the greater the need for investment. Obviously, too, the heaviest expenses will come in the first stages; private investment is not likely to pick up until it has seen a convincing demonstration that a government is determined and able to maintain purchasing power permanently. On the other hand, creation of such an atmosphere might create such a boom that *for a short period* public investment could taper off almost to nothing. The only guess that may be ventured at this stage of my argument is that public investment must be more nearly on a scale comparable to that achieved by Germany in the last few years than that of England and the United States.

Another question which cannot be answered dogmatically concerns the financing of the public investment. We saw in a previous chapter that there is no reason to raise the bogeyman of inflation merely because budgets are unbalanced. And it was suggested that a considerable injection of new money might be advisable during the early stages of a return to full production, but that when such a stage was reached there must be a balance between purchasing power and the goods and services offered for sale. The basic monetary problem is to maintain investment at the rate of saving. Several alternatives present themselves, and probably a sound political economy would make use of all three. First, the government can tax the larger incomes so heavily that no hoarding occurs. Second, it could tax hoardings to discourage their accumulation. Third, it could borrow as fast as hoardings accumulated.

But here a new difficulty arises. Because of the nature of the banking system and its check-book money, the government can borrow from the banks without reducing the "idle balances" that may be on deposit there, for the banks can create new "deposits" for the government. So long as those private deposits remain idle no harm will be done. In effect the government and the banks will be creating new money to take the place of that withdrawn from active circulation. But the piling up of further "idle balances" (and with full employment they might pile up at a very much more rapid rate) raises the problem of potential inflation if their owners ever sought to spend them all at once.

It would seem as if the best solution of this difficulty would be to provide safeguards against "dis-hoardings" rather than penalties on hoardings. A simple procedure might be to require banks to treat all deposits of more than a certain amount as savings deposits, putting them in special accounts where they would be invested in government bonds or other proper securities, and where they would not be subject to withdrawal without thirty or sixty days' notice. To make such provisions watertight it would probably be necessary to provide penalties against hoarding currency (such as are now provided in the United States against hoarding gold), and against evasion by the scattering of deposits in several banks.

The net effect of such measures would be to assure that the government could tax and borrow funds for investment equal to those saved and not privately invested. The choice as between taxation and borrowing is an arbitrary one, largely to be determined by political and social rather than economic considerations. Too heavy a tax program in the beginning would defeat the "rules for transition" I laid down earlier. The interest burden on outstanding government securities is, as I previously pointed out, not very serious. In the United States, if the tax exemption on government securities is removed, the procedure is merely one of paying out interest with one hand and taking it back by taxation, perhaps largely from the same people, with the other.

In pre-depression days, savings were channeled into investment and new money was created as necessary, in the course of issuing scores of billions of dollars' worth of securities and the creation of scores of billions of debts by private enterprise. Now that the process of adequate private borrowing has ended, there is nothing "unsound" in governmental enterprise doing the same thing. A hundred billion or two hundred billion dollars' worth of government bonds outstanding, backed by the taxing power, are no more "unsound" than an equal amount of private securities, backed only by the dubious prospect of "taxing" the consumer.

The question remains whether all this new fiscal policy to maintain equilibrium between savings and investment, and between purchasing power and productive capacity, can be carried through without nationalizing the banking system. How can the right amount of money—subject to no unforeseeable fluctuations of volume or velocity—be assured, while private bankers retain the power to create credit money at will?

The answer seems to be that if the government controls the "central bank" and the investment banking system, commercial banking can be safely left in private hands. As we saw, private commercial banks perform most of their functions adequately—bookkeeping, safekeeping of funds, the maintenance of checking accounts, the bringing together of individual savings, the issuance of commercial loans for the production and distribution of goods. But if they are deprived of their investment business (this need not mean that they cannot buy outstanding securities, but that they cannot float securities, or lend money for capital expansion), and thus deprived of their domination of business and industry, their power to create credit money is rendered harmless. Commercial loans, as I have pointed out, carry no danger of inflation. While in time of depression their volume is not large enough to make banking profitable, and most large businesses in effect do their own short-term financing, the expansion of business to prosperity levels, plus the restrictions on hoardings previously mentioned, would greatly expand such borrowing; and the interest on commercial loans provides a legitimate means of payment for the bookkeeping services which the banks maintain free in connection with checking facilities.

Thus private banking, deprived of its power for harm, takes its proper place as a comparatively minor but legitimate form of private enterprise.*

One further point arises in connection with this program for public management of the monetary and credit features of our economy: the effect on them of foreign trade. The integration of industry, to assure sound price policies, which is the first part of this program, is also likely to be upset if foreign trade remains outside the controls set up.

* It is interesting to recall that the Nazi planners began by insisting on a high degree of centralized control over banking. But once their autarchic Four Year Plan for military effectiveness was solving the three problems of full employment, a balance of purchasing power and consumer goods, and a proper rate of investment, they relaxed their hold over the banking system.

Many liberals who call for management of other parts of the economy, even such a drastic step as nationalization of banking, cling to the old-fashioned notion that greater "freedom" of trade is desirable. Yet it should be obvious that the present trend is toward a controlled trade in every part of the world. Economic nationalism, autarchy, varying degrees of collectivism, are everywhere accompanied by a shift to trade by planned exchange rather than by laissez faire. The barter agreements entered into by the totalitarian states, and in a lesser degree the reciprocal trade treaties entered into by free-trader Secretary Hull, are halting steps toward an intelligently balanced world trade planned by collective agreement.

If trade by the haphazard competition of private business men in pursuit of profit seems preferable, it should be remembered that it was this economic practice which led to the conflict of imperialistic ambitions in 1914. The present trend carries its own type of imperialistic menace too. But it also contains the promise of a sane world order. And the conscious integration of exports and imports with the needs of the domestic economy is in every country coming to be essential.

The achievement of a managed foreign trade, along with a managed money, can protect the domestic economy from economic disturbances in other countries. All the uncertainties and fluctuations and disruptions arising in the jungle of present international relations—loss of foreign markets through high tariffs and quotas, dumping of cheap foreign goods on the home market, changes in world prices of staple commodities like wheat, sudden fluxes of gold in or out of a country, export and import of investment funds—these need no longer plague an intelligently managed national economy.

### *The Radical, the Millionaire and the Citizen*

The program of reforms I have outlined may seem drastic at certain points to a conservative, but there is nothing likely to startle an advanced liberal. On the other hand, the radical may raise impatient objections that I am merely seeking to perpetuate capitalism. None of the usual elements of a socialist program are present: public ownership of banking and the public services, to say nothing of industry, is omitted. With no limitations imposed on profits, and no emphasis on the taxation of large incomes or property, the wealthy class seems to retain its privileges.

I myself, if presented with such a program a few years ago, would have scoffed at it as an utterly inadequate set of inconsequential reforms, of the type so frequently tried in the past without success. I would have thought it impossible that so brief and prosaic a list of familiar measures could have accomplished the glorious transformation of our sick social order, and the creation of an "economy of abundance."

Even the reader who has followed my analysis of the complexities to be mastered in achieving an equilibrium in the present system, may feel that I have oversimplified the solution. It is true that I have so far merely sketched the broad outlines of the necessary policies. In the next chapter they will be elaborated, in terms of specific legislation which might be advanced by progressives in New Deal America, and some of the complexities involved will more clearly appear.

Yet the essential job to be done is comparatively simple, once it has been decided to use the existing market mechanism, merely furnishing it with guidance, rather than attempting the construction of a completely new mechanism, as the orthodox socialists have advocated. The measures suggested would make possible a steady rate of investment, at a level adequate to maintain full employment, and would assure a steady flow of purchasing power to take the goods and services off the market, as they were made available, without shortages or overproduction or inflation.

In the beginning there would be merely our familiar capitalist system, somewhat more rationalized than any yet witnessed, brought up to a point of full employment and held there. Full employment such as this (which should include no useless "made work" or "leaf-raking") means a vast increase in the national income. And the wage provisions and social dividends provided for will assure the abolition of poverty.

But there will still be "private ownership," and incomes from property. In fact the incomes from property in a system of permanent prosperity will at first be on a scale comparable to 1929. Will this not mean the same corruption of taste, the same mad scramble for speculative profits, the same inflation of security values, the same excess of savings over real investment, and the same final crash?

I have already stressed that the evils of great wealth are of two kinds: on the one hand ethical and aesthetic and on the other economic. So far as the ethical and aesthetic considerations are concerned it is to be hoped that our social conscience will continue to grow, and gradually take more drastic action, probably through taxation. Though there is a case to be made for the millionaire as a creator of new standards of consumption, I think it a pretty weak case, and should be glad to see the millionaire become extinct. But to legislate such changes before the public is educated up to them might be as unwise as was the prohibition experiment.

On the other hand, the economic effects of great wealth may not be serious, given the program of changes outlined above. In fact, a natural process of social leveling may be expected by natural economic processes. As funds for investment are always available from government sources, their yield can be driven down to any percentage desired. Recipients of great wealth will bid up existing securities, as they did in 1929, and this will provide, as it did then, a great reservoir of idle funds. But the government can make up all discrepancies of purchasing power in the ways suggested. Mere inflation of security prices may be kept to the limits of a harmless pastime by various safeguarding regulations, eliminating marginal trading and brokers' loans, requiring special accounts which can be liquidated only gradually. In so far as the other aspects of the program succeed in making the system depression-proof, there need be no worry over panics.

What else do rich people do with their money, besides invest it? They spend it on mansions and yachts and racing stables and other hobbies, which are expensive because they involve the employment of immense numbers of servants to keep up. As I suggested earlier, in an economy in which there was opportunity for useful work for everyone at good wages, it would be increasingly difficult to get servants. Their wages would be raised immensely, to compensate for their menial social status. Yachts and great private estates would become too expensive, even for millionaires. With poverty abolished, riches will lose much of their significance.

In addition to saving and extravagant spending the wealthy turn their money into power. They get control of businesses, banks, railroads; they buy newspapers and radio stations and influence public opinion; occasionally they buy political power. It is the argument of the Marxist that, regardless of economic equilibrium or ethical considerations, great wealth must be abolished because it means power of the few over the many. This is a valid argument. But the kind of organization and co-ordination of industry we have imagined, as well as the public control of money and credit predicated, would largely eliminate the power of wealth for economic harm, and there remain only the questions of power over public opinion and politics.

I cannot help feeling that the whole tendency of the times in our American democracy is to diminish these aspects of the power of wealth. It would take me too far afield to analyze this tendency here. I can only say that from my contact with people of wealth, I am convinced they *believe* their power is waning. As the daughter of a powerful Wall Street banker once put it to me in conversation: "I felt like writing my Congressman to protest; but then I realized I had no Congressman today!"

The most important consideration in weighing the dwindling power of private wealth is the fact that its actual dollar interest is increasingly overshadowed by the dollar interest of the government itself. If it is the dominant economic interest which rules in any social order, then in the present system, and far more in the system that would develop if the program here outlined were adopted, it is the government salariat rather than the recipients of property income which would be the ruling class. This may or may not be a good thing, but there is no stopping it.

I am making this argument for the increasing harmlessness of the wealthy partly because I have a special personal interest in not seeing them suffer. I know a good number of wealthy people; they are mostly quite harmless, quite well-intentioned, and quite charming. But I have reasons that should be more convincing. If the power for harm of the industrialist and the financier is not too crucial, let us leave them alone. Anyone will fight nastily when cornered. If their intelligence and managing abilities can be utilized, if their co-operation can be secured during the transition period, it will be better for everyone. In the long run, by natural evolutionary processes already at work, the power of private wealth will tend toward extinction. I am far from advocating that progressive income and inheritance taxes should not be pushed ahead: in so far as democracy becomes more effective they will be, though less as economic than as social measures. But the economic effects of achieving abundance will ease the millionaire much more painlessly out of the picture.

Since there would be room for all in productive work, unproductive work, such as unnecessary domestic service, would, as I suggested, diminish, and with it the chief prerogative of wealth. While large fortunes would become increasingly meaningless, poverty would have been eliminated, and the whole population would step into the comfortable middle-class income group. Only the true enterpriser and "captain of industry" and the owners of existing securities would continue to draw large incomes. With the government controlling the issue of new securities, and driving the interest rate toward zero through its monopoly of capital loans, it would be possible to carry through the gradual extinction of the rentier, as predicted by Keynes. With the people as a whole substantially in control of their economic system they could end property income any time they felt it desirable. There is no reason to think they would do so at all promptly.

Finally there is the effect on inequalities of wealth that would arise from the great expansion of public services. I have predicated a vast annual investment by the government, but have said little of the purposes for which it would be used. From an economic point of view, armaments may be as effective as parks and playgrounds. But in so far as intelligent uses are possible, the expenditure can go directly into raising the living standards of all the people. Housing is the most obvious field for public investment, and there are other public works that may be revenue-producing. But looking farther into the future, with the immense reserves of productive capacity that would in this way become available for improving our estate, it is not wholly Utopian to think more of parks and gardens and free public services than of armaments or dams.

A garden is one of those curious economic goods in which the limits of consumption are quickly found. No man can walk on more than one garden path at once. In enjoying the sight of trees and flowers he in no way takes away from his neighbor's enjoyment. In a city's parks no more than ordinary courtesy and self-restraint are called for to permit thousands to be accommodated. A city's parks may be inadequate but they cannot be misappropriated by those who do enjoy them. In other words, no rationing is needed to make sure that the demand keeps down to the supply, hence no price of admittance must be charged.

Such "free goods" are, as I have noted before, a growing feature of our economy. No one can safely take more than his share of the highway system, no one can use more than his share of street lighting and other municipal services, no child can occupy two seats in school.

It is probable that these free goods and services will multiply rapidly in the coming years. Most city transport services, like New York's subway system, could take care of all the traffic even if it were free—and thus dispense with all the wasted effort of collecting fares. We shall soon see free milk for all children: why should any future citizen be penalized because of circumstances he had no part in choosing? So with other staple foods and clothes. Everything has to be paid for, of course, in human effort, and these costs will be borne by taxation on the market areas of the total economy. But the spreading of the area of free goods and services, in those fields where consumption cannot be misappropriated, and where only ordinary training in consideration for others' welfare is adequate to avoid abuse, will bring nearer the end of the peculiar science of economics.

Economics means economizing, to be economical of scarce goods. There is nothing so cramping as to have to economize. There is no limitation on liberty so absolute and complete as an empty pocketbook. There is no freedom like the freedom from want.

With the extension of free goods the price system by so far begins to lapse. It can still be made to govern through its dominance in other fields, as the "market socialists" have shown. Some goods will remain forever scarce, and some form of rationing by price system or lot or merit will always be required, except in the case of those rarities which by being put in museums or libraries or in other public places are at once enjoyable by all. But most goods in an emerging economy of abundance can eventually be put on the free list. Until, as earlier suggested, the needed labor becomes voluntary, some pressure to get the work done is essential, and a money and wage system is probably better than any other form of compulsion. But perhaps we can look forward to a not-too-distant generation which will have free labor as well as free goods.

Is it a coincidence that the word "free" can in this way be used both for goods and for human beings?

The economic problem is concerned with the securing for man of a sufficiency of goods. When that sufficiency is at last permanently assured, economy becomes unnecessary. Man at last is free when his goods are free.

I have known most of my life what that kind of freedom is. I could always have what I wanted free, with no more ado than writing a check. I have worked all my life under other than monetary compulsions. There is nothing "Utopian" about it in the sense that it is inconceivable or that it runs counter to human nature. I was merely brought up in that kind of world, and I cannot limit my perspectives of the future to anything short of that for my fellow-men. Moreover, I know that the achievement of this kind of freedom is not any final goal. It is merely a beginning. Perhaps indeed all that has gone before—man's competition with the other animals, his struggles with nature's hostility, his mastery of himself and his environment—merely constitutes "pre-history," and that "history" begins on that date when man becomes full master of his estate. It may be sooner than you think.

# Chapter Eighteen

## A "NEW" NEW DEAL

AMERICA, until 1929, was a land of hope. It was fabulously rich in resources. It offered lots of room to the enterpriser. Uninhibited by a feudal past, except in the Deep South, the tradition of social equality was still so strong that class-conscious politics found no permanent acceptance. The state was almost universally believed, even by those who corrupted it to their own profit, to represent all the people.

Actually, in that year of the Grand Crash, the American government was far behind the other major powers in the development of institutions for social planning and control. But its political and social traditions were more favorably disposed for action that could make a reality of economic democracy than those of any other country.

The very weight of America's wealth meant a heavier crash when it fell. And the gap between its best recent performance, in 1937, when eight or ten million were still unemployed, and full production, is (and, as Keynes shows, must be) greater than in any other country. Hence we have had to move more rapidly in the acquisition of the necessary social controls. In large measure this pace is due to our having the unusually aggressive leadership of Franklin Roosevelt. But even without Roosevelt we should have moved rapidly.

For the successful solution of the economic problems raised in this book, America is in an amazingly fortunate position. Physically and spiritually we "have what it takes." Though today the sicknesses of this historical period have reduced a larger portion of our population to hopelessness than in any other country, the dominant philosophy is still an absolute faith in progress and in the destiny of the common man.

Physically we have the only integrated continental economy outside of the Soviet Union; but unlike the Soviet Union our industrial plant is largely built. Our plant could turn out "abundance" almost from the start of its full and intelligent use, with no belt-tightening necessary during the construction period.

It is easy to forget what advantages geography has given us. Apologists for the "American system" (by which is usually meant the industrial *status quo*) often claim the credit for a standard of living that is in reality largely traceable to natural resources: other countries, with a similar "system" and an equal glorification of "individual initiative," have lagged far behind. With vast stores of the essential minerals easily accessible—iron, coal, oil—with a great network of natural transportation facilities available in our rivers and lakes, with immense stretches of incomparably rich soil, apparently limitless forests, and great power sites from Niagara to the Colorado, we could hardly escape success. Today, in spite of an orgy of waste as devastating as a dozen great wars, we still have so much of our natural heritage left that, if we learn how to use it and how to conserve it, countless generations may live on this continent with never a fear of want.

Spiritually, too, our heritage is one that warrants no pessimism. It is true that American democracy has never been perfect or secure. But time after time the fundamental American concepts have been asserted and reasserted. We gained independence of England only to be endangered by the Federalists' aristocracy of the "rich and well-born." But Jefferson's humanist spirit and Jackson's muddy boots accomplished a second revolution which, by 1840, according to George Counts, carried the idea of human equality higher in most of the United States than it ever reached in any other time or place. Slavery remained to be eradicated; its aftermath in race subjection is with us yet; but progress is being made there, too. It is true that, between the Civil War and the turn of the century, a new aristocracy of wealth set back democracy once more. Plutocracy and its corrupt political bosses reigned supreme in most of the new smoke-blackened cities, in the venal state capitals, and at Washington. But in the nation's villages and small towns, which were feeding the ravenous cities, and out in the still open West, the old spirit lingered on. At the same time the conscience of the literate was goaded by the muck-rakers. The Populists, Bryan, the city reformers, the Trust-Busters, the pre-war Socialists, kept the tradition vigorous. The plutocracy, even when triumphant, was on the defensive, forced to justify itself.

In the twentieth century the plutocracy, though still growing arithmetically, began relatively to lose ground. The social conscience, once awake to the contrast between the "pursuit of happiness" in the Declaration of Independence, and the pursuit of wealth of a Rockefeller or a Morgan, refused to be lulled back to sleep. A labor movement, able more and more to keep its hat on in the presence of the boss, reasserted the old principle of equality.* The mass production standard of living, which idealized "a car in every garage" and which in the twenties tended to put every worker in the new industries psychologically into a white collar, and on a level with the new middle classes of the professions and service trades, went far to bring the whole population in spirit not down to but up to a common social class. It was often difficult to tell the worker and the boss apart if you met them on the street.

It seems to me that George Counts' recent book, *Prospects for American Democracy*, though a magnificent study of the rise and decline of American democracy, gives too little recognition to its resurgence in the last thirty or forty years. It is true that the early promise was blighted by plutocracy, and that even at the height of the "new era" in the twenties there were vast areas and vast strata of the population little better than feudal serfs; and of course, since 1929, the devastation wrought by poverty and unemployment has smeared the face of our vaunted American dream. But even in my own lifetime I think I have seen a marked increase in the democratic spirit. The snobbery in which I was raised is becoming extinct. "Good" servants are hard to find, as every wealthy housewife knows. Sharecropper peonage is a national shame, not an accepted part of the order of things.

The vitality of our classless heritage goes further than merely

* When the Steel Workers Organizing Committee in 1937 rented a lavish suite in a Pittsburgh skyscraper for its unionization campaign, a few floors above the offices of the Iron and Steel Institute, the outward trappings of social equality were re-established with dramatic finality.

the protection of ancient liberties or the reassertion of a lost social equality. It holds every promise of being able to carry through a social transformation in a way denied to European peoples. In *Insurgent America* I tried to show how the buoyant "middle-class psychology" of this country, while discouragingly incapable of being aroused to a "class struggle" along the proletarian-capitalist lines of the Marxist teaching, is capable of a new insurgency. The dream of the "more abundant life," as a universal right, may be potent social dynamite.

We are a little ashamed of our crack-pot movements. And the consistent fumbling of the New Deal has, at the moment of writing at the end of 1938, lost much of the people's enthusiasm. But what European country in these critical years has seen anything to compare in buoyant optimism with such symbols as the Blue Eagle, "Every Man a King," "Thirty Dollars Every Thursday"?

There are darker symbols to be sure. There are feudal satrapies in Maine and Arkansas and Florida. There are Liberty Leagues and Tom Girdlers and the vigilante "Associated Farmers." But who will say these are not back eddies, who will say these are in the main stream of American life today?

The New Deal itself is the best possible example of why we may have hope in the vitality of American democracy. Pragmatic, experimental, almost happy-go-lucky, it has blithely gone ahead with measures of the most profound radicalism (in comparison with its antecedents) without arousing effective opposition. Many of its measures have been ill-considered, vacillating, unrelated to each other. It has encouraged monopoly and then attacked it. It has taken surplus land out of cultivation and reclaimed new surplus land for cultivation. It has sought the co-operation of business and finance and then called them names. The result has been a failure to achieve prosperity, a growing loss of confidence on the part of the middle classes, and a growing hatred on the part of the old ruling class. Yet if you consider that its first political setback in the fall of 1938 was at the hands of Republicans who almost everywhere were endorsing the New Deal aims (merely attacking its "methods") and who even went beyond it in certain instances, such as the frequent endorsement of the Townsend Plan, then you must admit that the New Deal has been astonishingly successful. It has won proletariat and middle classes together to the *essential idea of positive governmental intervention to assure the popular welfare.* The only division of classes it has created has been of a loose and comparatively harmless sort: the richer you are the less you like Roosevelt. Nothing more (nor less) serious than that.

Whether the New Deal represents a sufficient alignment of forces to permit further change, and what general political strategy may be able to carry through the specific changes suggested in this book, will be briefly considered later in this chapter. What I have wanted to stress here is the extent to which the New Deal has prepared America for change, shaken it out of its smug lethargy, demonstrated the potentialities of American political methods. Those pessimists who still repeat the formulae about the state as the "executive committee of the ruling class" must now labor long hours to prove its validity, in the face of a political regime which commands the loyalty of but 28 per cent of the "prosperous." American democracy has proved that it has the youthful vigor to do the job that European democracy has bungled.

## *The New Deal Foundation*

Almost all the types of governmental response to the increasing difficulties of laissez faire capitalism, which I considered earlier in general terms, have been exemplified in the United States in the years since the Grand Crash of 1929. In the RFC the government went into banking and lent money on easy terms. In the AAA the government tried to meet the discrepancy of flexible agricultural prices as against monopolistic industrial prices, by enabling the farmers to set up their own monopoly for administering prices. In the RA and FSA it tried to meet the discrepancy between flexible agricultural prices and rigidity of farm enterprise by helping farmers to move off submarginal land and resettling them elsewhere.

In the NRA it tried to meet the discrepancy between rigid monopolistic prices and the flexible ones of "chiselers," sweatshops, and price-cutters, by forcing all businesses into monopolistic trade associations masquerading as "code authorities." With the failure of the NRA it began anti-trust prosecutions to force all businesses back to price-cutting practices.

In the FERA, CWA, PWA, and WPA it tried to fill the vacuum in people's stomachs and in the nation's stream of purchasing power caused by the cessation of private investment, by corralling people's timid savings and by creating "new money"—pump-priming to the tune of a twenty-billion-dollar increase in the national debt (the British achieved the same result by taxing instead of borrowing); it in effect took over the function of investment itself. In the process it has incidentally given the public new roads, schools, parks, concerts, and a host of other new free public services.

In the TVA it sought to induce a particularly rigid and particularly unintelligent monopoly price—that of electric power—to a level where a vast new demand could be opened up. Incidentally it began to rehabilitate a whole run-down area, and it learned much about the technique of the autonomous government corporation.

In occasional "breathing spells" it has sought to encourage private enterprise to restore the old levels of private investment, but everything else it was doing kept "confidence" from returning. Then it would turn to an "excess profits" tax, to force business either to invest its reserves ("liquidity preference" being unduly high) or to distribute them back into the spending stream, only to have a new collapse of confidence. Then as the burden on its own administrative machinery became increasingly heavy it sought "reorganization" only to confirm the worst fears of the business community that what it sought was a Soviet dictatorship, at which, in a panic, capital "went on strike," and a new depression started the whole process on a second round.

The New Deal has not succeeded in putting the unemployed back to work, in rehabilitating the forgotten "third," in solving the basic economic dilemmas. Yet, if the economic analysis of this book is correct, its measures have for the most part been sound. If it has failed it is because these measures were not pushed far enough and were not integrated into a single comprehensive assault on capitalist failure. In certain respects this is less the fault of the New Deal than of the enemies who emasculated its measures when they could not defeat them. Yet in the final analysis the fault is perhaps simply that even the most intelligent New Dealers were working in the dark, responding to pressures without a clear understanding of the problem and its solution.

Without worrying further over the reason for previous failures, let us look once more at some of the assets which the New Deal has to date made available for future planners. It has laid down the principle that no one shall starve, that no one shall be permitted to fall below a certain minimum standard of living, and that every employable person is entitled to a job. As we saw in an earlier chapter, this principle carries especially important connotations in a country conditioned to the idea of abundance.

Moreover, the more technical principles of monetary and credit and investment control are likewise on the way to acceptance. The Federal Reserve Board is dominated by the government, money is frankly "managed," investment banking is officially divorced from commercial banking, and the Securities Exchange Commission has begun making over the investment markets. The necessary changes have not gone far enough to be beyond the recall of a sudden return to Harding "normalcy." But no signs point to another Harding.

As for the necessary integration of industry, the undue haste and the inevitable mistakes of the NRA resulted in a serious setback. It took two years to restore Section 7a of the extinct NIRA, and the Wagner Labor Relations Act is still liable to revision, thanks to the A. F. of L.-C.I.O. feud. It took three years to restore the wages and hours provisions of the codes. And the present emphasis on the evils of monopoly suggests that it may be even longer before the problem of "administered prices" can be intelligently faced again. But if there has been some loss of ground there has also been some ground gained.

Since the Blue Eagle era, a considerable new administrative personnel has been trained in Washington. The confusion of new governmental agencies not knowing each other's limits and eternally coming into conflict or giving the public the "run-around" has had time to straighten itself out. And, though the continuing division of labor's ranks remains an obstacle, the vastly increased strength and experience of the labor movement means that if "code authorities" were re-established today there would no longer be a dumb acquiescence on the part of labor's spokesmen.

Furthermore, the liberal trend in Supreme Court decisions, which reached its high point in the favorable decision on the

Wagner Labor Relations Act (the legal lights of the American Bar Association could not have been more flabbergasted if they had seen a hammer and sickle suddenly sprout on the roof of the new Supreme Court Building), means that no serious constitutional problems are now likely to arise. If the interstate commerce clause covers the manufacture of goods which enter interstate commerce, the back of legal opposition to government control of business is broken. A new NRA need not be declared unconstitutional.

The reaction of the New Dealers themselves to the monopolistic trends in the NRA remains the most serious obstacle to further progress in integrating our economy. There has been a conflict from the beginning between two kinds of New Dealers—or rather it has been a conflict, within the mind of each one of the New Dealers, between two approaches.

On the one hand is the older liberalism, which identified laissez faire competition with liberty, and therefore viewed the basic problem as one of eradicating the abuses of monopoly. This was in the legitimate line of descent from Jefferson, Jackson and Bryan, through Theodore Roosevelt, the elder La Follette and Justice Brandeis.

The other tradition was the socialist tradition. Marx may have been a distant ancestor, but so were Fourier and Brook Farm and Robert Owen. More recently Bellamy and Veblen and the "technocrats" represented a special American branch of socialist thought. The concept of our economy as a machine, which must be operated on engineering principles to produce the most mileage per gallon, seemed to call for central planning.

It has been one of the theses of this book that there need be no conflict between these two approaches, that the best planned economy will be one which is as automatic and "free" as the perfect equilibrium of pure laissez faire theory.

But the conflict is still waged in Washington. And doubtless it is coming nearest actual blows within the Temporary National Economic Committee, set up to study monopolistic practices following the revived anti-monopoly crusade in the winter of 1937-38. It appears that the anti-monopolists are in the ascendant—certainly they will be when the issue is presented to Congress—and it may be that the Committee's labors will result merely in certain revisions of the patent laws and a few new restrictions on the interlocking of corporate controls. But it is unlikely the other solution will be passed over, or long postponed. The integration of our industrial structure to produce steadily at capacity can be achieved only through a return to the NRA method. But instead of the scramble for monopoly advantage witnessed under the first NRA, we may hope for the type of industrial organization suggested above, which will not only subordinate the claims of ownership to the claims of labor and the consuming public, but will subordinate the claims of each industry to the harmonious co-operation of all.

### *The Next Stage in Industrial Organization*

It is not necessary for me to confine myself to generalizations in discussing the program which the New Deal or some successor must adopt if we are to go forward. Almost all the elements of the program I have urged as the logical goal of democratic collectivism have been offered in concrete, if necessarily still imperfect, form (and without relation to each other) by some of the more advanced progressives in Washington.

The most important is a proposal for a new organization of industry along the lines I have discussed. It already has had an interesting history. In its original form it was advanced by Mordecai Ezekiel, economic adviser to the Secretary of Agriculture, early in 1936, in his book *$2,500 a Year;* he there attempted an application of the AAA method of production planning to industry, but "in reverse," to produce "plenty rather than scarcity." Starting with the established facts of vast unused capacity in industry, and the legitimate assumption that a fuller rate of operation would mean increasing returns (through the spreading of overhead costs over a larger production), Ezekiel proposed that the government take the initiative in getting all major industries to begin an expansion program together. If industries were recalcitrant, compliance could be induced by the device of a refundable processing tax, as under the original AAA. In return, the government could guarantee a market for the increased production, since its integrating blueprint would balance lower prices, higher wages, and a vastly expanded total payroll against the increased production offered for sale.*

This ingenious if somewhat mechanical conception received little public attention till it was incorporated in the program of a small "abundance" group in New York, the Commonwealth Federation, of which I was a member. The Commonwealth Federation persuaded a group of progressive Congressmen to take up the proposal, and it was drafted and introduced in Congress as the "Industrial Expansion Bill" by Representatives Robert G. Allen, Amlie, Maverick and Voorhis, in the spring of 1937. It began to attract attention, both from alarmists like Hugh Johnson who saw it as an insidious New Deal plot to try to do what he had not been permitted to do in the NRA, and from left-wing critics who pointed out that it proposed a potentially complete regimentation of industry, without tackling the investment and monetary aspects of the problem of full production.

A considerably improved bill was introduced in June, 1938, by the same sponsors, for further study and criticism. This expressly covered the planning of capital expansion, and provided improved techniques for integrating the consumer and capital goods industries.

Meanwhile another organization, the American Association for Economic Freedom, representing advanced liberal opinion inside and outside the New Deal, was revising the whole proposal along somewhat different lines. It frankly recognized the monopolistic features of the present economy, and proposed to treat monopoly

* In the most recent exposition of his proposal Dr. Ezekiel thus outlines its main features: "The essential idea of Industrial Expansion is to have each of the key basic industries prepare tentative programs for expanding its operations and pay roll in the year ahead, and then to check and revise those tentative programs against each other to be sure they fit properly. Then each concern in these industries will be given advanced orders for the planned production, through contracts with a special government agency. These contracts will provide for the public purchase, at a discount, of any portion of the programmed production which remains unsold. Under these contracts each concern will be safe in going ahead with the planned expansion in production and employment. The nation, in turn, will incur little risk in having the government underwrite the expansion in production, for the programs will be so drawn and fitted together that the increase in production in each industry will just about match the increased demand for the products of that industry." *Jobs For All*, page 17 (1939).

by subjecting it to the rigid supervision of government. While continuing the Code Authorities of the NRA and the Industry Councils of the Industrial Expansion Bill, the new proposal would have these bodies purely advisory, and give the enforcement and administration of the expansion and co-ordination programs wholly into government hands. A supervisory authority and planning board were set up with all necessary powers. They would assure that no undue profits would be made with the new administration of prices. Moreover, the new proposal abandoned the processing tax as a sanction, since this aspect of the old AAA had been discredited, and substituted the licensing provision of the Borah-O'Mahoney "anti-monopoly" bill as a means of compelling compliance. Finally, it added a completely new provision for the nationalization of investment banking. While the main assumption of the drafters of this provision seemed to be that this was necessary to break banker-domination of industry, and that till that control was broken there could be no integration of industry in the public interest, still this new provision obviously greatly increased the possibility of control of the essential investment process.*

None of these proposals can yet be considered anything but tentative. None has clearly understood the nature of monopolistic competition and administered prices, though they all provide a mechanism for making the administration of prices socially responsible.

The objective here, if the analysis pursued in this book is correct, is not so much the rigid enforcement of centrally drawn blueprints for the expansion of industrial production, but the building of a permanent structure for intelligently administering both wages and prices, facilitating the gathering and dissemination of statistical information, so that business men can go forward with "confidence," and giving the government supervisory powers, particularly over new investment, so that it can prevent the dispro-

* The bill being drafted by the American Association for Economic Freedom, as this book is going to press, has been called the Industrial Reconstruction bill. From present indications it will be introduced in Congress before this book appears; the chief aim at present is to publicize and improve it; even the most sanguine of its promoters hardly hope for its passage in the present Congress.

portions and maladjustments to which an uncorrelated business system is so subject.

The measure or measures that seem to be emerging from the tentative approaches described would, if carried through into practice, fulfill most of the requirements for dynamic equilibrium I have set forth. In the first place, the organization of all important industries under government auspices would give them all alike the advantages of "monopolistic competition," not in some extralegal semi-darkness where they must grope for an intelligent price level, or cling stupidly to a conventional price for fear of the unknown consequences of a change, cracking down meanwhile in crude fashion on "chiselers"—but all in the full light of day, with the best of market estimates to aid them. In some cases there may be increased flexibility, but on the whole the effect will be to stabilize prices: rigidity and stability are, as I have tried to point out, different concepts.

The second great achievement of such a method of industrial organization would be its ability to plan for and maintain a steady rate of new industrial investment in actual capital construction. It could try to balance employment-creating investment with investment designed to save labor.

The other feature mentioned might turn out to be of only secondary importance. The guarantee of ultimate sale would rarely be needed after the first psychological effect in getting recovery well under way. The question of sanctions and enforcement and inducement, and how much power to leave in the hands of industry itself, can only be worked out by trial and error method.

Since the whole emphasis of modern socialist theory is, I believe, to leave a large measure of freedom of enterprise to the individual or corporate producer, and since, in my opinion, property ownership and private profit are of minor importance, given the necessary central guidance, therefore it seems quite probable that the individual business man will feel little more restraint than he does today. To be sure, all enterprises will be permitted (and compelled) to participate in "self-government" of the industry: the little fellow cannot be squeezed out nor silenced, but neither can he demoralize wages or prices. To be sure, also, all enterprises will come under collective bargaining contracts, almost necessarily on industry-wide bases, on matters of wages and working conditions, and labor's representatives will increasingly be heard in the planning councils of each industry. But many business men are already used to this type of conventional co-operation. For the most part, what is proposed here is business operation in all important industries at the high level of "industrial statesmanship" already made familiar in a few advanced industries, rather than the imposition of completely new and hitherto unknown standards.

It is probable that the emphasis on definite expansion programs as it appeared in Dr. Ezekiel's first proposal will be of less importance than imagined. If the aspects of the proposal that would restore "confidence" to business are effective, and a high order of predictability of wages, prices and markets is assured, and if at the same time the other measures required to assure a balanced expansion of our purchasing power, as outlined below, are successfully tied in with the program of industrial organization, then no special effort will be necessary to get industries to expand their production. They will expand without outside pressure, to meet an expanding purchasing power.*

### *Rounding Out a Program*

The other measures essential, if my previous analysis is correct, require less elaboration than the scheme for industrial organization. They may be considered under five heads: public investment, agriculture, social dividends, banking, and foreign trade.

1. *Public Investment.* It is legitimate to assume, following Keynes and other leading modern economists, that private investment in new capital construction will never again reach great heights. Conceivably we could cut down hours of labor proportionately to the needs of our consumer goods industries alone, and enjoy our leisure without attempting to reach a standard of living higher than our productive capacity now makes possible. But there is so much to do, so much debris left over from the days of unmitigated capitalist exploitation, so much to be rebuilt in our cities and our countryside, if we are to be happily adjusted to our en-

* While this book was in press I learned of a very similar measure introduced in Parliament in England by Harold Macmillan, M.P. His recent book, *The Middle Way* (Macmillan, 1938), discusses that measure in relation to a general economic approach astonishingly similar to my own here set forth.

vironment, that an immense amount of public investment is called for. (And, for some time to come, our country, no less than others, will be pouring its energies into armament, the easiest form of public investment.)

The best concrete proposal I know of in this direction is one that originated with a group of economists in New York as a projected "National Development Act," and was subsequently introduced in Congress by Representative Voorhis in two complementary bills (75th Congress, 3d Session, H.R. 10516 and 10520). The purpose of the proposal is to take up any existing slack in the economic system, due to the failure of private enterprise to employ any of those desiring employment. The undertakings proposed are in general similar to present public works, except that there is an express emphasis on the necessity that all projects shall be of genuine social value. A constant record is to be kept of employment, and public enterprises are to be immediately expanded as soon as any new unemployment appears. Workers may always find jobs in public employment and are not to be considered relief clients.

The bills provide for the extension of credit at low interest to any public or private enterprises that promise an increase in employment and offer reasonable security for repayment.

Funds in the Voorhis proposal are to be derived from a direct creation of credit, up to five billion dollars, for all self-liquidating projects; the Treasury would buy the bonds of a Public Works Finance Corporation (which would repay the amount gradually from revenues accruing from the projects), and set up credit accounts in the Federal Reserve Banks to the equivalent amount. All non-self-liquidating projects would be financed out of taxation. These provisions would avoid an increase in the national debt, and the obligation to pay interest to the banks for the mere creation of credit money.

The Voorhis bills contain many admirable features. There seems no valid reason except political expediency, however, for limiting the creation of new money to five billion, nor for the ban on further expansion of the national debt. If a measure of this kind is part of a general program of economic expansion and co-ordination there will be a vast amount of real savings seeking investment in government bonds at almost nominal rates of interest. Surely it is easier and pleasanter to get this money, whether for self-liquidating or non-self-liquidating projects, by borrowing it than taking it in taxation. The social problem created by the accumulation of large private fortunes in government bonds is hardly serious, as I have intimated earlier.

Another possible fault with the Voorhis proposal is its failure to emphasize housing as a field where public enterprise is long overdue. It can be argued, however, that a private construction boom of large proportions would follow from the general revival of prosperity, flowing from full employment in industry, with consequent rises in the average family income; and if loans at low interest were always available from the government to assist such private construction, no large-scale public housing program might be necessary. My guess would be that a boom in private construction would take place under such circumstances; but it would be of the utmost importance, before it got under way, to have local and state authorities given increased power to direct building programs along better lines than the jerry-built monstrosities of the last housing boom: this probably could be done simply by setting conditions to all grants of federal money, as well as supervising the issue of all mortgage bonds.

With public investment going to housing or other public construction, and a policy of additional public lending to public or private enterprise at a "yardstick" interest rate, there may be an end of unemployment, for any slack appearing in private enterprise will always be taken up as a matter of course under the Voorhis bills. This public money will serve an additional function, moreover, in setting standards for private enterprise in the matter of wages and working conditions. If work relief is not considered a disgrace, nor thought of as an "emergency" program, then private enterprise will have to bid against the government for labor. It is likely that no further minimum wage legislation will be necessary.

2. *Agriculture.* We might if we wished permit agriculture to work out its own salvation according to laissez faire principles, once the rest of the economy was stabilized as assumed. If everyone seeking work could find it, either in private or public enterprise, and at a good wage, a considerable part of our farming population would leave the land. With the menace of overproduction from marginal and submarginal farmers removed, and with pur-

chasing power in the cities and towns rising to new heights, the remaining farmers would gradually find prosperity. But it would be an uncertain and fitful prosperity so long as the price of what the farmer produces is determined by speculation in Liverpool and other commodity markets. And there is no reason to ask the farmer to wait till the rest of the country becomes prosperous before giving him his share.

The "cost of production" measure first proposed in 1925 represents the most probable line of development, since there is greatest pressure from the advanced farm groups behind it. It calls for "cost of production" on the portion of a farmer's production going to domestic consumption: if he chooses to grow more he must take his chance with the world price on the rest. The marketing of the principal agricultural commodities becomes, under the bill once more before Congress, virtually a public responsibility.

The weakness of the bill as it stands is that it provides no check on the growing of surpluses. Farmers would grow as much as possible, since they would get the cost of production on a fixed *percentage* of their crop regardless of how much each one planted, and thus, though they would be better off than before, they would still be cutting each other's throats to the extent that they grew more than needed domestically, and so long as world prices were below "cost of production" (as they almost certainly would be).

However, if the present production controls were retained, as they stand in the Farm Act of 1938 (the many intricate devices are unimportant here), then to add the "cost of production" proposal would seem to provide all that is needed to restore a prosperous agriculture, except for the question of foreign trade considered below.

The definition of "cost of production" by the government marketing agencies will necessarily be arbitrary, since as in the current measure it should include wages of management, as well as interest and depreciation on capital; and it is not clear whether marginal costs or average costs are to be taken. But this will work itself out by trial and error. It has not been a serious problem where tried elsewhere, as in France, Australia, and, I believe, in somewhat similar fashion in our own sugar industry.

No collectivization of agriculture beyond this program is necessary, even should we wish to socialize our industry. We already have established democratic procedures for the necessary controls: for taking polls on crop or marketing schemes and for allocating and enforcing production quotas to individual farmers by means of their own county committees, organized by the County Agents. We already have the machinery for planning our agricultural production to meet our needs. If purchasing power in the whole economy is assured, real needs and not mere market demand can for the first time find expression. Then if, at the same time, new legislation establishes a rational administration of agricultural prices, the income of the farmer can be assured.

The old individualistic farmer, who grew most of what he needed for himself, is gone forever. The modern one-crop farmer has neither individualism nor security. There has been much romantic talk in the cities about farming as a "way of life." Yet, since colonial times, it has never furnished a real living. Until 1921 the chief income of the farmers was in the form of "capital gains" on the value of their land: they homesteaded free land, they mined the soil, they sold out and moved on. Since 1921 they have lived on their dwindling capital, and on government subsidy. The farmer of the near future will still be able to farm his own land on his own time and in his own way (provided he does not ravage the soil); but through his own democratic machinery for administering prices and planning total production, the acres for which he will share responsibility will stretch to far wider horizons than his own. For the first time in modern America, farming may become a "way of life."

3. *Social Dividends.* Once again we might, if we chose, leave the question of the support of those unable to work to laissez faire methods, if a stable economy at full employment were achieved. With no worker forced to quit at forty-five or fifty because he was "too old," with husbands assured of a living wage on which they could support a wife and bring up children, with ample incomes from which it would be easy to save "for a rainy day" and buy generous insurance policies, it might be possible to forget the social security programs devised for an era of insecurity.

Yet we have already embarked on the other road. There are many advantages to be derived from social security and social dividends. And there is no reason to wait till the rest of our program is finally successful before assuring at least certain minimum protections against unnecessary suffering.

There is no need to consider here any special additional legislation. Our present social security program is bound to be made increasingly generous, put on a "pay as you go" basis, and made to include health among the other hazards for which society must take responsibility if only to protect itself.

From the economic point of view there are two considerations.

The first is that by linking together a taxation program with a program of social payments (pensions, insurances, bonuses, allowances of various kinds), a final check is provided on the maintenance and distribution of the supply of purchasing power, as I suggested on an earlier page. As we perfect our methods of economic planning, both taxation and social dividends may play a dwindling economic role, though their importance for effectuating desired social policies is likely to last longer.

The second consideration is that the extension of social dividends in the guise of free goods and services (schools, roads, parks, playgrounds, cultural opportunities and the like) is likely to become an increasingly important sector of our economy, as compared to production for sale on the market. Construction and maintenance of these public enterprises require revenue, and, unless the government goes in for an at present unexpected expansion of revenue-producing activities, most of this revenue will come from taxation. (The goods and services are free only in the sense that everybody pays for them, not merely those who use them; but the elimination of a sales mechanism may greatly reduce their cost.) I suggested earlier that these social dividends may in the very long run completely transform the economic and social order.

4. *Banking*. There have been a great number of specific proposals before Congress for making our banking system more socially responsible. If the rest of the program outlined here is adopted, with its controls over the flow of purchasing power to consumers and to new investment, it is likely that little will need to be done to the banking system. It performs its other functions, as I have said, with reasonable efficiency.

There has been much pressure in Washington for the public ownership of the central banking system. Such a measure as the Patman bill for public ownership of the twelve Federal Reserve

Banks has considerable following. But since it is control that is important rather than ownership, it might seem that if any closer direction of policy was desired it could be achieved with the present Board of Governors of the Federal Reserve System, the majority of whom have been since 1933 appointed by and responsible to the government.

The argument that the power to create credit out of thin air should be a sovereign prerogative, like the right of coinage, and that to leave this power in the banks is to give them power to levy tribute on the whole population, and to give them a pernicious hold over debtor business, has likewise frequently been heard in Congress since the days of the Populists. The Binderup bill, introduced in the last Congress by Representative Binderup of Nebraska, is an intelligent measure for limiting this power along lines demanded by a growing number of economists. It provides for taking over the Federal Reserve Banks and establishing a 100 per cent reserve requirement in all private banking, thus preventing unpredictable fluctuations in the quantity of money.*

But if our previous controls have been adopted there is little to fear from the remaining power of the bankers. Let us recall the previous answer to this argument. Banker control as much as any other kind of control of industry will have to conform to the requirements of industrial organization contained in our first proposal. If the government is to lend money at low interest to all businesses for expansion or other capital purposes, interest can be made to play its proper role. Commercial banking, limited to the actual financing of specific goods in process of production and distribution, tends to maintain at all times a balance between new money and new goods, and should therefore be relatively harmless. If the government takes it over and leaves merely the checking and depositing and bookkeeping services to private banks, these services will have to be otherwise paid for; so nothing is gained.

The one important new safeguard required against the economic power for harm of the private banking system would seem to be a restriction of the lending function to genuine commercial loans

* Similar controls are carried even farther in another measure, drafted by Irving B. Altman, which would gradually replace all private banking by public banking.

(say of the type accepted for rediscount by the Federal Reserve Banks). All loans for housing or other long-term purposes should be made through the government investment banking system, such as is proposed in the new version of the Industrial Expansion Bill outlined above.

As regards the separation of investment and commercial banking, this is at least nominally accomplished already, under the Banking Act of 1933. To what extent the power of commercial banks to loan money against securities or to buy outstanding securities might be retained, if at all, in making this separation really effective, I am not prepared to say. All I am concerned with here is that the commercial banks should not have the power to create long-term credit or make loans for capital purposes.

In addition, if the analysis of the preceding chapter is sound, and adequate measures are to be taken to prevent a stagnation of business through the stagnation of funds awaiting investment, the new regulations of banking procedures should include provisions either against hoarding, or against the danger of "dis-hoarding." The suggestion will be recalled that deposits of more than a certain size, remaining for more than a certain period, be transferred to special savings accounts; the banks might be required to make these "hoards" available to the public investment banking system, or for the purchase of government securities, with adequate provision for thirty or sixty days' notice before withdrawal by the owner.

It was also suggested earlier that restrictions be placed on loans for speculative purposes, to prevent the inflation of security values by credit which can be as easily destroyed as created. Stock market booms are not necessarily harmful (especially if new money is created to take the place of that withdrawn for speculation); it is the crashes which do the harm.

In the course of time it is reasonable to suppose banking will become a purely public function. The great days of banking came to an end in 1929. Resistance to gradual absorption by public agencies is likely to diminish, as men of ambition are no longer attracted to the humdrum functions left. Better, then, to let it slowly lapse into government hands, rather than to raise a fierce "totempolemic" against all change by threatening anything so radical-sounding as "nationalization."

5. *Foreign Trade.* In view of the liberal prejudice in America

against a planned and organized foreign trade, mentioned a few pages back, we might as well reconcile ourselves to the probability that the necessary controls will be imposed here after all the other items we have mentioned. Monetary disturbances, in view of our huge gold stocks and the ability to "sterilize" them, are slight enough, even today. Inter-industry planning could take exports and imports into account in such a way as to minimize their unpredictable effects. And before long pressure would put through some measure for keeping tabs on foreign trade—for instance, by requiring the passing of all payments through the Import-Export Bank. Ultimately we shall undoubtedly come to an integrated planning and control of all our foreign trade.

If we can afford to be lax for a while in the matter of trade in industrial products, however, we cannot leave agricultural exports to the mercies of the world market. Since we have already proposed that domestic marketing of the chief agricultural commodities become a public function (largely under the co-operative administration of the farmers themselves), it is natural to put the same controls over the export market. There is no reason why American farmers should produce cotton or wheat for export, at a loss. At present they cannot help themselves. Let the government take the risk; the "export subsidy" method is sound enough, except when it proposes to abandon production controls. In return the farmers may well be asked to give the government power to limit production for export each year in accordance with the principles of an "ever normal" domestic granary and in the light of conditions on the world market.

### *Integration and Democracy*

Few of the foregoing proposals suggest anything drastically unfamiliar. The most important new features are control over total purchasing power and over new investment. Even as to these, there have been tentative attempts at control, as in NRA and PWA, which failed only because they were not bold enough nor sufficiently integrated in a single program.

The need for integration should be given additional emphasis. If such a program as that here formulated is ever enacted as a coherent whole, then the policy-making authorities in each department may have a sufficient understanding of the common goal so that no supreme economic authority will be necessary. Any such scheme for industrial organization as that elaborated above will have a central planning agency to co-ordinate the various industries; and this agency will have to take into account all the public spending and investing policies, and the total purchasing power as affected by taxation, social dividends, farm income and the like. It might function as the general co-ordinating body for the whole economy.

It should be remembered, however, that the whole objective of the economic program laid out here is to set up a mechanism that can function automatically rather than arbitrarily. Arbitrary decisions there will have to be, of course. But on the whole what is wanted is co-ordination according to self-applying general rules, dependent on full knowledge. For example, the Public Works Authority should operate under the general instruction to expand its operations (having its blueprints for new projects all waiting for immediate utilization) as soon as current statistics of involuntary unemployment show a rise. There would be little occasion for arbitrary discretion.

What is needed, then, is simply a central advisory body that would watch all statistics coming in from the various agencies of economic control, and advise the executive when any potentially dangerous discrepancies or maladjustments occurred. Since the best ultimate checks are monetary, this advisory body might well work as an adjunct of the Treasury and the Federal Reserve Board.

The fact that the necessary degree of integration can be achieved without any new centralization of arbitrary power, and within the existing constitutional framework, itself gives assurance that collective economic planning will mean no loss of democracy. On the contrary, the whole program is designed expressly to achieve more democracy in the economic field.

There has been much argument for "economic democracy" and "industrial democracy" lately, as though it were some clear-cut phenomenon that could be isolated.

It is unfortunate that the term "industrial democracy" has been so widely identified with collective bargaining. Sometimes there is nothing democratic about collective bargaining, as when a racketeer union, or a union whose constitution provides no effective check on the officers, negotiates with an employer. The bargaining process presumes a commodity for sale on the market, the labor or labor power of the workers. In so far as the market ceases to be the determining factor in economic processes, collective bargaining may in a sense tend to disappear. Will this mean that there will not be unions, or that "industrial democracy" will be destroyed? Will it mean that the "right to strike" will be taken away?

So far as an economy of abundance is approached, there will follow a great increase in outward equality: if everybody has good food and good clothes and good houses, the whole environment will encourage the democratic attitude. So far as this is achieved gradually and without dislocation, and with a constant effort to work through democratic procedures, it will mean an immense achievement in "economic democracy." In the scheme for industrial organization proposed, each industrial plan, which provides among other things for wages, employment, and working conditions, will be drawn up by the representatives of the owners, the employees, and the consumers, and thus will allow much more scope for "industrial democracy," even collective bargaining, than the usual collective bargaining contract. There is no reason why, under such a scheme, or any other democratically conceived scheme for economic planning, the right to strike as a means of protesting a grievance should be abrogated: but as rational adjustments take the place of the crude strike weapon—and the strike is even more costly for workers than employers—it will tend to be ever more rarely employed.

### *Who Is to Do the Job?*

Most of the program we have now outlined is merely a continuation and rationalization of the New Deal. Though the total conception is bolder and some of the measures more drastic than anything emanating from President Roosevelt or his administration advisers so far, there is no reason why the logic of events should not push them on to this point.

But I am writing this at the end of 1938. The present Administration has only two years of life left. The fall elections indicated a resurgent Republican party, and were hailed as an indication that the public is no longer enthusiastic over unbalanced budgets and New Deal "radicalism." As suggested earlier, the general New Deal attitudes and approach are now accepted by the younger and more progressive Republicans, but it would be fatuous to expect that if a Republican administration returns in 1940, it could initiate a program more radical than that of the Roosevelt Administration.

It has not been my purpose in this book to analyze the political aspects of social dynamics. I might logically leave the program as it stands, merely to indicate the type of adjustment that is most likely in the course of time to be pursued, by a democracy making reasonably intelligent use of its ability to learn by its own successes and mistakes. Moreover, I attempted in *Insurgent America* to deal with the social forces that might be counted on to bring economic change, and to suggest a political strategy. However, much has happened since that book appeared, and a more realistic appraisal of the political methods most likely to facilitate an intelligent program is now possible. No further important changes in the political set-up seem likely between the time of writing and 1940. And since my whole aim is to estimate the possibilities for immediate practical action, a few paragraphs about political methods may not be out of place.

The events of 1938 seem to have scotched the possibilities for a clear-cut political alignment on basic issues. Roosevelt's attempt to "purge" his own party of reactionaries and drive them into the arms of the Republicans was unsuccessful (except in the case of House Rules Committee Chairman O'Connor). The Republican candidates widely accepted the New Deal "aims," and in some instances it even appeared that conservative Democrats had been replaced by more liberal Republicans. Virtually none of the "Old Guard" Republicans, who once ran the party for the benefit of Big Business, are in evidence. The possibility that the two old parties would be or could be remodeled so that one stood definitely for progressivism and the other for conservatism seems to have passed. The difference between the actual party structures (discounting Mr. Roosevelt's personal leadership) is no greater than it was in the twenties. But both parties are considerably to the "left" of where they were.

At the same time the possibility that a new alignment would develop through the emergence of a new party has declined. In spite of continuing efforts by a number of organizations and individuals, the most ambitious of which was Governor Phil La Follette's launching of the National Progressives in the spring of 1938, no effective new party has gained a foothold in any state in these tense years, with the exception of the American Labor party in New York. Even in Wisconsin the Progressive party is scarcely a new party, being merely a split-off of the La Follette organization from the old Republican party; its defeat in the 1938 elections is thought by many to end the immediate prospect of the La Follettes' new national party. The Minnesota Farmer-Labor party, also defeated in 1938, is hardly in a position to expand its field of operations.

The American Labor party is caught in a disconcerting dilemma. It has been unable to make marked progress with independent candidates, except within New York City, and at the same time its efforts to play off one old party against the other, while reasonably successful in compelling the Democratic party to put up a liberal and pro-labor slate, have tended to demoralize its following. Moreover, as an affiliate of Labor's Non-Partisan League, initiated and largely dominated by C.I.O. unions, the American Labor party is handicapped by A. F. of L. opposition. There is little immediate likelihood that the party will organize effectively on an independent national basis. Even the C.I.O. convention at the end of 1938 gave little consideration to the formation of a national Labor party.

The only hope of a powerful third party in 1940 springs from the possibility that the Roosevelt forces, defeated in the Democratic National Convention in 1940, will take the lead, Bull Moose style, in launching a new Progressive party to carry on the New Deal. Such a move would have some considerable advantages over Theodore Roosevelt's venture: Franklin is probably an even more popular national figure than was his cousin; and the existence of strong organization nuclei in the Wisconsin and Minnesota third parties, the American Labor party, and Labor's Non-Partisan League, would make the effort more effective than was that of 1912. Fiorello H. LaGuardia or young Bob La Follette would be logical standard-bearers for such a party, if Franklin Roosevelt did not run himself.

A political development of this kind, if successful, could very easily push on from the existing foundation of New Deal legislation to some such program as outlined in this chapter.

The danger of such an attempt would lie in its tendency to consolidate conservatives in power in both old parties; if the new party failed to win, a period of genuine reaction might set in, with intelligent gradualism indefinitely postponed.

The events of 1938 have tended to confirm in me a new belief in the two-party system. If the Republicans vie with the Democrats in progressive appeals, the possibility seems to open up that we may continue to have gradual progress to the left regardless of which party is in power. If a reasonable measure of liberalism continues to pervade both old parties to a comparable extent, then there would seem to be an excellent chance that democracy can achieve social progress more consistently and more effectively in this country than in any other. There need be no fear of fascism. For there will be neither acute class struggle nor the political stalemate and consequent demoralization that arose in Germany and Italy out of the conflicts of sharply opposed parties.

It would certainly be preferable that the Democratic party carry on in 1940 than that the Republicans should come to power, for the Democratic party's traditions are healthier. And it would certainly be preferable that the Democratic party's next candidate should be a thorough New Dealer rather than a conservative. Unfortunately, no candidate now stands out, except Mr. Roosevelt himself, with the necessary combination of political charm and progressive principle. Whether the obvious objections to a third term are to be ignored will depend on all the other alternatives open.

The probabilities seem to indicate that there will be neither third party nor third term, but a mildly liberal administration under one of the old parties in 1940. What then becomes of the New Deal, and of the "new New Deal" proposed in these pages?

Here again it might be logical to advise a laissez faire attitude. The internal pressures of our social and economic organism will compel the changes in due course of time. Yet the possibilities of delay, suffering, potential calamity, are too great in the modern world for any of us to be willing to stand still. What then?

It is to be expected that there will be a growing awareness of the nature of the economic problem on the part of progressive elements throughout the country. The lessons of Europe are hammering insistently at our ears. The "Monopoly Committee" is likely to bring much that is fundamental to the surface of public discussion. The very instinct for survival on the part of the New Dealers should make them readier in the remaining two years of the present administration to look boldly for a way out of the present stalemate.

Much could be accomplished if the progressive elements in the federal administration, in the states, in the labor movement and elsewhere, were to come to an increasing agreement on what needs to be done. Whether or not any concrete formulation of progressive policy or organization emerges within the next two years, to make more certain that the New Deal carries on, is perhaps of less importance. But it might be worth attempting.

President Roosevelt was probably right when he told Upton Sinclair in 1934 that he was going ahead as fast as he could carry the people with him. If the New Deal is still far from its objectives it is less the fault of its leadership than of enlightened public opinion generally. With no clear understanding of the nature of the basic economic problems, and no general agreement on the "left" on what course should be pursued, it would have been a miracle if more success had been achieved.

Today it is becoming increasingly possible to diagnose and prescribe. Great experiments in economic practice are available; they can test and be tested by a growing body of sound economic theory. If enough people understand what sort of program is called for to accomplish needed changes democratically, then perhaps our existing political institutions will themselves carry the burden. In that case questions of a new political alignment, a third term, a third party, and the integration of progressive forces, will solve themselves without undue stress.

It is to lend such aid as I can to that process of public understanding, that this book is written.

There remain to be considered only the general implications of the social and economic theories I have advanced, for international developments and the prospects of peace.

# Chapter Nineteen

## NOT FOR OURSELVES ALONE

BETWEEN a neighbor and a statistic there is a vast difference. For most of us the population of Bulgaria or China is only a statistical one. It is in fact difficult to think of people as neighbors except when they are so familiar that we can visualize them as separate human beings, even to their distinguishing facial features, homely but specific. Anyone who has traveled abroad at a leisurely enough pace so that the particular individuals in a foreign country begin to come into sharp focus must be conscious of that difference.

I recall a particular Chinese soldier. It was in the days before the Japanese conquest, when Chiang Kai-shek was fighting the Communists, that I traveled up to the provincial city which was then his headquarters. Wounded were coming back from the front. I was invited to see a military hospital in a school building, and in the course of the inspection had an opportunity to watch an operation performed on a soldier who had a bullet in his lung. Only a local anaesthetic was used. The soldier was afraid, though stoical, and I was afraid for him. He was in pain, and as I watched I was in pain too. His eyes wandered dumbly around the room looking for comfort, and for an instant met mine.

There are some four hundred million inhabitants in China—or were before the Japanese invasion. It has sometimes shocked me to discover how easily one can toss off millions when they are abstract figures. Until recently it was not uncommon to read that a million had died of famine in some Chinese province, that five million had been rendered destitute by a Yangtze flood, that so many thousand had been killed in a battle with the "Reds." Since the Japanese war the figures are on a grander scale—dead, wounded, homeless, starving. All the statistics are less vivid to me than the suffering of that one soldier in the hospital with whom I suffered.

With such individuals, who have in a sense become part of you, it is no longer possible to think in statistical terms. You realize that human beings are very much alike, without profound racial differences. There are greater differences between the people who live on my street in New York than between people of similar taste and temperament in the far corners of the world.

I suppose the Christian ideal of a world in which all men are truly neighbors to each other is impossible of complete attainment. But if you accept the humanist approach and assume that every human being is an individual personality worthy of respect, then you must at least aim at that larger concept of world brotherhood. It is impossible, for instance, to think of the economic program which I have just outlined as an isolated program for the United States without respect to the rest of the world.

Indeed every approach to the problem of human organization involves an attitude to the rest of the world. The Russian communist faith keeps coming back to the world revolution, when the workers of the world will throw off their chains everywhere, smite their oppressors, and set up the rule of the "human race." The Nazis dream of a world dominated by a race of Nordic supermen, to whom all the lesser races do happy homage. Even our "American dream" has its world outlook: we went to war in 1917, as we thought, to make the world safe for our special set of democratic institutions; not until every nation adopts the equivalent of our own Constitution would most of us consider the goal of the Founding Fathers achieved.

Today, more than ever before, in spite of the wars and rumors of wars that fill men everywhere with dread, there is a world-consciousness. Nazis and Communists and democrats alike talk of saving "civilization." We concern ourselves with the lot of "future generations." On a lesser scale people in Europe talk of behaving like "good Europeans," the nations of the Western Hemisphere dream of a pan-American comity, in the Far East an "Asiatic" consciousness is fostered by Japan for her own ends. Behind these lesser slogans there is probably a keener sense of the basic unity of the human species and the inseparability of its fate on this planet than ever before. The very horror with which we approach the next war indicates how war now goes against the grain.

From the philosophical point of view, our concern with the human race and its future is certainly legitimate. But for centuries prophets and dreamers have felt that concern without its greatly affecting the course of history. Now it is reinforced by a very real and practical consideration—that "next war." The more extreme alarmists may be unjustified in fearing that "civilization itself will be wiped out," at least in one war. But the brutalization and demoralization that must accompany an increasing ferocity of human relations, and the totalitarianizing of thought which, under the necessities of any military regime, stifles the essential rationalism on which our civilization is based, may well set back the clock for centuries.

The interpretation of present world trends which I have attempted in this book necessarily carries wider consequences than a mere program of economic legislation for American progressives. In this last chapter I am attempting to draw the wider conclusions—to fit communism and fascism into a world perspective, to consider how best we may hope that the ills of world capitalism can transmute themselves into a new social order, to estimate the prospects for war and peace, both for ourselves and for our children. And finally I want to look at some of the more remote implications of my approach.

Yet perhaps I should first sound a note of warning. Concern over remote consequences often stifles action. American conservatives have been rightly pilloried by Thurman Arnold for their inordinate worries over the future generations who might be affected by a bold and honest attack on present problems. By feeding the hungry we are "weakening the nation's fiber." By writing red figures in a ledger we are "burdening posterity." By laying rough hands on the "American system of free enterprise" we are dooming our children and grandchildren to slow decay. Another aspect of this concern with what is far away is the prior emphasis given by many to international relations. The free trade enthusiasts see no hope for improving domestic conditions till the world's barriers are down. The Communists tend to postpone "the revolution" at home till after fascism has been destroyed abroad. Many of us have unconsciously justified our failure to solve our own problems by blaming the unsettled state of the world. We protest "the rape" of Ethiopia or Czechoslovakia, or the persecution of the German Jews, with a vehemence we no longer can evoke against Negro discrimination here, or the sufferings of our own unemployed.

Our own job must come first. We cannot save democracy abroad while we fumble our own. We can show our concern for the rest of the world and for civilization and for future generations in no way more effectively than by discovering how to plan for abundance and how to find freedom for ourselves.

## *Democracy on the Home Front*

Suppose the controls for the planning of purchasing power and investment, as outlined in the previous chapter, were successfully imposed by a "new New Deal" administration within the next few years. Suppose we abolished unemployment, established a high minimum family income in line with our productive capacity, controlled the flow of income, savings and new investment so that maladjustments and discrepancies quickly regulated themselves without bringing on depression. And suppose we did all this with no more social friction or loss of democratic procedures than we have experienced since the New Deal came to power.

Within twelve months from the inauguration of such a program, 1929 levels of production and income should be passed. The millions of workers, mostly unskilled, who in 1929 were employed in industry and construction, and are now no longer required by private industry because of new techniques and the adequacy of our existing factories and office buildings, will be employed in vast public construction, chiefly of housing. Within five years, while our monetary income may no longer be rising as rapidly as at first, the amenities of decent living will be multiplying at an increasing rate: longer vacations, more recreational facilities, slums going down not by the block but by the acre, sunshine coming in new windows, all main roads taking on the well-groomed look of parkways.

Goebbels' newspapers would have increasing difficulty in finding pictures of ragged unemployed sleeping in subways, scavengers on garbage dumps, lynchings, battles between strikers and vigilantes: he would have to use old and increasingly familiar pictures to show the Germans how much better off they are than the inhabitants of this "third-rate democracy."

Where opinion is still free our successes would have an irresistible effect. While today American periodicals run articles on English housing schemes, Swedish depression-proof fiscal policies, Danish co-operatives, at some future date foreign publicists and political leaders and economists would begin to point to American experiments (as they did in the early days of the New Deal). In so far as our measures proved workable and were imitated, the morale of the now harassed world would begin to mount.

To be sure, a picture of Europe suddenly waking up to find America had solved the problem of depression is a little fanciful. For all countries tend to move together under the same pressures, and before we reached a clearly recognizable degree of success other countries would be taking the same road. But my main point stands: give the democracies a cure for unemployment and economic insecurity, and the fear of totalitarian ideologies, whether communist or fascist, will begin to fade like a bad dream. The panic of the Western world in this year 1939 is due to its inner sickness, its guilty conscience, its ineffectiveness in the face of the dictatorships. Even as regards the brutal realities of armament we cannot keep up with the efficient pace of Germany today; but let us find a workable technique of economic organization, and our greater resources could soon outdistance her even in that fatuous race.

Suppose further that the democracies have found it necessary to abandon their laissez faire ideas of foreign trade for profit, and to plan for exchange of what they need on a rationalized basis. Suppose France and England should so concentrate their energies on developing their own resources and productive capacity that the influence of those who live on investments in their colonies began to be submerged. It would become possible for the first time to bargain on a basis of mutual benefit, not only between the great powers themselves, but between them and the regions they have in the past exploited. Perhaps I am looking into too distant a future to imagine a day when India will receive as much from England as England receives from India, and empires based on exploitation dissolve. But that is the only way to ultimate peace.

It is true that if England and France and the United States were democratic planned economies, and could plan for and predict what raw materials they would need each year from tropical regions and from each other, and what they could most advantageously give in return, their economic rivalry would not be at an end. It would in fact take on a more official character than when their competition is left to irresponsible salesmen, promoters and surreptitious imperialists. But for the first time they could bargain openly and frankly and completely. No longer would a trade agreement merely set the limit of the penalty imposed on foreign business men for the right to sell in the other's market. Each country would seek to secure as much of the world's wealth from the other as possible; and if there is any validity in foreign trade, because of difference in cost, then each would gain. Under such circumstances a trade agreement would be an unmitigated advantage to all concerned.

As the practice of a rational and planned interchange of the world's products spread, the basic international tensions would relax. As agreements became increasingly multilateral it would become possible to bring all those willing to co-operate around one council table. The resources of the world could be jointly assessed. All assets would be frankly acknowledged. Colonies, spheres of influence, foreign investments, access to raw materials, all the exclusive prerogatives which are the international trappings of domestic scarcity, could be shed by nations newly strong at home, and an intelligent world order at last begun.

But all of this will be cited as idle day-dreaming by those who see in fascism (or those who see in communism) an imminent threat to civilization and peace. Suppose at the best that the democratic powers could eventually learn how to solve their basic economic problems without abandoning their democracy, how will they have time or opportunity, in the face of advancing totalitarianism?

To answer that question requires an estimate of the immediate future of Soviet communism and the fascist states.

*Economic Nationalism*

If it is true that the economic methods as well as the political systems of Soviet Russia and the fascist powers tend to become more and more alike, as I have argued in previous chapters, then this question rises: Why is Soviet Russia so obviously a force for peace, without aggressive designs, as unbiased observers unanimously agree, whereas the fascist powers seem to be addicted to war? The answer lies perhaps in recognizing that the kind of national collective economy they are all building within their own boundaries is capable of successful achievement only when those boundaries enclose enough natural wealth. The other powers—Germany, Italy and Japan—are too meagerly endowed with natural resources.

Soviet Russia avers its belief in internationalism, and its partisans argue that it cannot on that account treat any other country as an enemy to be conquered. By the same token it is argued that the fascist powers, inflated with national egotism, are necessarily belligerent. But on both sides this argument may be irrelevant. The very internationalism of the Comintern, which works ostensibly for the overthrow of bourgeois governments, at one time made the Soviet Union militantly aggressive. If its armies had not been stopped at the gates of Warsaw in 1920 they might have overrun all Europe, as the armies of the French Revolution did before them. If the imperial conquests of the Czars, in the oil fields of the Caucasus, the cotton lands of Turkestan, the cattle country of middle Asia, and the distant frontier territories of Mongolia and eastern Siberia, had not fallen once more before the military power of the Soviet government, the Soviet Union might be now a belligerently "have not" country like Germany. And conversely, if and when Germany obtains full control over the mineral and agricultural resources of the Danube and the Balkan states, Germany may become as much a *status quo* country as the Soviet Union.

"But what about *Mein Kampf?*" is the quick rejoinder of those who see civilization in permanent peril till Nazism is exterminated. It is true that Hitler's romantic dreams envisage the complete domination of Europe, if not of the world, by Germany.

But the Communists, who are loudest in their insistence that Nazism *delenda est*, have, with Marx for their teacher, least ground for their alarm. No romantic dreams are likely to influence history unless real economic pressures bear them out, or unless they have the valid mass appeal of the French and Russian Revolutions. Hitler won control of Germany because economic pressures made *Mein Kampf* seem like a gospel of salvation to millions of Germans. Hitler took Austria and the Sudeten region, and will bring other and richer territories under his sway, because Germany's hunger is not yet appeased. But, however limitless Hitler's own dreams may be, there is no reason to suppose that in the economic logic of history, Germany's appetite for conquest is limitless.

Italy and Japan are somewhat different problems, though the same general rule should hold good. Italy is so poor in resources that even the control of the whole eastern Mediterranean would not sate her; probably not even with northern Africa and Spain thrown in would she feel the same confidence in her strength that the Soviet Union today feels, or that a German Mittel-Europa might feel. But neither is she as much a threat to peace as Germany: she could not wage an aggressive war alone.

Japan, on the other hand, if she is to consolidate her hold on China, is not likely to engage in further conquest, for a long time at least. Her only threat to the European democracies and to the United States is to their trade, and the profits from that trade, which should hardly concern us here.

The three major "aggressor powers," then, have great spheres of influence, into which they may expand during the next few years without direct threat to the major democratic powers or even to the Soviet Union.

With the surrender of France and England to Hitler at Munich no further opportunities for calling a halt to fascist expansion are likely to arise. France and England will fight if their own territory is invaded, or if their imperial prerogatives are menaced at too rude a pace. But there is no need for the fascist powers to run that risk.

In this period of economic nationalism there is much danger of local wars, which may reach major proportions. But there may be less danger of a general world war than many of us have feared.

Time and again the powerful nations have backed away from a crisis which, before 1914, would have led without doubt to a general war. As long as the "have" nations continue willing to let the "have not" nations pursue their aggressions without armed interference, and so long as these aggressions do not too nearly threaten the integrity of the "have" nations within their own territories, there need be no general war. The process of aggression may cease of its own accord when a certain point of saturation is reached.

Of course the power of myths and the ideals of international morality may prove greater than intelligent economic interest. The democratic powers may insist on taking up the challenge of the fascist powers, regardless of the fact that the result would not be moral but merely more universal brutalization. Or the fascist powers may have their myths of national superiority so inflated that they will not know when to stop, and they may go on from the conquest of territories and resources which their national economies need, to attempt the conquest of territories not essential to them but essential to one of the other camp. But America did not take all of Mexico in the days of our "manifest destiny"; and England's "white man's burden" found the limits of its arrogance. So why should we envision the "Rising Sun" in California, or "Aryan supremacy" driving north from Mexico?

The chances seem fairly good that for the next few years France and England, and much more the United States, will be able to work out their own salvation without war. A few great powers will be found to have parceled out the earth's resources, Japan, the Soviet Union, Germany, the British, French and Italian Empires, the United States, with the smaller states generally in one or another economic orbit. There is no reason why all seven should not collaborate as peacefully as the four that are in the "have" class today. If the democracies achieve the necessary domestic controls, international economic arrangements will become increasingly possible: and under the circumstances—all being *status quo* nations—agreements would not need to be one-sided, and mutual satisfaction should be possible.

Before many years a stable world settlement between national states all more or less collective may become a reality. Whether it is a settlement that will encourage not only the survival but the ultimate universalization of democracy will depend on what the democratic powers do with their peace in the meantime.

Of course any estimate of the future is rash. There are too many unpredictables, accidents, personal emotions, imponderable social and economic developments to make any forecast more than good guesswork. But even if war should supervene, the progress which the democratic powers can make in economic reorganization before it begins will be all to the good. If they must defend themselves with arms, then the nearer to full production and full use of man-power their economies can come, the better for them and for the democracy they would preserve.

### *Nationalism and Internationalism*

Yet at best such an outlook may seem a precarious one. For the United States, along with the other non-totalitarian states, to develop efficient economic techniques along purely national lines, might seem to perpetuate the very dangers from which the world is suffering. If this is "socialism," even though not altogether like the "socialism" practiced in the Soviet Union, it still has an ominous resemblance to the "national socialism" which, written with capital letters, is generally thought our chiefest enemy. True-blue Marxists will insist socialism is a travesty unless it is international. Many a liberal, untouched by Marxism, will insist that a peaceful ordered international system must be achieved before we can make even America safe for democracy.

National states are at present the logical units of economic organization, rather than regions or continents or the entire world—out of historical necessity. But their potentialities for effective economic organization necessarily vary greatly. The more dependent they may be on resources outside their own boundaries, the less able to achieve a completely integrated and internally stable economy; the more self-sufficient, the more able to "build socialism in one country."

England with her empire may plan for a balanced economy. So may France with hers. Continental Europe can only achieve economic stability through some degree of continental integration. Under laissez faire theory this integration can be approached so long as trade for profit is comparatively "free." With the permanent passing of the laissez faire era there is no possibility of economic stability in central Europe save by enforced integration under either communist or fascist control. The Communists lost their chance by 1920. Where they failed, because capitalist opposition was too strong, the fascists are succeeding; capitalist opposition is now too weak to resist, even if the fascists had not first bought it off, in contrast to the Communists who had tried to kill it off.

The objection that such a unification of central Europe will involve the destruction of lesser nations (Austria was the first victim) is not logically tenable, especially by Americans. National sovereignties are not worth preserving for their own sake; otherwise why are we so willing to accept the fact that the "sovereignty" of the "states" of the United States has been gradually reduced to nothing since 1776? The value of small states is in cultural diversity, which ought to remain unaffected, and as convenient units for administrative decentralization. Even in the authoritarian collective state of Soviet Russia, most of the 182 nationalities have their own languages, their own literature, their own culture, and the bewildering complexity of the myriad organizations through which collectivism functions in the Soviet Union is further complicated by the maintenance of national territories and "autonomous" areas. There is no reason to feel that civilization would lose by the merging of Rumanian sovereignty, for example, half into the Soviet Union, half into a super-German state, except in so far as those states might repress the Rumanian people more than they were repressed by their own governing groups.

I realize that the myth of "national independence" is so strong that to suggest the partition of Rumania, even as a theoretical example, may sound offensive. Yet if we are to work toward a world order, national sovereignties will have to go, and this method of absorption of the smaller by the larger may be the only way. You can't have your cake and eat it too.

Nevertheless, though this development of self-sufficient economic empires represents in a sense the triumph of the national state, it also marks a stage in its disappearance. The Kingdom of Muscovy became the Russian Empire, with many races and peoples subject to the Russian national state; the Bolsheviks in their own way completed the "Russification" of the whole territory, to achieve a larger national unity, but they did far more: they achieved a federation of autonomous nationalities which they hold out as the model for the federation of the world. Likewise the British Empire, starting with national conquest and subjection, has been emerging as the British Commonwealth of Nations. If and when Germany is complete master of Mittel-Europa the first aspect of her empire may be helot provinces exploited by the "Blond Beast"; but in so far as the economic pattern tends to assume the form of socialist planning on the Soviet model, the national state may begin to evolve as a United States of Central Europe.

In such merging of lesser national groups, not as imperial subjects, but as participants in a larger whole, lies the hope for a natural growth of internationalism and an ultimate world power. There will be a growing pressure for integration as national planning becomes more prevalent. I do not overlook the possibility, mentioned earlier, that national rivalry on a new basis may rise as a counter-danger. When two planned national economies both want the same territory containing rich resources—say the Ukraine—they may fight if those resources are indispensable. But German interest in the Ukraine appears to be more political (or "ideological") than economic. If Germany had complete domination of Hungary and Rumania it is hard to see what economic interest she would have in the more distant Ukraine. Moreover, as I emphasized earlier, economic conflicts are potentially far easier to settle between planned economies than between the less open and more diffuse ambitions of capitalist states. The Soviet Union had exemplary trade relations with Mussolini and, in his early years, even with Hitler, relations that were only disrupted when the ideologues took the initiative away from the economic planners.

One of the most intelligent and complete proposals for international planning yet offered was the "World Reorganization on Corporative Lines" by one of Mussolini's senators, De Michelis. Some of its excellent suggestions for migration and the allocation of raw materials, to relieve population pressures and rationalize the world's wealth, were brought periodically before the League of Nations: France and the British Empire were of course not interested; the proposals won little attention; Italy withdrew from the League; Senator de Michelis' intelligent pattern passed into limbo.

There is nothing in the *economics* of fascism incompatible with internationalism. There is much in its doctrinal atmosphere that is, however; for fascism is nothing if not militantly nationalistic. If we go along with Marx, at least so far as to admit that economic pressures are of major importance in historical evolution, then is it too much to hope that if fascist economics finds fulfillment in world planning ("on corporative lines," let us say), fascism as a religious doctrine will fade?

Other forces, too, may be counted on to foster the infant faith of international solidarity. The independent labor movements—and not all because of Marx—have clung to the concept that workers were bound more closely to their fellow-workers than to their bosses. Liberals of the humanist tradition have contributed to a whole cultural development which takes for granted the essential likeness of human beings and their aspirations. Intellectuals, scientists, technicians, where not totalitarianized, think and work in a world without national boundaries. Even the capitalists of the departing imperialist era made the world the theater of their operations, and deplored as honestly as any humanitarian the wars they unconsciously brewed.

The forces that would associate all human beings on our planet in a joint enterprise move slowly but are none the less powerful. The League of Nations was a noble dream that became a half-cynical, half-sentimental pretense because it came too soon. The victors of Versailles were still thinking of the profitable investments and markets and spheres of influence of the moneyed men whose rivalries had brought on the war. The idealists like Lord Cecil, who gave their energies to building "the parliament of man, the federation of the world," were being used by governments which considered the League merely a policeman to protect their least noble interests abroad. But the failure of the League does not mean the necessary return to the rule of might, for it had not replaced that rule, only perpetuated some of its settlements. It means we are in the process of sweeping aside a lot of glittering sham. When next it becomes possible to create an international organization—if another war does not intervene—

it may be done with more realism and honesty, and with more chance of success.

Out of Russian "socialism in one country" and German "National Socialism" and the Italian "corporative state" and the "armament economies" of the *status quo* empires, and all the other halting attempts at collectivism within autarchic national boundaries, there may yet come the "international socialism" preached by a few men ahead of their time.

It will mean no "super-state." We need fear no world Caesar, giving unappealable commands to all the denizens of earth. If collectivism within national boundaries, as it has been analyzed in this book, can approach the laissez faire ideal of an automatic mechanism to regulate the affairs of free individuals, then a world collectivism can do the same in the affairs of free nations. The sovereign liberties of nations to wage war upon each other will be curtailed. A stronger people will no longer be "free" to subjugate a weaker. But the economic interdependence and political fraternization of the United States and Canada, depending on no super-state or international "policeman," may become a model for the flexible ties that will bind the nations of the world in an unimposed co-operation.

## *A Peace Policy*

The chief barrier to progress along these hopeful lines is not Hitler, or fascism. Nor is it Stalin, or communism. Nor any other leader or ism. In a large sense it is not even the possibility of war that stands in the way of our natural evolution, for war is only a symptom of ignorance and fear and hatred, and the abandonment of rational human ways. Back of this fear and hatred is what I might call the mania of righteousness. It springs from intolerance, and intolerance is strongest in absolutist creeds. If war, international or civil, is what we fear most, it is because it makes fanaticism supreme.

There is a natural strength in fanaticism. The supreme effort required by revolutionary change calls forth (and is called forth by) a crusading zeal which, in the midst of its new temple to man, sets up an idol gory with sacrifice.

Perhaps when a social order becomes too decadent it is well

to have zealots in control for a while. For all their cruelty they will sweep clean, and their successors can move ahead unencumbered by useless clutter from the past. But fanaticism is a purifying fire hard to stamp out once its work is done. Just because it acts irrationally it may destroy the possibilities of later rationality.

No revolutionary movement has ever had more horrible features than Nazism. Its racial dogmas seem capable of destroying the essential humanist spirit. The neurotic romanticism it derived from Nietzsche, Wagner, and Hitler himself, has led to the burning of books, the virtual destruction of universities, the dethronement of reason itself. The wolf-pack sadism of the culminating assault on the Jews in November, 1938, seemed final proof that Nazism is the incarnation of evil.

It is easy to forget that all revolutionary periods are cruel, even sadistic. The very vitality of Nazism should indicate that it is not merely reactionary or decadent. In a larger sense, and seen in its historical perspective alongside the Soviet revolution, even the Nazi revolution is an aspect of the trend that started with the liberal humanistic awakening of the last two centuries. Many of its institutional procedures reflect the aspiration toward a brotherhood of equals (labor service, for instance, is compulsory regardless of status or income, and the Nazi party as the ruling elite is theoretically open to all members of the community, though the community is thought of in terms of racial exclusiveness). It is certainly too early to say that fascism cannot return to a humanistic view.

After all, the specific crimes of cruelty and anti-intellectualism under fascism can be matched in the history of the Soviet Union. True, the absolutist creed of the Bolsheviks sprang directly out of the rationalism and humanism in which Marx and later Lenin were impregnated, while fascism is immediately and preponderantly influenced by the decadent romantic reaction. But, on the other hand, Russia was closer to barbarism to begin with, and the survival of a humanist attitude in spite of brutality might perhaps be less expected there than in a country of Germany's cultural past.

The tens of thousands of "white Russians" scattered over the face of the earth can tell tales of sadism, the persecution of the innocent, the hounding of helpless men, women and children (because they were "capitalists" or "aristocrats," hence things of "evil"), the decimating of the intellectual class, the totalitarianizing of universities, the banning of books, all because they represented a system that was condemned.

In the early years of the Russian Revolution the "civilized world" rose up in horror, sent its armies to exterminate "the accursed thing," sought to ring bolshevism with a *cordon sanitaire*. Finally it grew accustomed to the novelty. Its tourists went to see and admire the "great Russian experiment." Its intellectuals extolled the new liberation of mankind—until a revival of the old mania of righteousness in Moscow called for new victims, and the "old Bolsheviks" began to exterminate each other. But meanwhile a new monster had arisen, on which the "civilized world" could vent its horror, the monster of fascism.

"Anti-Fascism" has now become a cult. It is almost as fanatical as fascism itself. Many are the former "liberals" who feel that the sooner a war to exterminate fascism may come the better. There is no room for sympathy, no will to understand, in this new sect.

Civilization is indeed threatened; but not by any particular group of cruel and anti-intellectual fanatics, rather by fanaticism itself, a fanaticism to which the whole world is prone. Not that anyone is to blame; it is rather that men are desperately seeking new techniques of social organization under the compulsion of technological progress, and when they do not know how to find what they seek, they grow a little mad.

What we have most to fear is war. It is the natural end of the "retreat from reason." It is the final triumph of absolutist faith in one's own righteousness.*

It will not be easy—perhaps it will be impossible—to give way gracefully before dynamic fascism. Communism at least was a more distant menace, half in Asia. Fascism looms over western Europe, seems to menace even the Americas. Often will we be tempted, as before the Munich settlement, to make the final test of guns and airplanes. Perhaps the fascist powers will themselves attack. But no good can possibly emerge from war to weigh

* Lancelot Hogben has better explained the current "retreat from reason" in his little book by that name than anyone else.

against the agony and the destruction and the danger of a complete loss of the ability to reason and understand.

The immediate problem for the democracies is to find a *modus vivendi,* a means of getting along in the same world with expanding and ruthless fascism. The governments of France and England are at the moment seeking such a settlement, at the cost of much humiliation and political strain, and without the imagination or the will to push the internal reforms which could make the price they are paying bearable. Yet the granting of a free hand to Hitler in southeastern Europe, and of increasing concessions to Mussolini in the Mediterranean, is probably essential. Meanwhile eastern Asia has been virtually written off as a total loss, so far as Western imperialist interests are concerned.

I have previously suggested that the democracies, along with their new internal plan-ways, must begin to look at their empires and foreign trade with new realism. Not until they are willing to plan for the mutual utilization of the world's scarce raw materials and natural products—minerals, foodstuffs, fibers, rubber, rare metals—can they make their peace with the fascist powers. To be specific, Hitler must be assured access to Rumanian oil, Hungarian wheat, Lorraine iron ore, Chilean nitrates, Brazilian coffee, Malay rubber; the old fetish of international free trade is worth nothing to him, subject as it is to the whims of politicians, the vagaries of the international money markets, the unpredictable potentialities for profit. If there is to be an international economic settlement, the democratic powers must be willing to scrap that fetish at the start.

In all of this America can take the lead. Even where the first steps toward planned utilization of the world's resources are possible, this country could take an initiative. So long as we cling to the free trade fetish we shall not do so, even though Germany and Italy need our cotton and our wheat and our oil and iron, and could give us much in return. So long as we let concepts of "sin" interfere with economic sense we shall merely perpetuate the suffering. The least we could do would be to arrange for the gradual absorption of all Germany's Jews; but till our economic program is well along, even that proposal must be thought fantastic, for all our humanitarianism.

At best the path this country has to travel in a warring world will be difficult and thorny. No simple rules without exceptions can be drawn. Neither collective security, nor power politics, nor the moralistic lecturing so dear to our hearts will do any good. If a general European war does start we shall have to make up our minds as best we may at the time, without preconceptions or prejudgments, whether or not civilization will be any the better served because we join in the slaughter. Where wars are already in progress, as in China and Spain, our chief interest is to avoid all possibilities of involvement, for this would be a greater calamity than any foreseeable outcome in those wars; it may still be possible without undue risk to aid the victims of aggression, as by embargoes or by lifting embargoes. Our neutrality legislation needs amendment, if only to minimize friction and "incidents."

Our foreign policy, like that of England and France, cannot but be an inglorious one at this time. We must live from day to day, making the best of bad bargains, tearing up unjust settlements to sign new ones equally unjust, cherishing our humanity in retreat, rather than making a defense in which we shall lose it beyond redemption. We cannot make a stand "to defend democracy" when the occasion for our stand will be the protection of some past robbery. Not until the vital homelands of the democratic tradition, the actual territory of France and England, are endangered, should we think of fighting, if ever; for only then is it possible that we will be fighting for things enough worth while to minimize the brutalization of battle.

Our foreign policy must necessarily be a domestic policy. Whatever may be the wide causes of war today, the causes that will embroil us are, as they were in 1917, the destruction of American lives and property, and the pressures of a growing trade with belligerents. If we ship cotton and machine guns to an "innocent" "democratic" nation, a victim of "aggression," American farmers, American manufacturers, American bankers, American workers, will acquire a direct economic stake in the war, and we shall be on our way in. If we believe in keeping out we must be prepared to pay the price of keeping out. The price is a virtual cessation of trade. Even if "normal" peacetime quotas are still traded, this can only be with one side, in a war that assumes world proportions, for one side will control the sea. So there will be an inevitable shrinkage of trade and consequent dislocation. The answer is economic planning to turn our productive capacity in the direction of home consumption. In brief, the measures proposed in the previous chapter as a transition to a controlled economy are also essential to maintenance of neutrality.

This is more than a coincidence. For it is still the world economic struggle which is the basic cause of the present war danger. The economic interests of the people of the different world powers are felt to be irreconcilable. This is not simply that "capitalism" produces wars, for those nations which lay the greatest emphasis on war preparation today are those which have left capitalist procedures farthest behind. But it is the fact that the basic economic maladjustments have not been solved that sends Mussolini into Ethiopia and Spain, Germany into southeastern Europe, the British fleet into the Mediterranean or out to Singapore to protect British "possessions," and the Soviet armies to the Amur to protect Soviet territory from hungry Japan. Until those basic economic maladjustments are solved, no peace is anything but suspense before a war. We have been discussing the solution in terms of an economy of plenty. The solution is as imperative here in America as anywhere, and here is the only field where we Americans can effectively work out the solution, not as an abstract exercise, but as a real problem in the real world. In so far as we do work it out this country becomes to that extent immune from war.

The secret of a warless world then becomes clear: it must be a world which has solved the basic economic problem. It must be a world which has so ordered its group activity that the capacity to produce has come up to the capacity to consume. The principle is as valid in China as in America: what may not be comparable for a long time is the capacity to produce. It is even possible that the poorer natural resources of the rest of the world outside the United States, in relation to the consumption needs of the population (as exemplified to the extreme degree in India and China), will prevent any world-wide correlation of production and consumptive need until population has been brought down by birth control to what the resources can support in abundant measure. Perhaps a division of labor will ultimately be worked out between the areas where extraction is predominant and those where processing is predominant. The problem we are seeking to solve by no means becomes impossible as one's perspective shifts to include the globe; it only becomes more difficult.

If our tolerance and humanity can survive the next ten years, whatever the cost in pride and prestige, there is every reason to hope that the next generation will live in a sane world. The basic economic problems are being solved, whether unconsciously or rationally, whether brutally or with good will. After all, poverty is the parent of the whole brood of troubles that plague us, revolution, reaction, civil war, international rivalries—ignorance, hatred, war itself.

If we can stave off war, peace can become every day more firmly grounded in reason and understanding. Give the Soviet Union another ten years, in which a really ample standard of living can emerge, with security and leisure for all, and the opportunity to learn and to assuage frenetic dogmatisms. Give Germany ten years in which to do the same in central Europe: Hitler has not permanently destroyed the spirit of German civilization. The re-emergence of decency in the Far East may be longer in coming, for Japan is still half-medieval in culture, and China, even before her cities were burned, was only just emerging into the modern world. India, too, has a long slow road ahead. But in the Western world the "economy of abundance" is coming by rapid strides. I cannot conceive of a generation brought up in conditions of abundance—materially well off, secure, leisured—remaining subject to an absolute dictator or an absolutist creed.

And if we are justified in thinking that the social tensions bred by poverty and insecurity will tend to relax as economic planning achieves well-being, then the international tensions likewise should in time relax. And if it is these tensions, derived preponderantly from economic crisis, whether or not of revolutionary acuteness, that foster the mad nationalisms which today are monsters run amok, then there is every hope, as economic crisis is resolved, for a return of reason and tolerance, and the willingness to work together.

Finally, if it is true that the economic planning necessary to resolve the crisis will mean not dictatorship but a more inclusive liberation than ever before possible, then we may expect the achievement of world peace, not as a new *pax Romana* under rigid discipline, but as a new triumph for democracy. Democracy is less a concrete good to be possessed and defended, than an opportunity for free men to work out ever new ways of freedom.

### *Dare We Look Ahead?*

Our Utopian dreams have often been the stars to which we hitched very practical wagons. Revolutionary periods have been particularly prolific of grand visions. The ardent communist today has no doubt of the reality of his vision: he sees it arising to unimaginable heights in the Soviet Union, and he will let no doubts "in the pale cast of thought" sully its perfection. The ardent fascist, with his trance-like faith in millennial empires peopled by heroes, finds that faith renewed and justified as each new triumph brings new glory home.

Only we of the democracies lack confidence in our aspirations. A recent symposium of enlightened British opinion probing this same question, *Dare We Look Ahead?*, saw only war and brutality and unreason in that future; its authors, leading exponents of the free mind and the worth of man, could offer those who would guard that humane heritage only the desperate counsel, Stand and fight!

If the way of freedom were dependent, as are the ways of the militant dictatorships, on the strength of its maintainers' faith, then we would be justified in scrapping it at once. Fortunately freedom has a strength of its own. Democracies are inefficient, but they are flexible, adaptable. They respond to pressures with a natural resiliency. They have the capacity for growth. Dictatorships are formidable, but brittle.

If this is not true, if we have been fooling ourselves in thinking that freedom releases powers bondage never can, if it is a false assumption that democracy in group organization gives that group a tough survival value by making every individual responsible for that survival, then let absolutism win. If democracy is a fragile flower, the luxury of accidental periods of social stability, then let discipline and dictatorship crush it out.

The whole drift of the argument of this book is that the basic ills of our economic system are curable and are being cured. The democracies take longer to change institutions than the dictatorships which were formed for that express purpose. But they are learning how to manage nevertheless. Only complete despair—such as would plunge them into war—can blight the promise of their progress.

As an antidote to pessimism, take a guarded look into the more promising possibilities beyond these next ten years (or, if we make too many blunders, twenty, or thirty), to a world that most of us may well live to see.

Already we have a real mastery of the forces of nature. If we apply the best that we know to the nurture of our soil and basic resources, to the planning of populations and their needs, to the building of our cities and industries and machines, we can achieve a full production of those necessities, luxuries and amenities that constitute the foundation of secure living. We are on the verge of gaining a new mastery of ourselves. Biology, physiology, psychology, are advancing with accelerating pace. Educational procedures are beginning to cope with the pseudo-sciences of propaganda, race culture, salesmanship, social dialectics, and sheer superstition, and as they become successful, people will be trained to stand on their own feet, equipped for freedom. Mastery of our social environment, dimly foreshadowed today in Soviet Five Year Plans, corporative economies, agencies for planning and controlling the flow of goods and services in consumption and investment, can then at last be fulfilled without dependence on institutional tyranny.

We have so long been accustomed to a world in which there was never enough to go around. For hundreds of generations we have been hungry and cold and afraid. Even today, over most of the earth's surface, abject poverty due to natural scarcity and undeveloped techniques is the order of nature for hundreds of millions of human beings. No wonder if, even in America, we still have the attitudes of scarcity and still call thrift a virtue.

Yet once a nation like the United States gets over the borderline between scarcity and plenty it should be able to proceed to a complete sufficiency of material goods in a very few years. In nine years, since the start of the Great Depression in 1929, it is probable that unemployment has averaged 10 million a year. That means we have wasted 90 million man-years of labor—180 billion man-hours—except for the limited works projects—without much actual physical suffering from want. Suppose we had done what the Soviet Union did during that period, taken all its surplus labor force and put it to capital construction, keeping its collective belt tightened the while? There seems no reason to doubt that we could have doubled our existing productive plant, factories, mines, mills, machines. But actually our plant was already in most respects adequate to the limit of our consumptive capacity. Suppose, where no conceivable consumer need could have been met by new factories, that the surplus labor force had built houses, schools, parks, playgrounds, roads, had rebuilt our cities and beautified our landscape. The achievements of work relief in the last few years have merely suggested some of the new community assets we could use.

We have such a huge margin of productive capacity that if we chose to hold consumption levels where they are and put that surplus into permanent improvements, we could transform the face of America almost overnight.

It is not likely that in the next ten or twenty years, when we find our stride, we shall reach any of the fantastic income levels predicted, say, by the "technocrats." A ten- or twenty-thousand-dollar-a-year income is possible only when concomitant poverty forces many to be servants; its allure is the specious one of a pecuniary economy.

It is more likely that with full employment and effective planning, and their corollaries in leisure and security and released energies, we shall think more of cultivating our garden than of building mansions. It will be a garden in which we can begin to grow human beings with as much devoted skill and artistry as a millionaire's gardener can now lavish on his flowers.

Perhaps the whole process can be illustrated in terms of Long Island.

My first visit to Jones Beach was like a glimpse into a Bellamy Utopia. I had known Long Island, from my private school and college days, as a place where one went to magnificent parties, in the fabulous mansions which the great American fortunes had built in imitation of English country houses. The estate owners had even built a private motor speedway, on which they paid toll to speed their exit from the slums and towers of New York. Now as you leave the city limits you find yourself on a parkway more magnificent than any private drive, beautifully landscaped, free of billboards, stretching on and on to the east. The private speedway has been abandoned.

As I drove over the public parkway that first time I passed playground after playground, lakes, picnic areas, bridle paths, tennis courts, public golf courses; nowhere was there a sign of commercialism or poverty or ugliness. Even the gas stations which make most highways hideous were set around with vines and trees and merged with the landscape. Thirty miles out, on the south shore of Long Island, across wide tidal flats, lies Jones Beach State Park. The beach is so long that, except on crowded Sundays, you can have a quarter of a mile to yourself if you wish. There are swimming pools, and concert stadiums, and dance halls, and restaurants, and terraced pavilions where you can sit under colored umbrellas and look at the ocean. The architecture of the buildings and the landscaping of the grounds are carried out with meticulous regard to the comfort and convenience of a hundred thousand visitors.

I have seen the private mansions and the private clubs where the rich take their ease. There is no doubt a satisfaction in the privacy and exclusiveness of your own cabaña at a thousand dollars for the season. But I have never seen anything that could compare with the radiance of Jones Beach. Early in the summer, when people are getting their first sunburn and are the color of newborn babes, it almost seems as if they felt themselves to be sharing in the delights of a newborn world.

There are country clubs, too, bought cheap in the depression, where the right to play is not dependent on a family name.

Robert Moses, scion of wealth himself, is the builder of New York's new parks, including the parkways and Jones Beach. He had to meet the opposition of the exotic beach clubs; and in the end he shunted them off to the ignominy and squalor of shacks across the railroad tracks. He had to meet the opposition of the estate owners whose forests he skirted. But they were worsted. And as they hide behind their shrubbery in all the splendor of past magnificence, and hear the passing traffic, they must feel that the people, now with their own estate, no longer look up to theirs.

To be sure, Mr. Moses has charged the public fees. And the possession of a car is almost an essential passport to admission to the more distant parks. The East Side slum-dwellers of New York still have to take the subway to garish Coney Island, though even that and the adjacent beaches are being made over by Mr. Moses. Not everybody can yet enjoy Jones Beach. But it is there, as a portent for the future. Give everybody the income of those who now frequent the parkways and Jones Beach, and new parkways, new Jones Beaches, will spring like mushrooms. Multiply them by the hundreds all over the country, by lake, mountain and seashore, and what nobler estate could any man desire?

*New York City,*
*March 17, 1939.*

# BIBLIOGRAPHICAL NOTES

(These Notes are intended to serve three purposes. First, they indicate the major sources of my ideas, from which the expert critic may determine how little I know, and the general reader may be impressed with how much I know. Second, the books and other materials mentioned may furnish some helpful suggestions to any reader interested in following up a topic more thoroughly than I could do here. And third, the page and line references furnish the sources from which most of the factual statements and conclusions in the text are derived and by which their validity can be tested: I have not wanted to make the text any more difficult to read than it is by interrupting it with footnote references. Occasionally I have included brief comments on the books mentioned, especially when I wanted to recommend them particularly, or justify my reliance on them.)

---

CHAPTER ONE

| Page | Line | |
|---|---|---|
| 12 | (fn.) | Alfred M. Bingham, *Insurgent America: The Revolt of the Middle-Classes* (1935). I wish to recommend this book particularly. |
| 14 | 2 | Thurman Arnold, *Folklore of Capitalism* (1937); Stuart Chase, *Tyranny of Words* (1938). These books, particularly Chase's, have been criticized by the learned (whose toes were much stepped on) for lack of originality and profundity. This is like criticizing Henry Ford for not having invented the internal combustion engine. |

CHAPTER TWO

| Page | Line | |
|---|---|---|
| 17 | 1 | This phrase was, I believe, first used in an article by Stuart Chase in *Common Sense*, December, 1932, under that title, but achieved currency as a result of his book, *The Economy of Abundance* (1934). My indebtedness to him will appear throughout this volume. |

| Page | Line | |
|---|---|---|
| 29 | 24 | The following books stick out in my memory as having profoundly influenced me at about this time: J. G. Frazer, *The Golden Bough* (1890, abr. 1922); W. E. H. Lecky, *History of European Morals* (1869); Walter Lippmann, *Preface to Morals* (1929); Harold J. Laski, *A Grammar of Politics* (1929); Sidney and Beatrice Webb, *The Decay of Capitalist Civilization* (1923); Bertrand Russell, *Proposed Roads to Freedom* (1918); Bernard Shaw, *The Intelligent Woman's Guide to Capitalism and Socialism* (1928); Upton Sinclair, *Oil* (1929). |
| | 30 | One of the few English books I found to counteract the Kipling myth was E. M. Forster, *A Passage to India* (1925). A reasonably good summary of the Gandhi movement at the time I was in India appeared in C. F. Andrews, *Mahatma Gandhi's Ideas* (1929). Jawaharlal Nehru wrote an *Autobiography* in prison not long ago (1936). For recent discussions of the socialist tendency in the India independence movement, see Basanta Koomar Roy, "Asia's New Man of Destiny," *Common Sense*, September, 1936; Chaman Lal, "Keep Your King in England!" *Common Sense*, October, 1937. |
| 30 | 9 | A somewhat sensationalized version of what was happening in the Far East at the time I was there appeared in Upton Close, *The Revolt of Asia* (1927). |
| 31 | 4 | A good example of the hysterical school of anti-Soviet writing, which I read just before my visit to the U.S.S.R., is Edmund A. Walsh, *The Last Stand* (1931). For general sources on the U.S.S.R. see notes to Chapters Five and Six below. |

## CHAPTER THREE

| Page | Line | |
|---|---|---|
| 41 | 21 | The classic statements of the two opposing concepts of capitalism are, of course, Adam Smith, *Wealth of Nations* (1776), and Marx and Engels, *Communist Manifesto* (1847). Outstanding recent treatments of the two approaches are Walter Lippmann, *The Good Society* (1937), and Harold J. Laski, *The State in Theory and Practice* (1935), and *The Rise of European Liberalism* (1936). |
| 43 | 35 | The descriptions in Marx's *Capital*, Chapters 8, 13 and 23, are as grim as any in print. Much of the material was taken from Frederick Engels, *Condition of the Working Classes in England* (1845). |
| 44 | 13 | For good recent descriptions of the relation of business and government in American history, see A. M. Simons, *Social Forces in American History* (1911); Jerome Davis, *Capitalism and Its Culture* (1935); Maurice Parmelee, *Fare-* |

| Page | Line | |
|---|---|---|
| | | *well to Poverty* (1935). For the earlier mercantilist phase see E. A. J. Johnson and Wesley C. Mitchell in Findlay MacKenzie's invaluable symposium, *Planning, Yesterday, Today and Tomorrow* (1937). |
| 49 | (fn.) | See Walton H. Hamilton, "Justice Black's First Year," *The New Republic*, June 8, 1938. |
| 50 | 21 | Berle and Means, *The Modern Corporation and Private Property* (1933), is the classic study in this field. |
| 55 | 7 | The most illuminating study of the economic and social role of labor unions I have encountered is Selig Perlman, *Theory of the Labor Movement* (1928). |
| 56 | 23 | Stuart Chase, *Government in Business* (1935), is the best summary of collectivism under capitalism, though little of its material deals with the pre-war era, or even the pre-depression era. |
| 61 | 24 | Seba Eldridge, "Socialism via the Consumer," *Common Sense*, February, 1934. |
| | 36 | Frank R. Kent, *The Great Game of Politics* (1923). |

## CHAPTER FOUR

| Page | Line | |
|---|---|---|
| 66 | 2 | John Dewey's *Liberalism and Social Action* (1935), is, to my mind, the outstanding contribution to a modern definition of "liberalism." Compare Harold J. Laski, *The Rise of European Liberalism* (1936); Walter Lippmann, *The Good Society* (1937); Herbert Hoover, *Challenge to Liberty* (1934); Earl Browder, *The People's Front* (1938). |
| 67 | 38 | The relation of liberalism and "free trade" is well set forth in Jerome Frank's *Save America First* (1938). |
| 68 | 2 | Compare Arthur Salter, *Recovery* (1932); the recent Van Zeeland report, and Secretary of State Hull's speeches are full of allusions to the dependence of peace on freer trade. |
| 69 | 27 | See Lillian Symes and Travers Clement, *Rebel America* (1934); John Chamberlain, *Farewell to Reform* (1933); Nathan Fine, *Farmer and Labor Parties in the United States* (1928); Eunice Clark, "The Socialist Party," *Common Sense*, October, 1934. |
| 75 | 9 | J. Walter Thompson Company, *A Primer of Capitalism* (1937). |
| | (fn.) | Norman Thomas, *Socialism on the Defensive* (1938). |
| 79 | 16 | The National Survey of Potential Product Capacity and the Brookings Institution both measured consumptive capacity as well as productive capacity, though in different ways. See references in Chapter Fifteen below. |
| 87 | 34 | Aldous Huxley, *Ends and Means* (1937); Ordway Tead, *The Case for Democracy* (1938). |

### CHAPTERS FIVE AND SIX

As mentioned on page 94, books on the Soviet Union have been mainly concerned with political and social rather than economic problems. The sources I found valuable were very few. I relied most on L. E. Hubbard, *Soviet Money and Finance* (1936). His later book, *Soviet Trade and Distribution* (1938), is almost as valuable, but it appeared too late for me to make much use of it. Arthur Z. Arnold, *Banks, Credit and Money in Soviet Russia* (1937), covers much the same ground as Hubbard, perhaps more fully but less imaginatively. W. B. Reddaway, *The Russian Financial System* (1935) is a good brief summary of Soviet monetary theory. Boris Brutzkus, *Economic Planning in Soviet Russia* (Eng. ed. 1935) and Calvin B. Hoover, *Economic Life of Soviet Russia* (1931) are valuable studies of the earlier years. Barbara Wootton, *Plan or No Plan* (1934) contains some brilliant chapters on Soviet planning.

For other than economic aspects of the Soviet Union, the leading recent books are, for the defense, Sidney and Beatrice Webb, *Soviet Communism, A New Civilization?* (1935); Albert Rhys Williams, *The Soviets* (1937); and, for the opposition, Eugene Lyons, *Assignment in Utopia* (1937); W. H. Chamberlin, *Russia's Iron Age* (1934), and *Collectivism* (1937).

For statistical sources see note to Table on page 114, below. Other sources appear in the page references.

| Page | Line | |
|---|---|---|
| 93 | 19 | John Reed, *Ten Days That Shook the World* (1919; Modern Library edition, 1935), p. 126. |
| | 23 | Quoted in Webb, p. 605. |
| 94 | 8 | Reed, p. 123. |
| | 26 | Hubbard (references are to his *Soviet Money and Finance* unless otherwise noted), pp. 24, 35; Reddaway, p. 73. |
| 96 | 39 | Lenin, *State and Revolution* (1917; Vanguard Press edition, 1926), p. 205. See Brutzkus, p. 99. |
| 97 | 8 | Arnold, p. 70. |
| | 25 | Brutzkus, p. 102; Wootton, p. 57. |
| 98 | 14 | Arnold, p. 217. |
| | 24 | Walter Duranty, *I Write As I Please* (1935). |
| 100 | 6 | Brutzkus, p. 115; Hoover, p. 305. |
| | 11 | Brutzkus, p. 116. |
| | 21 | Hubbard, p. 26. |
| 101 | 4 | Hubbard, pp. 9-11. |
| | 13 | Hubbard, p. 13. |
| | 19 | Hubbard, p. 81; Arnold, Chap. XV. |
| | 22 | Brutzkus, p. 131. |
| | 33 | Brutzkus, pp. 124-125. |

| *Page* | *Line* | |
|---|---|---|
| 105 | 9 | Brutzkus, p. 177. |
| 106 | 5 | Hoover, p. 316. |
| | 19 | Hubbard, pp. 6, 7. |
| | 29 | Hubbard, p. 17; Arnold, p. 345. |
| 107 | 2 | Hubbard, p. 79. |
| | (fn.) | Hubbard, pp. 145, 336; Hoover, p. 206; League of Nations, *Statistical Yearbook; Socialist Construction in the U.S.S.R.* (Moscow, 1936), pp. 8, 500. |
| 108 | 15 | *Socialist Construction*, pp. 286, 428. |
| 109 | 9 | *Socialist Construction*, pp. 305; *Research Bulletin on the Soviet Union*, April, 1937, p. 37. |
| | 20 | *Foreign Policy Reports*, June 1, 1938, p. 73. |
| | 26 | Wootton, p. 84. |
| 110 | 3 | Hubbard, p. 122; Reddaway, p. 50; Brutzkus, p. 184. |
| | 17 | *Socialist Construction*, p. 5. |
| | 24 | Hubbard, pp. 34, 317; but compare Hoover, p. 33. |
| | 36 | Hoover, p. 25. |
| 111 | 16 | *Socialist Construction*, p. 4; *Research Bulletin*, p. 37. |
| | 22 | *Socialist Construction*, p. 73. |
| | (fn.) | Hubbard, p. 333; Hubbard, *Soviet Trade and Distribution*, Part VI; Chamberlin, pp. 84-90; Brutzkus, p. 228. |
| 112 | 6 | Arnold, p. 457. |
| | 15 | Arnold, p. 434; Hubbard, p. 238. |
| 113 | 3 | Hubbard, pp. 43-50. |
| | 31 | Bassett Jones, *Horses and Apples* (1934). |
| | 38 | These summaries are derived from many sources; see next note on statistical Table. |
| 114 | (Table) | There are no completely satisfactory sources for Soviet statistics. The index of industrial production in the Table is that of the League of Nations *Monthly Bulletin of Statistics*, which also furnishes monthly figures for some of the heavy industries, secured of course from official Soviet sources. Most of the figures in columns 1, 2, and 4 are from *Socialist Construction in the U.S.S.R.*, published by the State Planning Commission (Moscow, 1936). For the figures in columns 3 and 5 on Plan objectives I have used the *Handbook* of the American-Russian Chamber of Commerce (1936), A. Z. Arnold, *Banks, Credit and Money in Soviet Russia* (1937), Boris Brutzkus, *Economic Planning in Soviet Russia* (Eng. ed., 1935), W. P. and Z. K. Coates, *The Second Five Year Plan* (1934), and the *Research Bulletin of the Soviet Union*. For the figures in column 6 I have used the *Monthly Review* of the U.S.S.R. Trade Delegation to the United Kingdom (1938), the Foreign Policy Association's *Reports* (June 1, 1938), the New York *Daily Worker*, as well as the periodical sources previously mentioned. The figures in col- |

| *Page* | *Line* | |
|---|---|---|
| | | umn 7 come from a United Press despatch from Moscow of January 30, 1939, and a despatch to the *Daily Worker* of the same date. |
| 117 | 2 | Hoover, pp. 20, 300. |
| | 18 | Hubbard, p. 45; *Research Bulletin*, 1937, p. 71. |
| 118 | 25 | Hubbard, p. 57. |
| 119 | 2 | Hubbard, p. 245. |
| | 17 | Arnold, p. 434. |
| 120 | 16 | Hubbard, pp. 250, 260. |
| 122 | 37 | *Socialist Construction*, p. 13. |
| 123 | 13 | *Socialist Construction*, pp. 4, 7. |
| | 16 | Hoover, p. 53; Hubbard, p. 112; *Research Bulletin*, p. 75. |
| 126 | (fn.) | Brutzkus, p. 203. |
| | 19 | Hubbard, p. 6; Hoover, p. 57. |
| | 28 | Hubbard, p. 179. |
| 127 | 25 | Hubbard, p. 202. |
| | 35 | Hubbard, p. 86; Labor Research Association, *Economic Notes*, February, 1939, p. 6. |
| 128 | 16 | Hubbard, p. 160. |
| | 38 | Figures derived from *Socialist Construction*, pp. 7, 500, 501; estimate of percentage of investment from Hubbard, p. 91. |
| 130 | 8 | Hubbard, p. 197. |
| 133 | 4 | Brutzkus, p. 236. |
| | 19 | Hoover, p. 187; Reddaway, pp. 40, 71; Hubbard, p. 263; Wootton, p. 96. |
| | 36 | Eduard Heimann, "Planning and the Market System," *Social Research*, November, 1934, suggests that the test can be disregarded only during the "undeveloped stage" when "any investment" is useful. |
| 136 | 9 | Hubbard, p. 298. |
| 138 | (fn.) | League of Nations, *Monthly Bulletin of Statistics*. |
| 139 | 7 | Hoover, pp. 330-340. *Letter from an Old Bolshevik* (Rand School Pamphlet, 1937), gives an apparently reliable and highly revealing inside picture of recent demoralization. |

### CHAPTERS SEVEN AND EIGHT

There are few objective studies on fascist economics, whether Italian or German. The most valuable single work I have found is "Germanicus," *Germany: The Last Four Years* (1937). For economic aspects of Italian Fascism the most informative volume is H. W. Schneider, *The Fascist Government of Italy* (1936), as his *Making of the Fascist State* (1928) is still the most informative for its social and political aspects. F. L. Schuman, *The Nazi Dictatorship* (1936), is a

*Page* *Line*

good factual study of German fascism, though marred by the Marxist bias. The best discussion of Nazi economic ideas appears in E. B. Ashton, *The Fascist: His State and His Mind* (1937). The following contribute somewhat less directly to an understanding of fascist economics:

*General:* Ascoli and Feiler, *Fascism For Whom?* (1938); M. T. Florinsky, *Fascism and National Socialism* (1936); Calvin B. Hoover, *Dictators and Democracies* (1937).

*Marxist:* R. Palme Dutt, *Fascism and Social Revolution* (1934); John Strachey, *The Menace of Fascism* (1934); Robert A. Brady, *Spirit and Structure of German Fascism* (1937).

*Italian Fascism:* Carmen Haider, *Capital and Labor Under Fascism* (1930); Carl T. Schmidt, *The Plough and the Sword* (1938); G. Lowell Field, *The Syndical and Corporative Institutions of Italian Fascism* (1938); Paul Einzig, *Economic Foundations of Fascism* (1933).

*German Fascism:* Konrad Heiden, *History of National Socialism* (1935); Henri Lichtenberger, *The Third Reich* (1937); J. B. Holt, *Under the Swastika* (1936); F. Morstein-Marx, *Government in the Third Reich* (1937); Paul Einzig, *Germany's Default: The Economics of Hitlerism* (1934); Edgar A. Mowrer, *Germany Sets the Clock Back* (1933); Calvin B. Hoover, *Germany Enters the Third Reich* (1934)

Other sources appear in the page references.

141 1 Florinsky, p. 8.

28 See "Marxist" references in general Bibliographical Note above.

32 Lewis Mumford's *Men Must Act* (1939) has become the definitive statement of this point of view; the attitude is documented in Aurel Kolnai, *The War Against the West* (1938), and dramatized in the current addresses and writings of Thomas Mann.

143 35 Mussolini's speeches may be found in *Source Book on European Governments* (1937).

145 3 Florinsky, pp. 97, 108; Morstein-Marx, p. 157.

146 18 Quoted in Findlay MacKenzie, *Planning, Yesterday, Today and Tomorrow* (1937), p. 805.

147 10 See Morstein-Marx, p. 64; Holt, p. 91; Fritz Ermarth, *The New Germany* (1936), p. 33.

30 Werner Sombart, *Deutscher Sozialismus* (1934), American edition under title *A New Social Philosophy* (1937), p. 287. The American translator, Karl F. Geiser, was decorated by Hitler in 1938.

148 3 Holt, p. 77.

| *Page* | *Line* | |
|---|---|---|
| 148 | 31 | "Economic Thinking in the New Germany," *Annals*, May, 1937, pp. 210, 211, 216. |
| 149 | 5 | Quoted in Findlay MacKenzie, p. 803, and in Florinsky, p. 73. |
| | 32 | See Lewis L. Lorwin, "Planning in Europe," *Bureau of Personnel Administration* (Conferences, 1931-32), p. 143. For a suggestion that the expulsion of Schacht in the winter of 1938-39 was at the hands of Rathenau's followers, see Peter F. Drucker in *Common Sense*, March, 1939. |
| 151 | 9 | See Gustav Cassel, "From Protectionism Through Planned Economy to Dictatorship," in Findlay MacKenzie, p. 775. |
| 152 | 34 | New York *Times Magazine*, February 27, 1938; Schneider, p. 127. |
| 153 | 3 | "Germanicus," p. 67. |
| | (fn.) | "Germanicus," pp. 15, 31, 37. Following the Munich crisis the tempo of "war socialism" speeded up considerably, according to the New York *Times*, December 22, 1938, and March 6, 1939. |
| 154 | 35 | Schneider, p. 101. |
| 155 | 12 | Einzig, *Economic Foundations*, pp. 88, 91; Florinsky, p. 98; Lorwin, p. 150. |
| | 19 | Schneider, p. 113. |
| | 33 | "Germanicus," p. 5. |
| 158 | 33 | Schuman, pp. 88, 140, 188, 268, 392; Ermath, p. 43. |
| 159 | 7 | Schuman, p. 470. |
| | 20 | John C. de Wilde, "Germany's Controlled Economy," *Foreign Policy Reports*, March 1, 1939, gives figures on property income; government expenditures are taken from the article in *Living Age* cited below, in note to Table, p. 167. |
| | 23 | For the status of the capitalist class see Frieda Wunderlich, "Germany's Deficit Economy and the Decay of Capitalism," *Quarterly Journal of Economics*, June, 1938; "V," "The Destruction of Capitalism in Germany," *Foreign Affairs*, July, 1937; Morstein-Marx, p. 157; Florinsky, p. 109. |
| 160 | 5 | New York *Post*, July 26-28, 1938. |
| | 8 | "Germanicus," p. 25. |
| | 11 | New York *Times*, May 16, 1938. |
| 163 | 17 | Schneider, pp. 101-120. |
| | 25 | F. E. Lawley, *Growth of Collective Economy* (1938), p. 117. Compare Einzig, *Economic Foundations*, pp. 88, 109; Florinsky, p. 203. |
| 164 | 35 | "Germanicus," p. 58. |
| 166 | 6 | See footnote, p. 182. |
| | 8 | See Emil Lederer, "Economic Doctrine of National Socialism," *Annals*, May, 1937. |

| Page | *Line* | |
|---|---|---|
| 167 | (Table) | All figures derived from "Germanicus," except 1937-38 from W. G. J. Knopf, "Behind the Nazi Facade," in the London *Banker*, reprinted *Living Age*, April, 1938. |
| | 11 | New York *Times*, May 16, 1938. |
| 168 | 6 | "Germanicus," pp. 78, 80. |
| | 14 | "Germanicus," p. 88. |
| | 24 | New York *Times*, October 25, 1938. |
| 169 | 6 | *Events*, July, 1938, p. 52. |
| | 25 | "Germanicus," p. 83. See also Holt, p. 231; New York *Times*, May 16, 1938. |
| | 38 | Schuman, p. 470; Florinsky, p. 110. |
| 170 | (fn.) | Quoted in *Living Age*, April, 1938, see note above, to Table, p. 167. See also Wunderlich; A. Vidakovic, "How Hitler Pays His Arms Bill," *The Nation*, January 30, 1937. |
| | 9 | New York *Times*, May 17, 1938. |
| 171 | 24 | Frederick T. Birchall, "Five Years of Nazism," New York *Times Magazine*, January 30, 1938; League of Nations, *Monthly Bulletin of Statistics.* |
| 172 | 4 | New York *Times*, August 20, 1938. |
| | 20 | New York *Times*, March 17, 1937. |
| 173 | 2 | Speech to the Peasants at Bueckeberg, October 4, 1937, and at Nuremberg Party Congress, September 13, 1937. |
| | 25 | Speech of March 23, 1936. *Source Book on European Governments*, III, p. 81. |
| 174 | 8 | Schneider, p. 121. |
| | 11 | Schuman, p. 270. |
| | 17 | Speech of March 23, 1933. *Source Book on European Governments*, IV, p. 122. |
| 175 | 6 | For material on the *Reichsnährstand*, and standards of food consumption, see Florinsky, p. 179; "Germanicus," pp. 40, 44, 96; Morstein-Marx, pp. 160-167; de Wilde, pp. 293-296. |
| | 38 | Schuman, *Germany Since 1918* (1937), p. 93. |
| 177 | 8 | New York *Times*, January 31, 1938; June 12, 1938. |
| | 11 | Wootton, p. 194; Hubbard, p. 276. |
| | 23 | Eduard Heimann, in his *Communism, Fascism or Democracy?* (1938) and his "Types and Potentialities of Economic Planning," *Social Research*, May, 1935, points out that "national socialism" is not wholly a misnomer for a war economy with planned investment, even if private ownership remains; yet Heimann is a German Socialist émigré. |
| | 34 | Schneider, p. 120. |
| 178 | 4 | Florinsky, p. 110. |
| | 24 | League of Nations, *Monthly Bulletin of Statistics.* |
| 179 | 12 | Morstein-Marx, p. 153. |

| Page | Line | |
|---|---|---|
| 183 | 21 | See Peter F. Drucker, "The Social Revolution in Austria," *The New Republic*, July 6, 1938. Tolischus reported in the New York *Times* early in 1939 a growing fear on the part of Aryan business men that the method of expropriating Jewish business men would soon be turned against them by the radical Nazis. |

CHAPTER NINE

| Page | Line | |
|---|---|---|
| 187 | 2 | Freda Utley, *Japan's Feet of Clay* (1936), p. 215. This is probably the best study of modern Japan in spite of its Marxist bias. |
| | 5 | *Fortune*, September, 1936. This entire issue was devoted to Japan, and is packed with statistical material. |
| | 16 | Utley, p. 72. |
| | 33 | Utley, p. 289. |
| 188 | 7 | Utley, p. 296. |
| | 14 | Quoted in W. H. Chamberlin, *Japan Over Asia* (1937), p. 241. This book is especially valuable for its light on the "collectivist" traditions that have made the shift to fascist ways so easy. See, especially, pp. 282-288. |
| | 32 | Quoted in G. Stein, "What Japan's Army Wants," *Asia*, June, 1937. |
| 189 | 9 | *Literary Digest*, August 15, 1936. |
| | 14 | Willard Price, *Children of the Rising Sun* (1938), provides the most sympatheic insight into the attitudes that have supported Japan's aggressive ambitions. |
| | 34 | The best material on the more recent government interferences with business in Japan I have found in *Business Week*, in the issues of July 25, 1936, June 26, July 31, and August 28, 1937, and March 26, 1938. See also New York *Herald Tribune*, June 17, 1937 on the Five Year Plan, and New York *Times*, November 30, 1938 on the Industry Mobilization Bill. |
| 192 | 3 | For a good brief description of Loyalist Spain and the social revolution see Anna Louise Strong, *Spain in Arms, 1937* (1937). |
| 193 | 27 | Reliable material on Franco Spain is scant. I have relied mainly on a series of despatches in the New York *Times* by Harold Callender, May 14-18, 1938. Two interviews by William P. Carney, New York *Times*, March 16, 1937, and January 9, 1938, give the point of view of some of the Insurgent leaders, as quoted in the text. See also Hanighen in *Common Sense*, April, 1939. |
| 197 | 34 | A significant interpretation of modern Turkey appears in Clark Foreman, *The New Internationalism* (1934). |

Page Line

198 17 See note to p. 29, line 30, for Indian sources.

22 Edgar Snow's *Red Star Over China* (1937), is already a classic in the literature on modern China.

27 *Fortune* carried a significant series of articles on South American countries, illustrating the trend to state capitalism, beginning in December, 1937.

199 16 For a good summary of present-day Mexico see Selden Rodman, "Mexico's Bloodless Revolution," *Common Sense*, October, 1937.

201 (fn.) See *New Republic*, May 25, 1938; *Common Sense*, December, 1938. See also, Mgr. John A. Ryan, *A Better Social Order* (1935). For the significant experiment in Catholic co-operatives in Nova Scotia, see B. B. Fowler, *The Lord Helps Those* (1938).

202 2 The Secretariado da Propaganda Nacional of the Portuguese Government publishes propaganda pamphlets in English. See *Political Constitution of the Portuguese Republic* (1937), and T. W. Fernandes, *Professor Oliveira Salazar's Record* (1936).

## CHAPTER TEN

206 5 Since Marquis Childs's book (1936) there has been much valuable material published about Sweden. The most recent and most complete is the symposium of the New Fabian Research Bureau, *Democratic Sweden* (1939). See also the collection of studies in *Annals*, May, 1938, "Social Problems and Policies in Sweden," and E. R. Bowen, *Sweden, Land of Economic Democracy* (Co-operative League pamphlet, 1937).

207 15 See *Annals*, May, 1938, p. 5.

31 See Finn Moe, *Does Norwegian Labor Seek the Middle Way?* (pamphlet, 1937).

37 See R. A. Goslin, *Changing Governments* (pamphlet, 1937), and chapter on Denmark in Marquis Childs.

208 16 For information on European co-operative movements, see Jacob Baker and others, *Report of the Inquiry on Co-operative Enterprise in Europe* (1937); Jacob Baker, *Co-operative Enterprise* (1937); Sydney R. Elliott, *English Co-operatives* (1937).

209 3 For a discussion of the American co-operative movement and the general implications of co-operation see John Daniels, *Co-operation, an American Way* (1938); R. A. Goslin, *Co-operation* (1937); Paul H. Douglas, *Co-operation, A Middle Way for America?* (pamphlet, 1937); and articles in *Annals*, May, 1937, "Consumers' Co-operation."

| Page | Line | |
|---|---|---|
| 211 | 19 | Charles W. Pipkin, *Social Politics and Modern Democracies* (1934) II, pp. 80-91. |
| | 24 | Robert Cahill, *Economic Conditions in France* (1934), p. 156. |
| | 33 | Cahill, p. 452. |
| | 35 | Pipkin, p. 200. |
| 212 | 6 | Cahill, pp. 627, 631. |
| | 18 | Alexander Werth, *Which Way France?* (1937), p. 329. |
| | 23 | Cahill, p. 645. |
| | 36 | Cahill, pp. 92-95, 201. |
| 213 | 6 | Cahill, p. 79. |
| | 24 | Richard L. Stokes, *Léon Blum* (1937), p. 232; Werth, p. 345. |
| | 34 | Werth, p. 346. |
| 214 | 13 | Werth, pp. 313-326. |
| 215 | 12 | Werth, *France in Ferment* (1935); Jacques Duboin, *En route vers l'Abondance* (1935). |
| | 16 | Henri de Man, *Planned Socialism* (New Fabian Research Bureau pamphlet, 1935); Paul Sering, *What is Folk-Socialism?* (League for Industrial Democracy pamphlet, 1937). |
| | 29 | Jerome Frank, *Save America First* (1938). |
| 216 | 1 | Gordon H. Hewart, *The New Despotism* (1929). |
| 217 | 35 | T. H. O'Brien, *British Experiments in Public Ownership and Control* (1938) is an excellent study of the Central Electricity Board, British Broadcasting Corporation and London Passenger Transport Board. |
| 219 | 7 | John Strachey, *What Are We To Do?* (1938) Chaps. V and VI. |
| 220 | 2 | By far the most realistic as well as optimistic outline of the possibilities for economic planning in England appears in Harold Macmillan, *The Middle Way* (1938) which came to my attention after writing the present volume (see footnote, p. 406). For instances of the present pessimism of the Fabians see *What Is Ahead of Us?* and *Dare We Look Ahead?*, the Fabian Lectures of 1937 and 1938, published in book form. |
| | 20 | Marx, *Capital* (Everyman edition) I, p. 667. |
| 221 | 3 | See "Canada the Siren," *Fortune*, September, 1937; Selden Rodman, "Canada Faces Two Ways," *Common Sense*, August, 1938; W. R. Maclaurin, *Economic Planning in Australia 1929-1936* (1937); C. Hartley Grattan, "They Knew What They Wanted in New Zealand," *Common Sense*, February, 1939; John A. Lee, *Socialism in New Zealand* (1939). |
| 222 | 22 | The following are among the best interpretations of the New Deal, particularly as seen by the New Dealers themselves: E. K. Lindley, *The Roosevelt Revolution* (1933); |

*Page* *Line*

"Unofficial Observer," *The New Dealers* (1934); Stolberg and Vinton, *Economic Consequences of the New Deal* (1935); Harold L. Ickes, *The New Democracy* (1934); Harry L. Hopkins, *Spending to Save* (1936); Henry A. Wallace, *America Must Choose* (1934), and *Whose Constitution?* (1936).

225 18 Brookings Institution, *America's Capacity to Consume* (1934), p. 148; *The Recovery Problem in the United States* (1936), pp. 313, 317.

227 (fn.) Stuart Chase, *Government in Business* (1935), p. 36. I have relied heavily on this highly informative and provocative book in the present section.

228 2 Henry T. Hunt, "Domesticating the Corporation," *Common Sense*, April, 1937.

229 (fn.) George W. Edwards, *The Evolution of Finance Capitalism* (1938), p. 309.

17 See the President's opening message and budget message to the new Congress, January, 1939, New York *Times*, January 5 and 6, 1939.

## CHAPTER ELEVEN

235 11 Vincent Sheean, *Personal History* (1935).

238 12 Angelo Herndon, *Let Me Live!* (1937).

239 37 Frederick Engels, *Socialism Utopian and Scientific* (George Allen & Unwin edition), p. 82: "From the kingdom of necessity to the kingdom of freedom."

242 31 Stuart Chase, *The Tyranny of Words* (1938); Lancelot Hogben, *Retreat From Reason* (1938).

243 9 Frederick Engels, *Socialism Utopian and Scientific*, Chap. II, and Marx's Preface to the Second German edition of *Capital* (included in the Everyman edition on p. 866) provide the readiest statements of "dialectical materialism."

11 See *Science and Society, a Marxian Quarterly*, and J. B. S. Haldane, *The Marxist Philosophy and the Sciences* (1939).

15 For critiques of the dialectic see Max Eastman, *Marx, Lenin and the Science of Revolution* (1926); Sidney Hook, "Dialectic and Nature," *Marxist Quarterly*, April-June, 1937; Edmund Wilson, "The Myth of the Marxist Dialectic," *Partisan Review*, Fall, 1938.

244 16 Marx and Engels, *Manifesto of the Communist Party* (Kerr edition), p. 13.

19 See my *Insurgent America*, and Lewis Corey, *Crisis of the Middle Class* (1935).

245 26 One of the few exceptions is Lewis Corey, *Decline of American Capitalism* (1934).

| Page | Line | |
|---|---|---|
| 246 | 26 | Lenin's *Imperialism* (1916) and *The State and Revolution* (1917) are brilliant restatements of parts of Marx's *Capital*, rather than original theses. |
| 247 | 32 | *Manifesto*, pp. 20, 29. |
| 248 | 19 | *Capital*, I, p. 874. References for the first volume of *Capital* are to the Everyman edition; for the second and third volumes, the Kerr edition. |
| | 25 | *Capital*, I, p. 886. |
| | 30 | *Capital*, III, p. 515n. |
| 250 | 16 | This Preface appears in the Everyman edition at p. 861. |
| 251 | 15 | *Capital*, I, p. 714. |
| | 20 | *Capital*, I, p. 846. |
| 253 | 25 | *Capital*, II, p. 324. |
| 254 | 1 | These formulas appear in somewhat different form at various places. When first worked out, I, pp. 208-212, the first formula uses C to mean "capital," though in previous pages (I, pp. 83, 131) it stands for "commodity." I have used the formulation that appears in III, pp. 38, 49, though the C is not specifically defined and seems to be understood in a double sense, as the capital advanced in the production of a commodity. The second formula appears in somewhat varying form likewise; as presented it is derived from II, pp. 59, 74. The elaborated form appears at II, p. 129. |

### CHAPTER TWELVE

| Page | Line | |
|---|---|---|
| 257 | 1 | Ludwig von Mises, *Socialism* (1922), p. 364. |
| 258 | 9 | See Cole's introduction to the Everyman edition of *Capital*, I, pp. xxiii, xxix. |
| | 14 | John Strachey, *The Nature of Capitalist Crisis* (1935), p. 177. |
| | 22 | See *Capital*, I, pp. xxi, 184-189. |
| 260 | 10 | See Marx, *Value, Price and Profit* (Kerr edition), p. 87; *Capital*, I, p. 580. |
| | 22 | Marx, *Critique of the Gotha Programme* (International Publishers edition), p. 27. |
| 263 | 32 | For somewhat divergent interpretations of occupational divisions see my *Insurgent America*, and Corey, *Crisis of the Middle Class*. |
| 264 | 30 | *Critique of the Gotha Programme*, pp. 39-40. |
| 266 | 19 | *The Formation of Capital*, p. 8. |
| 267 | 26 | The quotations in italics on this and the following pages are paraphrases rather than direct quotations. |
| 268 | 13 | Twentieth Century Fund, *Big Business, Its Growth and Its Place* (1937), pp. 9, 95. |

| Page | Line | |
|---|---|---|
| 268 | 32 | Berle and Means, *Modern Corporation and Private Property*, p. 373; *Insurgent America*, pp. 68, 82. |
| 270 | 5 | See *Capital*, III, pp. 517-519; Engels, *Socialism Utopian and Scientific*, pp. 69-71; Lenin, *Imperialism*, p. 71. |
| 272 | (fn.) | Compare Engels, *Socialism Utopian and Scientific*, pp. 60-63. |
| 273 | 1 | Compare Marx, *Value, Price and Profit*, pp. 60, 96. |
| | 38 | John Strachey, in *The Nature of Capitalist Crisis*, p. 297, ridicules Hayek's solution of unemployment by a lengthening of the structure of production, but he does not claim it would increase unemployment; and in the Soviet Union, as I pointed out above, unemployment is absent while the structure of production is lengthened without a corresponding increase in consumption. |
| 276 | 31 | Compare H. B. Parkes, "Some Marxist Fallacies," *Southern Review*, Winter, 1939. |
| | (fn.) | Brookings Institution, *America's Capacity to Consume*, p. 158; 1935 figure from Department of Commerce, *National Income*, 1929-35, Table 3, in proportion. |

CHAPTER THIRTEEN

| Page | Line | |
|---|---|---|
| 278 | 10 | See also *Manifesto*, pp. 14-18. |
| 279 | 9 | So in R. Palme Dutt, *Fascism and Social Revolution*; John Strachey, *The Coming Struggle for Power*, and *The Menace of Fascism*; Ernst Henri, *Hitler Over Europe*. |
| | 33 | Brookings Institution, *The Formation of Capital*, p. 199; Stuart Chase, *The New Western Front* (1939), p. 99. |
| 281 | 30 | *The Formation of Capital*, p. 159. |
| 282 | 26 | John Strachey is less critical than Engels: he considers Marx to have achieved "the definitive account of the effects of the development of a credit system upon capitalism." *The Nature of Capitalist Crisis*, p. 309. |
| 284 | 25 | See Brutzkus, pp. 18-23; von Mises, p. 133. |
| 286 | 19 | Marx, *Value, Price and Profit*, pp. 89-92. |

CHAPTER FOURTEEN

| Page | Line | |
|---|---|---|
| 294 | 30 | Henry Adams, *The Education of Henry Adams* (1907). |
| 297 | (fn.) | See also his *Retreat from Reason* (1937). |
| | 29 | Aldous Huxley, *Ends and Means* (1937) is the best recent statement of this point of view. |
| 298 | 27 | Bertrand Russell, *Power* (1938); Harold Lasswell, *Politics; Who Gets What, When, How* (1936). |
| 299 | 25 | Brooks Adams, *Theory of Social Revolutions* (1913). |

| Page | Line | |
|---|---|---|
| 307 | 11 | For two wholly different formulations of this emphasis compare Kropotkin's *Mutual Aid, A Factor in Evolution* (1902), and John R. Commons, *Institutional Economics* (1934), especially Chapter X, "Reasonable Value." |
| | 25 | Stanley Casson, *Progress and Catastrophe* (1936). |
| 309 | 12 | Albert Jay Nock, *Our Enemy the State* (1935). |

CHAPTER FIFTEEN

| Page | Line | |
|---|---|---|
| 317 | 5 | See Stuart Chase, *Technocracy* (1933); and Wayne Parrish, articles in the *New Outlook*, November, December, 1932. |
| | 20 | Walter N. Polakov, *The Power Age* (1933). |
| | 21 | Bassett Jones, *Debt and Production* (1933). |
| | 28 | This idea was first suggested by Thorstein Veblen in *The Engineers and the Price System* (1921). |
| 318 | (fn.) | *Report of the National Survey of Potential Product Capacity* (1935); Harold Loeb and Associates, *The Chart of Plenty* (1935); Mordecai Ezekiel, *$2500 a Year* (1936); John Strachey, *Theory and Practice of Socialism* (1936); Harold Loeb, *Production for Use* (1936). |
| 319 | 18 | Continental Committee on Technocracy, *The Plan of Plenty* (1934). |
| 320 | 33 | Brookings Institution, *America's Capacity to Produce* (1934). |
| 321 | 5 | In his *Economy of Abundance.* |
| | 35 | *Common Sense*, May, June, 1935; Upton Sinclair, *I, Governor of California, and How I Ended Poverty* (1934). A somewhat similar "dual" system was persuasively presented in William Beard, *Create the Wealth* (1936). |
| 322 | 19 | The interest in planning became very great in the years 1931-1935. The best general studies of the problem are Barbara Wootton, *Plan or No Plan* (1934); G. D. H. Cole, *Economic Planning* (1935); George Soule, *A Planned Society* (1932). |
| 324 | 5 | William Morris, *News From Nowhere* (1891). |
| | 9 | Marx, *Critique of the Gotha Programme*, p. 31. |
| | 12 | Barbara Wootton, *Plan or No Plan*, p. 11. |
| 329 | 29 | John R. Commons, *Institutional Economics* (1934), pp. 472, 549. |
| 331 | 19 | There are some helpful brief critiques of the under-consumption theories in Brookings Institution, *The Formation of Capital*, Appendix A, and in Alvin H. Hansen, *Full Recovery or Stagnation?* (1938) Chapter IV, "The Social Credit Proposals of Major Douglas." |
| 332 | 21 | John Maynard Keynes, *The General Theory of Employment, Interest and Money* (1936). For a helpful critique of |

Page Line

Keynes and his terminology see Hansen, *Full Recovery or Stagnation?* Chapter I, "Keynes on Underemployment Equilibrium."

334 21 Arthur Salter, *Recovery* (1932).

30 Keynes's earlier work was *A Treatise on Money* (1930).

335 14 See note to page 385, line 4.

336 4 Harold Loeb recently pointed out in an article in *Common Sense* (January, 1939) that failure of monopolistic industries to lower prices as costs fall has the effect of creating a money shortage.

338 16 Eduard Heimann, "Types and Potentialities of Economic Planning," *Social Research*, May, 1935, considers this equilibrium one of the most crucial.

339 (fn.) Brookings Institution, *The Formation of Capital*, p. 146.

342 27 The leading recent proponents of use of the government's spending power to maintain equilibrium are Paul H. Douglas, *Controlling Depressions* (1935); James Harvey Rogers, *Capitalism in Crisis* (1938); and "Seven Harvard and Tufts Economists," *An Economic Program for American Democracy* (1938). Compare J. W. Sundelson, "Socio-Economic Control and the Fiscal System," in Findlay MacKenzie.

348 (fn.) Alexander Gourvitch, "The Problem of Prices and Valuation in the Soviet System," *American Economic Review*, XXVI Supp., p. 279

CHAPTER SIXTEEN

352 (fn.) See note to page 133, line 19.

353 35 See Eduard Heimann, *Communism, Fascism or Democracy?* (1938).

(fn.) League of Nations, *Monthly Bulletin of Statistics*.

355 5 Joan Robinson, *The Economics of Imperfect Competition* (1933); Edward Chamberlin, *The Theory of Monopolistic Competition* (1933). I have followed the latter in terminology and approach.

22 Brookings Institution, *Industrial Price Policies and Economic Progress* (1938) is the best study available of price administration in practice, with a particularly illuminating example in the case of aluminum. The first study in this field was Gardiner C. Means, *Industrial Prices and Their Relative Inflexibility*, U. S. Senate Document No. 13, 74th Congress, 1st Session (1935).

357 26 Ware and Means, *The Modern Economy in Action* (1936), p. 58. This is the best popular presentation of the problem of administered prices.

34 Jerome Frank, *Save America First* (1938) and the Brook-

*Page* *Line*

ings study last cited are the only books, to my knowledge, which have brought out the significance of the difference between an intelligently administered and a stupidly administered price.

362 33 For an excellent summary of post-war "interventionism" see P. W. Martin, "Present Status of Economic Planning," *International Labor Review*, XXXIII, p. 619, and XXXV, p. 177.

365 27 For an excellent bibliography of the literature of "market socialism" see Eduard Heimann, "Literature on the Theory of a Socialist Economy," *Social Research*, February, 1939. I have relied principally on Lange and Taylor, *The Economic Theory of Socialism* (1938). A good summary of the theory appears in three articles by Robert Mossé, Gerhard Meyer and Carl Landauer in *Plan Age*, October, 1937. The most complete presentation is R. L. Hall, *The Economic System in a Socialist State* (1937). Barbara Wootton, *Lament for Economics* (1938) offers a trenchant critique of "market socialism" from the "left." A. C. Pigou, *Socialism versus Capitalism* (1937) is an equally competent critique from the "right."

31 Ludwig von Mises, *Socialism* (1922). A briefer statement of von Mises' position, with other statements of the conservative argument, appears in F. A. von Hayek, *Collectivist Economic Planning* (1935). Brutzkus' work on the Soviet Union, which I have frequently cited, actually anticipated von Mises, though it was only published in English as a companion volume to Hayek's in 1935.

366 9 Barbara Wootton, *Plan or No Plan*, p. 111.

367 1 Compare, for a similar approach by a non-socialist, H. S. Person, "Planning and Consumption" in Findlay MacKenzie.

5 Compare Eduard Heimann, "Planning and the Market System," *Social Research*, November, 1934; Frank Knight, "The Place of Marginal Economics in a Collectivist System"; Alexander Gourvitch, "The Problem of Prices and Valuation in the Soviet System," *American Economic Review*, XXVI Supp., pp. 254, 267. See also Heimann, "Types and Potentialities of Economic Planning," *Social Research*, May, 1935, where "planning" and "socialism" are distinguished.

33 The only "market socialists" who have given any hint that public ownership may not be necessary are Heimann and Mossé. See especially Heimann, "Planning and the Market System," p. 494, where the possibility of monopoly prices is suggested, and Mossé, *Plan Age*, October, 1937, p. 197, where mention is made of the French C. G. T.'s emphasis on public supervision rather than ownership. This latter emphasis is also made by Henri de Man, see above p. 215.

## CHAPTER SEVENTEEN

| Page | Line | |
|---|---|---|
| 371 | 10 | See Barbara Wootton, *Lament for Economics* (1938); Jerome Frank, *Save America First* (1938). |
| 378 | 12 | Compare Harry L. Scherman, *The Promises Men Live By* (1938). |
| 381 | 34 | Keynes, *General Theory*, pp. 320, 378. |
| 382 | 23 | See W. Jett Lauck, "Practical Possibilities for Economic Planning," *Common Sense*, September, 1938. |
| 383 | 1 | See "That Wonderful Swedish Budget," *Fortune*, September, 1938; Ernst Wigforss, "The Financial Policy During Depression and Boom," *Annals*, May, 1938. |
| | 37 | For a theoretical discussion of the role of social dividends in a planned economy, see John H. G. Pierson, *An Essay on the Possibilities of Monetary Control* (manuscript, Yale Library, 1937). |
| 384 | 29 | The second alternative is the main thesis of Edward Dahlberg, *Capital on Strike* (1938). |
| 385 | 4 | See D. H. Robertson's definition, quoted in Hansen, *Full Recovery or Stagnation?*, p. 22: "Hoarding (dis-hoarding) may be alternatively defined as acting in such a way as to decrease (increase) the velocity of circulation of money against output." |
| 386 | 4 | This is the question asked by such divergent economists as Hayek and Irving Fisher. See Henry C. Simons, *A Positive Program for Laissez Faire* (pamphlet, 1937). |
| | 18 | See H. Parker Willis, "Banking and Credit in a Planned Society," *Bureau of Personnel Administration* (Conferences, 1931-32), p. 178. |
| | (fn.) | See reference to p. 169, line 25 above. |
| 387 | 18 | Clark Foreman, *The New Internationalism* (1934) is the most cogent analysis of the relation of autarchy and foreign trade. Among the most persuasive arguments for basing American policy on such an approach are Charles A. Beard, *The Open Door at Home* (1934); Jerome Frank, *Save America First* (1938); Stuart Chase, *The New Western Front* (1939). See also Keynes, *General Theory*, Chap. 23. |
| 388 | 22 | Eduard Heimann is one of the few socialists who has come to much the same conclusion. See *Communism, Fascism or Democracy?* (1938), and "Planning and the Market," *Social Research*, November, 1934. |
| 389 | 13 | In the *Fortune* "survey," February, 1939, less than 30 per cent of the population were shown to favor any top limit to private fortunes. |
| 391 | 18 | Keynes, *General Theory*, pp. 220, 376. |
| 392 | 34 | See Lange, 140; Mossé, p. 207. |

## CHAPTER EIGHTEEN

| Page | Line | |
|---|---|---|
| 395 | 24 | For the background of "Americanism" from the liberal point of view see especially George S. Counts, *The Prospects of American Democracy* (1938); Morris L. Ernst, *The Ultimate Power* (1937); Max Lerner, *It Is Later Than You Think* (1938); Herbert Agar, *Land of The Free* (1935); Alexander Meiklejohn, *What Does America Mean?* (1935); John Chamberlain, *Farewell to Reform* (1933); Symes and Clement, *Rebel America* (1934). |
| 396 | 13 | Herbert Harris, *American Labor* (1938) is the most realistic recent history of the American labor movement. |
| | 33 | See "The Servant Problem," *Fortune*, March, 1938. |
| 398 | 15 | See the *Fortune* and Gallup surveys. |
| | 18 | Louis M. Hacker, *American Problems of Today* (1939) contains an excellent survey of New Deal measures and agencies. |
| 401 | 15 | See William Harlan Hale, "The Men Behind the President," *Common Sense*, May-July, 1938. |
| 402 | 24 | See also Mordecai Ezekiel, "AAA in Reverse," *Common Sense*, June, 1937. |
| 403 | 9 | H.R. 7332, 75th Congress, First Session. |
| | 16 | See especially, Herbert Harris, "This Bill Bears Watching," *Survey Graphic*, April, 1938. |
| | 17 | H.R. 10924, 75th Congress, Third Session. |
| 406 | 6 | See Brookings Institution, *Industrial Price Policies and Economic Progress* (1938), Chap. II. |
| 407 | 7 | See *Dynamic America*, March, 1938. |
| 409 | 15 | See Smith W. Brookhart, "Half Slave and Half Free," *Common Sense*, April, 1938, for a discussion of the "cost of production" proposal. The present bill, introduced in the Senate by eighteen Senators, is S. 570, 76th Congress, First Session. |
| | 37 | See O. W. Willcox, "An Abundance Program for Agriculture," *Common Sense*, March, 1938. For a hostile criticism of these efforts see Jules Bachman, "Government Control of Prices," in Findlay MacKenzie. |
| 410 | 4 | For an excellent description of the County Agent and the democratic controls he typifies, see *Fortune*, July, 1938. |
| | 19 | See Thomas R. Amlie, *The Forgotten Man's Handbook* (1936), pp. 7-18, for a statistical study of the collapse of agriculture. |
| 411 | 38 | H.R. 7230, 75th Congress, First Session. |
| 412 | 13 | H.R. 8585, 75th Congress, Second Session. A similar bill has been introduced in the new Congress by Representative Voorhis, H.R. 4931, 76th Congress, First Session. |

| Page | Line | |
|---|---|---|
| 412 | (fn.) | See *People's Money*, December, 1935; *Annals*, January, 1936, p. 157; and reference to p. 386, line 4. |
| 413 | 37 | "Totempolemic" was coined by Jerome Frank in *Save America First*. |
| 416 | 21 | See Mordecai Ezekiel, *Jobs for All* (1939), pp. 37-76, for a discussion of the effect of "industrial expansion" on the labor movement. |

CHAPTER NINETEEN

| Page | Line | |
|---|---|---|
| 425 | 33 | O. W. Willcox is the outstanding proponent of the theory that even England could grow its own food. See his *Nations Can Live at Home* (1935). |
| 432 | 35 | G. De Michelis, *World Reorganization on Corporative Lines* (1935). |
| 436 | 17 | See note to page 141, line 32. |
| 438 | 13 | The outstanding proposal for more effective neutrality legislation is that prepared by a group of experts for the Economic and Social Planning Association and published in *Plan Age*, November, 1937. |
| 441 | 14 | Russell, Bartlett, Cole, Cripps, Morrison, Laski, *Dare We Look Ahead?* (1938). |
| | 31 | Edward Bellamy, *Looking Backward* (1888) and *Equality* (1897) still present the soundest "Utopia" of modern times. |

# ACKNOWLEDGMENTS

I wish to record a special indebtedness to Stuart Chase, Eduard Heimann, Harold Loeb, and John H. G. Pierson for material contributions to the theoretical analysis involved in this book. The last three read sections of the manuscript, as did also Irving B. Altman, Herbert Harris, Selden Rodman, and Charles W. Yost, and for their generous help I am deeply grateful. Members of my family have contributed in various ways, obvious and not so obvious, to these pages, and to them I wish to express my affectionate appreciation. Finally a word of acknowledgment is due my publisher, whose encouragement has made the book possible. Neither he, nor any of the others, however, is to be considered responsible for the ideas set forth.

# INDEX